D1569077

TRAINING BEHAVIOUR THERAPISTS

Methods, Evaluation and Implementation with Parents, Nurses and Teachers

DEREK MILNE

CROOM HELM
London & Sydney

BROOKLINE BOOKS
Cambridge, Massachusetts

Croom Helm Ltd, Provident House, Burrell Row,
Beckenham, Kent BR3 1AT
Croom Helm Australia Pty Ltd, Suite 4, 6th Floor,
64–76 Kippax Street, Surry Hills, NSW 2010, Australia

British Library Cataloguing in Publication Data

Milne, Derek
Training behaviour therapists: methods, evaluation and implementation with parents, nurses and teachers.
1. Behaviour therapy 2. Medical personnel — Training of
I. Title
616.89'142'07 RC489.B4

ISBN 0–7099–3515–3

Brookline Books, PO Box 1046,
Cambridge, MA. 02238

Library of Congress Cataloging in Publication Data

Milne, Derek 1949–
Training behaviour therapists.
Includes bibliographies and index.
1. Behavior therapy—Study and teaching. I. Title.
[DNLM: 1. Behavior therapy—education. WM 18 M659t]
RC489.B4M55 1986 616.89'142 85-30879
ISBN 0-914797-22-0

Phototypeset by Sunrise Setting, Torquay, Devon
Printed and bound in Great Britain by
Biddles Ltd, Guildford and King's Lynn

CONTENTS

This book is dedicated to Keith Turner in recognition of his supervision, support and psychology

FOREWORD

The research literature on training behaviour change agents, although of recent origin, is already quite extensive. Although all or part of that extensive literature has been reviewed in several papers, those papers are limited by size constraints from fully exploring the intricacies of the topic.

This book meets the need for a thorough exploration of the training literature that is unconstrained by size limits and is informed by the author's extensive expertise as both a practitioner and a researcher in the area. Derek Milne's command of the subject is evident in everything he writes.

Perhaps most important, this volume emphasises both specificity and context while viewing both from an empirical perspective. The case is made for increased specificity of description and analysis of training methods, change agents and their environments as well as for increased rigour which relates the training process to outcomes defined by behaviours not only of change agents but also of those they serve.

Milne analyses the training literature with a keen eye for detail, but he never lets us forget the importance of the context in which training occurs. Thus we find extensive discussions of setting events which may influence training, and of the need to examine unintended effects of training such as the effects of change agents on those who train them (e.g. 'superstitious supervision'). In general, the emphasis is on the multiple interactions among environments, those who train, those who receive training, and those who are served by trainees. We are constantly reminded that training is not something you do to people, nor does it occur in a vacuum.

The inclusion of the chapters that describe existing training programmes for nurses, teachers and parents in detail gives a reality base to the discussion of contextual and methodological issues. Further, it helps the reader to see that although we have much to learn about training, we have made substantial progress.

In his closing chapter Dr Milne points out that 'psychotherapy has a long and undistinguished scientific history, notable for the passing fads and fancies of various quacks and therapists'. This book is a major step towards making the training of behaviour change agents a science rather than a fad. It will have considerable interest for anyone engaged in giving psychology away as an empirical endeavour.

Gail S. Bernstein
Denver, Colorado

ACKNOWLEDGEMENTS

I am indebted to many people for their help in instigating and facilitating this book. Prominent among these are my wife Judy, for her unflagging encouragement and tolerant editing; and Charles Burdett, my erstwhile colleague and champion. My general inspiration to think about, write about and apply psychology comes first from my father, Alec Milne, of the Kingston Clinic; and more recently from Keith Turner (Leicester District Psychologist). More material help was provided with typing, especially by Shirley Goodison, and also by Eileen Greaves, Grace Greenall, Elaine Bootnan and Michaela Frizelle.

Valuable assistance in the form of commenting on draft chapters of this book was provided by Phil Barker, John Hall, Keith Topping, Peter Farrell, Keith Turner, Ruth Turner, Kelvin MacKrell, Roger Blunden, Stephen Morley, Cecily Miller and an anonymous reviewer. Tim Burton drew the illustrations and also gave me a new perspective on editorial deadlines. Carol Greatrick and Wakefield Health Authority helped with a desk and miscellaneous letters and typing. Mary Sanderson of the Information and Education Services at Pinderfields Hospital, Wakefield, sustained me with an endless supply of books and articles. My colleague Linda Walker also assisted with valuable articles. Susan White and Marthie Malik helped to sort out the bibliography, and Mary Sayers carried out the task of copy-editing the typescript. Dennis Milne advised on the methods of champagne production.

My own attempts at training behaviour therapists (summarised in Chapter 6) were greatly facilitated by Gordon Sivewright, then Divisional Nursing Officer, Carlton Hayes Hospital, Leicester; and by his Nursing Officers, Rose Maud and George Barnsley. I also appreciated the support of Norman Kaye, Consultant Psychiatrist at the same Hospital, and of Ray Meddis, my Ph.D. Supervisor at the University of Technology, Loughborough.

Several undergraduate psychologists aided me with my data-gathering at Carlton Hayes, including Amanda Hodd, Shirley Roe, Clare Watson, Nick Jones, Helen Edgar and Sue Potter. John Beckett (Computer Laboratory, University of Leicester) then provided expert and patient help with the data analyses. My former colleagues in Leicester were also supportive during this research programme, particularly Mike Corp, Angela Holland and Gwyn Frazer, as was the Leicester Health Authority in sponsoring my Ph.D. registration. Latterly the Wakefield Health Authority sustained this sponsorship and I received support from my new colleagues, particularly Iain Burnside and Rosemary Jones.

Lastly, I am grateful to Tim Hardwick for the opportunity to write this book and for his encouragement during its maturation.

PREFACE

This book derives from a full-blooded involvement in training behaviour therapists over the best part of a decade. My commitment to learning and training goes back further, to some difficult passages in my own education. In retrospect these seem attributable to faulty evaluation, incompatible goals and inappropriate learning opportunities. I think that this history contributed substantially to my enthusiasm for training, aided by a deepening concern for the quality of care in institutions and more generally for the widening gulf between client needs and helping services.

Behavioural approaches seemed to me to represent a very promising way of responding to these concerns. They offered a way of analysing, interpreting and evaluating the training ventures that appeared necessary to effect improvements in our helping services. They were free of the dreaded implications of illness and blame which had tarnished many such services in the past; and they could reduce the gulf between needs and services because they were often simple procedures, easily grasped and implemented. This opened the door to 'non-professional' therapists in a way that had not previously been considered possible or desirable, and ushered in what must be regarded as one of the major recent innovations in health care and education.

The aim of this book is to offer a behavioural analysis of the training that has been provided to this new wave of therapists, namely parents, nurses and teachers. We first consider some core issues as a backdrop to the actual contents and methods of training. These include the 'Triadic model', which provides the framework for behavioural training, the relationship between training and learning, and the ethics of 'non-professional' therapists. (On this latter point I was much amused to read a recent article on resuscitation, in which only 8 per cent of 'professionals' — doctors — were deemed competent in a technique which 'non-professionals' acquired in 3 hours of specialised training (Casey, 1984). Perhaps this highlights one of the major flaws in the typically fruitless debate on professionalism — the assumed but rarely quantified competence of the traditional 'professional'.)

A second introductory chapter goes on to consider some issues which often pass unmentioned in research reports, such as the respective contingencies bearing on all those involved in a training intervention, and the obstacles to innovations of this kind. The chapter is essentially a behavioural analysis of training, in which a variety of contextual or 'system' variables are related to the training enterprise. It is argued that such an analysis is necessary if we are to understand and overcome the obstacles to training.

The six following chapters (3 to 8) provide reviews and detailed examples of research involving parents, nurses and teachers. There is now a voluminous literature on these behaviour therapy 'mediators', amounting to some 800 empirical studies. The reviews of research were, therefore, not intended to offer an exhaustive account of this work, but were rather an attempt to capture some of the main themes and developments. Each review is complemented by a detailed account of one research programme, which elaborates some of these developments. The principal reason for including these accounts and an appendix was to offer interested readers enough information to enable them to make a decision about replicating the programmes or to facilitate their development of their own versions of these training programmes.

Three major issues are addressed in both the research reviews and the illustrative programmes. They are the training methods, the evaluative procedures, and the problems of successfully implementing training in hospitals, schools and homes. They are highlighted because they are regarded as the essentials of training and hence as the topics lying closest to the needs of those who conduct training. In this sense it is very much hoped that this book will provide a valuable 'handbook' to trainers, as well as a thorough analysis of the literature for those concerned more broadly with training and learning in terms of these sorts of setting.

The concluding chapter integrates the material from the rest of the book so as to tease out some general themes and findings. These include the importance of carefully structured active learning opportunities for skill acquisition, the relative value of alternative evaluation procedures, and promising strategies for procuring the acceptance and generalisation of training programmes. Finally, there is a summary of some of the outstanding requirements for future research involving parents, nurses and teachers; and some suggestions as to how this might be pursued.

Derek Milne

NOTES ON CONTRIBUTORS

Gail Bernstein, Ph.D.: Assistant Professor, Adult Services, University of Colorado Health Sciences Center, Campus Box C234, 4200 East Ninth Avenue, Denver, Colorado 80252, USA

Bruce Baker, Ph.D.: Professor, Department of Psychology, University of California, Los Angeles, California 90024, USA

Peter Farrell, Ph.D.: Department of Education, University of Manchester, Manchester M13 9PL, England.

Derek Milne, Ph.D.: Senior Clinical Psychologist, Stanley Royd Hospital, Wakefield, West Yorkshire WF1 4DQ, England and Honorary Lecturer and Regional Tutor, Leeds University M.Sc. in Clinical Psychology.

1 'GIVING PSYCHOLOGY AWAY': AN INTRODUCTION

1.1 Aims of the Book

One of the most significant recent developments in the field of behavioural problems has been the rise of the non-professional therapist. Following relatively brief periods of training, mothers, teachers, fellow patients, nurses and many others have been able to take a therapeutic role. The result has been an enormous expansion in the availability and use of psychotherapy, especially of behaviour therapy, and an impressive list of successful applications with such groups as problem children and chronic psychiatric patients has accumulated. This development has far-reaching implications for us all, in terms of improvements in the health and educational services, and in terms of technology.

The technology issue concerns the application of behavioural science to pressing social problems for which conventional practice has offered no solution: there are simply too few trained therapists to deal with demands, and no prospect of substantially increasing those numbers. An alternative strategy has been to 'give psychology away' to non-professionals (Hawks, 1981).

The aim of this book is to examine some of the major issues surrounding this development, and particularly to analyse such technological problems as the training and evaluation of therapists. These include the following questions. What are the best methods of helping people to learn therapy techniques? How do we determine what they need to know? Which evaluation strategies and measures are best given to groups of therapists? How does the training of the different groups compare?

These questions are dealt with in the context of the system in which the problems arise and where therapeutic solutions are attempted. In the case of the problem child, the system includes the home and other linked environments, such as the neighbourhood. In the case of the chronic psychiatric patient, the system is the ward and the hospital. For each group of therapists that we consider, attention will be given to this context in order to develop a more complete account of therapy skills. The aim of the book is to attend to these issues through a detailed, thorough analysis of existing research.

This broad review and analysis will draw on research involving parents, nurses and teachers in order to develop an integrated perspective on the assessment, implementation and training of therapy skills. As such, the goal of the book is to provide those who train others and those who receive training with a useful resource on therapy skills. It offers a summary of the experimental literature, with all the ideas that this generates, and a number of derived guidelines on running and evaluating training courses. The book is, therefore, an academic and applied resource, one that will, it is hoped, prove most valuable to those interested in giving or receiving behavioural therapy skills. However, the issues it raises are also germane to other therapeutic approaches.

1.2 General Introduction

In the Dark Ages and in the Middle Ages it was very common to find untrained people acting as self-appointed therapists, thriving on the gullibility of their clients. These 'quacks' enjoyed the displeasure of the medical profession as well as a profitable sideline to their more readily recognised roles, which included those of shepherd, conjuror, water-peddler, gypsy or sieve-maker. Despite their indignation, reputable physicians were unable to remove 'the spectacle of such a gallant array of charlatans, recruited from the ranks of illiterate tramps and vagrants, the very scum of society, from thriving by reason of the popular credulity' (Lawrence, 1910).

This strong sense of division between doctor and layman has not been entirely eroded, although Freud (1927) for one has argued that the right to practice psychotherapy should be acquired by specialised training rather than by medical status. As a result, he redefined 'quack' as 'anyone who undertakes a treatment without possessing the knowledge and capacities necessary for it'; this encouraged him to go on to assert that 'doctors form a prepondering contingent of quacks in analysis'. He felt that doctors received a training in medical school that was more or less opposite to that required as a preparation for psychoanalysis, with its emphasis on the interpersonal relationship.

During the 'enlightened ages', dating from the 1960s, there has been a very rapid expansion of non-medical therapies, carried out by a growing variety of professional and lay people. Unlike their predecessors, these latter-day lay therapists not only receive training but are also a valuable ally to professionals.

In addition to the development of the approved 'para-professional' therapist, two other important trends during the past two decades have been the extensive application of the principles and techniques of behaviour therapy; and a related onus on careful evaluations of services, particularly those based on behaviour therapy (Hokanson, 1983).

1.3 The Behavioural Approach

One major reason for the trend towards giving psychology away has been the advent of behaviour therapy. In contrast to Freud's psychoanalysis, behaviour therapy does not require an intensive, lengthy period of individual training, which is then only applicable over an equally extended period of years on a one-to-one basis and usually at considerable financial cost to the patient. Rather, behavioural approaches meet the need for simple, readily acquired and clinically effective techniques in a wide variety of settings. These techniques can be taught to groups of lay people, such as parents, in short training periods with a minimum involvement from qualified professionals. They are generally more acceptable to intending therapists because they assume neither the medical emphasis on disease or 'sickness' nor the analytic onus on unconscious motivation (Reiff, 1966). Instead, the role of learning and environment are regarded as paramount (O'Dell, 1974). In contrast to other approaches, such as client-centred therapy, in which 'personality' is seen as the determinant of behaviour (Rogers, 1951), the behavioural emphasis includes both the one-to-one relationships and other social and physical factors that influence behaviour in the 'natural environment'.

As a consequence, behavioural strategies are now applied to a staggering range of important social issues, with considerable success. For example, during 1983 the *Journal of Applied Behavioural Analysis*, a journal especially committed to reporting these issues, contained scientific studies evaluating such diverse behavioural applications as reducing speeding and accidents, teaching job-interview skills to the mentally handicapped, motivating autistic children, controlling disruptive and aggressive behaviour, treating drug abuse, training family therapists, improving parental care-giving and reducing cigarette smoking.

However, the contemporary 'behaviour therapy' underlying these strategies eludes a simple definition. It is often used synonymously with the term 'behaviour modification', and distinctions tend to lead into a 'terminological wilderness' (Franzini and Tilker, 1972). In general we will prefer the term 'behaviour therapy', since it refers to a wider range of procedures, foci and methodologies than 'behaviour modification'. But since it clearly suggests pathology and cure, we will prefer the latter term when discussing the educational system. Our definition of these terms is broadly based on the continuity of behavioural approaches with the principles, procedures and findings of psychology as an experimental science. Specifically this entails the use of explicit, testable hypotheses; interventions derived from or consistent with experimental clinical psychology; techniques that can be precisely described and objectively measured; and experimental evaluation (Wilson, 1982).

Why should we apply behavioural strategies to the training of para-professional therapists? There are three main reasons. First, there is the *prevention* argument, which stresses the role of those, such as parents, who directly influence the development of psychological problems. As we will see later when we examine the parent training research (Chapter 3) the influence of the immediate care-giver on the developing child is profound, ranging from the relatively discrete control of cues and consequences to the more lasting effects of enduring patterns of parent-child interaction (Wahler *et al.*, 1965).

A second argument concerns *impact*. It is only through the people who provide the context in which problems develop that we can truly expect to have any real influence. There are so many psychological problems in the homes, schools and hospitals that the few specialists who do exist cannot begin to tackle the problem alone. For example, Rutter *et al.* (1970) reported that the frequency of emotional and behavioural disorders in a sample of schoolchildren drawn from the general population included 22 per cent who were 'worried' and 20 per cent who were 'fearful', based on their teachers' questionnaire replies. In terms of the adult population it appears that there are also large numbers of people with psychological problems. A questionnaire survey of 76 general practitioners indicated that some 75 per cent of them requested help with their patients' marital and sexual problems and 79 per cent wanted assistance with phobic and obsessional disorders, in addition to eight further problem categories, for each of which 20 per cent or more of the GPs requested the help of a clinical psychologist (Davidson, 1977).

As there are only very few specialists who can respond to these potential demands, it is self-evident that they cannot deal with them by the traditional strategy of direct contact. In terms of the ratio of psychologists (of any specialisation) to the population, Fichter and Wittchen (1980) presented figures ranging from 0.5 per 100000 population (Poland) to 13.5 per 100000 (Great Britain). The United States with a ratio of 9.1 per 100000 and West Germany (12.3) also had relatively good ratios. Furthermore, a survey conducted in the USA (Vandenbos *et al.*, 1981) indicated that psychologists in post spent only about half of their time in direct client contact, so exaggerating the difficulty of providing direct professional contact.

The third and closely related argument for developing 'para-professional' therapists is that of *effectiveness*. Unlike the disease or personality views of psychological problems, the behavioural approach regards these problems as arising out of an individual's current predicament and learning history. The various influences under which the individual learns to behave in a problematic way are regarded as the crucial factors, and these are only observable and understandable in the 'natural environment'. This means that therapeutic success depends on assessing and altering problems in the context in which they have developed and been maintained. This leads to the view that people in the natural environment need to be trained in order to alter the basic learning conditions for themselves and others, in the same way that they are helped to acquire other skills of living. For although many such skills are carefully nurtured, the ones such as 'parenting' are not usually among them. This has led some researchers to suggest that the retraining of parents may frequently be desirable and often absolutely necessary (Patterson *et al.*, 1964), and that mandatory parent-training programmes should be instituted (Hawkins, 1972).

1.4 The Triadic Model

So far we have used the term 'therapist' or 'non-professional' to refer to the person in the natural environment who acts as the behaviour therapist. An alternative is 'mediator', which implies that the person who actually applies the therapeutic techniques 'mediates' between the professional therapist and the person with the problem. This results in a three-way interaction, which is called the *triadic model*. It is schematised in Figure 1.1 below.

The professional therapist or 'supervisor' is anyone who can provide the necessary expertise to 'give the therapy away' to the mediator. In turn, the mediator is someone in the natural environment in which the problem arises, someone who as a result tends to have an important relationship with the patient or 'trainee'. The trainee's problem is the target of the therapy.

The triadic model can be contrasted with its predecessor, the dyadic model. This is the traditional doctor–patient relationship, which typically entailed consultation in a clinic. The differences were therefore that in the dyadic model the problem was seen, or more likely heard, out of its context by someone who would not have had a 'natural' relationship with the patient. They would not be able to consult with more than a very limited number of patients and so could not expect to have any real impact on the number of problems that were present in the community.

Figure 1.1: The Triadic Model. The arrows indicate reciprocal influence

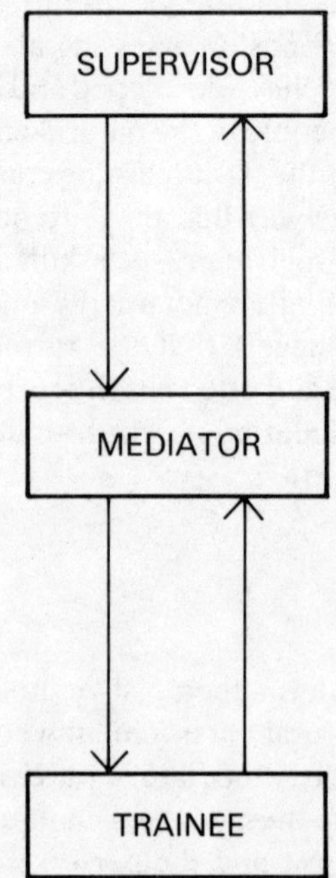

The original outline of the triadic model came from Sigmund Freud (1909). He acted as supervisor to the father (mediator) of the famous Little Hans (trainee). Freud indicated that the father was entirely responsible for the implementation of the treatment process, under his expert supervision, and stated that the father's natural relationship with his son was important in the treatment.

In presenting their masterful thesis on behaviour therapy in the natural environment, Tharp and Wetzel (1969) regarded the triadic model as the 'organizational convergence of the thrusts of behaviourism, of deprofessionalization, and the utilization of natural relationships'. They offered a list of the possible trios involved in the convergence, of the kind given in Table 1.1.

Tharp and Wetzel (1969) made it clear that the position of any agent in this triadic model was based on their resources and functions rather than their status. Thus, the 'supervisor' is anyone who has the necessary skills, knowledge and time to assist the mediator. In turn, the mediator is anyone who has a natural or important relationship with the trainee, and who therefore tends to have a powerful influence on them. The trainee is anyone who has a problem that the mediator and supervisor agree to tackle. Incidentally, Tharp and Wetzel (1969) used the terms 'consultant', 'mediator' and 'target' to refer to the three members of the triadic approach, a convention adopted by most other writers on the subject. These terms seem less appropriate in the UK, where a 'consultant' in the health services refers to a senior member of the medical profession. There is therefore likely to be confusion in adopting this term in this book, since medical consultants have formed only a very small minority of supervisors in the research on the triadic model. One can also question the acceptability of the term 'target', since in addition to its

Table 1.1: Some Triadic Relationships

Supervisor	*Mediator*	*Trainee*
Nurse Therapist	Psychiatric Nurse	Psychiatric Patient
Educational Psychologist	Teacher	Pupil
General Practitioner	Wife	Husband
Social Worker	Mother	Child

pejorative tone it implies a lack of interaction: it is something at which things (treatments) are 'fired'. In the triadic model the 'target' fires back! 'Patient' is the most frequently used term for people seeking help with problems, although this is also loaded with medical overtones, and, as we have mentioned, the medical model is incompatible with the therapeutic triad. It therefore seems best to adopt the term 'trainee' since this comes closest to the emphasis give in the triadic model to learning and skill acquisition.

Latterly, the triadic approach has evolved into a 'quadratic' model, particularly in the USA. This appears to stem from the availability of graduate students, who act as intermediaries between the supervisor and mediator. Such agents are usually referred to as 'behavioural engineers'. Bernstein (1982) has provided a helpful breakdown of the various triadic and quadratic variations to the basic model. However, for the purposes of this book, few distinctions between these variations are made. This is largely because they still share the same functional relationship of a supervisor who provides mediator training and a mediator who works directly with the trainee. The fact that the supervisor may utilise an 'engineer' to effect mediator training does not alter this fundamental relationship, although it does afford new research opportunities. A secondary reason for minimising triadic-quadratic distinctions is that information on the training activities of either supervisors or engineers is very much lacking in research reports. This makes general distinctions between them rather pointless, given the present state of research. We will, however, discuss the quadratic model in those few studies where the distinction between supervisor and engineer is specified and of practical significance, as in manipulations of supervisor behaviour.

One of the earliest behavioural examples of the triadic model was given by Ayllon and Michael (1959). They instructed psychiatric nurses to attend only to their patients' appropriate behaviour, ignoring all other activities. These nurses were given no theory or training in the use of this approach, technically known as 'differential reinforcement'. None the less, they were able to alter a number of problems successfully, including patients' over-frequent entry into the nurses' office, psychotic talk, violence towards other patients, hoarding rubbish, and refusal to eat.

However, it should be noted that the triadic model was never regarded as quite such a static, one-way form of influence. Tharp and Wetzel (1969) went on to outline the reflexive, dynamic nature of the relationships between mediator, trainee and supervisor, and to make it clear that, depending on the identified 'problem', any one of these three agents might be the focus of therapeutic attention. In this way such problems as resistances on the part of the mediator might temporarily become 'the problem', for instance because they rejected the deterministic base to behaviour therapy, regarded it as bribery, or lacked the self-control to be an effective mediator. Equally the supervisor might lack the necessary skills to facilitate the mediator's learning of therapy techniques, and despite experience and success within the dyadic model might have a problem when 'once-removed' and forced to work through an intermediary. Other supervisors may have a 'philosophical revulsion' to give psychology away, for example out of professional jealousy or for ethical reasons. For instance, Rioch (1966) predicted that the innovative training of housewives as therapists might cause feelings of envy among professionals, as well as the struggles for power and prestige that are common within professions (Miller and Wexler, 1969). This had led to suspicions that some para-professionals merely play at therapy, which may lead to the exploitation of patients (Gruver, 1971), associated with a general animosity on the part of the professionals expressed in such terms as 'scabs' and 'do-gooders' (Hopkinson and Hurley, 1976).

1.5 'Para-professional' Therapists

Most people would regard as absurd the idea that therapeutic skills need to be developed in parents and other groups. The traditional view of parenting, and to some extent also of teaching and other professional skills, is that we are born with a predisposition to be 'good' with people, and this unfolds with motivation, opportunity and the application of common sense.

The evidence suggests otherwise, since such groups as parents and teachers who are given training in relevant skills are seen to become more successful therapists. This evidence is reviewed in detail in subsequent chapters, but we can deal here with the role of 'common sense' as an illustration of one of the popular misconceptions concerning therapy. One of the characteristics of common sense is that it defies definition: some have regarded it simply as a feature of those who agree with us (Duc de la Rochefoucauld); some saw it as the most widely distributed commodity in the world (Descartes); and still others regard the training and organisation of common sense as scientific thinking (T. H. Huxley). Some of the best examples of the confusion between common sense and science are to be found in social psychology (Furnham, 1983): one the one hand, the unremarkable and generally favourable findings of social psychology are viewed as self-evident; on the other hand, less favourable depictions of man are a basis of public outcry. Instances include Milgram's (1974) evidence that ordinary citizens would administer (simulated) fatal electric shocks to complete strangers as a result of instructions from an authority figure. Zimbardo *et al.* (1973) added unsavoury data on how ordinary citizens behaved when they role-played jailors. Other studies also illustrate the effect that certain environments can have on behaviour. 'Common sense' would not have predicted these disquieting findings, and would not wish to accept them. Even when such findings are favourable, 'common sense fails to notice what it later finds obvious' (Fisher *et al.*, 1978). In short, common sense may at times *appear* to be a firm base for understanding and controlling behaviour, but on closer inspection is usually incoherent, ambiguous and occasionally contradictory (Heider, 1958). Not least, say the scientists, it is short on the kind of factual data that would 'completely upset the speculation and the wonderful dream castles so laboriously constructed by the layman' (Eysenck, 1957). Perhaps, then, the value of common sense lies in the ideas and beliefs it generates about behaviour; although to be useful they must be evaluated scientifically.

One of the important implications of this view is that much of psychology is not common sense at all, thereby being something that can usefully be 'given away'. As suggested earlier, the most crucial people to receive psychology are the para-professionals, as they are numerous enough, significant enough and most appropriately placed to use the refined common sense that is behaviour therapy. At the same time it must again be emphasised that these mediators have an interdependent relationship with the supervisors who train and support them and with the trainees with whom they work. We will therefore regard the following discussion in the light of this interactive triad, and in the next chapter develop a larger context incorporating the triad into a systems framework.

The 'quacks' so vividly described by Lawrence (1910) were also defined as such by Freud (1927) because they lacked the 'knowledge and capacities' for therapy. Latter-day definitions are consistent with this emphasis on specialised training. In a major review of the comparative effectiveness of professional and para-professional therapists, Durlak (1979) regarded the professionals as those who had received a post graduate, formal, clinical training in such disciplines as psychology, psychiatry and social work. By contrast, the para-professionals tend to be psychiatric nurses, students, parents, teachers and any other therapists not meeting Durlak's definition. For example, Balch and Soloman (1976) reviewed the training of such para-professional therapists as child-care workers, community volunteers and fellow patients.

This division, however, between 'professional' or 'para-professional', is perhaps a simplistic and misleading one, since there are many levels of training and therapeutic sophistication within each category. Indeed, some para-professionals receive training in some aspects of behaviour therapy that is superior to that received by professionals. For example, the 'nurse-therapist' does not meet Durlak's definition of a professional, since nurses in the UK are (unlike their American counterparts) rarely graduates. But they do receive an extensive, specialised training in behaviour therapy (Marks *et al.*, 1977). As a result, their expertise is often greater than that of the 'professional' psychologist, who is always a graduate but not necessarily in receipt of specialised behaviour therapy training. The 'knowledge and capacities' of these different 'professions', therefore, is not as distinctive as might be expected, with the result that there has been considerable role change among the helping professions (Hall, 1979).

Within the para-professional body of therapists it is also possible to distinguish various levels of training and competence. Some of the different levels of behavioural sophistication to which parents and nurses have been trained are given in Table 1.2.

On the next level, the most sophisticated behaviour therapist is the 'nurse therapist', who will be regarded as a professional for the purposes of this book. The reason for this is simply a behavioural one, where people are defined in terms of their activities rather than by some arbitrary criterion such as their status. Nurse therapists function autonomously, assessing and treating sexual, phobic, obsessional-compulsive and other general disorders from out-patients' bases. There are no sound behavioural grounds for placing them in the para-professional category since their training and subsequent effectiveness are as good as any other professional group, such as psychologists and psychiatrists (Ginsberg and Marks,

Table 1.2: Some of the Different Levels of Behaviour Therapy Sophistication among Para-professionals

Level of sophistication	Para-professional group	Function	Author describing the training
'Applicator'	Teachers	Uses simple and very specific contingencies under highly structured supervision	Robinson *et al.* (1981)
'Technician'	Parents	Applies a small number of techniques with moderate structure and supervision	Salzinger *et al.* (1970)
'Specialist'	Nurses	A wider range of techniques with programme structure but little supervision	Horner (1973)
'Generalist'	Nurses	A wider range of techniques than the specialist. Also greater range of problems, and little supervision	Horner (1973)

1977; Hall, 1979).

In addition to the wide range of 'knowledge and capacities' held by trained professionals, there is also an issue concerning the 'untrained' people who make up the rest of society. If we pursue our argument about the suitability of behaviour therapy for interventions in the natural environment, then it follows that no one can be excluded from processes of influence: the people who make up the natural environment *will* influence behaviour, whether or not they have received any form of specialised training. In this sense it may be more meaningful to regard individuals as differing in terms of the amount of influence they exert and how deliberately they use it. Those who carefully plan and monitor therapy programmes are the sophisticated ones, the 'professionals', whereas those who are unaware of their effect on others are the 'non-professionals'. No doubt this kind of definition of therapists would result in an even greater number of levels of sophistication both within and between professional and para-professional groups, but it would at least reflect the complexity of influences in the real world, rather than conforming to such preconceived categories as 'professional' and 'para-professional'. In psychoanalysis these complexities tended to be described in terms of mental dynamics, even when it was being 'given away' to new groups. Miller (1921), for instance, argued that

> acquaintance with the methods and the findings of analytical psychology will help the teacher both to understand the mental processes of the child and to avoid some of these dangers of unconscious bias and prejudice in himself that are sometimes at work in contradiction to his conscious purpose.

Freud (1927) also discussed the idea of providing an analytic training for 'social workers' so that they could become 'a band of helpers for combating the neuroses of civilization'. More recently, Balint (1964) has urged GPs to develop analytic perspectives in order to join this band of helpers.

There is, then, a considerable history and wealth of advice for non-experts wishing to learn therapeutic techniques. It will provide us with a backdrop for examining the findings on the training of a variety of therapists.

Evaluations of para-professional behaviour therapists have to date been very positive (e.g. Guerney, 1969; Johnson and Katz, 1973; O'Dell, 1974). For example, Durlak (1979) considered 42 studies comparing professional and para-professional groups and concluded that para-professionals achieved clinical outcomes equal to or significantly better than those obtained by professionals. There are some difficulties in accepting Durlak's conclusion, since he included studies with weak experimental designs and had difficulty assigning therapists to professional or para-professional categories. This led Nietzel and Fisher (1981) to conclude that only five of the original 42 studies actually provided acceptable evidence on comparative effectiveness. These five studies offered tentative evidence that only those para-professionals working with psychiatric in-patients and under close professional supervision achieved clinical outcomes equal to or better than those achieved by professionals.

Further qualifications were suggested by Hattie *et al.* (1984). They conducted an analysis of 39 studies. Although they also concluded from this analysis that para-professionals achieved clinical outcomes equal to or better than those obtained by professionals, the differences were only evident on the ratings of either the therapist or the client. When specific behavioural measures were used, the difference between professionals and para-professionals disappeared. Furthermore, the more experienced and longer-trained para-professionals were most effective in relation to professionals, whereas the recently trained professionals had more success than their colleagues who had a more distant training. This again suggests that the status of therapists is less important than their respective training and experience. However, these findings are still very tentative, as Hattie *et al.* acknowledge. For one thing, their 'meta-analysis' did not consider client variables in relation to the obtained outcomes. It is quite plausible that professionals deal with more difficult clients in less advantageous environments, such as the chronic psychiatric in-patient. Clearly, future reviews of this kind should consider all relevant variables in reaching their conclusions. This may help to shift the debate away from status clashes and towards more helpful information on the important elements of therapy — for all concerned.

The comparative effectiveness of professionals and para-professionals is, however, only half the story, since the arguments that follow from the triadic model suggest that we also need to attend to other relationships in the natural environment. In this sense, we need to contrast the relative effectiveness of those who have not received any training at all in therapeutic techniques with the various levels of sophistication shown by para- and professional groups. To rephrase, the option is not 'to be or not to be' a therapist, but rather to recognise that, like it or not, we all influence the behaviour of others in our environment, no matter what level our 'knowledge and capacities'. The professionals and para-professionals are only distinguished by their efforts to develop their skills and enhance their understanding of this influence, and by the more formal nature of their relationship to the trainee.

Unfortunately, such relatively complex views of therapeutic influence in the natural environment are not reflected in the research literature (Hersen, 1981). Recently, Agras and Berkowitz (1980) reviewed the status of behaviour therapy and found that evaluations of training, dissemination methods and field efficacy figured in an average of less than 1 per cent of articles appearing in two major journals during the years 1970 to 1978. It is surprising that so little systematic research has been carried out on the effects of training behaviour therapists, since many critics might point to the possible dangers of letting mediators 'loose' with such powerful techniques of control. Let us now consider more of the ethical issues in 'giving psychology away'.

1.6 Ethical Issues

Giving away potent therapeutic techniques carries with it the risk that these techniques will be misapplied or abused. This raises the ethical issue of whether it is appropriate to involve change agents such as mediators, since their understanding of the techniques is necessarily limited and therefore liable to lead to their misuse.

One early view was that, unlike the quacks who meddled with physical complaints, the quack psychotherapist was a relatively harmless creature, and so no ethical problems were raised. This followed from the belief that the subconscious mind would reject any evil suggestions from the practitioner who strives to use his powers for malign purposes: 'instructive morality comes to the aid of the genuine psycho-therapist, and refuses its co-operation to the counterfeit' (Lawrence, 1910, p. 236).

This might be consistent with more recent psychoanalytic perspectives, but it is at variance with a behavioural formulation, which asserts that processes of influence are always present. This influence can be 'good' or 'bad'. For instance, it can shape up a range of behaviours on the part of nurses or parents that are not therapeutic. Illustrations of such processes will be provided in the next chapter, when we consider a number of the factors that influence therapy. The task for the professionals who give psychology away is to understand and control the influences that bear on the development of therapeutic 'knowledge and capacities'.

For this reason, it is especially important to evaluate the training of such groups as the 'para-professionals'. A study by Brooker and Wiggins (1983) provides a good illustration of how such an evaluation can be conducted and how ethically important the findings can prove to be. They examined the clinical outcomes achieved by eight trainee nurse therapists who had treated 251 patients. They found that three of the therapists had not brought about any significant improvements with the group of 87 patients that they had seen, whereas their five colleagues did achieve successful results. No doubt similar results would be found regarding individuals in other professions, but what is important about the Brooker and Wiggins (1983) study lies in their careful assessment of the *effects* of training therapists. It would be difficult to find equivalent data on the training of other professionals, and it is therefore to the credit of these nurse therapists that they made their findings public. This seems to be the essence of ethical therapeutic conduct, for it is only through evaluations of this kind that one learns about one's strengths and weaknesses.

It follows that the essentially unethical form of conduct is to apply therapeutic techniques in the absence of any evaluations or feedback. This is especially the case where brief courses of therapy training have been introduced, as typically occurs with mediators. Such a training offers the danger of 'a mindless technology', where superficial teaching methods and simplistic behaviour analyses are not followed by observation of the application of the technique by the fledgling therapist (Berger, 1979). A more ethical strategy for giving psychology away is to allow the trainee therapist to progress gradually through a systematic course of training entailing regular demonstrations of competence as a condition for moving on to the next stage of learning (Stein, 1975). It is paradoxical that such care is sometimes taken in training para-professionals such as mothers (e.g. Patterson *et al.*, 1970) or nurses (e.g. Paul and Lentz, 1977), but is rarely found in the training of supervising professionals, such as clinical psychologists (Milne, 1983a).

The ethical issues therefore include not only *monitoring* one's own therapeutic efforts, but also *evaluating* the effects of training others and of utilising mediators. Looking to the future, it may be that *inadequately* prepared mediators or professionals will be ineffective therapists, whose work will then be extinguished. This will retard the development of a broadly based and accessible therapy service, so there is clearly a premium on systematic approaches to 'giving psychology away'.

In addition to a concern with intra- and interprofessional issues, there is also a need to ensure that techniques are acceptable to the patient and more generally to society. There is a particular danger in some institutional programmes, for instance, of losing sight of essential human values. Lucero *et al.* (1968) reported that these programmes have included the use of electric-shock grids, physical restraints (tying a patient to a bed or chair), prolonged seclusion and deprivation of food or sleep.

Such programmes have led to the establishment of ethical guidelines for behaviour therapy (e.g. the 'Zangwill report': Zangwill, 1980, and the reports by the British Psychological Society in 1974, and the British Association for Behavioural Psychotherapy in 1980). In general there is a great deal of agreement between British and American guidelines. The main themes that relate to training-therapy skills are the importance of adjusting the treatment programme to the needs of individual patients, and the need for the therapists to work within their limitations, seeking advice and assistance where these limits are reached. For example the 'Zangwill report' (Zangwill, 1980) regarded the continuing evaluation of a mediator's performance as essential, and that the supervisors themselves must develop substantial theoretical knowledge and practical experience. On this basis the report recommended further development of in-service training schemes and interdisciplinary workshops in order to promote wider understanding and active use of behaviour therapy. They also recommended that supervisors should foster an appreciation of the need for clearly stated aims and adequate methods for evaluating results.

In terms of specific procedures, all these reports urge that aversive and deprivation techniques be avoided unless all other strategies prove ineffective. Instead, the emphasis is on *positive* reinforcement procedures, where, for example, undesirable behaviours can be ameliorated indirectly by reinforcing behaviours that are incompatible with the problematic activity. For example, rather than punishing a child for a temper tantrum, he might only be rewarded for other behaviours.

It is important to realise that the ethical issues arising in the case of behaviour therapy are no different from those that apply to any other therapeutic technique. It is unfortunate that behaviour therapy, or more particularly 'behaviour modification', has been associated with the sorts of aversive technique cited above. When such unethical procedures have been investigated, it has usually transpired that 'behaviour modification' was simply a handy label for some of the preferred practices of the institution, or were simply a misunderstanding of what was entailed by a behavioural approach (Miron, 1968). In contrast, a carefully constructed programme of behaviour therapy that judges aversive techniques to be appropriate may be a vital resource, in which case it might be unethical *not* to consider applying such a programme. For instance, when Lovaas *et al.* (1965) were faced with a child who persistently injured himself, they succeeded in stopping his behaviour by the careful use of electric shocks. The actual treatment only lasted a few minutes, and at a 3-year follow-up the problem had not recurred. Similarly, Lang and Melamed (1969) used electric shocks in order to reduce persistent vomiting and chronic rumination in a 9-month-old child. Other approaches to this life-threatening problem had been unsuccessful, but aversion therapy brought about a rapid improvement and saved a life.

There is an additional ethical issue we have not yet considered: that of civil liberties. Is it acceptable, for instance, that chronic psychiatric patients should be denied access to such programmes as token economies, which require work in exchange for basic rights such as food, if these 'tough' approaches are an important way of opening the door to the community (Cotter, 1967)? Does the 'normal' psychiatric hospital routine, which deprives the patients of opportunities to make simple choices and decisions relating to everyday life, not provide a clearer example of an unethical and aversive 'programme'? These issues are relevant since they draw our attention to the *relative* acceptability of various treatment or non-treatment strategies, and require a considered response in terms of personal, professional, institutional and societal values. Again, the most important consideration is the analysis on which the use of aversive or other techniques is based, the skilful application of these techniques, and an ongoing and systematic assessment of the effects of the technique. Perhaps the fundamental ethical issue is whether the end justifies the means, and having a patient earn cigarettes in order to buy better mental health may be a good bargain (Cahoon, 1968). It also seems remarkably like a natural relationship, such as that between teacher and pupil or mother and child, full of painful but helpful lessons (Bragg and Wagner, 1968).

1.7 Training and Learning

One theme that has emerged from the preceding sections is the importance of ensuring that therapists, whether professional or para-professional, are adequately trained and supervised. Not only is there an ethical constraint on the trainer to ensure that any given level of competence is actually attained and maintained successfully: if the initial training is unsuccessful, then it is very likely that trainees will fail in their attempts to obtain changes in their patients and subsequently will abandon their new skills completely. This represents a comparable failure on the part of the trainer to give psychology away. At the heart of this problem are the interrelated themes of *training* and *learning* which can be found at both levels of the triadic model, either between supervisor and mediator, or between mediator and trainee. All three agents in this model are in training or learning positions, since on the one hand they are trying to train one another, while on the other hand they are well placed to learn about that training effort through feedback.

This suggests that we effectively give training 'downwards' and learn about the training effectiveness 'upwards'. It is vital to regard these two processes as interdependent, since the success of one depends on the success of the other; we cannot become effective supervisors or mediators if we do not learn about the effects of our training. That there is 'no learning without feedback' is a truism, yet in the sphere of giving psychology away this has not been implemented. Although psychologists have spent large portions of their professional time training mediators, there is relatively little information on the effects of all this training. We may be reminded of the old common-sense saying that 'practice makes perfect'; but it is only practice, *the results of which are known*, that makes perfect. This elementary fact has not had much influence on supervisors, who generally do not arrange for knowledge of results in order to improve their own performance.

As a consequence, the acid test of training is rarely applied, namely that the trainee learns and *enjoys* learning (Stones, 1979). In turn, if the supervisor obtains no reliable or valid feedback, he may develop 'superstitious' supervisor behaviours. This refers to the emergence of training activities that are not functionally related to the sought-after change in the mediator, but which are shaped up by coincidental reinforcement (Loeber and Weisman, 1975). One illustration may well be the popularity of 'satisfaction' ratings of training courses, which tend to be so general that the supervisors may be reinforced for activities that are irrelevant to the mediator's learning. In contrast, more precise evaluations provide feedback on detailed elements of the training, facilitating the supervisor's learning of functionally related behaviours. An example is 'micro-counselling' (Ivey *et al.*, 1968) where great care is taken to pinpoint and develop counselling skills.

To indicate the general lack of commitment to evaluation, consider the training of psychiatric and mental handicap nurses in behaviour therapy. A survey of hospitals in the UK revealed that some 22 hospitals were operating in-service training courses in behaviour therapy (Hall, 1974). Of these, only eight courses had been evaluated, and even then only by general 'satisfaction' ratings and questionnaires. Supplementing these findings, there are only four published articles that report in-service evaluations of training in behaviour therapy in the UK. These publications provide one of the few formal learning opportunities to supervisors and guidance on such issues as the course content and teaching methods.

Considering the research literature on other mediators, such as parents and teachers, and incorporating all the English language research literature, there are only a small minority of articles that *systematically* relate the training of mediators to their success in helping clients. One of these rare studies is that of Bouchard *et al.* (1980), who taught professionals to apply social skills training. In addition to assessing the effects of their attempt to train the therapists, they also examined the related outcomes achieved by the therapists with their socially unskilled clients. And, as they state, it is ironical that so little controlled research has been carried out with such groups as these professionals, since they are the people who are entrusted with passing on the therapeutic skills. Others have commented on the current situation in professional education, in which psychologists are expected to learn training skills by osmosis or magic (Buttrum, 1976).

This paradoxical situation seems to be widespread, as well as having a considerable history. Over 25 years ago, Rogers (1957) said:

> considering the fact that one-third of present-day psychologists have a special interest in the field of psychotherapy, we would expect that a great deal of attention might be given to the problem of training individuals to engage in the therapeutic process . . . for the most part this field is characterised by a rarity of research and a plenitude of platitudes.

More recently, Loeber and Weisman (1975) concluded that whereas the actual techniques of behaviour therapy had become increasingly sophisticated, there was still no comparable development in the study of the trainers and therapists who used these techniques.

If the necessary training is not provided to the supervisors, then what hope is there for the mediator or trainee? Fortunately, it is not essential to place all our emphasis on a 'downwards' training process. Indeed, perhaps the most valuable process is the 'upwards' one, in which the supervisor can learn about training from the mediator. This may itself seem rather paradoxical, given that the supervisor is supposed to be the one with all the skills and knowledge. However, one of the key supervisor skills is to arrange for feedback on training efforts. This means that the supervisors are both training and learning, and through this process enhancing their expertise. For instance, supervisors can obtain feedback on the teaching methods used or the tasks set, and revise these in the light of subjective (e.g. the mediator's comments) as well as objective criteria (e.g. measures of skill and knowledge). In a less formal sense the relationship between training and learning is dynamic, with opportunities at every turn for both to occur.

Perhaps the clearest illustration of a learning opportunity is the classic school situation in which the supervisor attempts to establish a common base from which to start teaching. He or she will usually ask if everyone is familiar with a certain basic idea, such as classical conditioning. The usual response is a few blank stares, some averting of audience eyes and one or two nods. The classic response of the supervisor is to then accept this as equivalent to some given, often preselected level of understanding that fits with his or her plans. Such a difficulty is all too common, not only in training mediators but also in 'dyadic' work with patients. Consider the findings on doctor-patient communication (Ley, 1977): although the 'supervisor' (doctor) believes that the audience (patient) has understood, the evidence shows that this is very often not the case. As a general rule, the findings from this kind of research show that experienced clinicians produce material that is too difficult for their patients, who are therefore unable to understand or remember what they were told, and who consequently fail to comply with instructions. However, to avoid the embarrassment of appearing unintelligent these patients will rarely say that they have not understood, so depriving the doctor of corrective feedback that would improve communication.

There is no reason to suppose that an audience of mediators is any more likely to automatically understand. One solution to this training-learning difficulty is to move from 'talk and chalk' to action-based learning. Instead of requiring a verbal response from the audience, which is a very delicate task at the best of times, the trainer can create a practical situation in which trainee therapists can *demonstrate* their level of understanding. This overcomes the problems associated with verbal responses, which can very rarely match the related practical skills in any case, and at the same time offers the trainer the most priceless feedback on what the trainee can actually *do*. During a course of training, this feedback lets the trainer know the effects of their instruction, and it is by this device that the most important learning takes place — on both sides. Some quotations may help to confirm this view:

> I hear and I forget. I see and I remember. I do and I understand. (Ancient Chinese proverb)

> [The wise teacher] does not bid you enter the house of his wisdom, but rather leads you to the threshold of your own mind (Gibran, 1926, p. 67)

> The teacher helps the student respond on a given occasion, and he helps him so that he will respond on similar occasions in the future. He must often give the first kind of help, but he is teaching only when he gives him the second. Unfortunately, the two are incompatible. To help a student learn, the teacher must as so far as possible refrain from helping him respond (Skinner, 1968, p. 216)

Of course, this emphasis on the importance of 'learning-by-discovery' is equally relevant to the relationship between mediator and trainee. It is one of the basic tenets of behaviour therapy that verbal responses are not accepted as equivalent to action, and this underlies the widespread use of *in vivo* desensitisation as the treatment of choice for most anxiety-based problems. Equally, the patient's report of exposure to difficult situations is not accepted to be as valid as the therapist's own direct observations. There is, therefore, a common thread running through training and learning. This thread links the principles of learning to the training situation via a shared premium on *overt behaviour* and *feedback*. The result is that we need not depend solely on 'downward' training experiences for the development of our therapeutic skills. We can also *learn* by structuring our training so that it yields information that can guide us in the future, making education an evolutionary process (Bolton, 1910). This applies equally to dyadic and triadic models, and returns us to some earlier issues: we may now like to regard a 'quack' or an unethical therapist as one who does not attempt to arrange some kind of systematic feedback from this training (or treatment) of others. One illustration of this is the use of electro-convulsive therapy (ECT), which until recently had been administered to many thousands of patients without any compelling evidence of its effectiveness. It was found that the training of doctors in the use of ECT and the maintenance of the equipment itself were often of such a low standard that the editors of the prestigious *Lancet* journal described it as 'a shameful state of affairs' (*Lancet* Editorial, 1981).

One might readily argue that the giving away of psychological techniques merits a similar verdict; the ECT example merely exemplifies the importance of determining carefully the precise effects of any therapy. One reason why ECT was apparently not accorded careful evaluation from the outset was its 'obvious' success in relieving depression (Kendall, 1981). But even if its overall success was self-evident, there still remained the question of systematic evaluation. For instance, what is the most effective shock intensity and duration, the correct number of ECT sessions in a course of treatment, and the kinds of 'depression' that respond best to ECT? Equally, in the training of therapists one can argue for comparable rigour, even if only because such training is 'obviously' going to help, and has benefits that no one would question.

1.8 Summary and Conclusions

There is nothing new in the widespread use of therapeutic techniques. What distinguishes the recent trend to 'give psychology away' is the attempt to provide a firm empirical base for this dissemination. This includes the internal consistency of behaviour therapy, which relates the importance of natural environments to readily acquired and effective techniques that are applicable to a diversity of problems and settings. The key feature of the natural environment is the relationship between direct-care individuals, such as parents, teachers and nurses, and those with problems. The behavioural approach predicts that these relationships will be crucial to any change programme and so attempts to develop them in a systematic fashion. The triadic model illustrates how this is implemented, with the supervisor providing training for the mediator who then applies the techniques to the trainee in the natural environment. The use of the triadic model has led to objections from the professional colleagues of supervisors, who express concern about the possible dangers of 'a little knowledge'.

However, there is reason to believe that among the wide variety of para-professional and professional therapists in practice there is a considerable overlap in their range of skills and good reason to believe that specialised training can prove to be safe and effective. An equally pressing ethical issue is whether we can justify withholding therapy when there is a reasonable likelihood of improving services to the public through such strategies as the triadic model.

In addition to the possible benefits of a fresh appraisal of how we provide therapy, we might also reconsider training itself. There is a general tendency to adopt 'easy' teaching formats, such as the lecture. Unfortunately, on its own this usually profits neither the supervisor nor mediator. It is more useful to regard training and learning as reflexive, to be understood and developed in terms of the general laws of learning. This includes the importance of *feedback* as the means by which the 'trainer', whether supervisor or mediator, learns about the effects of their training. The popularity of passive methods of instruction, such as reading assignments and discussions, are unlikely to promote this learning on their own, as the correspondence between saying and doing is usually weak. The consequence of only having verbal feedback is that the trainer may develop 'superstitious' behaviours at the expense of functionally important skills. The value of more objective evaluations is apparent in terms of all the topics in this chapter, since it provides the feedback necessary for developments in our understanding of the triadic model. In this sense the concerns of professionals about giving psychology away are misplaced and short-sighted. As the ancient Zen masters might have put it, you only get to keep what you give away (Kopp, 1973).

2 PLACING BEHAVIOUR THERAPISTS IN CONTEXT

2.1 Introduction

The previous chapter stressed the interdependent roles of supervisor, mediator and trainee in the triadic model. It was necessary to consider their respective contributions in order to understand issues such as how therapists acquire skills and how therapy services can be run efficiently.

We can extend this understanding to the system that hosts the triad, such as the hospital or school, and in this way we can develop an awareness of some of the many factors that exert a powerful influence on the development and maintenance of therapist skills. The main theme of this chapter, then, is that everything occurs in a context, and it is impossible to understand therapy skills fully until one grasps how they are influenced by the situation in which they occur. One of the most widely used terms for describing relationships of this kind is 'system'. This has been defined as any entity that consists of interdependent parts. In this sense a car is a system, and so is a hospital or a school. Some of the basic concepts of a system are that all levels of the system are interdependent, that there is order despite complexity, that cause-effect relationships are not straightforward, and that living organisms and social structures interact with other systems (Ackoff, 1969).

This chapter outlines some of the important factors in systems where therapy commonly takes place. These factors (or 'constraints') include politics, the physical environment, the organisational structure, the learning potential of trainees, and the interactions between supervisors and mediators. We will then consider innovation, namely the attempt to overcome these constraints and to introduce planned and beneficial change. Behaviour therapy has encountered a range of constraints which are typical of those that face any innovation. Unfortunately we know very little about securing successful innovations involving behaviour therapy, and all we have are lists of guidelines based on the experiences of pioneers. Following a review of these guidelines and the research that has been done on bringing about change in an established system, we will discuss the nature of systems in order to attempt a behavioural analysis of therapy skills.

Some of the clearest illustrations of the nature of systems come from ecology, the study of the interdependencies between organisms and environments. Many of man's attempts to alter his environment have resulted in 'side-effects'. These have highlighted unexpected interrelationships. One of the most common examples was the use of insecticides to control insect-borne diseases and save precious crops. Although short-term results were good, it gradually became evident that newer and larger outbreaks of insect pests were replacing the initial ones, as predators were killed off and food chains were disrupted. Some insect strains were becoming resistant to the insecticides, and so high concentrations of the poison were being accumulated further up the food chain, threatening birds of prey that were not intended to suffer (Odum, 1963).

Willems (1973, 1974, 1979) has offered some more striking examples from such changes to the environment as the building of the Aswan Dam on the Nile. The dam was designed to supply water for irrigation and to generate electricity, but it also produced 'side-effects', including an increase in schistosomiasis among the people living along the Nile, since the now still waters harboured snails carrying more virulent flukes than occurred in running water. This disease causes fever, internal bleeding and inflammation, leading in some cases to permanent damage of the liver and bladder.

Many other instances of how our technologies go awry are regularly reported in our media, and it is now common to find groups opposing new developments on the grounds that it will lead to unacceptable side-effects, for example from nuclear power. There has not, however, been any such group concerned about the possible side-effects of 'giving away' the technology of psychology. Perhaps this follows from the relatively small commitment that psychologists and other social scientists have made to social problems on a large scale, allied to a lack of research that would elucidate any side-effects of vigorously applying psychology to socially important problems. As Willems (1973) has put it, 'the question of larger and unintended effects within the interpersonal and environmental contexts and over long periods of time beg for evaluation and research' (p. 97). This research needs to assume that side-effects *will* occur following behavioural interventions and to be prepared to take them into account.

In this chapter we will consider some research that has adopted an ecological perspective. This perspective, allied to a behavioural analysis framework, has been called 'behavioural ecology' (Rogers-Warren and Warren, 1977) and, as we shall see, it has thrown light on how our interventions influence and are influenced by the environment in which they occur.

2.2 Systems: Research Problems in Natural Environments

Anyone who has 'given psychology away' will have experienced the gulf between what we actually do in therapy and the world of the textbook. They seem at times to be separate realities, since straightforward techniques and rapid cures are only present in the literature (Berger, 1975). An image of precision and control is maintained in journals and to a lesser extent at conferences and other public discussions of behaviour therapy. The political, personal and environmental problems that precede any research and impede its effectiveness are rarely stated (Clark *et al.*, 1972). Repucci and Saunders (1974) in a classic paper addressing this issue stated:

> although claims of the success of applied behaviour modification as a vehicle of institutional and individual change are widespread, convincing empirical evidence is limited to laboratory and to highly financed, small demonstration projects. Thus, the usefulness of behaviour modification techniques in natural settings is unclear. (p. 658)

There is little reason to update this statement a decade on. There remains a 'disturbing gap' between research and practice (Wilson, 1982, p. 291). For instance, there has been almost no research attention given to the 'best' methods of teaching behavioural approaches, to training methods and to evaluations of the effects of techniques in natural (i.e. 'real world') environments. Agras and Berkowitz (1980), summarising a random sample of articles in two major behaviour therapy journals during the 1970s, reported that the three topics above, when combined together, were present in *less than 1 per cent* of articles. Furthermore, long-term clinical outcome studies were present in only 1 per cent of articles. In contrast, 41 per cent of articles were classified as laboratory studies by these authors. The state of research outside the laboratory is no better represented in other journals, such as the *Journal of Applied Behaviour Analysis*

(Warren, 1977) or the *American Journal of Community Psychology* (Novaco and Monahan, 1980), leading one to suspect that claims of an advanced state of applied behavioural research is a fantasy akin to Skinner's *Walden Two* Utopia.

The paucity of applied research itself provides a useful illustration of how the academic system works: we are witnessing the effects of brief research grants and the premium on publications regardless of utility, to mention only two constraints. Similarly, applied psychologists are given few inducements to conduct research relevant to their work issues, since the onus is on first 'seeing patients'.

In addition the applied researcher is faced with what often seem like insurmountable obstacles. For instance, Watson (1979) recalled how nurses resisted his attempts to make observations in homes for elderly disabled patients by de-focusing cameras and by pointing them away from the intended subject. Morrison *et al.* (1968) found that attempts to introduce nursing staff to the use of behavioural techniques with autistic children floundered due to 'interpersonal problems'. These included the nurses' reluctance to control the food given to a six-year-old autistic child because they considered that it entailed 'emotional suffering' for the child, in the form of crying and depression. As a result these nurses tended to exceed food limits when the child cried, so undermining the behaviour therapy programme. Educationalists have also expressed disapproval of behavioural approaches, which have been described as a regression to the traditional classroom view of education: 'Be still, be quiet, be docile' (Sullivan, 1975). In addition to these difficulties in gathering data and obtaining staff support, there are a vast range of obstacles arising from the situation in which the clinical problem occurs. This problem is usually related to the social interactions that take place in the natural environment. In this way the relationships between fellow-patients, pupils, children and so on will typically have a more powerful effect on the problem than the therapist can hope to have. Indeed, this was put forward as one of the *advantages* of the triadic model in the first chapter. Unfortunately, many therapists have tried to directly influence their trainees without altering natural relationships. The consequence is usually that the trainee remains under the control of his peers, who tend to reinforce an alternative or incompatible set of goals to those of the therapist. This kind of process is particularly evident in long-stay institutions, such as prisons, where the friendship between prisoners (the 'inmate subculture') exerts a powerful influence on the behaviour of staff and inmates. This power derives largely from the prison system itself, which reduces contact between staff and inmates and forces both groups to turn to their own peers for support (Ohlin and Lawrence, 1959). As we shall see shortly, such processes are also present in hospital and school settings.

With these kinds of difficulties it is not surprising to find that so little research has been conducted in these settings. However, there is an alternative to the avoidance of applied research, and this is to develop 'coping strategies' (Kraemer, 1981). This entails adjustments to the sampling, measurement, design and implementation so that research can start and can reach a conclusion. This process provides the therapist and the system with feedback, helping us to make informed adjustments (Suchman, 1967). It also provides reinforcement for the therapist's research behaviour. As Salmon (1983) has pointed out, this reinforcement does not come from some vague satisfaction with 'understanding the world', but from the reactions of our colleagues, having work published, and so on.

2.3 Systems: Some of the Constraints on Training

Research has just provided us with an example of academic and applied systems that influence the behaviour of scientists. But such an analysis is equally applicable to behaviour therapy training. Consider the supervisor who tries to 'give psychology away' in an institutional system. The most celebrated account of this is provided by Georgiades and Phillimore (1975), whose provocative article illustrated the futility of a 'hero-innovator' approach. They pointed out that such pioneers of change are 'eaten for breakfast' by large institutions, and suggested that rather than attempting to alter these systems by staff training it might be more fruitful to use less confrontational approaches. In reaching this conclusion they drew on the research of Morrison and McIntyre (1969), who had studied the effectiveness of teacher training and found that attitudes encouraged during a three-year training, such as 'tender-mindedness', were rapidly lost once the teachers went into practice in the school. Georgiades and Phillimore recounted other examples of attempts to alter organisations by training, and concluded that they had been uniformly unsuccessful because they used oversimplistic strategies to introduce change. Repucci and Saunders (1974) highlighted the 'social psychology' of behaviour therapy and in particular some of the factors that are present in systems and that prevent training ventures from achieving more successful outcomes. They include political constraints (Richards, 1975), poor staff and patient selection (Hall and Baker, 1973), adverse living environments (Buehler *et al.*, 1966), restrictive management practices (Raynes *et al.*, 1979), bureaucracy, unions and public relations (Repucci, 1977). In short, places like hospitals and schools are 'very complex social systems' (Thompson and Grabowski, 1972).

Although there are, no doubt, differences in complexity, all social systems harbour constraints and difficulties for the innovator. For instance, Ferber *et al.* (1974) found that their attempts to train the parents of 'problem children' were compromised by the child's training of the parent: in one illustration a child was able to control his mother's interactions with him by minimising contact with her. Wahler (1980) recounted the difficulties mothers had in dealing with their children's 'oppositional behaviour', correlating it with a lack of social contacts and support. This led Wahler to list the kinds of social interaction that influenced the parents' behaviour towards their children. For instance, one maternal grandmother was experienced

Figure 2.1: A Reproduction of an Old Cartoon, Depicting One of the Constraints of Training ('Counter-control')

by a parent as 'making me feel like a kid again' and another mother reported 'Well, you've got to do what they say.' On the other hand, the supervisor and some friends provided support for the mothers' attempts to control their children by applying their behaviour therapy training. These differences in social support accounted for the poor maintenance of the parent training programme among 'insular' parents, even though those parents were initially successful at altering their children's behaviour.

A further illustration can be found from attempts at implementing the 'engineered classroom' (Martin, 1977). As with the insular parents just described, it has proved possible to obtain short-term changes with pupils who do not pay attention in the classroom by first 'engineering' changes in the teacher. This included greater restrictions on the teacher's behaviour, as in not allowing pupils who have finished ahead of others to just sit or read a book and in not blaming children for their learning difficulties. Abidin (1971) has added a list of problems associated with the introduction of behaviour therapy to the classroom, including the need for 'mildly compulsive' teachers, since greater than average demands are made on their organisational ability. Abidin has also emphasised the importance of ensuring the supervisor's support for any changes. He has found that weekly or daily encouragement and recognition of the teacher's effort by the supervisor and the head-teacher were effective reinforcers, as was the evidence from graphed records of changes in the pupils' problem behaviour.

It is worth stressing the significance of the use of reinforcement in the above example, in contrast with the more traditional emphasis on punishment, as in detention, lines and the belt. Skinner (1968) described the 'sullen, stubborn and unresponsive' students that result from attempts to alter the educational system by the use of aversive methods, such as ridicule and coercion. He points out that this form of inaction by the students is often a form of escape because it entails less punishment than compliance with the new system. The greater punishment is the pressures that other pupils exert when a pupil deviates from the norm, and the reinforcement that is given for conformity. This phenomenon is present in all systems, for instance in preventing change in therapy (Ohlin and Lawrence, 1959).

The advent of computer-based education could prove revolutionary in that it could circumvent a lot of these difficulties. If learning were to be removed from the classroom situation, then students would be freed from the obstacles and embarrassments engendered by traditional classroom systems. Some experts anticipate that in the not too distant future the great majority of learning will take place at home. This will have profound implications for both teachers and parents since many of the behavioural problems and solutions discussed in this book will probably be altered radically. Consider the difference between the bored school pupil who has 'nothing to do' in class but cause mischief, and the engrossed learner who has to be dragged away from the computer. There are likely to be big changes in the short-term consequences of such enjoyable and efficient learning, such as increased appropriate reinforcement and decreased punitiveness from teachers and parents, and an increase in the child's general self-esteem and self-efficacy. And if teachers are encouraged to adopt a more tutorial or 'democratic' style of instruction, rather than resisting the advance of technology because someone in the room is more knowledgeable about computers than they are, then we would have a 'quantum leap' out of the old system. This would undoubtedly pose new therapeutic problems, but on balance one might hazard a guess that we would all be better off for the innovation.

2.4 A Behavioural Analysis of Training

The behaviour of the researchers, teachers and therapists outlined above has been presented in a way which highlights the control that the environment exerts over their activities. In the same way that we can carry out an analysis of pupils' behaviour in terms of the things that reinforce or constrain it in the classroom, so we can also examine the behaviour of supervisors and mediators in terms of their environment. This perspective is rare in discussions of therapy training, as traditional accounts of educators in general, whether teachers or therapists, tend to focus on their personality characteristics. Let us now pursue the alternative account, one which relates therapists' behaviour to the environment in which they both train and exercise their skills.

In a fascinating study of a penal institution, Sanson-Fisher and Jenkins (1978) reported that delinquent girls coerced staff into behaving in ways that were contrary to the therapeutic aims of the institution. In place of the so-called 'therapeutic opportunities' (which occurred as seldom as 2 per cent of the time), the staff were influenced by the inmates so that they spent 88 per cent of their time in ways that were non-threatening to the inmates. This included 'passively watching' and 'talking positively' to the girls. The reason for interpreting these findings in terms of a coercion process was that the girls were positively attending to the staff's work behaviour 97 per cent of the time. This work included sweeping the floor and washing dishes, which should have been shared by the one or two staff members and the ten girls. However, not only were the staff reinforced by the inmates' positive attention for doing these household chores; they also reported that trying to get the girls to do these tasks was aversive. Similarly, the girls gave 'negative attention' (swearing, physical threats, etc.) to 75 per cent of the opportunities for therapeutic interactions with staff. This is similar to the coercion process described by Patterson and Reid (1970) as a 'general facet' of social systems, and suggests that the behaviour of staff is shaped by their environment, in this case the inmates.

The advantage of this kind of explanation is that it suggests some ways of altering interactions. Sanson-Fisher and Jenkins (1978) emphasised the need to train these para-professional therapists (i.e. prison staff) in order that they may discriminate between appropriate and inappropriate inmate behaviour, and learn how to control their own reactions to it. They also suggested that these therapists be taught self-control tactics for coping with coercion and how to gain the necessary support. These suggestions again reflect the view that the therapist is part of a system that controls their behaviour, rather than a 'personality', controlled from within. There is every reason to suppose that therapists in other contexts would experience the same kind of environmental 'pressure', and may be equally unaware of the reasons for their behaviour. Nurses who experience 'burnout' (Cherniss, 1980) may attribute their vocational apathy and pessimism to their innate unsuitability for the job. But, rather than viewing themselves as being temperamentally unsuited, or other 'personality' explanations, it will often make sense to regard burnout as 'learned helplessness' (Seligman, 1971). This is a sense of being unable to influence what happens and derives from experiences of failing to alter the system.

As we have seen, systems rarely provide positive reinforcement for those who attempt to promote change. The typical argument involves procrastination, such as 'perfectionism' ('If it can't be done properly we won't do it at all') or more commonly, by stating that 'It doesn't work: we've tried it before and it failed.' If the change agent is not deterred by procrastination, he or she will be influenced by the consequences that a system provides for attempting to introduce change.

One major consequence is punishment: change may be so aversive that the would-be therapist is 'frozen' between the wish to introduce changes that may be therapeutic and the resistance of the system to these changes (Seligman, 1971). The cost of change may be measured in terms of pressure from colleagues and more generally from the commitment of systems to routines. Any alteration to routine inevitably upsets a variety of people who then exert pressure for a return to the original routine. This makes it personally expensive to bring about the kinds of change advocated in the training of teachers, nurses and so on, in terms of the penalties imposed by the school or hospital system.

Loeber and Weisman (1975) have provided a thorough review and model for analysing the behaviour of supervisors and mediators. They point out that, to be understood, training has to be regarded within the context of the system in which it occurs. This includes not only short-term influences such as the trainee's reaction to therapy, but also the reaction to other influences often distant in time and space. These less obvious influences have been referred to as 'setting events', being a variety of complex conditions such as the trainee's hunger, tiredness or preoccupation with earlier or ongoing events (Wahler and Fox, 1981).

The effects of these setting events are still subject to the standard empirical evaluation, namely to observations of their actual *effect* on training. They cannot be assumed to have a straightforward or steady influence.

Some illustrations of these events have already been provided. For example, Wahler (1980) found that parents who experienced essentially critical and unrewarding relationships with their relatives, friends and therapists were unlikely to apply the behavioural techniques they had learnt to their children's oppositional actions. These parents' interactions with others were correlated with systematic changes in their use of aversive methods to control their children later that day. In addition to social influences, setting events also include physical factors such as the availability of suitable training rooms and equipment, historical factors such as the prior behaviour of trainees, supervisors and mediators, and such pervasive elements of the system as rules, regulations and routines (Thomas *et al.*, 1982). These and other factors are presented in Table 2.1.

Table 2.1: Some Setting Events for the Application of Therapy Skills

	Setting-event dimensions	Some illustrations and issues
1.	Physical, social and historical	Absence of training room; pressure from peers to change or stay the same; previous training innovations and the mediator's experiences of particular therapies and outcomes; previous behaviour of trainees
2.	Trainee variables	Response to therapy; motivation to change; physical status
3.	Mediator variables	Existing skills, knowledge and attitudes; co-operation with training; previous experience; peer subculture
4.	Supervisor variables	Career development; the therapeutic model utilised; discipline (whether 'outsider' or not); consultation and participative decision-making
5.	Therapy programmes	Cues (tokens, record sheets); consequences (visitors, response of superiors in staff hierarchy)
6.	Ongoing events	Pay disputes; Christmas; re-organisation
7.	Feedback	Trainee changes; system changes

There is now a growing literature on the influence of these factors on our attempts to change systems. The literature consists of anecdotal accounts of some of these setting events (e.g. Repucci and Saunders, 1974; Richards, 1975; Repucci, 1977; Hersen, 1979), and only a small number of empirical studies, such as those of Wahler (1980), as described earlier, and Woods and Cullen (1983). The latter article considered how the rate and permanency of behaviour change in the trainee altered the mediator's behaviour. It is commonly understood that the results we achieve as therapists will influence how we work: it is very difficult, for example, to continue prompting when the trainee is unresponsive. Woods and Cullen summarised some evidence from work with the mentally handicapped in long-term care that illustrated how the very slow changes that were obtained in toilet training were imperceptible to the nursing staff, who therefore asked for the training to be abandoned. The researchers concluded from this, together with examples from team management and token economies, that the nursing staff's therapeutic behaviour required the trainees to show perceivable, beneficial changes. Not only this, the authors guessed that senior nurses and outside interest had been crucial in maintaining the nurses' behaviour. Once regular observations by the psychologists and the interest of outsiders declined, then so did the nurses' attempts at therapy, since changes in the trainees themselves were not sufficiently reinforcing.

Loeber (1971) also assessed the effect of changes in the trainee on mediator behaviour and contrasted this with providing financial reinforcement to the therapist. He found that nurses significantly improved their use of tokens to reduce a patient's head-banging only when promised a reward themselves. Improvements in the patient alone did not result in improved therapist behaviour. As Loeber concluded, this may have been due to the artificiality of the experiment, in which the nurses only listened to a tape of the patient's head-banging and pressed buttons. It may be that mediators perform better when they have a personal relationship with their trainees. Indeed, Hogg *et al.* (1981) have indicated that nurses working with profoundly retarded children were reinforced by the extent of progress in the children's behaviour, and we have found in our research with psychiatric patients that nurses who achieve success tend to increase their involvement in training (see Chapter 6).

There is clearly no simple relationship between trainee and mediator behaviour, and in addition there are a host of other factors to consider. An interesting illustration of these has been provided by Baker (1980). He trained the parents of mentally handicapped children and assessed the relationship between a list of nine obstacles and the parents' persistence. He reported that parents who did not continue to apply the behavioural techniques reported significantly more obstacles than other parents. The major obstacles were disruptive events (e.g. serious illness), lack of time, and daily interruptions (e.g. telephone calls). These parents did not differ in their ratings of their children's progress, encouragement from the rest of the family, or their knowledge of managing behaviour problems.

Clarification of these findings probably awaits observational studies of the actual effects of these variables, rather than the ratings or opinions of participants. The Woods and Cullen (1983) research, summarised above, revealed the discrepancy between opinions and objective data on trainee change. In addition to assessing changes in the trainee there is a comparable interest concerning what prompts or 'cues' the therapist into action. Tokens are a good example, and they have been found to significantly increase the frequency and duration of nurses' interactions with chronic psychiatric patients (Rezin *et al.*, 1983). Similarly, the room management procedure requires the mediator to note appropriate trainee behaviour. This then serves as a cue for the mediator to provide reinforcement (Porterfield *et al.*, 1980).

It is clear that the search for simple causal relationships between the behaviours of supervisor, mediator and trainee is misguided. It fails to take into account the complexity of natural systems, such as the hospital ward, or to recognise the subtle relationships between these three agents. On the other hand, a systems framework such as the behavioural-ecological perspective offers a way of understanding the events that control therapy behaviour. We shall be offering illustrations of this perspective in the succeeding chapters, but to conclude this chapter let us consider an issue that is closely related to a systems analysis, namely the adoption of innovations in systems.

2.5 Innovation Strategies

It is because systems are so complex, misunderstood or uncontrollable that even the most successful and famous behavioural programmes have floundered (Stolz, 1981). But even though small systems such as schools are 'fantastically complicated' (Sarasen, 1967) we may still be able to make an analysis and arrive at practical options for altering them.

The outstanding illustration of such an approach in the field of mental health has been provided by Fairweather and his colleagues (1967, 1969, 1974). They call their approach 'experimental social innovation'. The fundamental characteristic is to define each phase in an innovation exercise and evaluate it in contrast to alternative strategies. The results provide information on what exactly affects the adoption of innovations. Fairweather *et al.* (1974) applied the experimental social innovation approach to 255 mental hospitals in the USA and noted how these institutions responded. Three strategies were used: demonstration projects, workshops and brochures. They concluded that true organisational change does not occur unless a specific set of techniques is established to facilitate change. These are presented as 11 principles or guidelines for those attempting changes in a system. The principles are summarised in Table 2.2.

Subsequent empirical studies by Tornatzky and Fergus (1982) and by Liberman *et al.* (1982) have borne out the significance of these kinds of variable and have particularly emphasised the role played by the innovator: active participation, personal contact and mutual respect were paramount among these innovation variables. Both groups of researchers regarded such social and political factors as more crucial to an innovation than the actual clinical success of the behavioural techniques themselves.

Many other researchers have presented their guidelines for innovation, but unlike Fairweather *et al.* they are simply retrospective lists of apparently important factors. They include Repucci and Saunders (1974), Georgiades and Phillimore (1975), Bennis *et al.* (1976), Wodarski (1976) and Zaltman and Duncan (1977).

A British study similar to Fairweather's work is that of Towell and his colleagues (1976, 1979), who attempted to isolate the problems psychiatric hospital staff experienced in caring for their patients, and to encourage the implementation of any changes that followed from their investigations. Nurses were most represented, but doctors, occupational therapists, psychologists, social workers and administrators were also involved. The results from all these researchers are remarkably similar to those of Fairweather *et al.* (1974) as summarised in Table 2.2. One of their many unifying themes is the great difficulty of procuring change in established systems, which is, of course, not a new problem:

> It must be considered that there is nothing more difficult to carry out, nor more doubtful of success, nor more dangerous to handle, than to initiate a new order of things. For the reformer has enemies in all those who profit by the old order, and only lukewarm defenders in all those who would profit by the new order, this lukewarmness arising partly from fear of their adversaries, who have the laws in their favour; and partly from the incredulity of mankind, who do not truly believe in anything new until they have had actual experience of it. (Machiavelli, *c.* 1513; in Glen, 1975)

The most common strategy that behavioural researchers have

Table 2.2: Fairweather's Innovation Principles

	Principles	Findings and Guidelines
1.	Perserverance	Hard work and tolerance of confusion are essential. Long time scales need to be adopted and relatively minor 'pay-offs' expected
2.	Discontinuity and independence	Many of the variables traditionally regarded as change-related turn out to be unimportant. These include conservatism and finance
3.	Outside intervention	Some 'outsider' needs to have an active, personal and frequent involvement in change. The outsider's role is to activate a process of change, i.e. to lead, or act as a catalyst
4.	Action-orientated intervention	The demonstration rehabilitation ward results in greatest change, in contrast to simple verbal acceptance of the idea. Innovation talk is not to be accepted as equivalent to institutional change
5.	Foot-in-the-door	The action-orientation often leads to institutional resistance, in contrast to verbal orientation such as persuasion. It may be best to focus on institutions that show a commitment to action, following a graded intervention from talk to action
6.	Limitations of formal power	There is very little evidence that change can be procured by control and coercion via the formal power structure. High status advocators makes no difference to adoption.
7.	Participation	One of the clearest and most consistant findings indicates that involvement across disciplines, status and social groups leads to the greatest change. Unilateral decisions do not lead to change
8.	Group action and implementation	A small 'social change group' within the organisation is necessary to provide leadership and mutual support
9.	Resistance to change	The amount of resistance to change is directly related to the amount of change necessitated by innovation. Role changes that require retraining are particularly prone to resistance
10.	Continuous experimental input	There is considerable local specificity to innovation, entailing a continuous evaluation of the important variables
11.	Activate diffusion centres	Once hospitals have adopted the innovation they become local diffusion centres. They should be given support over a follow-up period

adopted in order to gain acceptance for their innovations is to alter the *consequences* that follow therapeutic behaviour (Stokes and Baer, 1977). In this vein nurses have been given time off work (Watson, 1972), money and trading stamps (Hollander and Plutchik, 1972, Katz *et al.*, 1972), supervisor approval (Montegar *et al.*, 1977), certificates (Watson and Uzzell, 1980), practical demonstrations (Wallace *et al.*, 1973) and feedback (Panyan *et al.*, 1970; Greene *et al.*, 1978), all contingent on their making more therapeutic effort. Parents have been required to pay deposits in order to receive training in behavioural techniques, with the contingency that should they not fulfil the course requirements the money is donated to 'an ideologically unattractive group' (Walder *et al.*, 1969).

Although these contingencies have been successful in developing and maintaining therapeutic behaviour, their application has typically been short-term. The result has been the 'hero-innovator' effect, namely that once these researchers and their contingencies have moved off in pursuit of their next 'positive reinforcement' (research publications, grants, professional posts, etc.) the schemes they set up collapse. In order to make our innovations 'stick', we may do well to turn our attention from 'artificial' contingencies, i.e. those arranged by researchers and hero-innovators, to 'natural' factors, namely the integral features of the innovation itself. Fawcett *et al.* (1980) have listed seven such criteria, based on a review of community schemes in behavioural technology, agriculture and other domains. These criteria are listed in Table 2.3. Fawcett *et al.* (1980) emphasise innovations that are appropriate to their settings. This provides a useful adjunct to Fairweather *et al.*'s (1974) guidelines, since the characteristics of the innovation itself need to be considered together with the means by which it can best be introduced into a system. Implications for training therapy skills follow readily from these authors' suggestions and provide a basis for experimental analysis of the guidelines as they apply to differing circumstances. This experimental step overcomes the naïve approach to innovation that has characterised much behavioural technology to date (Repucci, 1977; Stolz, 1981), and promises us a better understanding and success rate in the future. Chapter 6 presents a case study in nurse training which is an illustration of one attempt to fulfil this promise.

Table 2.3: Criteria for Successful Innovation (Fawcett *et al.*, 1980)

Innovation Criteria	Examples
1. Effective	The major attribute of an innovation is that its benefits exceed its costs and that it is a better idea than the existing approach. 'Better' is best judged by the observations of *all* those involved in the change event. Small, delayed or irrelevant changes are unlikely to persist
2. Inexpensive	Effective changes should be widely accessible and not prohibitively expensive. For example, the cost of parent training should not exceed available funds. The cost to the institution also needs to be evaluated
3. Decentralised	Appropriate technologies should be suited to small-scale application. This allows the preceding two criteria to come into effect and minimises the likelihood of failure. One reason for this is that decentralisation encourages local decision-making
4. Flexible	Rigidly administered technologies tend towards non-adoption, for instance, training counsellors in an unalterable sequence of activities when there is no compelling evidence to so restrict the training. In contrast, a 'menu' of options promotes 'creative involvement' and 'ownership'
5. Sustainable	Scarce resources, such as the contingencies of money and time-off for carrying out therapy, need to be used sparingly. Local resources, such as innovation 'leaders' and positive reinforcers, are more likely to result in maintenance of change
6. Simple	There is a negative correlation between the perceived complexity of innovations and their rate of adoption. Sophisticated technologies may simply promote procrastination
7. Compatible	Innovations that are consistent with the existing values, past experiences and needs of the potential adopter are less prone to rejection

2.6 Summary and Conclusion

The main theme of this chapter has been to show how the development and adoption of therapy skills is inevitably embedded in a system of contingencies. Rather than ignoring these constraints, as typically occurs in reports of applied research, we can increase our understanding of such systems as schools or hospitals by using our psychology reflexively. Of particular utility may be the behavioural-ecological perspective which draws our attention to some of the unpredictable but inevitable 'side-effects' of giving psychology away. These side-effects are amenable to the same basic kinds of analysis that we customarily use with smaller problems, such as a child's temper tantrum. That is, tantrums and therapy skills are influenced by the immediate antecedents and consequences that their environment supplies as well as by the less obvious 'setting events' that may also have a powerful bearing on them.

By pursuing this kind of functional analysis we can develop ways of understanding the constraints that often immobilise new therapeutic schemes. In addition, we would be well advised to attend to two other variables. These are the *appropriateness* of the new technology, and the manner in which we *approach* the system with therapy innovations.

3 PARENTS AS THERAPISTS: A REVIEW OF RESEARCH

3.1 Introduction

In the first chapter we discussed the triadic model as the basis for 'giving psychology away' to non-psychologists. The difficulties in so doing were outlined in Chapter 2. We will now consider those issues in terms of the training of parents as therapists for their own children.

The employment of parents as therapy mediators has a lengthy history. Graziano, in his review of parent training (1977), dated it back to the nineteenth century. As we have already seen in Chapter 1, Freud and others made occasional use of parents as therapists, and, in general, many professionals have seen advantages in directly involving parents in the treatment of their own children. However, the routine and widespread use of parents in this way has been a relatively recent development. One of the earliest accounts of parent training in behaviour therapy emphasised the reasons for this development. These were: the opportunity to observe directly the child's problematic behaviour, rather than relying solely on the parents' self-report; the option of also observing the *parents'* behaviour towards the child; the capacity to observe the parents' understanding of any practical suggestions that are made by the therapist; and to build up an impression of the responsiveness of the child's behaviour to these changes (Hawkins *et al.*, 1966).

On the basis of these, Hawkins' group described an attempt at parent training. They made use of three prompts to guide a mother who had complained of being 'helpless' in dealing with her 4-year-old son's tantrums and disobedience. They were intended to control the nature of the mother's interactions with her son, and included prompts to tell him to stop what he was doing, to give him attention, praise and affectionate physical contact, and to put him in his room for five minutes. These three reactions of the mother were directed at nine of the child's problematic behaviours, such as kicking himself or others, threatening to damage objects or persons and throwing objects. The experimenters (or 'supervisors') visited the house two to three times a week for about an hour each time and sat in a central position where they could unobtrusively observe the interactions between mother and son. They then prompted the mother to give one of the three reactions to her son, depending on his behaviour. They found that the problematic behaviours decreased rapidly once the mother utilised these reactions appropriately, and this improvement was subsequently maintained without the supervisor's prompts.

This early example of parent training has been followed by a large number of replications and variations: in less than a decade a further 70 studies had been carried out (O'Dell, 1974), and there is a continued growth of interest in this field which shows no sign of abating even yet.

The present chapter is intended to give an outline of this development by focusing on some of the main characteristics of parent training efforts to date. For the purpose of this book these principally include the methods used to develop parents' skills and understanding and the approaches used to evaluate this training. Also of interest will be the range of problems that commonly arise, and the content of training and characteristics of the parents as they relate to the acquisition and utilisation of therapy skills. No attempt will be made to review all the literature on parent training, since the amount of research on this topic is too great for a book such as this to accommodate. We will, however, try to highlight the variety and direction of research in this area with respect to the main themes of the book. Those who are interested in more comprehensive reviews are referred to Johnson and Katz (1973), O'Dell (1974), Yule (1975), Forehand and Atkeson (1977), Graziano (1977), Baker (1980), Callias (1980), Wells and Forehand (1981), Isaacs (1982) and Dangel and Polster (1984a).

3.2 Training Methods

The early parent-training experiments typically involved a very brief account of the training procedure, the involvement of only one parent and child, and a focus on a discrete problem behaviour. The paucity of information on the training of the parent, such as the number and duration of sessions or the instructional method, made it difficult to replicate these exploratory studies (Berry and Woods, 1981). Often they simply entailed instructions to the parent. Williams (1959), for instance, asked the parents of a child displaying temper tantrums to ignore these episodes. Within 2 weeks of treatment the tantrums had ceased. Equally simple educational approaches have been described with equally successful outcomes (Boardman, 1962; Wolf *et al.*, 1964; Patterson and Brodsky, 1966; O'Leary *et al.*, 1967). This early, 'exploratory' phase of parent training was followed by an expansion into group training procedures, using more systematic instructional and evaluative methods, and focusing on multiple behaviour problems. We shall now consider illustrations of these developments, which we might regard as the 'technological' phase of parent training.

One of the largest programmes of parent training has been described by Patterson and his colleagues (1967, 1973, 1975, 1982). Their standard training format involves having parents first read a self-instructional text (Patterson and Gullion, 1968) covering the principles of social learning theory. Next, parents are taught individually how to pinpoint problems and to record and graph behaviour. Only when they have actually gathered these data on their own child are they allowed to proceed to the group training phase. This training then includes attention to the nature of parent-child interactions at home and how these may be influencing the problem behaviour. In Patterson's work this has frequently been 'aggression'. We will be returning to Patterson's work in the succeeding sections. For the moment we will focus on research that has examined closely the relative effects of alternative training methods.

Another major figure in parent training who has taken a great interest in this topic has been O'Dell. With his colleagues (O'Dell *et al.*, 1979a) he described a comparison of five training methods designed to teach parents how to use the 'time-out' technique. This entails telling the child what to stop doing, giving a firm, unemotional warning of what will happen if the child fails to comply, and then placing the child in 'time-out' if they still fail to comply. Time-out refers to separating the child from any source of pleasure or 'reinforcement', as for example in taking him away from his toys and placing him in the corner of the room, facing the wall. This time-out usually lasts for up to five minutes, with the child being brought back as soon as the problem behaviour has diminished.

In their experiment, O'Dell *et al.* (1979a) randomly assigned 60 parents to either a no-training control group or training by one of five methods. The first of these was simply reading a manual; the second entailed watching a film; the third consisted of the film plus a brief individual supervision; the fourth was based on individual training by following the therapist's demonstrations ('modelling') and practising the time-out technique under his guidance ('rehearsal'); and the last method was a brief version of individual modelling and rehearsal. They reported that all five methods produced equivalent understanding and skill in a role-play assessment, and that this was greater than the control group scores on either of these measures. On a third measure, based on their actual use of the time-out technique, they found that the film plus individual supervision was the most successful method.

A very similar comparison was reported by Nay (1975), who trained 77 mothers to use time-out by a manual, by lectures, by videotaped modelling, or by videotaped modelling plus role-play. Using a different measure of the parents' understanding of time-out, he reported that all four methods produced similar results. But a second, audiotaped simulation measure indicated that the parents in the modelling plus role-play group were the most skilful.

The difficulties in interpreting these different findings include the lack of a clear specification of the actual training method and content, and the different measures of the parents' learning. For example, O'Dell *et al.* (1977) had trained another group of 40 parents and found that those receiving a 'workshop' training, emphasising behavioural rehearsal, did best on measures of implementing the training at home. These included writing out definitions of their child's problem behaviours and plotting the frequency of the problem on graphs. On the measures of the parents' knowledge or attitudes, there were no differences between the methods of training, indicating that in this case the use of rehearsal training was beneficial. Such apparently inconsistent findings cannot be readily clarified however, because although O'Dell *et al.* (1977) utilised some *30 measures*, none of these was re-administered in their later study (O'Dell *et al.*, 1979a), nor were they present in a subsequent study (O'Dell *et al.*, 1982). In this latter piece of research, 100 parents were randomly assigned to either a control group or training by one of four methods: written manual, audiotape, videotaped modelling, or live modelling and rehearsal. The manual was 3000 words long, written at an eighth-grade reading level (13 years of age) in a conversational tone. It could be read in 20 minutes and presented detailed examples of parent-child interactions with dialogue. The audiotaped training group simply listened to a reading of the manual, while the videotaped group viewed a 26-minute enactment of the manual. A narrator presented the relevant information as five different sets of parents modelled the principles in the manual. In the individual modelling and rehearsal group, parents viewed live role-played demonstrations of the principles, and then rehearsed them during the 30-minute session. As with all training formats, every effort was made to ensure that this group received the same coverage of the principles as the other groups. All training sessions were followed by a 'booster' session in the home, where the parents received essentially a repeat of the clinic training. Some differences existed, as in the 'live modelling with rehearsal' group, who practised the therapy principles with their own children rather than role-playing them with the supervisor as they had done in the clinic. O'Dell *et al.* (1982) reported that all trained groups did better on a semi-structured play assessment than the control group, and that those parents receiving the audiotaped presentation did significantly less well than parents having either the written presentation (manual) or the live modelling and rehearsal. There were no other significant differences between any two training methods.

When the researchers examined these results in terms of the parents' characteristics, they found that there was a general tendency for training outcome to be positively correlated with higher levels of education, socio-economic status and reading level. However, training was interpreted as having reduced the relationship between the parents' therapy skills and their demographic characteristics, and it was suggested that these characteristics interacted with the method of training. Videotape presentation, for example, seemed to reduce or eliminate the association between parents' characteristics and their therapy skills. These findings led O'Dell to conclude that for a high proportion of parents, perhaps those who are well motivated and educated, the actual method of training does not appear to be as crucial as other issues, such as the 'efficiency' of training. Thus a less costly method such as videotaped modelling affords an efficient training method for this group of parents because it achieves comparable results with minimal supervision time.

Christensen *et al.* (1982) have conducted an evaluation of the efficiency of three parent-training methods. They assessed the amount of supervisor time required to train parents whose children displayed a range of behaviour problems, and related the training methods to the outcomes. Individual training, group training and a self-instructional manual were compared. Each method was based on Patterson and Gullion's (1968) programmed book, *Living with*

Children, which parents had to read prior to focusing on their children's specific problem behaviours. The self-instructional group met the supervisor only once and were encouraged to work through the book and the application of it to their own children as far as possible on their own. In the two other groups the parents met the supervisor weekly, either one-to-one (individual training group) or six parents to one supervisor (group training). Parents in all groups maintained telephone contact with the supervisor and the two clinic-trained groups also made audiotape recordings of their attempts at implementing their new skills. This provided the supervisor with accurate feedback, which was then discussed in the clinic sessions.

Christensen reported that the 36 families, equally divided into the three training groups, had all improved by their post-training evaluation. Whereas all parents perceived their children as having benefited equally, specific observational measures indicated that only the two clinic-trained groups were associated with significant decreases in the children's problem behaviour at home. The average amount of supervisor time per family was 11 hours and 44 minutes in the individual training condition; 5 hours and 6 minutes in the group condition; and 49 minutes in the manual condition. In addition, telephone contact added a further 69, 2 and 4 minutes, respectively, for these groups. In sum, compared with individual training, the manual received about 10 per cent and group training 50 per cent of supervisor time. None the less, the manual group ended up with attitudes towards their children that were equivalent to those of the two more supervisor-intensive groups. Given the view that it is the parental *attitude* towards the child rather than simply the child's problematic behaviour itself that is the important determinant of treatment-seeking (Lobitz and Johnson, 1975), such an outcome could readily be argued as a major goal of training, since it reduces the problem of demand for professional help at which the training enterprise is directed. In this sense the self-instructional manual was very efficient and may be the most appropriate training method for some parents. Another possible role for manuals could be in maintaining parenting skills acquired by the individual, or group training methods as have been described above.

Video-based parent training also has great potential as an efficient use of supervisor time and may have a complementary role to play alongside manuals. Webster-Stratton (1981) successfully used a standard video-plus-discussion format to train parents to reduce their own dominating and non-acceptance responses and to increase lead-taking and positive affect with their children. She reported behavioural and attitudinal improvements in these parents as a result of the video-based training and related discussions. As she pointed out, it was unclear whether discussions with the supervisor and the video-presentation of 'good' and 'bad' parenting models were responsible for this change, and like most other studies there remains the task of evaluating the effectiveness of individual components of training 'packages', such as the video alone or one parent alone (Adesso and Lipson, 1981).

Hudson (1982) reported a very similar study to that of O'Dell *et al.* (1982) described earlier. He compared verbal instruction, verbal instruction plus the teaching of behavioural principles, and verbal instruction plus modelling and role-playing. These three groups were contrasted with one another and with a waiting-list control group, the mothers being randomly assigned to each of the four groups. The training groups met once a week for 3 hours over a 10-week period. In the verbal-instructions-alone group the parents began by selecting a specific deficit behaviour for their child and were then told how to start recording baseline data, including the construction of record sheets for these data. Next the parents were instructed how to teach the given skill to the child. The parents were required to run daily training sessions for their children, each session consisting of ten trials. New deficit behaviours were added during the course as prior ones were successfully trained.

In the instructions-plus-principles group the parents were given the above format with the addition of lectures on the principles of behaviour analysis and the behavioural approach to teaching. One hour of the weekly three-hour sessions was devoted to lectures on the topics of functional analysis, prompting, shaping, backward chaining and time-out. The instructions plus modelling and role-playing group also received the same basic format, with the addition of the attendance of the children at the training sessions. This allowed the supervisor to create a 'learning environment' consisting of the supervisor's modelling of the relevant skill, direct observation of the mother's imitating the application of this skill, followed by a corrective feedback phase when the supervisor role-played the child. Thus, the reason for the child's presence was apparently to allow the supervisor to demonstrate training techniques to the mother, rather than to give her supervised practice in the clinic.

Hudson (1982) then used multiple measures to assess the relative effects of these three training methods. He found that the teaching of behavioural principles did not contribute at all to training outcome, although the group receiving this component did score more than the control group on a knowledge test. However, the addition of modelling and role-playing was effective in significantly raising the skills level and in increasing the number of home-based child training sessions, and led to better clinical progress than the control group. Also, this group had acquired a knowledge of behavioural principles comparable with that of the group receiving lectures, suggesting that, in addition to the superior outcomes just mentioned, they had 'incidentally' learnt some of the underlying principles during child training. Hudson (1982) concluded that for parents of markedly handicapped children the use of modelling and role-playing was necessary for *skill* development.

A technological extension of the prompting technique of training has been the 'bug-in-the-ear'. This is a miniature remote radio receiver worn by the parent during interactions with the problematic child. The supervisors can prompt the parent via this radio contact. One illustration was provided by Wolfe *et al.* (1982). They began by observing a mother's interactions with her three children in the clinic, before extending these to the home. The supervisors mostly attempted to replace her 'hostile prompts' to her children (e.g. 'Don't be stupid') with 'positive prompts' (e.g. 'You're doing a good job'), using the radio link. Gradually the reliance on this link was reduced, and the results indicated that this training method substantially decreased the parent's hostile prompts and increased positive prompts. Furthermore, these encouraging findings were maintained when instruction was stopped altogether. These results were also broadly corroborated by the home observations, providing evidence that the parent's new skills had generalised from the clinic to the home. In addition, the researchers reported that during a 2-month follow-up period the family's caseworker and paediatrician had recorded no evidence of child-abuse and that the mother had improved her compliance with the treatment of her children's epileptic disorder.

A considerable number of large-scale parent training packages have been developed latterly, incorporating many of the methods outlined above. A summary of these can be found in Dangel and Polster (1984a). They include some new training features, which we will now outline. One such development has been a 'pyramid training' approach, in which parents who were formerly mediators take on a supervisory role. Hall's (1984) 'responsive parenting' programme provides these ex-clients with subsequent training so that they can act as 'apprentice' leaders of groups of parents newly entering the programme. An 8-week course of training is provided to these 'apprentices', during which time they extend their understanding of behavioural principles by extra reading assignments, assisting the supervisor and the parents, and completing a behaviour-change project. They also attend a workshop in which they are trained in such supervisor skills as demonstrating role-plays and managing problems that may arise in the group sessions. Video tapes and a manual are among the methods used in the workshop.

Shearer and Loftin (1984) have also trained parents to train other parents, and like Hall they are enthusiastic about the advantages accruing to this approach. These include cost-effectiveness, the availability of parents to act as home teachers, a more supportive community network, and enhanced acceptability of the programme.

An extension of the pyramid-training approach has been the 'teaching family' (Braukmann *et al.*, 1984). This consists of a group home run by 'teaching parents' who live in a family-style community home with about six 'delinquent' teenagers. These teenagers would otherwise be liable to custodial care in an institution, but instead spend an average of 10 months in the home receiving 'parenting' designed to promote more adaptive alternatives to their delinquent behaviours. The teachings parents receive a one-year series of skill-centred workshops, incorporating such training methods as manuals, video-tape models, and behavioural rehearsal with systematic and detailed feedback. The workshops are arranged so that 'parenting' skills are gradually developed. The steps in this process include observing experienced teaching parents at work, as well as receiving comments from them on their own subsequent efforts. Interestingly, the youths also provide feedback to the novice teaching parents. Supervision of the parents is then gradually faded during their first year of running a group home.

A grander extension of the methods used to train parents has been the preparation of a self-instructional package consisting of a video tape, written materials, quiz and practice assignments (Dangel and Polster, 1984a, b). This package was disseminated to 8717 public libraries in the USA, allowing many parents the opportunity to study the behavioural approach to parenting at their convenience.

Self-instructional manuals for parents are a feature of many recent programmes, and indeed written advice on child management dates back many centuries. Beckman (1977) found suggestions dating back 2000 years, and cites as evidence of their popularity the number of manuals and pamphlets currently available (800). One such resource, Spock's *Baby and Child Care* (1945) has sold 28 million copies. Behavioural parent trainers have joined the ranks of those offering written advice (Patterson and Gullion, 1968; Christopherson, 1977), and have characteristically placed their manuals on an empirical footing. O'Dell *et al.* (1980), for example, contrasted parents who learnt the time-out technique by manual alone, manual plus film, or manual plus individual modelling and rehearsal. He found that all three methods were equally successful in developing the parents' knowledge and skill.

A survey of 26 behavioural parent training manuals (Bernal and North, 1978) concluded that there was a dearth of such manual evaluations, but where these existed they indicated that manuals were most effective when the child's problem was very circumscribed, as in toilet training. More general or multiple problems required professional guidance. They also pointed out that very few data existed on the effects of supervisor training manuals (e.g. Herbert, 1981) and called for more evaluation, reflecting the scientific training of those who wrote the manuals.

Summary

Parent training methods have clearly advanced at a rapid rate during the last two decades, proceeding from small-scale, supervisor-intensive interventions to semi-automated programmes disseminated on a large scale. There now exist a considerable number of carefully developed training 'packages', each combining a range of instructional procedures. Prominent among them are some traditional methods, such as educational role-play and written material. However, there has also been an emphasis on more recently developed methods, such as audio prompting by way of a 'bug-in-the-ear' radio receiver, and video-presented modelling and feedback, etc. Simultaneously, interest has been shown in the relative efficacy of the different amounts and kinds of supervisor involvement in training, and in parent characteristics. This has led to some challenging findings for traditional methods, such as the success of minimal supervisor packages, utilising a manual, video modelling and group meetings with a supervisor. Furthermore, the relative insignificance of the kind of training method employed with parents who are of higher socio-economic and educational backgrounds throws some doubt on the efficiency of 'standard' supervisor-intensive programmes. Variability of this kind can be accommodated by such recent developments as the 'apprentice' pyramid training approach, in which parents who have successfully completed a programme act as individual trainers for parents first entering the programme.

The main weakness of this research lies, paradoxically, in breaking one of its core principles, that of behavioural specificity. As a consequence, it is impossible for others to replicate their programmes, rendering them neither entirely believable nor viable. A minority of researchers have overcome this weakness by providing detailed manuals for supervisors, indicating precisely what should be done under such terms as 'role-play' or 'feedback'. Even in these cases there remains a need for data indicating the finer processes of supervision, such as the qualitative features of the methods dictated by the manual. Supervisors, like their clients, will vary along this broad dimension and this is likely to influence the outcome in rarely qualified ways. Thus, problems in replicating parent training programmes may arise because of either inadequate specificity or supervisor variables in applying the programme, such as the tone or timing of supervisor feedback, as reported by Isaacs *et al.* (1982). Both areas seem likely to repay research efforts, as do attempts to develop more efficient packages by improving the 'compatibility' of training methods and parents, or by systematically streamlining the packages.

3.3 Evaluation Methods

A very extensive range of methods have been used to evaluate the effects of parent training exercises. They have largely focused on the behaviour of the child, but some researchers have also evaluated the parents' behaviours, knowledge and attitudes. In contrast, very few evaluations of the supervisor's behaviour have been reported. These evaluations have occurred in the clinic and the school, but mostly in the child's home. This range of procedures and measures will now be described in terms of the main areas that have been subjected to evaluation.

Evaluations of Behavioural Change in the Trainee

The early, exploratory investigations of parent training placed their emphasis entirely on changes in the child's behaviour. O'Leary *et al.* (1967), for instance, focused on the frequency of three general classes of child behaviour, namely 'deviant', 'cooperative' and 'isolate'. Deviant behaviour referred to kicking, hitting, pushing and so on; cooperative behaviour included conversation, asking for a toy and requesting help; and the absence of verbal, physical or visual interaction was designated as 'isolate behaviour'. The researchers then recorded the frequency of these behaviours during two baseline and two experimental phases, the latter consisting of training the parent to apply a token economy and time-out procedures.

In a similar vein, Hawkins *et al.* (1966) recorded the frequency of a 4-year-old boy's 'objectionable behaviour'. This included biting, kicking, hitting, throwing objects and pushing his sister. In this case and the O'Leary *et al.* (1967) example, the researchers reported reductions in the frequencies of the undesirable behaviours only during the experimental (i.e. parent training) phases. This style of evaluation has been extended to psychosomatic complaints: Neisworth and Moore (1972), for example, recorded the duration of a 7-year-old boy's asthmatic attacks. They chose to record duration rather than frequency because the components of asthma consisted of overlapping events, such as coughing, wheezing and gasping. They found that the duration of these attacks reduced from a baseline of around 65 minutes per night to less than 10 minutes during the two experimental periods. During these periods the parents discontinued their attention during asthmatic attack and provided positive reinforcement for non-asthmatic behaviour. The problem continued to decline, and when reassessed 10 months later, attacks were only lasting about 1 minute per night.

A most thorough programme of parent training and evaluation has been reported by Patterson and his colleagues (Patterson, 1980). They noted that among the multiple goals in training parents, the primary one is a significant reduction in the deviant behaviour of the problem child. For example, Patterson (1974) trained the parents of socially aggressive and/or stealing children and evaluated the effect of training by observing the children's behaviour. Fourteen categories of problem or 'coercive' behaviour were observed, namely: 'disapproval', 'destructive', 'dependence', 'ignore', 'non-comply', 'humiliate', 'tease', 'yell', 'whine', 'physical negative', 'high rates', 'command negative', 'negativism', and 'cry'. These subcategories are summarised into a 'total deviant' (TD) score. Patterson and his co-workers tend to report the TD score along with parents' observations of their children's problem behaviour. This second behavioural measure they call the 'Parent Daily Report' (PDR). The PDR was originally concerned with a number of specific problems that the parents had identified during an initial interview and six subcategories from the TD measure (namely 'cry', 'yell', 'whine', 'non-comply', 'tease' and 'destruct'). Latterly, however, the PDR has evolved into a 34-item problem-behaviour checklist designed to assess the frequency or non-occurrence of problem behaviours. The checklist is administered daily over the telephone by an independent interviewer (Patterson *et al.*, 1982). Bernal *et al.* (1980) have developed a similar measure. The Patterson group have also latterly made use of Reid's (1978) 29-category observation system known as the Family Interaction Coding System (FICS). This sequentially samples a range of family interactions and is therefore a broader evaluation device than the TD measure, extending beyond but incorporating the 14 social aggression categories enumerated above. The PDR and TD are highly correlated, are accurate in classifying samples of children as clinical (i.e. 'deviant') or non-clinical (i.e. 'normal'), and have adequate test-retest and inter-rater reliability (Patterson and Fleischman, 1979). These findings therefore suggest that the PDR and TD measures are reliable and valid. They were also sensitive to changes in the main target of the intervention, namely reductions in coercive child behaviour.

Flanagan *et al.* (1979) provide an illustration of the categories in an observational scale such as the TD measure. In their study of parental use of time-out, they coded four behaviours. These were

(1) *Parental commands:* rated as either (a) 'indirect or unclear' (e.g. instruction given in the form of a question); or (b) 'direct and clear' (e.g. not a conditional statement).
(2) *Child behaviour:* rated as either (a) 'compliance' (child carries out parent's instruction within 5 seconds of command); or (b) 'non-compliance' (failure of child to comply within 5 seconds).
(3) *Warning:* either (a) 'clear, brief' (any statement indicating that time-out will occur if the child does not comply immediately); or (b) 'no warning or other action' (e.g. extended lecturing, pleading, warning).
(4) *Parental use of time-out:* either (a) 'immediate and correct' (parent takes or sends child to time-out following non-compliance to the warning); or (b) 'other action or incorrect' (e.g. continuing lecture to child once he is in time-out).

Flanagan *et al.* (1979) had two undergraduate students as observers. They used the above scale to rate the parents during five standard commands to their child in their home (e.g. 'Have child return building blocks to bag'). Inter-rater reliability was good and the scale was sensitive to changes as a result of training in parental skill in applying time-out.

An extension of this type of scale and of the use of parental observations such as Patterson's PDR is to have parents complete extensive checklists. These provide a fine-grained assessment of the child's behaviour. Baker *et al.* (1980) have described a set of Behavioural Assessment Scales (BAS) that illustrate this form of evaluation. The BAS consists of a 29-page set of checklists relating to the mentally handicapped child, and contains scales concerned with language, behaviour problems and self-help skills. An illustration of a self-help skill checklist focuses on 'drinking from a cup' and lists eight levels of skill. These range from 'cannot hold a cup at all' (score 0) to 'drinks from a variety of cups and glasses, completely on his own' (score 7). The BAS was used in conjunction with an interview and questionnaires to assess the Read project, a project designed to train parents to become more effective teachers of their mentally handicapped children. Manuals formed the basis of this training, provided to 160 families over a 20-week period (Heifetz, 1977).

Baker *et al.* (1980) reported one-year follow-up results from the BAS for 86 families, indicating that the significant gains made by children in the self-help skills scale during training were maintained for three of their four training groups. (The successful methods were group training, manual only and groups plus visits; the group that failed to maintain its post-training improvements only received instructions over the phone.) They reported that the parents' completion of the BAS correlated very highly with independent, trained observers, and that the BAS was sensitive to developments in the children's self-help skills.

The BAS is similar to the more famous Portage checklists. The Portage project was developed in Portage, Wisconsin, by Shearer and Shearer (1972) utilising a 'precision teaching' model. This entails careful specification of the mentally handicapped child's behavioural strengths and weaknesses, and the involvement of the parents in regular, home-based training of the child. A home adviser provides supervision during weekly visits, deciding with the parents what skills to teach and how to teach them. The Portage checklist covers the developmental areas of self-help, motor activity, socialisation, language and cognition. There are 580 'curriculum cards' covering all the steps in the five developmental areas. Each card includes a behavioural description of a skill and suggests materials for teaching it to the child.

During the first visits the home adviser (or 'supervisor') completed the checklist in order to establish the baseline level of the child's functioning. The parents and supervisor then selected a goal that could be achieved in the next week. At the next visit the supervisor assessed progress with this goal and adjusted the next week's goal. The educational basis of the supervision was written activity charts which were left with the parents each week. These charts described a behavioural goal, how often the selected skill was to be practised, what behaviour was to be reinforced and how it was to be reinforced. Shearer and Shearer reported from one study that 75 mentally handicapped children taking part in the Portage project progressed above their expected developmental rate and that their parents were able to initiate, observe and accurately record this change on the checklists. For example, the 'socialisation' area requires the parents to record the developmental level of their child in terms of some of the 83 behaviours listed in this area of the checklist. These behaviours span the age range 0–6 years, and range from 'watches person moving directly in line of vision' and 'smiles in response to attention by adult' (cards 1 and 2) through to 'states goals for himself and carries out activity' and 'acts out parts of a story, playing part or using puppets' (cards 82 and 83; Bluma *et al.*, 1976).

The Portage model has also been evaluated in the UK. Revill and Blunden (1979) reported a project conducted in South Glamorgan, Wales, involving 19 mentally handicapped children and their parents. They found that all children benefited, regardless of their degree of handicap: of 306 tests set, 88 per cent were learned, 67 per cent of them within one week. Only 5 per cent of tasks were abandoned. They concluded that this home training scheme was a very effective way of teaching mentally handicapped children new skills.

A variation on the Portage model, entitled 'Partnership with Parents', has been developed at the Hester Adrian Research Centre, University of Manchester, UK. The focus remains on the pre-school mentally handicapped child. However, in place of the Portage checklists, the project utilised developmental charts and an alternative parent training approach: individual visits to parents and children were supplemented by fortnightly group sessions at which basic teaching skills were developed by a variety of methods (McConkey and Jeffree, 1975). In addition to these parents, a larger group were involved with the project through specially prepared teaching programmes, presented in book format. These programmes, or 'learning games' were carried out by the parents, following a decision as to their child's developmental level. For instance, the speech development programme ('Let me speak'; Jeffree and McConkey, 1976) includes activities to encourage the child's babbling, such as blowing and sucking exercises utilising straws for drinking, and blowing out candles or matches. A number of these games are suggested for each developmental level. Parents are encouraged to record their child's progress on the developmental charts, ticking off each item that has been successfully taught. In the case of 'babbling', the items include 'makes throaty noises', 'coos and babbles to self' and two or more sounds which the child repeats.

Another approach to gathering observational data in the home has been to use audio tapes. Christensen *et al.* (1980), for instance, placed a small microphone transmitter on the belt of the problem child, with a receiver, tape recorder and timer stored in the home. The microphone picked up the verbal activity of the child and of those in the immediate environment. At the intake interview the parents selected two time periods for tape recordings, covering a total of 4 hours a day. From this period three 15-minute recordings were randomly selected. The parents were given 'censorship rights' to protect their privacy. This included disconnecting the receiver, and listening to and erasing any part of a recording prior to their being listened to and coded by observers. Christensen *et al.* (1980) reported that only two families of the 36 who started the training programme used the censor switch (once each), none requested to listen to the tapes, and one family asked for the equipment to be removed. On average, 3 hours and 13 minutes of audio recordings were collected for each child over the 3-week pre-assessment period and the 2-week post-assessment period.

An observational code was used to categorise the data. The coding system contained 25 discrete behaviours coded sequentially in 10-second blocks. Each behaviour code was noted along with the persons doing the talking and the listening. These 25 behaviours were then summarised into three groups: 'mother negative behaviour', 'negative behaviour of the problem child', and the 'noncompliance ratio of the child to the mother'. For example, in the case of 'mother negative behaviour' the behaviours 'disapproval', 'disapproving tone', 'threat', 'verbal negative', 'whine', 'yell', 'tease' and 'physical negative' were added together.

Christensen *et al.* used the observational data to evaluate the cost-effectiveness of three parent training approaches, namely individual training, group training, or reading a self-help text plus one meeting with the supervisor. They found that the audio recordings indicated a significant reduction in the 'child negative behaviour' category as a result of only the group and individual approaches. In contrast, observational data recorded by the parents indicated that 100 per cent of individually trained cases, 88 per cent of group-trained and 70 per cent of the self-help text group achieved the generally accepted criterion of a 30 per cent reduction in the child's problematic behaviour by the end of an average of 6 hours of training per family.

Evaluations of Behavioural Change in the Mediator

Neither the commitment nor the sophistication that is apparent in observations of problem children is evident in the observations of related parental behaviour. This is a rather strange state of affairs, considering that parent training programmes are based on the belief that changes in the *parents'* behaviour are crucial to reductions in child problem behaviours. Of course, it is usually argued that ultimately the most important criterion of success *is* improvement in the child's behaviour. Without entering into this mildly debatable issue (e.g. it has been argued that in fact changes in the *parents' attitudes* are the most important goal in training; Lobitz and Johnson, 1975), there still remains a need to demonstrate that changes in the child's behaviour are indeed due to changes in the parents' behaviour. It may well be that a child's problematic behaviour alters following training as a result of other variables, such as parental enthusiasm, or the child's 'faking good' for observers during the period of the experiment (Johnson and Bolstad, 1973). Furthermore, ignoring the effect of training in terms of its immediate impact on parental behaviour greatly reduces our 'feedback' about the training procedure. It has been found, for instance, that characteristics of the parents interact with training methods, so obscuring the effect of such training on their child management (O'Dell *et al.*, 1982).

Also, there is compelling evidence (in addition to common sense) to indicate the importance of studying the parents' behaviour. For instance, it has been found that children with conduct problems had parents whose command rates were very highly correlated with their child's misconduct. Furthermore, these parents tended to give more negative commands than another group of parents who identified their children as 'normal' (Delfini *et al.*, 1976; Bernal *et al.*, 1980).

There have, however, been only a few evaluations of the parents' behaviour as a result of training. Berkowitz and Graziano (1972) describe the work of Walder *et al.* between 1966 and 1971, who used both 'before' and 'after' measures of the parents' proficiency in behaviour therapy by means of video-tape measures, although these were not specified, nor were any data presented. Other early examples include the observations of parents by Herbert and Baer (1972) and Patterson *et al.* (1982). More recently, Strain *et al.* (1982) observed the frequency of parents' use of such behaviours as 'adult command', 'positive social reinforcement' and 'negative feedback'. Their parent training programme was based on texts, modelling, role-play, rehearsal and feedback. They found that the parents were able to achieve a score of 85 per cent for 'appropriate therapy behaviour' by the end of training and that this was associated with improvements in their child's behaviour. Furthermore, a long-term follow-up evaluation of parents and children carried out up to 9 years after training indicated that these improvements had been maintained. For example, parents were providing positive social reinforcement for their child's compliance with a frequency similar to that achieved at the end of training.

One of the few evaluations that has considered this 'intervening variable' of parental behaviour with the kind of detail accorded to trainee behaviour was reported by Watson and Bassinger (1974). They provided a summary of a training programme that had been applied to 40 mothers and 54 children, consisting of 'academic' and 'practicum' training. The academic training was based on a programmed text, exams, lectures and slides. Parents were required to obtain a mark of at least 90 per cent in order to proceed through this phase and into the 'practicum' (practical) phase of training. In this latter phase, parents followed step-by-step programmes focusing on their child's self-help, language, social and recreational, co-operative and problematic behaviour, as appropriate. A 'home training specialist' (i.e. the supervisor) assisted the parents in their own homes, ensuring understanding of the programmes and objectively evaluating the parents' use of techniques such as reinforcement and shaping by administering a Training Proficiency Scale (TPS). The TPS is a 40-item, 5-point rating scale designed to assess a person's behaviour therapy skills. The rating scale and items are summarised in Table 3.1.

The TPS was completed by the supervisor during the practicum phase of parent training. The criterion for passing the TPS evaluation was 95 per cent. Not surprisingly, Watson and Bassinger (1974) reported that nobody passed the test first time. To help the parents to reach the criterion, the supervisors went over the items on which the parents did poorly and the evaluation was repeated until they passed.

This training-then-evaluation and feedback procedure began with the self-help skills programme and was repeated with the remaining four programmes. In total, this practicum phase of training took approximately 10 hours. Once the parents had successfully completed training they started to apply the techniques to their children's problems. For instance, one parent trained her child to

Table 3.1: An Illustrative Summary of Watson's Training Proficiency Scale (TPS)

	Therapy skill categories	Illustrations
1.	Shaping child behaviour	• Parent uses the proper sequence of steps • Parent returns to previously successful step if necessary
2.	Reinforcing child behaviour	• Parent finds an effective reinforcement • Parent gives the reinforcement quickly
3.	Communicating	• Parent uses child's name before command • Parent fades physical prompts according to child's progress
4.	Data collection	• Records child's progress as he/she trains • Parent uses Frequency Data sheet correctly
5.	Rapport and miscellaneous	• Parent shows adequate patience during training • Parent trains one task at a time

Rating of parents' proficiency

1 = Did not demonstrate the item
2 = Seldom demonstrated the item
3 = Demonstrated the item more than half the time
4 = Demonstrated the item nearly all of the time
5 = Demonstrated the item every time

take off its shirt and trousers. Watson (1972) has described an instrument for evaluating these and other changes in a child's behaviour, known as the Self-help Skill Assessment Checklist (SSAC). Like the TPS this is a 5-category, 5-point rating scale instrument and is based on direct observation.

In conclusion, Watson and Bassinger (1974) regarded their 'Parent Training Technology System' as a promising and inexpensive approach to helping children.

Hudson (1982) also made use of the TPS to assess a group of 40 parents of mentally handicapped children. He made video-tape recordings of the parents teaching their children three tasks that were covered in training. Two independent raters then used a shortened, 13-item TPS to gauge the parents' proficiency. Hudson found that the group of parents taught by modelling and role-play methods obtained significantly higher scores after training than a control group.

O'Dell *et al.* (1982) trained 100 parents by one of four methods. The goal of training was to improve their reinforcement skills and these were evaluated by observation of the parents interacting with their children during a 20-minute play session. Some of the 13 observational categories and their definitions are listed in Table 3.2. In addition to these 13 categories the raters made a final judgement on the *quality* of the parents' use of reinforcement (as opposed to the frequency or *quantity* as measured by the reinforcement skill measure in Table 3.2). To do this, they utilised a 5-point rating scale, ranging from 'cold and unloving' to 'warm and loving'. The results indicated that the four trained groups all used the reinforcement skills significantly more often than a control group. The reinforcement categories that most clearly distinguished the trained and untrained groups were 'verbal reinforcement', 'verbal punishment' and 'enthusiastic'. The overall rating of reinforcement quality was also significantly different for the trained and untrained groups.

An alternative way of evaluating the parents' behaviour to that of observations is to apply simulated or analogue situations that require parents to exercise the skills they have acquired through training. Flanagan *et al.* (1979) described the use of a 12-item audio tape to assess the skill of their group of parents in applying the time-out technique. The audio tape presented an example of a typical time-out situation and an opportunity for the parent to apply an appropriate part of the time-out procedure to deal with this problem.

Table 3.2: Some Categories and Definitions of the Reinforcement Skills Measure (O'Dell *et al.*, 1982)

	Category	Definition
1.	Verbal reinforcement	Parent emits verbal response apparently intended as a contingent reward for the child's appropriate behaviour
2.	Immediate	Verbal reinforcement delivered within five seconds of termination of child's response
3.	Enthusiastic	Verbal reinforcement delivered in an 'energetic' interested manner, i.e. words stated with higher than average volume and/or emphasis
4.	Described behaviour	Verbal reinforcement delivered along with a specification of the desired behaviour
5.	Not duplicated	Reinforcement not the same as either of the last two reinforcements given by the parent
6.	Food reinforcement	Food given to child as a reward for an appropriate behaviour within 10 seconds of that behaviour

Forty-five seconds were allowed for the parent to choose their response from six listed options, such as 'ignore' or 'warn'. Parents also had the opportunity to write down what they would say and do to deal with the child's problem behaviour. The audio-tape test results of these groups of parents were significantly higher than those of an untrained group. However, they reported only a negligible correlation between this analogue measure and observational measures administered in the home, when the parents were applying time-out with their children. Flanagan *et al.* (1979) concluded that caution was required in generalising from analogue tests to parenting skills under natural home conditions. However, it may have been that these two different kinds of measure tapped slightly different aspects of the time-out skill, or were more or less sensitive to the same skill. Until we clarify what analogue measures actually do measure, their value as evaluation alternatives or additions must remain suspect, and naturalistic observation remains the most valid alternative. A more promising option is to assess subsets of the actual behaviour therapy skills being trained. For instance, O'Dell *et al.* (1977) conducted an evaluation of parents' proficiency in graphing. This required the parents to plot raw data points, note what and when consequences were employed, and decide if the consequences were effective by judging the slope of the graph. Predetermined criteria were used to rate the graphs in terms of accuracy of drawing and interpretation. In a similar vein, they also had the parents view a video and write out as many of the small steps in the behaviour chain as possible ('task analysis').

These measures are obviously relevant to most training programmes and may be conducted in a manner that closely approximates the way they would be carried out in the home. Such measures therefore provide a useful option either when naturalistic observation is impractical or when researchers wish to give close scrutiny to certain skills that may not be readily evaluated by observation. Comparisons between scores on a variety of such measures may also lead to a gradual refinement in the evaluation process, as for example in eliminating measures that add little to the information already obtained.

Evaluations of Parents' Knowledge of Behaviour Therapy

In contrast to the paucity of information on parents' therapeutic *skills*, the effect of training on their *understanding* of behaviour therapy has been more frequently and thoroughly evaluated. Such understanding is generally considered to be important because it provides parents with rules about controlling their children. Once these rules are learned, then theoretically the parents can exert control in a variety of settings and over a range of behaviours.

This 'generalisation' effect is very important for the triadic approach, since it bears on the extent to which the skills developed in training are utilised (Forehand and Atkeson, 1977): if a parent only uses time-out for one problematic behaviour without seeing how the same technique applies to other problems, then the effect of training is unnecessarily restricted. If, on the other hand, they grasp the idea that behaviour in general can be controlled by such consequences as ignoring or praising, then they are in a position to apply this understanding to a large range of behaviours. It should be borne in mind, however, that this knowledge or understanding is not enough on its own to lead to improvements in the parents' behaviour. The consequences that parents themselves experience when they try to change their own behaviour are probably more potent, as discussed in Chapter 2 and later in this chapter.

However, improvements in their understanding may well be necessary for improvements in parenting skills. Studies by Glogower and Sloop (1976) and McMahon *et al.* (1981) both reported an enhancement of training effects after including an emphasis on the principles of behaviour therapy, giving substance to the widely held belief that understanding serves an important function in the parents' acquisition and generalisation of skills. However, the precise role of understanding is as yet unclear, and some studies have failed to find an enhancement of training skills by emphasising principles (e.g. O'Dell *et al.*, 1977; Hudson, 1982).

In one study (Hudson, 1982) the mothers of 40 mentally handicapped children received 10 weekly training sessions of 3 hours apiece from educational psychologists. Measures of knowledge included a ten-item multiple-choice 'knowledge of principles' test and an 'ability to generalise' test. No details were provided of the multiple-choice test, but the generalisation test was described as a task requiring parents to write out the steps they would follow in dealing with two 'new' problems, i.e. problems not covered in training. The parents' replies were independently assessed by two experienced psychologists and points were awarded for including each of a predetermined set of components that were considered necessary for a successful programme. These included taking a baseline, selecting and fading out prompts, and the choice of reinforcers. The two raters achieved a very high degree of agreement on the scores they gave parents.

The results for the knowledge of principles test and the generalisation test indicated that all three trained groups of parents scored more highly than a control group who subsequently received training, but that there were no significant differences between the three training groups. This was surprising, as one group's training had included particular attention to the behavioural principles assessed by these two measures. Hudson (1982) suggested that the parents in the other groups may have learned the principles 'incidentally', that is, as a result of practising the techniques that were based on these self-same principles. He also pointed out that the knowledge of principles test was relatively easy (the control group achieved a mean score of 73 per cent) and so may have been insensitive to group differences. He suggested that a longer knowledge questionnaire might have overcome this 'ceiling' effect. It is also possible that a within-subjects research design, where each group were administered the ten-item test before and after training, would have helped in the interpretation of the findings. Instead, Hudson restricted his design to a between-groups, post-test-only comparison. With small numbers ($N = 10$ per group) it is possible that the randomisation of parents to training groups produced biased samples, which then annulled differential training effects.

O'Dell *et al.* (1979b) developed a lengthier measure of parents' understanding, called the 'Knowledge of Behavioural Principles as Applied to Children' (KBPAC). It is an outstanding measure by virtue of its detailed and careful development. In contrast, the more common tendency is to provide only the starkest details of the knowledge tests used by researchers. For example, Nay (1975) allocated two sentences to describing 'an 18-item multiple choice questionnaïre [that] covered all aspects of the information on time-out procedures' (p. 15), and Flanagan *et al.* (1979), using the same measure, offered no further enlightenment. Such information as the selection of items for the test ('content validity') and the response format (e.g. number of choices) would help readers to judge the value of the measures.

O'Dell *et al.*'s (1979b) KBPAC was developed from two phases of item-selection. In the first phase, 105 questions representing 60 behavioural principles were pooled from the four books: *Parents are Teachers* (Becker, 1971b), *Managing Behaviour 2* (Hall, 1971), *Living with Children* (Patterson and Gullion, 1968) and *Families* (Patterson, 1971). The principles included those referring to reinforcement and punishment, schedules, shaping, counting and recording, differential attention and extinction. The 105 items were rated by four behaviourally orientated psychologists and the 70 most highly rated items became the first version of the KBPAC. A group of 102 respondents, covering a wide range of knowledge of behavioural principles, then completed the questionnaire. Analysis of the correlation between their individual answers and their overall test score, together with the original item ratings, led to the selection of 41 items. To this pool were added a further 64 items and a second phase of questionnaire analysis was conducted, just as the first. This included having 147 parents, teachers, students in psychology and mental-health professionals complete the revised questionnaire. The 50 questions having the highest correlations with the total score were retained to comprise the final KBPAC measure. The KBPAC was assumed to provide a real measure of knowledge (i.e. it had 'content validity') because 70 per cent of the original 60 behavioural principles had survived the two phases of instrument development. The KBPAC was therefore assessing what other authors considered to be the important principles in behaviour therapy with children.

The 147 people completing the KBPAC during the second phase scored an average of 24.4 for the 50 items (49 per cent). When O'Dell *et al.* compared the responses to the odd- and even-numbered items,

Table 3.3: Instructions and Sample Items from the Knowledge of Behavioural Principles as Applied to Children Questionnaire (KBPAC; O'Dell *et al.*, 1979). The correct answers are indicated by the filled squares

---

Directions:
Read each question and each of its four possible answers. Sometimes more than one answer could be correct under certain circumstances; however, you should select the best answer or the answer that is most generally true. Completely fill in the square beside the answer with a pencil. Be sure to fill in only one square for each question. Be sure to answer every question even if you must guess.

1. Desirable and undesirable behaviours are most alike in that they are:
   - ☐ The result of emotions and feelings
   - ☐ Habits and therefore difficult to change
   - ☐ Ways the child expresses himself
   - ■ The result of learning

2. A child begins to whine and cry when his parent explains why he can't go outside. How should the parent react?
   - ☐ Ask the child why going outside is so important to him
   - ☐ Explain that it is a parent's right to make such decisions
   - ☐ Explain again why he should not go outside
   - ■ Ignore the whining and crying

---

they found a very high 'split-half' correlation. This high level of internal consistency made it possible to use the 25 odd- or even-numbered questions to provide a shorter measure of parents' knowledge. An illustration of the KBPAC is given in Table 3.3.

O'Dell *et al.* found that the KBPAC was sensitive to the effects of training a group of 34 parents in behaviour therapy. Their scores increased from 48 per cent at the pre-training baseline assessment to 85 per cent after 5 hours of training. O'Dell *et al.* also reported giving 91 psychology students the training. Their KBPAC scores were 57 per cent and 85 per cent before and after training.

With respect to the points raised earlier in discussing the research of Hudson (1982), the value of the baseline assessment was that it allowed O'Dell to exclude from training those parents whose KBPAC scores were already very high and whose relative expertise might therefore have obscured the actual effects of training. This would lead in turn to erroneous interpretations about the relative value of different training methods.

Table 3.4: A Sample Item from the Behavioural Vignettes Test (BVT: Baker *et al.*, 1980)

Billy is constantly out of his seat in class. A new programme is introduced that gives Billy a token every time he stays in his seat for 5 minutes. Which of the following would best suggest that a star is a good reward for Billy?

(a) Billy stays in his seat longer on each of the next three days.
(b) Billy proudly shows his stars to teachers and visitors.
(c) Billy trades his tokens at the class store for candy.
(d) Billy asks his teacher for extra stars.

An alternative approach to assessing parents' understanding of behavioural principles is to present vignettes (or 'word pictures'). Baker *et al.* (1980) describe a Behavioural Vignettes Test (BVT) which they used to evaluate the Read project outlined earlier in this chapter (Heifetz, 1977). The BVT consists of 20 items designed to assess a parent's knowledge of behavioural teaching principles. A brief description of a teaching or behavioural management situation is given to parents, who are then asked to choose one of four courses of action. A sample item is presented in Table 3.4.

Baker *et al.* (1980) found that parents receiving group training plus visits scored the most highly of the four groups by post-testing (baseline approximately 41 per cent; post-training approximately 74 per cent) and maintained their results best at a one-year follow-up assessment (67 per cent).

Evaluation of Parents' Attitudes

Attitudes have been described as the 'primary buildingstone in the edifice of social psychology' (Allport, 1954), and have led to the growth of an extensive literature on their formation and change. Attitudes have been popularly regarded as enduring, generalised, learned predispositions to behave in certain ways, and as such have often been given prominence in studies of therapeutic processes. However, there are so many different definitions of the word that it is difficult to validate the concept (DeFleur and Westie, 1963). Furthermore, relating them to behaviour therapy skills creates the added problem of integrating an unobservable, inferred construct with a science of behaviour. One strategy has been to eschew them altogether, on the evidence that the consistencies we observe in people's behaviour and attribute to their underlying 'attitudes' are in fact due to consistencies in the environment (Mischel, 1968). This strategy is supported by evidence on the lack of correspondence between expressed attitudes and overt behaviour. Reviewing 31 empirical studies, Wicker (1969) concluded that it was considerably more likely that attitudes will be unrelated or only slightly related to overt behaviours than that they will be closely related to actions. He found that correlations between attitudes and actions ranged from 0.30 downwards and suggested that only rarely can as much as 10 per cent of the variance in overt behavioural measures be accounted for by attitudinal data.

Nevertheless, researchers have continued to assess attitudes, despite the theoretical difficulties of incorporating them into behaviour therapy, and not to mention the evidence that indicates their irrelevance to the therapy's principle focus (i.e. overt behaviour). This has also been the case with parent training, although the foregoing difficulties may explain the relatively infrequent use of attitudinal measures in this area.

Most attitude measures have in fact been brief, *ad hoc* assessments, given little prominence in research reports. Wahler and Fox (1980), for example, had parents rate their children's behaviour on a seven-point scale. This rating varied with changes in that behaviour, but the authors did not even mention the attitudinal data in their discussion. O'Dell *et al.* (1979) briefly referred to a three-item, seven-point rating scale concerning the parents' attitudes towards training. The three items were: the parents' overall impression of the training; how well they felt they understood the content; and how likely they would be to use the time-out technique they had been taught. They reported very positive ratings on all three items by the parents, but they omitted to discuss the implications of the results.

In a subsequent study (O'Dell *et al.*, 1982), they used a seven-point rating scale for the same three items and not only omitted to discuss the attitude measure but also omitted the results of the evaluation. In all these three cases, the authors instead gave their attention to measures of behaviour, reflecting the overwhelming bias towards overt, observable data and away from subjective, covert data.

There is one attitudinal measure, however, that has received considerable use and enjoyed more prominence in research reports than others, namely Becker's Adjective Checklist (BAC: Becker,

1960). This assesses the parents' perceptions of their children using a list of bipolar, seven-point rating scales with antonym pairs of adjectives defining the extremes of the scale. In the 1960 paper the child rating schedule contained 72 scales completed on the same children by their mothers, fathers and two sets of teachers, allowing for four separate factor analyses. These analyses yielded five salient variables. The factors and the five adjective pairs with the heaviest average factor loadings are presented in Table 3.5.

Bernal *et al.* (1980) used the BAC to assess parents' perceptions of their children's aggressiveness by combining factors 1, 3 and 5 following Patterson and Fagot (1967). Bernal *et al.* (1980) had fathers and mothers complete the BAC on their children before and after client-centred counselling or behaviour therapy training. They found that the behavioural group of parents had a significantly more favourable perception of their child at the end of training than the client-centred group and a waiting-list control group. Most interestingly, this difference between training groups was *not* reflected in the behavioural home-observation measure, although parents receiving the behaviour therapy training actually reported less problems with their child following training. This perceptual bias in the parents' reports was also present in their BAC results, but these two measures both returned to a level consistent with the home-observation data at a two-year follow-up evaluation. The authors explained this bias in terms of the greater attention that these behaviourally trained parents gave to their children's problems. The implication that Bernal *et al.* drew out of this bias was to be cautious when relying on parental reports of change.

Eyberg and Johnson (1974) used the BAC as part of a multiple-measure evaluation of parent training. Contrasting pre- and post-training scores, they reported significantly improved parental attitudes to their children as a function of the 12-week course. They also reported that these attitude changes were associated with comparably positive observational data and clinical outcomes. However, they discussed the possibility that all measures were to some extent imprecise since, for example, the training may have altered their attitudes to a more tolerant position, from which they reported fewer child-behaviour problems. Other possibilities included the parents and children 'faking good' for the observations conducted by independent raters at the beginning of training (Johnson and Lobitz, 1972); and that this observational measure did not directly assess the treated problems, since these were situation

Table 3.5: Becker's (1960) Adjective Checklist (BAC): Main Factors and the Five Rated Adjectives with Heaviest Loadings

	Factor	Adjectives
1.	'Hostile—withdrawal'	• Sociable—Unsociable • Warm—Cold • Happy—Depressed • Responsive—Aloof • Loving—Not loving
2.	'Relaxed disposition'	• Tense—Relaxed • Nervous—Placid • Excitable—Calm • Emotional—Objective • Anxious—Nonchalant
3.	'Lack of aggression'	• Demanding—Not demanding • Prone to anger—Not prone to anger • Jealous—Not jealous • Prone to tantrums—Not prone to tantrums • Impatient—Patient
4.	'Submission'	• Strong-willed—Weak-willed • Independent—Dependent • Dominant—Submissive • Adventurous—Timid • Tough—Insensitive
5.	'Conduct problems'	• Obedient—Disobedient • Responsible—Irresponsible • Co-operative—Obstructive • Easily disciplined—Difficult to discipline • Organised—Disorganised

and time specific (e.g. at bedtime or with neighbourhood peers). Thus, although the multiple measures tended to converge and show that training had been successful, there remained difficulties in establishing the validity of individual measures, such as the BAC.

O'Dell *et al.* (1977) used a revised BAC to assess parents' attitudes to their children before and after training, as well as devising their own brief rating scale concerning the parents' attitudes to the course. They failed to find any differential effect of the three pre-training methods on BAC scores, and, like Eyberg and Johnson (1974) found that the attitudinal data agreed with behavioural and knowledge measures.

Alternatives to the BAC include the Parent Attitude Test (PAT:

Cowen *et al.*, 1970) and the Parent Attitude Survey (PAS: Hereford, 1963). The PAT consists of three scales: a home attitude scale which has seven items indicating the parents' perceptions of the child's home adjustment; a behaviour rating scale which requires parents to specify the occurrence and severity of 23 problem behaviours; and an adjective checklist scale containing 33 personality adjectives rated on a 3-point scale. Baum and Forehand (1981) used the PAT in conjunction with behavioural observations to examine the long-term maintenance of a parent training programme. Thirty-four parents who had completed training up to $4\frac{1}{2}$ years earlier were reassessed, and found to have maintained their perceptions that their children were better adjusted. This was in accord with the observational data. No differences were found as a function of the follow-up period.

The Parent Attitude Survey (Hereford, 1963) is a 75-item measure believed to characterise the parents' perceptions of parent-child interaction. Five dimensions have been identified: confidence, causation, acceptance, understanding and trust. Webster-Stratton (1981) reported that 35 parents trained by a brief video-tape modelling procedure did not change their attitudes as measured by the PAS as a result of this four-week training. Like Wahler and Fox (1980) — and indeed most behaviourists — Webster-Stratton interpreted the absence of a significant attitude change in terms of the lag between changes in behaviour and the changes in attitudes that are generally considered to follow on some time later. In her case, a six-week follow-up assessment was not a sufficiently long interval to allow attitude change to emerge.

Another possible reason for the non-significant findings that Webster-Stratton considered was that the PAS was insensitive and outmoded. The general impression from the studies and measures reviewed above is that the evaluation of parental attitudes is generally fraught with conceptual, methodological and interpretative difficulties. This possibly explains the low frequency with which behavioural researchers have used attitude measures. However, one promising area lies in the relationship between attitudes and parents' use of the helping professions. Lobitz and Johnson (1975), for instance, found that parental attitudes were better predictors of referral than was problematic child behaviour. Research investigating this and other issues in parenting training will no doubt benefit from using instruments which measure more precisely defined 'attitudes'. The main task created by the sceptics is to then demonstrate a functional relationship between attitude scores and any other valid measure of overt behaviour change (Wicker, 1969).

Evaluation of the Supervisor

The triadic model that provides us with our rationale for parent training is based on the interactions between all three members of the triad. It is inconsistent, therefore, to minimise the role that each of those agents plays in the process of training and learning. As we have already seen from Chapter 1, the role of the supervisor is by no means a simple one, requiring great skill in facilitating the mediator's learning. This in turn influences the child's learning.

Given this perspective on parent training, it is alarming to find so little data on the knowledge, attitudes or skills of supervisors (O'Dell, 1974). Bernal *et al.* (1980) drew attention to the possibility that the designation 'graduate student', 'Ph.D. level', and so on to supervisors did not automatically bestow competence on them. This possibility might not surprise readers who have themselves floundered in a supervisory role and have realised the shortcomings of their own training. They are not alone: Garfield and Kurtz (1976) surveyed clinical psychologists and found 25 per cent of respondents dissatisfied with their training and feeling insufficiently prepared for such aspects of professional practice as supervision. A very similar finding was obtained for clinical psychologists in the UK (Milne, 1983a).

This discomfort with professional training may go some way to explaining why the commitment to evaluating the triadic model of parent training has been so heavily biased towards the behaviour of the trainee. Very little research attention has been given to mediators and almost none to supervisors. In the general field of supervision there has been a corresponding lack of data, but a growing acceptance that supervision skills are not after all acquired by osmosis or magic (Buttrum, 1976), rather through the same processes of change that occur with mediators and trainees.

There have been some research studies of training supervisors that emphasise formats that are similar to those applied to mediators. They include graded exposure to clinical casework through non-participant observation, role-play, sitting in, bug-in-the-ear prompting and finally audio- and video-tape feedback (Levine and Tilker, 1974); the application of a micro-teaching approach for counsellors (Kuna, 1975); and a broader ranging course for clinical psychologists as teachers (Hall and Brooks, 1976). In general, these and other studies have indicated that the laws of learning do indeed extend to professionals, and that, as with other groups of learners, certain training methods and forms of supervision yield better results. An outstanding example is the study by Bouchard *et al.* (1980), who demonstrated the superiority of a 'structured learning format' approach over a traditional seminar format in training professionals to become social skills therapists.

In the parent training literature there also appears to be a growing expression of concern over the training and evaluation of supervisors, but as yet very little data. One exception has been the research of Isaacs *et al.* (1982) who trained five family therapists to give instructions, information and praise to parents. They utilised a training programme consisting of 4 hours of briefing, introduction to a training manual, video-tape models and behavioural rehearsal. The contents of these components were described in some detail. Next, supervisors read a book on assisting parents with child-management problems (*Little People*: Christopherson, 1977), before receiving prompting and feedback on *their* work with parents and children.

Before commencing this training, however, Isaacs *et al.* (1982) gathered baseline data on the supervisors' proficiency and their interactions with the parent and child attending the clinic. Their respective behaviours were recorded through one-way mirrors, as summarised in Table 3.6, during a standard instructional training task.

During the baseline phase the supervisors were asked to begin offering assistance to the parents, calling on their past experiences and training. In other words they behaved in a way that may be considered representative of supervisors who have not received special training in supervision. The data from this baseline phase led Isaacs *et al.* to state that the supervisors were 'largely ineffective . . . and produced negligible changes in the parent/child behaviours' (p. 517). It is salutory to note at this point that these supervisors included 'graduate students' who had professional posts in the fields of social work and pre-school teaching and counselling, as well as a second-year student in clinical psychology training who had worked for 18 months as a therapist. Their 'ineffectiveness' prior to specialised training in supervision must be regarded as firm evidence that vocational titles or degree attainments do not themselves guarantee proficiency in supervision. Following the training outlined earlier

Table 3.6: A Summary of the Isaacs *et al.* (1982) Assessment Procedure for the Therapeutic Triad

	Agent in triadic model		Behaviours observed and recorded
1.	Supervisor ('trainee' professional)	(a)	Instructions to carry out procedures immediately
		(b)	Praise of parent performance
		(c)	Information statements about child management techniques, child development and child-rearing practices
2.	Mediator (mother)	(a)	Contingent attention to compliance
		(b)	Attention to non-compliance
		(c)	Parental instructions
		(d)	Parental praise
3.	Trainee (child)	(a)	Compliance
		(b)	Non-compliance

they increased their use of appropriate supervisory behaviours, as listed in Table 3.6, which was then accompanied by improvements in parent-child interactions. Isaacs *et al.* noted that one important change in their supervision was closer attendance to parents' behaviour, resulting in adjustments to the tone, timing and content of their prompts and praise.

This research is valuable as it substantiates the concern expressed about the general quality of supervision that can be expected without specialised training. It also provides a coherent framework for giving this training while relating it to changes in the parent and child. Such a framework permits the systematic evaluation of the relationship between key variables in parent training, such as subject characteristics and training methods, and should be pursued vigorously. One obvious next step is to extend the evaluation framework into the home environment. This may then promote our understanding of other crucial factors that interact with training, such as social support and other setting events. These will be discussed shortly.

Summary

Evaluations of parent training have focused very largely on the trainee, often utilising comprehensive observation procedures to determine the effect of such training. In contrast, very few studies have considered the equally important behaviours of the parents and supervisors who initiate these changes. As the existing research indicates that supervisors may be ineffective without themselves first receiving training, this disproportionate research emphasis requires urgent correction. Similarly, the research on parental changes, as determinants of changes in their children, has generally shied away from hard observational data, although often offering data on their attitudes, characteristics and understanding *in lieu*. However, the parents' perceptions of the social validity of training is one of the more promising forms of self-report since it bears on their use of the service and may help to shape its future form. Other promising measures that could be applied to supervisors or parents are direct observations of a restricted but crucial subset of behaviours. These minimise some of the difficulties inherent in observation while retaining the emphasis on objective data. For instance, Budd and Fabry (1984) have developed a brief observation system which allows supervisors to evaluate parent training reliably yet relatively easily.

3.4 Implementation Issues: 'Making it Stick'

This section concerns the problems that arise in parent training, especially those that occur when efforts are made to ensure that after training the parents actually apply their newly refined techniques. We are therefore interested in the 'systems' issues discussed in Chapter 2, as they apply to parent training. These issues may help us to understand why there has typically been only a short-lived training effect (O'Dell, 1974; Wahler, 1980) and little generalisation of parent or child behaviours (Johnson and Katz, 1973). In short, a study of these implementation problems may help us to make our innovations 'stick' (Stolz, 1981).

(a) Trainee Response to Training

One of the difficulties that was highlighted in Chapter 2 was the role played by trainees in controlling mediator behaviour. Woods and Cullen(1982) and Loeber and Weisman (1975) have emphasised the significance of trainee variables, such as unresponsiveness to training.

In general, researchers have not reported any initial difficulty in obtaining a significant improvement in child behaviour, even with minimal parent training efforts on their part. Patterson (1974) and Patterson *et al.* (1982) have reported reductions in the mean rate of child deviant behaviour ranging from 42 to 63 per cent, based on an average of 17 hours of training. These findings have been replicated (Fleischman, 1981) and are typical of the outcomes achieved by researchers using other approaches, as reviewed above. In sum, there is little indication that parents have problems with their children's response to training when evaluated in terms of the immediate, circumscribed effects.

A more subtle approach is to consider problems with the same child, which differ in their responsiveness to training. With this gradient of training difficulty ranging across the child's problems, it should be possible to assess whether this 'difficulty dimension' is associated with different levels of parental involvement in training. It is a rule of thumb in behaviour therapy to start with the child's easiest problem, so as to reinforce changes quickly in the parents' behaviour. Eyberg and Johnson (1974) evaluated the role of training difficulty by having parents start either with the child's easiest or hardest problem. They predicted that the parents' co-operation, as measured by attendance at training session, keeping diary records of problems and supervisor ratings, would be greatest in the 'easy' training group. However, they reported no effect arising from this 'easy-difficult' variable on any of the three co-operation factors. But, when they assessed the effect of other contingencies, they found that these had a powerful effect on co-operation: a group of parents who paid an extra 'contract deposit fee' in advance and were given extra time by the supervisor contingent on completion of task assignment and attendance were significantly more co-operative on all measures than a comparable but non-contingent group. Although not formally assessed, they also showed signs of completing training more rapidly, whereas the non-contingent group seemed to require a longer time to complete the required sessions though giving acceptable excuses. They also took longer to treat their children's problems, so that in fact fewer problems were treated.

It seems, then, that the trainee's response to training is secondary to the contingencies existing between mediator and supervisor. The apparent insignificance of training difficulty may not, however, hold for different groups of children. As Woods and Cullen (1982) have shown with the severely mentally handicapped child, change can occur so slowly as to be imperceptible to mediators, in this case nurses. In such a situation, trainee responsiveness may be functionally unrelated or actually punish the parents' therapeutic behaviour. There is therefore a need to carry out more research in order to clarify the role of trainee variables as determinants of the mediator's behaviour. This can be accomplished by systematically relating trainee variables to outcomes, as Clark and Baker (1983) have done, or by conducting detailed single-case studies of the effects that the trainee's response to training has on the mediator.

(b) Predicting the Parents' Response to Training

Another topic that has involved subject variables has been the relationship between parental characteristics and training. Clark *et al.* (1982), for instance, reported that educational status and previous group and behaviour therapy experience were all strongly associated with the learning of a group of 49 parents, as measured on the behavioural vignettes test described earlier. When they reanalysed the results, they found that the BVT score, together with the number of training sessions attended, would have correctly predicted 69 per cent of the parents who did not implement the training and 77 per cent of the group who did make use of it.

Drawing out the implications of this study, Clark *et al.* (1982) suggested that those parents who were expected to do well in training could be given the inexpensive group format, whereas parents expected to do poorly could be offered a potentially more effective but costly alternative. However, they stress that such equations are premature and should not as yet be used to exclude parents from training. For instance, they found that some parents who, they predicted, would do poorly actually did well. They also reported that child variables, such as functional level and age, were not strongly related to the parents' implementation of the training.

In a subsequent study, Clark and Baker (1983) included a broader range of 22 predictor variables, a more comprehensive measure of proficiency and a larger sample ($N = 103$). They again reported that BVT scores were related to predictions, this time of parents dropping out of training, and that the educational level of the parent and their prior exposure to behaviour therapy were important discriminators of 'high' and 'low' proficiency parents, and 'high' versus 'low' implementers. Other useful predictors of 'good' mediators (i.e high proficiency after training and high rates of implementation) were that the parents had a spouse, were of higher socio-economic status, expected fewer problems in teaching their child, and had already done more teaching of their child. On the basis of all variables, Clark and Baker (1983) correctly classified 76 per cent of parents into their respective 'high' or 'low' implementation groups, and 74 per cent into the 'high' or 'low' proficiency groups, following training.

These characteristics of mediator and trainee merit further research since they have clear practical implications: they bear on the issue of training content, methods, outcome and efficiency and so could substantially refine our approach to parent training. It is also helpful that these researchers have looked beyond the variables associated with the *trainee* (e.g. age, skills and problems) to those associated with the *mediator*. Of particular interest, in terms of the emphasis on the systems approach outlined in Chapter 2, is their attention to training obstacles. As we saw earlier, such 'obstacles' are powerful determinants of a mediator's therapeutic behaviour. Although they only considered the parents' *expectation* of such obstacles, Clark and Baker (1983) found that this very strongly discriminated between the 'high' and 'low' groups of parents. We will return to this issue later in this chapter. For the moment, we can note from the descriptions of the training process itself, reviewed above, that even these sophisticated and thorough evaluations of training omit the trainer from the analysis. This omission is all the more striking when one realises that trainer variables such as experience, empathy and similarity with the trainee have been found to be important factors influencing outcome in psychotherapy generally (Luborsky *et al.*, 1971).

This point holds for O'Dell *et al.*'s (1982) examination of four training methods, in which they considered eight parent characteristics and one child characteristic (age). Like Clark and Baker (1983), they reported a positive relationship between training effects and those parents having a better education and a higher socio-economic status. However, O'Dell *et al.* (1982) found that the training method they used *interacted* with parent characteristics. Thus, although less parental education was generally associated with less learning, video-tape presentations of course material seemed to reduce or even eliminate the effect of this characteristic on parents' learning of how to use reinforcement with their children. This interaction effect led O'Dell *et al.* (1982) to suggest that the conclusions of previous research regarding training methods may have been 'oversimplifications'. They argued, furthermore, that tentative guidelines on the selection of parents for training were consistently emerging from research studies. These indicated that for a high proportion of parents, namely those who were satisfactorily motivated and educated, the method of training was not crucial and that other issues, such as efficiency, were more important. This suggests that a greater emphasis on methods utilising video tapes, audio tapes and written materials would be effective with such parents, although only requiring minimal supervisor effort.

(c) The Training Format

Another factor that may be important in the maintenance and generalisation of training is the nature of the training process itself. In general, it is extremely difficult to determine the significance of this variable, because research reports provide so little detail as to what actually took place. Researchers typically use such terms as 'modelling' or 'behavioural rehearsal' without elaboration. We also find that few studies have then proceeded to evaluate the maintenance and generalisation effect of their training programmes. This is unsatisfactory since attention to the training process itself is of great practical importance, and of all the variables that supervisors might control to influence change, it is surely the most accessible. The implication of this is that the training process should receive more time and consideration than other less manipulable variables, such as the parents' socio-economic status or educational attainments.

Baum and Forehand (1981) carried out follow-up assessments gauging the maintenance of training effects up to $4\frac{1}{2}$ years after training. They pointed out that only six studies, until then, had reported maintenance data up to one year after training termination. Their findings indicated that both the parents and their children had maintained improvements overall, but that some parental behaviours, namely 'attends and rewards' and 'contingent attention', had actually *decreased* significantly in frequency. The relationship between this finding and the training process is impossible to discern from the report, as only two brief paragraphs were allocated to providing an account of the training. Although Baum and Forehand (1981) point the reader to a more complete description of the programme in another report (Webster-Stratton,

1981) it would be helpful if researchers in general gave more information on their training procedures, since it is to this that they attribute changes in parental and child behaviours. The lack of details about independent variables is unfortunately common in behaviour therapy (Peterson *et al.*, 1982) and tends to be overcompensated for in extensive accounts of the dependent variables (i.e. child behaviour). Manuals overcome this difficulty, but are typically assessed as part of a *package* of training methods.

These points regarding the maintenance of training effects are also true in the case of generalisation. In their review, Forehand and Atkeson (1977) found only two studies that had examined the effect of different training procedures with respect to the generalisation of behaviour. One of these studies (O'Dell *et al.*, 1977) found no differential effect between groups of parents receiving lectures covering the principles of behaviour therapy and groups who did not receive these lectures, although their evaluation was limited to parents' self-reports and behaviour in simulated situations. In the second study, Glogower and Sloop (1976) did find a generalisation effect for the parents receiving lectures, based on parents' records of their children's behaviour. This finding indicated that a knowledge of behaviour therapy principles facilitated the parents' application of their training to new child behaviour problems. The discrepancy between the studies may be attributable to the different measures of change or else to differences in the actual training process, in this case the content and method of lectures. To underscore the earlier point on the general lack of specification of training variables, these studies do not permit the reader to judge the respective contributions of each aspect of training and so obscure the role of training in the maintenance and generalisation of parents' therapeutic skills. There is evidence that such training alterations significantly affect these outcomes when nurses have served as mediators (e.g. Gardner, 1972; Milne, 1982; 1984e). These findings will be discussed along with details of the training process in Chapters 5 and 6.

(d) Social Support

Even if parents are expertly trained and produce highly significant results at the end of a course of training, actual *use* of their new skills will depend on other factors. One illustration of this, discussed in Chapter 2, is the role of social support: Wahler (1980) described the powerful effect of aversive and positive ratings by family, friends and therapists on parents' recently acquired therapy skills; and Wahler *et al.* (1979) studied the community social contacts of parents who did or did not profit from a training programme. In both cases he found that those parents who did not obtain improvements from their children had much fewer and less satisfying contacts with their social support system. In particular, the quality of parent-social support interactions seemed to reflect the kind of coercive process found in mother-child problems (Patterson and Reid, 1970). For instance, a member of the mother's social system might ask her to stop or start certain behaviours, which, when complied with, lead to reinforcement for both parties: the parent escapes from or terminates the nagging, accusations and ridiculing of the family member (including the problematic child) by carrying out their demands; and that member is positively reinforced by the mother's compliance. As a consequence, the mother's interactions with her child are less influenced by the child's responsiveness or the training process and are more under the control of her social environment.

Supporting those views, Wahler *et al.* (1979) found that parents who implemented their behavioural training successfully rated their social contacts as more frequent and positively reinforcing, thereby avoiding the 'coercion trap'. An empirical examination of these views was conducted by Wahler (1980) in which he systematically related child and parenting behaviours to 'low' and 'high' social support. He found that mothers who received high levels of support, that is an average of 9.5 interactions with people outside the family circle every day (as compared to 2.6 in the 'low support' group), were able to procure and maintain child improvement, associated with their using fewer coercive methods of controlling their children. This 'friendship factor' could predict daily fluctuations in the mother's coercive child control techniques (e.g. yelling). As expected, the child's behaviour reflected this 'friendship' factor, with reductions in child opposition most pronounced on 'high friendship' days. This change was not due to the parents simply spending less time with their children on high friendship days and thus of having less time to engage in interaction problems, since the amount of caretaking appeared to be constant across all days.

In a subsequent article, Wahler and Graves (1983) extended the argument on social factors by introducing the notion of 'setting events'. This refers to environmental conditions that influence later stimulus-response interactions, such as illness or marital discord. In the case of parent training, the 'setting events' include the friendship variable described above and any other factors that influence the parent-child interactions. Wahler and Graves suggest that these setting events may account for the lack of consistency in results of parent training. As illustrations they cite Reisinger *et al.* (1976), who found that marital problems reduced the effect of training, and Wahler and Afton (1980), who found that socio-economic disadvantage impeded training effects. Such problems underline the need to assess not only those factors that control the *child's* behaviour, such as parental attention, but also the factors that influence the *parents'* behaviour. For instance, Patterson and Fleischman (1979) pointed out that training effects were undermined by what they termed 'floods of aversive inputs' to the parents, such as unemployment, separation, divorce, poverty and clinical problems such as a parent's depression.

One way of assessing these factors is to have parents themselves rate how much their social support and the other 'setting events' interrupted their behavioural work with their child. Baker (1980) and Clark *et al.* (1982) have developed an 'Obstacles Checklist' consisting of 24 factors to assess the problems parents faced in attempting to train their mentally handicapped children. The parents rated a series of common problems on a three-point scale, ranging from 'not an obstacle' to 'very much an obstacle'. A summary of the Obstacles Checklist with parents' responses is given in Table 3.7.

Baker (1980) found that parents who implemented their training reported significantly fewer obstacles and had lower total scores on the checklist. As he pointed out, this could have reflected either less stress on the parent or a more organised approach to training their mentally handicapped children. The data provided by Wahler (1980) would indicate that stress was a more salient factor than lack of organisation, but these variables usually interact, as illustrated by the studies that have encouraged parents to develop self-control (discussed below).

Consistent with the emphasis on the interactional nature of the triadic model, some researchers have considered the social support provided to *supervisors*. This complements Wahler's (1980) attention to social support for the mediator and Sanson-Fisher and Jenkins' (1978) evidence on the powerful effect of peer support for trainee's problem behaviour.

Patterson *et al.* (1982) have argued that, in addition to a parent training technology, successful interventions require supervisors

Table 3.7: A Summary of the Ten Most Highly Ranked Problems Parents Experienced: from the Obstacles Checklist (Baker, 1980; Clark *et al.*, 1982)

Parents' ranking of obstacles	Obstacle Checklist item
1	Limited time to teach
2	Too many interruptions (e.g. phones, other children)
3	Unable to manage behaviour problems
4	My child's lack of skills
5	Unanticipated interruptions (e.g. illness, divorce)
6	Getting stuck and not knowing what to do
7	Lack of professional consultation
8	Not knowing what to teach next
9	Lack of support from my other children
10	Lack of progress in my child

with the clinical skills to cope with mediator resistance, and supervisors who themselves have a 'support structure'. Incidentally, they use these three necessary conditions for effective parent training to argue that some of the inconsistent findings can be attributed to poorly trained, novice therapists. They did not, however, elaborate on what the proposed support structure might be. One might conjecture that a successful support structure (that is, one that positively reinforces supervision behaviour) would involve the same range of variables identified for the other members of the triadic model. Thus, factors such as social support and obstacles will be important, although perhaps represented by different kinds of events. For example, the support a supervisor receives from colleagues and from the wider research community (in terms of publications, interest, conference papers, etc.) will play an important part in his future involvement in parent training. Fortunately, this does not necessarily imply an eternal regression to some ultimate deity as a source of support, but rather illustrates the role that supervisors can play in arranging for the environment to control their *own* supervision behaviour. One example would be arranging for regular groups meetings to discuss supervision problems, in much the same way as parents have been successful in helping and supporting one another through groups (Herbert and Ivaniec, 1981).

(e) Parental Self-control

In an attempt to improve parents' control of their own children, supervisors may first have to improve the parents' control over themselves. Some researchers have done just this by tackling such setting events as maternal distress (Forehand *et al.*, 1984) in addition to the more immediate difficulties that arise in dealing with children. For example, Patterson *et al.* (1975) and Wahler (1980) developed parents' skills in controlling other family members and so avoiding the 'coercion trap'.

Denicola and Sandler (1980) have examined potential self-control in detail with two families referred for child abuse. In addition to training the parents in behaviour techniques, they introduced a second training component concerned with the parents' ability to cope with their own aggressive impulses and feelings of anger and frustration. This 'coping skills' component consisted of training in deep muscle relaxation and techniques of modifying what they said to themselves in difficult situations. This included heightening their awareness of self-deprecating thoughts (e.g. 'I can't cope') and using such statements as cues for problem-solving and relaxation. In this way they learnt to respond in a more controlled manner to their children's provocation. Both parental self-report and observations in the home indicated that the training in behavioural techniques and coping skills was effective in improving the parents' interactions with their children. The relative contribution of these two components could not be discerned in this study, since both forms of training were associated with an equally marked decline in parent and child aversive behaviour. However, Denicola and Sandler did not apply a direct measure of the parents' coping skills, raising the possibility that coping skills training may have had its observed effect on interactions through such factors as the parents' expectancy of improvement, rather than through actual changes in their self-control skills. A similar study by Sanders (1982) also failed to provide these data.

Robin (1981) also trained parents in a self-control strategy. He allocated 33 families reporting parent-adolescent conflict to a problem-solving communication training group, to a range of alternative family therapy groups (psychodynamic, eclectic and family systems), or to a waiting-list control group. The problem-solving group of families were taught a four-step model, consisting of:

(a) defining the problem precisely and without accusations;
(b) generating alternative solutions;
(c) deciding on a mutually satisfactory solution by examining both the positive and negative consequences for each possible solution, and adopting one or more solutions when these are agreed by everyone; and
(d) specifying the details for implementing the agreed solution/s.

To develop these behaviours the supervisors provided feedback, instructions, prompts, modelling and behaviour rehearsal around a series of topics. Using a battery of six measures, the results confirmed the effectiveness of this problem-solving training in reducing parent-adolescent conflict.

These self-control strategies could be expected to increase training results in the home. They also demonstrate how we must view the triadic model as *interactive* and *complex*: simple, unicausal relationships are likely to be uncommon, and the aim of parent training should be to assess any variables that have an effect on the behaviour of supervisors, mediators or trainees. Wahler's work is important in highlighting the complexity of parent training, and particularly in encouraging supervisors and researchers to note the often subtle and reflexive nature of parents' behaviour. As he has pointed out, this entails a considerable expansion of the traditional behavioural view of training and evaluation.

3.5 Summary and Conclusions

In this chapter we have looked at some of the training and evaluation methods applied in training parents as behaviour therapists for their own children. We have also examined the problems that have been reported in implementing these training programmes. From these reviews it has become clear that parent training is a complex process, entailing subtle interactions between each member of the triadic model.

Unfortunately, we see from the reviewed literature that research and training practice have not reflected this complexity. We are offered a plethora of studies demonstrating the relative success of different teaching methods over control groups, but little or no data on the actual training process itself, or on the effects that it has across time, persons or behaviours.

Regarding the research on training methods that we have considered, some general conclusions seem in order. There have been very few comparisons of behavioural and alternative training approaches. Those that have been conducted have indicated comparable success in terms of changes in parents' attitudes and their reports of improvements in their children. More comparative studies are required to clarify the relative value of different models of assisting parents. It may be that some aspects of these models enhance the effect of the behavioural approach, such as the 'client-centred' emphasis on counselling the parents. These effects need to be measured in terms of the parents' use of professional services and their perception of their children's behaviour, as well as in terms of the actual learning that results from training.

In contrast, there have been a large number of comparisons of teaching methods, relating to such issues as the efficiency of training. The general conclusion of this review is that videos, self-instructional manuals and other 'cheap' methods do increase parents' understanding and that these are just as effective as more time-consuming methods. However, the development and application of behavioural skills seem to require direct professional guidance, at least at the level of small group training where 'active' learning procedures such as role-play, rehearsal and performance-based feedback can be practised. There appears to be considerable scope for the judicious use of manuals and videos for certain groups of parents and the problems presented by the child: the more highly educated and motivated parent may prove to be well suited to a simple manual training format for a discrete difficulty such as temper tantrums. There are, therefore, great practical benefits to be gained by refining our knowledge of these interacting factors.

We considered how our understanding of these issues had not advanced because of the lack of detail that typically accompanied the accounts of parent training procedures. To be told that 'modelling' or 'role-play' was used is hardly a very revealing description of the training process, and may explain some of the inconsistent findings that have emerged. This state of affairs seems especially unsatisfactory since the training itself forms the basis of the research intervention.

Another major weakness in the accounts of training is the lack of information on the related issues of supervisor and mediator behaviour. Whereas there are a few studies of mediator behaviour, data on supervisor behaviour have generally been restricted to labels such as 'experienced' or 'Ph.D. level'. The irony of this state of affairs is acute, given that the underlying rationale for parent training centres on the interaction arising between supervisor and mediator. In a rare study of the relationship between the training of supervisors and mediators, Isaacs *et al.* (1982) regarded the patterning and sequencing of aspects of supervisor behaviour, such as comments and instructions, to be an important area for future analysis. They found that their 'graduate students' were ineffective supervisors until they themselves had received training. In this sense it is surely important to go beyond mere labels to specifying precisely a supervisor's background and behaviour. This is particularly important as the main independent variable is in fact the supervisor's training behaviour. Studies of teachers in classrooms illustrate how we might go about this data-gathering exercise (e.g. Flanders, 1970; Perrot, 1982). Other relevant options include the use of supervision manuals, which might delimit the range of supervision behaviours but not describe them; and turning mediator assessment measures, such as the Training Proficiency Scale (TPS) on to the supervisor. This would tap the assumption that as the laws of learning are general what represents proficient parenting would also, broadly speaking, represent 'good' supervision. In this sense the supervisor's use of prompts, of contingent and appropriate reinforcement and so on, should be recorded. Such data on the *process* of training would complement data on the *content* of training. As these are two distinct variables, it would lead us to a position where we could specify not simply the relationship between the training method and changes in the mediator, but also the contribution made by the way in which that method was conducted. This is, of course, a difficult task both methodologically and professionally. However, as Patterson *et al.* (1982) have implied, parent training technology depends on such developments as training supervisors and they may well prove to be very important in improving results and explaining inconsistent outcomes.

At the end of the training process there remains a still more exacting research task, namely to clarify the variables determining implementation. The 'setting events' which so clearly influence parents' use of therapy skills are likely to prove very helpful in promoting our understanding of maintenance and generalisation. Indeed, most parent training programmes are based on the principle that the consequences for behaving therapeutically would control their future use of these skills. The paucity of research on this topic again indicates an unreflexive relationship between theory and practice in parent training.

It would help our understanding if the instruments used to evaluate either the setting events or the more immediate effects of training were applied consistently across a programme of research. As we saw earlier, O'Dell and his colleagues carried out a series of experiments on training methods, but tended to use a new set of measures with each successive study. Where there already exist outstandingly well-developed measures, such as O'Dell's knowledge test, Becker's attitude scale and Reid's observation system, it would be helpful to incorporate these alongside any measures that individual researchers preferred. We would then be in a position to compare training programmes directly.

On a more positive note, parent training programmes have tended towards careful and objective evaluations of their main goal, i.e. changes in the child's problem behaviour. As we shall see in the case of nurse training programmes, this degree of commitment to rigorous measurements is not a general feature of mediator training and so cannot be taken for granted.

Also, parent training programmes demonstrate by their very existence and popularity that researchers take the problems of service delivery seriously, as outlined in the first chapter of this book. When some 75 per cent of mentally handicapped children are cared for at home by their parents (Kushlick, 1968) and the remainder of the child population spend most of their time at home, it becomes desirable that researchers respond to those areas of pressing need on the grounds of both remediation and prevention.

Another strength of the research we have reviewed in this chapter is the wide range of problems that have been addressed. This has included a focus on the undesirable 'side-effects' that tend to follow any intervention into a system. Wahler (1969) found that some training interventions can actually *accentuate* a child's problem behaviours. Such an interest in the wider repercussions of training may be commendable, not least since an awareness of our past 'mistakes' may be the best way to develop the parent training technology (Holman, 1977).

Some promising areas of research include a growing acceptance of the need to provide data on the 'cost' of parent training, as well as indications of the outcome (e.g. Christensen *et al.*, 1980). The 'social validity' of training may also be an interesting and potentially important parameter, incorporating as it does the *parents'* evaluation of the goals, procedures and effects of training (e.g. Forehand *et al.*, 1980). This in turn will have repercussions for their use of services, as will the parents' perceptions of their children's problems. Some studies have already shown that there is no simple relationship between the parents' perceptions of these problems and the actual child behaviour causing concern (e.g. Doleys *et al.*, 1976), raising the important possibility that parents use services for reasons other than the child's problems (Rickard *et al.*, 1981). Griest and Wells (1983) review these and other emerging issues concerning parent variables, which lead them to propose an expanded parent training module, called 'family therapy'. This incorporates the parent variables mentioned, as well as the wider social ones discussed earlier. Such an approach promises to direct research attention to some of the tremendous gaps in our understanding of childhood disorders, and points to 'multi-modal' family therapy which focuses on all the relevant variables controlling these disorders.

In addition to considering interactions within the family system, research has also progressed towards an analysis of overlapping systems, such as the school and home (e.g. Blechman *et al.*, 1981; Forehand *et al.*, 1981). These developments augur well for the continued understanding and success of parent training programmes, particularly for the major remaining problems of generalisation and sustained implementation (Sanders and James, 1983). There is an emerging concern that a '*training technology*' alone is not a sufficient basis for parents to apply their therapy skills. They also require *support* when they use them. This support has been described in terms of the social consequences of applying behaviour therapy, such as the amount of friendly contacts a parent has in a day and the 'coercion traps' that exist to undermine change. As an adjunct to therapy skills the parents can be trained to minimise coercion and to develop ways of supporting each other. These 'self-control' components include problem-solving, marital therapy and the reduction of nervous tension that leads to aversive interactions with the child. The third and final requirement of successful parent training is the *clinical skill* of the supervisor. This refers not simply to expertise in the training methods themselves, but also to the supervisor's ability to elicit and overcome problems of parental resistance to change. These include the kinds of factor mentioned above and summarised in Table 3.7, the presence of which may well destroy the effects of even the most accomplished training process.

Considerable clinical skill is required to judge what 'the problem' is at any one point in time. Although the problem is initially presented as one of unacceptable child behaviour, it will often transpire that other 'problems' exist and require interventions by the parents, as in self-control training. The prevailing use of 'trainee' supervisors for this most demanding task means that parents are often offered an unnecessarily restricted service. The Patterson model, based on well-trained supervisors who tackle problems in series as they emerge, is a response to this difficulty and seems much more likely to lead to lasting and beneficial changes in parent-child interactions.

4 PARENTS AS TEACHERS: A PROGRAMME OF APPLIED RESEARCH

Bruce L. Baker

4.1 Introduction

Children with developmental disabilities bring to their families extraordinary needs, and bring out in their families more reactions than writers have been able to enumerate. They bring to their parents and siblings a measure of joy, fulfilment and compassion as any child does, and they teach very special lessons of patience and caring. We must not lose sight of these positive effects as we, from our professional perspective, focus on emotional burden, child-rearing demands, and lifelong uncertainties. None the less, these stresses are real, and much attention is being paid to defining stressors, examining coping strategies, and understanding of how professionals can play a meaningful role in supplementing and strengthening the family's own coping resources (Blacher, 1984).

This chapter emphasises one professional undertaking, providing educational programmes that build upon the parents' role as teachers of their developmentally disabled child. Formerly the psychiatric emphasis was on the traumatic emotional sequelae of the birth of a handicapped child and the parents' need for therapy. This is giving way to an acknowledgement of the daily stress produced by the child's skill deficiencies and behaviour problems and the parents' need for training. A developmentally disabled child raises, for any family, difficulties that can be met better with some special skills.

The rationale for training parents to increase their capabilities as teachers is compelling. There have always been too few special education professionals, and parents of retarded children are an abundant natural resource for supplementing professional services. Moreover, parents are able to make unique contributions. The manner in which children are taught at home during the pre-school years will affect their readiness to enter school and their ability to learn there. Further, the family setting is the best place to teach some skills, such as self-help. And, of course, the family can provide the crucial link in helping a child to practise new behaviours learned in school, at home, and in the community (Baker, 1983).

In this chapter I will describe a programme of applied research on behavioural training for parents of young developmentally disabled children. The intention is to provide the reader with a rather detailed account of one parent training programme as a complement to Chapter 3's comprehensive review of parent training research. I will describe the Parents as Teachers programme — its aims, curriculum, evaluation procedures, outcomes, research issues, and dissemination — with emphasis on the programme as it is presently implemented. Its origins, however, are in the Read project, carried out at Harvard University in the early 1970s, and in activities from 1975 to the present by our Project for Developmental Disabilities at the University of California, Los Angeles.

4.2 Parents as Teachers Programme

This section will briefly describe aspects of the Parents as Teachers training programme. Table 4.1 summarises the content of each meeting.

Aims

The overall aim is to facilitate retarded children's development by increasing their parents' ability to implement behavioural programmes. The focus is on training for parents, so that they can play a central role in the education of their young developmentally disabled child. Parents are taught to: enhance the child's attention to learning tasks and participation in them, reduce problem behaviours, build basic self-help skills, and, to a lesser extent, build play and speech-and-language skills.

We expect that, when a family becomes involved in teaching their developmentally disabled child, there are benefits in addition to the child's increased independence. Parents may be able to apply skills that they have learned in our programme to problems experienced with their other children as well. Moreover, parents may adopt more positive attitudes towards the developmentally disabled child and his or her potential. There may be increased co-operation among family members and between the family and the child's other teachers. Finally, there may be a decreased tendency to place the developmentally disabled child out of the home. Although we have anecdotal evidence for all of these broader effects, we will limit our presentation in this chapter to the more direct effects of training, where our evaluations have been more systematic.

Table 4.1: Primary Content of the Parents as Teachers Programme

Prior to training:

Orientation
Pre-assessment

Training sessions

(1) Self-help skills: introduction to behaviour modification; targeting a self-help skill
(2) Self-help skills: basic behavioural teaching principles
(3) Self-help skills: reinforcement
(4) Self-help skills: troubleshooting
(5) Self-help skills: individual session with child, to demonstrate self-help skill teaching and receive feedback
(6) Behaviour problems: definition, observation, functional analysis
(7) Behaviour problems: consequences and locating a better consequence; planning a programme
(8) Behaviour problems: additional techniques and troubleshooting ongoing programmes
(9) Generalising the principles to play skills; incorporating teaching into the daily routine
(10) Generalising the principles to speech and language, or review and future planning

Parameters

The Parents as Teachers programme was developed for families with moderately to severely retarded children about 3 to 13 years old. Training typically involves three individual assessments with parents and child (before, during and after the group meetings), and nine 2-hour group sessions for parents only. We have followed families in several ways once formal training has ended; we will discuss these in a later section. Training takes place in community agencies, and group meetings are held in the evening to facilitate attendance by working parents. Usually there are two co-leaders, who conduct training for a group of eight to ten families. In two-parent families, both are encouraged to attend. Single parents are urged to bring a friend or relative to participate in training with them.

Recruitment

Regional Centers for the Developmentally Disabled refer families to us. In California, a system of 21 of these Regional Centers registers developmentally disabled persons and provides services to them, either by referral to community agencies or to individual providers. Our project originally recruited families from the community at large, through TV coverage, newspaper articles, talks to community groups, and directed mailings. There were two major disadvantages to this approach: it was very time consuming, and parents who called were distributed across a wide geographical area. The latter meant that groups had to be formed on a geographical basis, with too few families in any one area for random assignment to different conditions. Moreover, some families decided against participating because the meeting sites were still too far away. Collaborating with Regional Centers has proven much more cost-effective. Counsellors inform families of the programme and compile a list of those who are interested, and the Regional Center provides meeting space. This collaboration between a University-based applied research programme and community service agencies provides benefits to both parties.

Curriculum

The group leader(s) guide parents through a standard curriculum (see Table 4.1). The first four sessions focus on teaching self-help skills. Parents learn assessment and basic teaching methods. They learn to set behavioural objectives, break skills down into component steps, and use reinforcement appropriately. In the fifth session, one or two families attend at a time with the developmentally disabled child. Parents demonstrate what they have been teaching at home and receive feedback from a leader and perhaps from other parents. Sometimes parents are videotaped during this session and the tape is replayed and discussed with them.

The next three group-training sessions focus on strategies for behaviour problem management, and toilet training when it is applicable. Parents learn to identify problems to work on, to observe and record the frequency or duration of problem behaviours, to analyse the problems in terms of antecedents and consequences, to develop and carry out a behaviour management or toileting programme, and to chart progress. Each family takes data on at least one problem behaviour before and during the execution of a home-based programme. The final two sessions deal with applying the principles and methods that parents have learned to additional areas of teaching, primarily play skills. These sessions also consider incidental teaching (working teaching into the daily routine at home) and future planning.

Orientation

The orientation of our training approach is cognitive-behavioural. The main focus is on teaching parents the application of basic behaviour modification principles to teaching activities, especially targeting a skill, doing a functional analysis, identifying and rearranging antecedents and consequences, and charting progress. In recent years, however, we have added a cognitive component to almost every meeting, focusing not only on what parents and their children do, but also on parents' cognitions — or 'self-talk' — about those activities. The general intention is to teach parents to be aware of negative or interfering self-talk and to develop problem-solving strategies that can override the kinds of negative cognition that so often impede progress.

In the first meeting, for example, parents are asked to list 'reasons to teach', and 'reasons not to teach'. The latter list might include statements such as 'He already gets too much pressure in school', 'I might do the wrong thing', or 'I don't have enough time'. It seems best to air such thoughts, because if unacknowledged they can effectively block progress. The group then attempts to come up with alternative, more positive, statements, or ways to solve the problem posed. Hence, the parent who is worried about doing the wrong thing may be advised to say to herself: 'I've already taught him many things', or 'I can ask members of the group for their ideas about teaching'. Similarly, the group can help the parent who complains of limited time to problem-solve on this subject until a workable plan is arrived at (e.g. 'I will teach at weekends and my husband will teach at night during the week'). Similar discussions take place in other meetings throughout training.

Instruction

Leaders use a variety of modalities to instruct parents. They use brief 'mini-lectures', small group problem-solving sessions, and focused discussions to present and elaborate ideas. They use action-oriented approaches such as demonstrations with each other and role-playing with parents to illustrate teaching techniques. In preparation for each group meeting, parents read parts of a self-instructional manual (see below). The leaders focus discussions around what parents have learned in the manuals, and supplement these with videotaped illustrations of teaching principles. Each concept, then, is presented in several different ways. To illustrate, one of the concepts parents learn in the second meeting is 'setting the stage' for teaching: arranging the antecedents so as to maximise success. Before the meeting they should have read about this notion in the manual. In the meeting, one leader will briefly describe this concept and lead a discussion about what parents understand of it. The leader will then show a five-minute video tape of several parents setting the stage to teach. Finally, the leader will ask each family to note one way in which they could set the stage to increase success with the skill that they have chosen to teach their child. Presenting each idea in this manner, using several different modalities, maximises parents' learning.

Media

The programme is built around the *Steps to Independence Series* of parent training manuals: *Early Self-help Skills, Advanced Self-help Skills*, *Behavior Problems*, and *Toilet Training* (Baker *et al.*, 1976–77), *Beginning Speech, Speech and Language* (Baker *et al.*, 1978), and *Toward Independent Living* (Baker *et al.*, 1981a). Parents first receive the self-help skill manual that is at the level appropriate for their child. The first half of each manual presents behaviour modification with retarded children in a light, easy-to-read manner (see Figure 4.1). The last half contains detailed programmes for teaching various self-help skills. For the second half of the programme, parents receive similar manuals on behaviour problems, play skills, and toilet training when relevant. In most meetings leaders use one or more examples from the *Parents as Teachers Videotapes* (Baker *et al.*, 1976), which contain ten brief (about 5-minute) segments illustrating various teaching and behaviour-management principles. In programme evaluations, parents assess the written and visual media very highly.

4.3 Assessment of Outcome

In this section we will present our primary evaluation measures. Our choice of outcome measures follows from our goals for families. Our ideal family after training would be able to select skills to teach, to develop strategies that are systematic and manageable, to implement these in a way that maximises success, and to know

Figure 4.1: Illustrative page from *Play Skills* Manual

Paying Attention

Nearly all types of play require your child to pay attention, either to you, to the toys or objects, to other children, or to the rules of the game. So, before you begin teaching even the most basic play activities, let's look at seven ways to increase your child's attention.

Stand near her

When speaking to your child, make sure she can see you and hear you. Expecting her to respond to something shouted from another room is certainly asking too much. Even talking to her from across the room may be too difficult in the beginning.

Get on her level

Position yourself so that she can see your face. That's what you want her to pay attention to. If she is sitting on the floor, squat down so she can see you. If she is sitting at a table, sit facing her. Make it as easy as possible for her to watch your face.

Call her name

One word your child likely recognizes is her name. Before asking her to do something, get her attention by calling her name—then she'll know you are talking to her. Wait until she turns to look at you before continuing. If she doesn't look, say her name again. Use proper names when you can. Understanding pronouns (I, you, me) is more difficult.

"*Jenny*, get the ball."
"Give *Dad* the ball."

Get eye contact

When you say his name and he turns toward you, look him in the eyes. If he is facing you but looking at the floor, he may be paying more attention to the floor than to you. If he doesn't look directly at you, put a finger gently on his chin and guide him to look at you.

Choose your words carefully

Use simple, familiar words and short sentences. "Come play" tells him in simple, clear terms exactly what you want him to do. It is better than "recess" or "playtime," which may have no meaning for your child.

whether they are working. This requires that parents be: (1) knowledgeable about behavioural principles; (2) able to apply behavioural principles in teaching interactions with their child; and (3) involved in implementing them at home. These goals have, in

Be consistent

Use the same words for people, places, and things all the time. Father should always be "Daddy" (or whatever you prefer), and not alternatively "Papa" one day and "Dad" the next.

Use gestures

Your child will more easily understand you and more readily pay attention to you if you accompany your words with helpful gestures:

Another way to increase your child's ability to pay attention is a variation on the old carnival shell game. The objects of this game are for your child to watch you hide food under one of three cups, to watch while you move the cups, and then to pick up the correct cup on the first try.

Source: Baker *et al.* (1983)

turn, led us to develop measures of parent knowledge, skills, and implementation. We are also interested in assessing other dimensions, such as changes in parental attitudes and child-rearing beliefs, but we have not made these a major focus of assessment.

We will describe each measure and indicate typical pre- and post-scores by reporting results from a recent sample of 35 families who completed five groups that used the cognitive-behavioural version of the programme described above. These families had moderately to severely retarded children averaging 5.6 years of age (range 3 to 13) at the beginning of the programme. In each family we determined the parent primarily involved in teaching; in all but one case this was the mother. These 'primary parents' averaged 32 years old, with 12.5 years of schooling; 41 per cent of these primary parents were working, and 20 per cent were single parents. These families represented a wide range of socio-economic status and ethnicity.

Parents' Knowledge of Behavioural Principles

Many behavioural programmes use a questionnaire to assess parents' knowledge of behaviour-change principles, and gains have been found consistently. Some programmes assess general knowledge of behavioural terms and principles without special reference to mental retardation (O'Dell *et al.*, 1979b; see also Chapter 3, this volume). The UCLA project uses the *Behavioural Vignettes Test* (BVT), which assesses knowledge of behaviour modification principles as they apply to teaching retarded children.

Twenty brief vignettes describe situations that reflect a range of common problems in the formulation and implementation of skill teaching and behaviour problem management programmes. Parents select the response that they think would be best from four alternatives (see example in Chapter 3).

Studies by our project and other researchers who have used the BVT have consistently found that parents gained significantly from pre- to post-training (Baker and Heifetz, 1976; Brightman *et al.*, 1982; Feldman *et al.*, 1982, 1983; Clark and Baker, 1983; Baker and Brightman, 1984). Two studies that compared trained families with untrained control families on the BVT found that trained families showed significantly greater gains; control families gained only minimally (Baker and Heifetz, 1976; Brightman *et al.*, 1982).

Table 4.2 shows pre- and post-training BVT scores for families in the cognitive-behavioural sample of 35 families. The average family scored about 50 per cent correct before training and 70 per cent correct after training. In addition to these group results, a clinically useful measure is the percentage of parents who reach a predetermined proficiency criterion. We have typically used 75 per cent or more correct (a score of 15 or greater out of 20) as a criterion

Table 4.2: Means and Ranges on Outcome Measures for Parents and Retarded Children before and after the Parents as Teachers Programme

Measure	Pre-training	Post-training
Behavioural Vignettes Test*	9.5 (range 2–16)	14.4 (range 5–20)
Teaching Proficiency Test*	7.1 (range 0–16)	12.8 (range 4–20)
Teaching Interview*	13.0	21.1
Performance Inventory**		
Self-help skills	15.6	20.4
Behaviour problems	51.4	36.3

* N = 35 families who completed five cognitive-behavioural Parents as Teachers groups.
** N = 46 families who completed the behavioural Parents as Teachers programme reported in Brightman *et al.*, 1982.

for proficiency. By this index, 7.3 per cent of families were proficient before training and 45.7 per cent were proficient after training. Although BVT scores are highly related to parents' education, there is some evidence that more parents would reach proficiency with further training (Brightman *et al.*, 1980).

Parents' Teaching Skills

Many programmes also assess whether parents can apply what they have learned in interactions with their child. Measures have been developed for rating behaviour-management interactions in families with conduct-disordered children (Patterson *et al.*, 1975; Christensen, 1979; Zebiob *et al.*, 1979; see also Chapter 3 this volume). These are not readily applicable to families with developmentally disabled children, however, where the emphasis is primarily on skill teaching. Several measures constructed for parents of developmentally disabled children tally a score based upon the number of behavioural techniques employed while teaching (Koegel *et al.*, 1977; Weitz, 1981). These suffer from not taking into account whether it is appropriate with a particular child to use a given technique — for example, with a high-functioning child, physical guidance may be unnecessary.

The UCLA project uses the *Teaching Proficiency Test* (Clark and Baker, 1982), a standardised assessment of a parent's ability to implement behaviour modification techniques while teaching. A parent is videotaped for 15 minutes teaching his or her developmentally disabled child two self-help skills and two play skills that the child can do some part of but has not mastered. Coders who are blind to the family's experimental condition or whether the administration was before or after training score the videotaped session on four dimensions: arrangement of the environment, task presentation, reinforcement, and behaviour problem management. A total of 21 points is possible. The coder scores the presence of specific parent behaviours as in other rating approaches; however, these are not simply tallied. Rather, various combinations of behaviours receive different scores, to reflect the relevance of a given teaching behaviour for the particular child and task. For example, a parent who does not remove distractions from the teaching environment will receive a lower score if, in fact, the child is distracted by them than if he is not. In turn, she can gain points if she notices that the child is distracted and corrects her error.

We have found very high intercoder reliabilities and significant changes in parents' teaching proficiency from pre- to post-training. In one study that compared 46 trained families with 13 control families, on an earlier version of the TPT, trained families showed significantly greater gains (Brightman *et al.*, 1982). TPT scores for cognitive-behavioural groups ($N = 35$) increased from 7.1 before training to 12.8 following training (see Table 4.2). Here, too, it is clinically useful to set a proficiency criterion, although it is more difficult on this measure since scores vary somewhat with the behaviour of the child as well as the parent (e.g. with a very inattentive child, a parent is limited in the number of points she can get). None the less, a score of 13 or above reflects teaching that is generally sound from a behavioural point of view and that promises to teach the child something. This criterion was met by 14.3 per cent of parents before training, compared with 61.8 per cent after training. The TPT correlates somewhat with parent education, although not as highly as the BVT knowledge measure.

The TPT has greater pre/post variability than the BVT, since it is a 'live' measure involving not only the parent but also the child. If the child is particularly disruptive or inattentive in one session, this can depress the score considerably. In individual training, the TPT can be done in every session, providing material for the trainer and the parent to discuss, and a more stable measure of change.

Parents' Implementation of Teaching at Home

A crucial question is whether parents use these teaching skills after training. We conduct a 30-minute Teaching Interview (Ambrose and Baker, 1979) before and after training and at follow-up (usually 3 or 6 months). Parents are interviewed by a staff member not known to the family, and are asked about teaching during the preceding 3 months. Interview categories include regular systematic teaching programmes (formal teaching), teaching that is more loosely integrated into daily routine (incidental teaching), and behaviour management. The interviews are tape-recorded, and coders who are blind to the family's experimental condition or whether the administration was before or after training score them for both extent of teaching and teaching sophistication (how well behavioural principles are used). Inter-rater reliabilities are very high on this measure, families show significant gains, and trained families have improved relative to controls (Prieto-Bayard and Baker, in press).

In the cognitive-behavioural sample of 35 families, Teaching Interview scores averaged 13.0 for the assessment taken just before training and 21.1 for the assessment immediately after training. This increase in the extent and sophistication of teaching reflects more and better teaching during the training period.

Child Behaviour Change. The demonstration of success of parent training in child change depends in part on the specificity of the measure. At one extreme, parent training programmes assess changes in specific child behaviours that parents have targeted, and typically find good results. Rose (1974) found that 90 per cent of parents modified at least one child behaviour 'to their own satisfaction', and O'Dell *et al.* (1977), using a stricter criterion for outcome, found 68 per cent completed one full modification project. Such specific measures, however, do not indicate whether training effects generalised to other child behaviours. On the other extreme, some studies that have used standardised intellectual or developmental measures have failed to show change relative to controls (Sebba, 1981; Clements *et al.*, 1982; Sandler *et al.*, 1983). These measures have taped too much beyond what the programme targeted and have, perhaps, masked successful, albeit more narrow, outcomes. Standard measures have consistently shown significant child gains when they were directly related to the content of training. For example, Harris *et al.* (1981) have used a language hierarchy to assess the effectiveness of their language training programme for parents of autistic children.

The UCLA Project has similarly assessed children on those

domains targeted in training. The *Performance Inventory Self-help Scale* measures child performance on 38 specific skills in the areas of dressing, eating, grooming, toileting, and housekeeping. The component parts of each skill are arranged in a hierarchical scale (ranging from 'Child cannot do any part of this skill' to 'Child can perform this skill completely independently'), and parents check the step that most accurately reflects the child's performance. Reliabilities have been high between staff and parents on this measure. On the *Performance Inventory Behavior Problem Scale*, parents estimate the frequency or duration of 51 behaviour problems commonly reported for retarded children. Items cover areas such as aggressive behaviours, stereotyped behaviours, and fears. Scores reflect the number of reported problems and their frequency of occurrence.

We have not yet completed analysis of these child measures for the cognitive-behavioural sample. However, several studies have shown increases in self-help skills and decreases in behaviour problems on the *Performance Inventory* following training (Baker and Heifetz, 1976; Brightman *et al.*, 1982; Feldman *et al.*, 1982, 1983). The Brightman *et al.* (1982) results are shown in Table 4.2, since they are the most recent available statistics from our project. The gains across all self-help skills totalled the equivalent of about five skills. Feldman and her colleagues (1982) used a multiple baseline design to show the relationship of gains to training. Baker and Heifetz (1976) distinguished between skills and behaviour problems that the parents programmed for and those that they had not programmed for; changes in both categories were significant relative to controls.

4.4 Short-term Gain: the Mann Family

The programme's expectations and outcome may be illustrated best by looking at one family's participation. We have chosen a family that was somewhat below average on the before-training assessment measures and about average in the amount of teaching that they did and the gains that they made.

Mr and Mrs Mann participated in the Parents as Teachers programme with seven other families at a Los Angeles County Regional Center. At the beginning of training, their son Jimmy, who has cerebral palsy, was seven years old. Gloria Mann was 25 years old, a housewife with a 10th-grade education and mother of two younger children besides Jimmy. Dennis Mann was 28 years old, with a high-school education and full-time employment as a bus driver. Both parents' rating of their marital harmony on the Locke Wallace Marital Adjustment Test (Locke and Wallace, 1959) was above average.

In their initial interview, the Manns acknowledged that they had no previous experience with either parent training or teaching using behaviour principles. The Manns did state that they had tried to teach Jimmy to perform various dressing skills and to balance without his crutches; however, they did not teach on a regular basis, and felt that they had seen little recent progress. On the Behavioural Vignettes Test, Gloria scored 8 (40 per cent) and Dennis scored only 4 (20 per cent); these scores were both below average for this measure, indicating very little awareness of behavioural principles. On the Teaching Proficiency Test, Gloria scored a 13 indicating reasonably good teaching; Dennis scored 10. The Manns scored 12 on the initial Teaching Interview, somewhat below average for this measure. The low scores on our three parent measures reflect, in part, the Manns' limited education and absence of behaviour modification experience.

During the ten-week programme the Manns attended every meeting and evaluated the programme highly. They learned how to observe Jimmy's behaviour, select appropriate skills to teach, and carry out a teaching programme. For their first self-help skill, the Manns chose to teach Jimmy to put on his pants, because he had already mastered some of this skill (he could pull his pants up from his knees after his parent had started them). At the training meetings Gloria and Dennis each reported teaching Jimmy daily, and they observed slow but steady progress.

By the end of the programme the Manns had developed some understanding of behavioural principles, as indicated by post-training Behavioural Vignettes Test scores of 12 for Gloria and 11 for Dennis; there was still room for improvement, but given their low starting scores these represent meaningful gains. Gloria's Teaching Proficiency Test score had risen to 16 and Dennis's to 12, indicating that both parents were teaching somewhat better.

By the last training session, they had successfully taught Jimmy to put on his pants without help. Also, they had started to teach a second dressing skill, putting on a pullover shirt. They had kept baseline data on Jimmy's hitting his younger siblings, and had carried out a behaviour-management programme with good initial success, reducing hitting by about 60 per cent. These programming efforts were reflected in a Teaching Inventory score of 26, indicating considerably more and better teaching during the training programme than in the comparable time before it. Both Gloria and Dennis felt proud of their accomplishments and were optimistic about continuing to teach now that the formal training programme was over.

4.5 Follow-up and Maintenance

A crucial question to ask of any intervention is whether the effects are maintained. The question of how to follow up families after training and to what extent gains are maintained is especially important for parent training programmes. The rationale for such programmes is usually presented in terms of increased parental teaching and coping — in terms that imply effects that carry beyond the training period. We have seen that parents like the Manns who have participated in our parent training programme typically demonstrate short-term gains in proficiency. The maintenance question really has two parts. First, will the knowledge and skills acquired be maintained? Secondly, will families continue with teaching and even begin new teaching programmes in the weeks and months after training?

We have some evidence that Behavioural Vignettes Test scores are about the same one year after training (Baker *et al.*, 1980), and we have conducted Teaching Proficiency Tests with some families six months after training with no loss in score. Hence in answer to the first question, it appears that knowledge and skills remain intact. It is the second question that gives us more reasons for concern. In several follow-up studies of six months (Ambrose and Baker, 1979) and one year (Baker *et al.*, 1980), we have found that when families teach, they rarely use formal teaching (regular, systematic teaching sessions); they are much more likely to use incidental teaching (working teaching into ongoing daily routines). In these studies only about one family in four was very actively involved in teaching. On the other extreme, one family in four was doing virtually no useful teaching. In the sample of families studied by Ambrose and Baker (1979), several voluntary group meetings were held after the formal training sessions. Only about half of the families attended, and although parents reported finding such follow-through of value, the meetings did not seem to enhance home teaching.

For the first two groups in the cognitive-behavioural sample, we administered the Teaching Interview before training, at the end of the three-month training period, and at a three-month follow-up. The group means for these three points were: 14.4, 22.1 and 17.8. Families increased in the extent and sophistication of teaching during the training, but by the three-month follow-up the level had fallen off to a point not significantly different from the pre-training level.

Post-training Intervention

In an attempt to promote maintenance of teaching, Kashima (1983) developed and evaluated a 'booster' intervention, consisting of an in-home planning session immediately following training and biweekly follow-through phone calls for three months. The next two cognitive-behavioural groups were smaller, with ten families who completed training. For a pilot test of the 'booster' intervention, these families were rank-ordered by predicted follow-through (based upon the Clark and Baker (1983) criteria); one member of each successive pair was assigned to the 'booster' follow-through ($N = 5$) and the other to a no-intervention follow-through ($N = 5$) for three months. I will briefly describe the intervention and initial results.

The planning session helped parents to set up goals and priorities, plan specific steps to take in meeting them, and anticipate obstacles. We used the Goal Attainment Scale developed by Kiresuk and Sherman (1968). Parents first choose three or four skills to teach or behaviour problems to reduce. Staff assisted parents in formulating goals so that they were stated clearly and were reasonable to attain (e.g. 'Learn to tie shoes in three months'). For each of these 'target' behaviours, the parents identified what they realistically expected they would do (e.g. 'Teach three times a week for ten to fifteen minutes each time'). They then identified one or two levels of effort that would be better than this, and one or two levels that would not be as good as this. Hence for each teaching goal the family developed performance criteria based upon their own expectations.

Following this, staff assisted parents in identifying the steps to follow in teaching, ways to reward themselves for following through, and obstacles that they might have expected to encounter. Staff and parents worked together to identify alternative 'self-talk' for

Figure 4.2: Before and after Training, and Follow-up Teaching Interview Scores for Families who Received the Booster Follow-through Intervention vs. no Follow-through Intervention. Scores reflect the extent and quality of teaching at home during the preceding 3 months

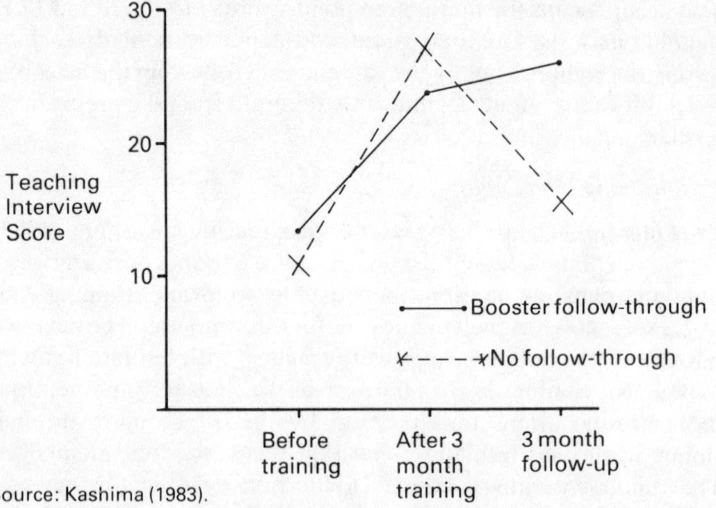

Source: Kashima (1983).

interfering thoughts and to problem-solve about ways to deal with realistic obstacles.

Biweekly telephone contacts lasting 10 to 15 minutes gave parents the opportunity to discuss their programming and obstacles they may have encountered. Each family who participated in the pilot booster programme reported at least once that their child was too ill to teach. When setbacks such as these were reported, the subgoals previously established were maintained or revised to accommodate the situation. In addition to contracting future subgoals with parents, staff offered teaching suggestions and encouragement.

The Teaching Interview scores from before training, after training, and at a three-month follow-up were compared for booster and no-booster group families (Kashima, 1983). These are shown in Figure 4.2. Using a multivariate analysis of variance for repeated measures, the group-by-time interaction was significant, $F(2,7) = 7.30$, $p < 0.25$. The no-booster group showed a drop in teaching at follow-up similar to reports of other authors and to our own earlier cognitive-behavioural groups. The booster groups, though, had maintained a high level of teaching. It remains to be seen, however, whether this level will persist in the absence of continuing contact.

Scores on the Goal Attainment Scale for the booster intervention group indicated that four of the five families attained or did better than their expected efforts at teaching. The one family in the booster programme that did not benefit from the additional programming was, according to the predictive equation developed by Clark and Baker (1983), the family that was predicted to do the least follow-through. The booster programme may prove to be most useful for parents with the capacity and inclination to teach but who need some further guidance and accountability.

4.6 Long-term Gains: the Manns, Continued

The Manns were randomly assigned to the booster condition. Two weeks after training, two project staff visited the Manns at home for the follow-up goal planning session. The Manns set the following four goals, stated in terms of behavioural outcomes: (1) Jimmy puts on a pullover shirt by himself; (2) Jimmy does not hit his siblings; (3) Jimmy washes his face; and (4) Jimmy balances without crutches. They understood that goals (3) and (4) might take a long time to reach, and developed subgoals (e.g. hitting is reduced to 25 per cent of baseline). The Manns discussed with the staff their teaching plans for each goal area and the obstacles to teaching that might arise. Gloria mentioned that at times she felt overwhelmed with the responsibility for all of her children. After some problem-solving, Gloria and Dennis agreed to divide the responsibilities more; in particular, when one was teaching Jimmy, the other would keep the other two children occupied. In addition, they made a plan to reward themselves for their teaching efforts each week by going out to dinner by themselves.

In the biweekly phone conversations, primarily with Gloria, progress and problems were discussed. At one point Jimmy was ill for a two-week period and no teaching took place. Three months following training, the Manns were interviewed again by a staff member who had not been involved in their training. Their total teaching interview score had increased to 36 (compared with 12 before training and 26 after training). Dennis had taken primary responsibility for teaching putting on the pullover shirt, and now stated that Jimmy could almost do every step himself. Also, the Manns reported that Jimmy was able to balance without his crutches for $1\frac{1}{2}$ minutes and had progressed in face washing. Hitting was still an occasional problem, although much reduced from pre-programme levels. Both parents expressed more optimism about Jimmy's learning ability and about their own ability to work together as a couple to teach him.

4.7 Research Issues

We have used variations of the Parents as Teachers programme to address a number of issues related to the implementation and outcome of training. This section will summarise research in three related areas: (1) understanding participants: joiners and completers; (2) choosing a training format; and (3) predicting outcome.

Understanding Participants: Joiners and Completers

Evaluations of parent training outcome are based upon those families who enter and go on to complete the training programme and the outcome measures. It is important, both methodologically and clinically, to inquire about how representative of families with developmentally disabled children are those who join and complete a programme. If only a small proportion of parents choose to join the programme, and, furthermore, if many drop out during the programme, the methodological concern is that outcome results are severely limited in generalisability. The clinical concern is that families are not finding the programme of value.

It is a common experience for us in talking with professionals about parent training to be told that 'We tried to get a group started, but there wasn't much response.' Most written reports of parent training are based upon small samples of volunteer families. Few mention how families were recruited into the training programme, what training options they were given, or how many families had to be invited in order to get the sample reported. Several papers do report joining rates, though we do not know how representative these studies are. Morris (1973) sent letters to 80 families with a retarded child, inviting participation in a free individual or group training programme; 41 agreed to participate but only 14 (18 per cent) attended the initial meeting. McConkey and McEvoy (1983) invited 101 families by letter to participate in an evening course on helping retarded children learn through play; 38 per cent joined. We sent letters offering the Parents as Teachers programme to all 74 families with a moderately to severely retarded child in a Los Angeles county public school for retarded children; 24 per cent joined the programme (Baker *et al.*, 1981b). The highest rate of joining that we know of was 63 per cent found by Shenk (1984), who offered a Spanish version of our programme to Spanish-speaking low socio-economic status families in Los Angeles. In contrast to recruitment through letters used in the above studies, Shenk personally invited 41 families to join one of two groups after project staff had visited them in their homes twice for another study.

We know very little about the characteristics of families who have chosen to join our programme. In the Baker *et al.* (1981b) study, compared with non-joiners, joiners were already more involved in school activities and were better educated. Also, they had children who were more retarded and had more behaviour problems that interfered with learning. Hence, if parent training were introduced into a continuing school programme, it is likely that many parents with less education and school involvement, or those whose children presently pose fewer problems, would probably not be motivated to participate. In Shenk's (1984) Spanish-speaking sample, joiners were also more involved with school activities. Shenk did not find differences in the actual skill and behaviour problem levels of retarded children in joiners' vs. non-joiners' families, but he did find that parents who joined reported more subjective distress from their children's skill deficiencies and behaviour problems.

Our criterion for completion has been attending at least half of the meetings and the post-training assessment. In an earlier sample, 94 of 103 families (91 per cent) were designated completers (Clark and Baker, 1983). In the cognitive-behavioural sample that we have been discussing, the 35 families who completed were from an initial 44 who began the program (81 per cent). Recruitment may partly account for the difference in completion rates; in the former sample, families were self-referred, and in the latter sample, they were referred by agency staff. The difference in dropouts between the two samples, however, was small and not statistically significant.

In these samples, dropouts did not differ from completers on measures of socio-economic status, parents' age or employment, distance families lived from the meeting place, marital adjustment, parent expectations, previous group membership, prior teaching, or child characteristics. They differed on only two variables: they were more likely to be single-parent families, and they scored lower initially on the Behavioural Vignettes Test. We now recommend that single parents go through the programme with a friend or relative, and we would recommend several individual sessions of pre-training before beginning the group for parents who evidence very limited behavioural knowledge. Correlates of programme completion must be considered tenuous, since dropout rates were low. With larger samples and/or with higher dropout rates, other variables might also differentiate those who stay and those who do not.

Choosing a Training Format

We have conducted several studies to assess the effectiveness of variations in the group Parents as Teachers programme that we described. The previous chapter reviewed results from the Read project (Baker and Heifetz, 1976; Heifetz, 1977; Baker *et al.*, 1980) which contrasted training by manuals alone and in combination with phone consultation, group meetings, and group meetings plus home visits. To review briefly, all training conditions proved superior to controls. The conditions produced similar outcomes in parent knowledge and child self-help skills, whereas programming for behaviour problems was more successful in the group conditions. Families in the manuals-only group, however, felt less competent as teachers and tended to be doing less teaching at a one-year follow-up, leading us to adopt a combined manuals and group curriculum for subsequent work. We wondered how this group curriculum compared with individual consultation, a model that is more frequently used in agencies; and carried out a study to investigate this question.

Group vs. Individual Training (Brightman *et al.*, 1982). Parents were randomly assigned to a modified group curriculum that involved no contact with the child (*N* = 37; 32 completed), an individual consultation format (*N* = 16; 14 completed) or a delayed-treatment control group (*N* = 13). In the individual condition, the parent(s) and child came to the clinic for nine hour-long sessions; training generally followed the same curriculum sequences as group training, except that many concepts were taught using parents' own videotaped teaching sessions. We hypothesised that group training would be superior in increasing knowledge of behavioural principles and that individual training would be superior in increasing actual performance in a teaching session, since the group format contained more information and the individual format involved more teaching experience and feedback.

In fact, however, parents and children in both training conditions demonstrated significant gains on all measures, and trained families differed from controls on all measures but one (child self-help skills). However, gains in the two training formats were almost identical. At a 6-month follow-up, group and individually trained families did not differ on the quantity or quality of their teaching since training. Group training requires about half the professional time per family as individual training, and therefore seemed a more cost-effective approach. We were left, however, with one lingering doubt. In this study, and in many studies that have made format comparisons, the conditions produced similar results. We wondered whether beneficial outcomes are specific to training programme content (as we would like to believe), or, rather, derive from non-specific factors, such as professionals' attention and encouragement. The latter, if true, might explain why different conditions seem to produce such similar outcomes. We designed a study to explore this question.

Programme-specific Outcomes (Baker and Brightman, 1984). We randomly assigned 15 families with a developmentally disabled child to either a seven-session version of the Parents as Teachers programme or the seven-session Parents as Advocates course, which teaches parents their legal rights and strategies for exercising them (Brightman, 1984). Measures of teaching (knowledge and skill) and advocacy (knowledge and skill) were administered to all parents before and after training. Fourteen (93 per cent) of parents completed the programme. The demonstrated gains were programme-specific on three of four indices of outcome. Gains on measures assessing advocacy-related knowledge (questionnaire) and skills (response to advocacy situations presented on video tape) were sizeable for those in the Parents as Advocates programme; parents in the Parents as Teachers programme showed some, though significantly less, change on these measures. Similarly, gain in knowledge of behavioural principles (Behavioural Vignettes Test) was considerable for those in the Parents as Teachers programme; parents in the Parents as Advocates programme changed little on this measure. In teaching skill (Teaching Proficiency Test), parents trained as teachers gained more but the difference failed to reach significance. We concluded that 'In general, gains were programme-specific. Parents did not change "across the board" as a result of being in a parent training programme. Rather, their gains reflected the unique content of each programme component' (Baker and Brightman, 1984, p. 259).

Prediction of Outcome

All families, of course, do not benefit equally from parent training: some do not attain teaching proficiency by the end of the programme and/or do not follow through well after training ends. We have been interested in identifying predictors of unsuccessful outcomes, so that we can develop alternative interventions for parents predicted to fare poorly in a standard group curriculum. We have reported two prediction studies (Clark *et al.*, 1982; Clark and Baker, 1983) that followed the strategy of classifying families into high- and low-proficiency groups at end of training and high- and low-implementation groups at follow-up. Groups were then compared on a number of variables (demographic, expectations, prior related experience and skills, child characteristics), and variables with significant univariate relationships to outcome were entered into discriminant analyses.

The findings of these two studies were summarised in Chapter 3. We followed the same procedures with the cognitive-behavioural sample that we have considered throughout this chapter. Taken together, these predictor studies find several consistent relationships. The best predictor of low proficiency after training (knowledge and teaching skill level) was low socio-economic status (SES), and a second strong predictor was no prior experience with behavioural groups. The best predictors of follow-through implementation were low post-training proficiency, little previous teaching (either before or during training) and being a single parent. It is interesting to note that child characteristics are not related to training outcome.

The finding that lower-SES families do less well is consistent with other prediction studies (see Baker, 1984, for review). Subsequent to our prediction studies, the UCLA project has explored several training variations in order to make training more accessible and beneficial for lower-SES families. We have conducted meetings at central and familiar locations, and counsellors have recruited families with whom they had a personal relationship. We have provided child care, provided or reimbursed transportation, included a lottery with tickets earned for attendance and homework, and given diplomas upon programme completion. The major curriculum change has been to supplement group meetings with modelling and supervised child teaching, as is done in school or home-based programmes.

We conducted two summer mini-camps, one for parents who had shown only limited benefits from group training (Brightman *et al.*, 1980) and one for parents predicted to be low proficiency based on Clark and Baker's (1983) predictors (Baker and McCurry, 1984). In both school-based programmes, parents were actively involved in observing children being taught and in teaching children, their own and others. Staff provided ongoing feedback and reviewed video tapes of teaching sessions with parents. These parents gained significantly in their knowledge of principles and in their teaching proficiency. In the Brightman *et al.* (1980) study, mini-camp-trained parents scored significantly higher than a comparison group who did not attend. We have also developed a programme for parents who speak only Spanish. In one study, where parents' education level averaged only the fifth grade, parents and children showed significant gains relative to a waiting-list control group (Prieto-Bayard and Baker, in press).

We are presently broadening our predictor battery to include measures of parental depression, marital adjustment, family adaptation and cohesiveness, and family coping strategies. We are hopeful that these will both increase our prediction of successful and unsuccessful families and suggest new directions for modifying training to better accommodate families.

Dissemination

While it is important to continue research on parent training, it is also true that the service delivery system does not reflect what we already know. Despite ready acknowledgement that training parents is or should be a top priority, few service agencies actually offer well-conceived parent training as a regular service. The typical parent of a young retarded child does not have access to a training programme.

This situation seems odd, since one assumes that intervention programmes are developed in order to be used. Yet in contrast to the considerable investment in evaluating mental health programme effectiveness, there has been scant attention to programme dissemination. The common route of publishing results and information about programmes, even demonstrably very effective ones, does not appear to be enough to inspire adoption by others

(Fairweather *et al.*, 1974; McClelland, 1978). Fairweather and his colleagues (1969), for example, pioneered a highly successful programme for moving psychiatric patients from the hospital to the community; yet despite the demonstration programme's national reputation, it was not even adopted by the hospital in which it took place! Similarly, in parent training there is a surprising lack of systematic programme adoption, despite promising reports in the literature.

A common approach to dissemination is in-service staff training. Yet this does not assure programme adoption. We trained 83 staff members from 24 agencies in Los Angeles to conduct parent training. Attendance at our training sessions was good, enthusiasm was high, and staff made demonstrable gains in their own behavioural skills. Yet little further implementation took place after the training programme had ended. High staff turnover rates, limited behavioural competency of staff, and perceived role discrepancy between most staff persons' jobs and the requirements of parent training resulted in even the best-intentioned staff or agency finding that they lacked the time and resources to train parents (Berlin and Baker, 1983).

There is a need for cost-effective and easily exportable programmes that (1) require much less knowledge of behavioural psychology and developmental disabilities on the leader's part; (2) work in a variety of organisational contexts; and (3) require little staff training, so that the wasted cost of training non-implementers will be minimal. In Ireland, McConkey and his colleagues (McConkey and O'Conner, 1982; McConkey and McEvoy, 1983) have developed and evaluated two video courses to teach parents of developmentally disabled children how to stimulate language and facilitate play. Course leaders have been easily trained, a high proportion of parents invited to participate have done so, and objective measures of child language and play have showed gains. Yet the promise of intervention through video-directed training remains generally unexplored. Hosford and Mills (1983), in their review of the video literature, noted that 'few quality video-based psychological interventions have been made available to the professional community' (p. 143).

We are presently approaching dissemination through video-directed training. We have produced four professional-quality colour video tapes that take a small group of families through the four-session self-help skill component of the Parents as Teachers programme. They require a group leader, but he or she need not be highly knowledgeable about behaviour modification, developmental disabilities, or group process. The group leader is responsible for the mechanics of the meetings (e.g. setting up the equipment, passing out manuals and handouts) and for limited facilitation of group discussions. We are presently contrasting this media-directed training with our standard leader-directed approach. If the video-directed group proves to be acceptable to parents and produces comparable outcomes, it will provide a model for us to follow in producing training tapes on other topics. It will also provide a means to facilitate adoption of our programme by others interested in implementing parent training.

Acknowledgements

This chapter is based upon activities of the UCLA Project for Developmental Disabilities. The research was primarily supported by the National Institute of Child and Human Development, Contract 72-2016 and Grants HD-42848 and HD-10962. The author gratefully acknowledges Ms Kathleen Kashima's contributions to this manuscript.

5 NURSES AS THERAPISTS: A REVIEW OF RESEARCH

5.1 An Introduction to Nurse Training in Behaviour Therapy

The involvement of nurses in behaviour therapy readily follows the guidelines laid down for the use of the triadic model for parents, as discussed in the preceding two chapters. This is particularly the case in long-stay hospitals, such as psychiatric and mental handicap units, where the nurse has a central role to play in the day-to-day care of patients. Because of this long-term involvement, nurses find themselves in a position in many ways similar to the parents' role. For instance, they develop an intimate understanding and shoulder the major responsibility for their patients' psychological growth and development. In many cases this continues over a period of several years. The nature of this parenting relationship is increased still further by the 'total' or self-contained quality of long-stay institutions (Goffman, 1961).

The research literature concerned with nurse training in behaviour therapy does not, however, sustain this parallel, as it is neither as voluminous nor as sophisticated as the parent training research that we have already reviewed. These research differences will be highlighted by considering the major themes of this book (training, evaluation and implementation) in terms of nurse training, nurse management and nurse development. These categories are used to illuminate three basic areas of research. It is realised that they are not, of course, logically exclusive, nor do they reflect a clear distinction emerging from the literature. In fact, most studies have failed to clarify their general aims, making it difficult in many cases to integrate them as a body of research. None the less, these categories help us to take account of the historical development of research into nurse training, and so afford a helpful perspective.

Those readers who are interested in reviews that have taken a different perspective on aspects of this research are referred to Gardner (1972, 1973), Le Bow (1976), Barker (1980), Miller and Lewin (1980), Reid and Whitman (1983), Bernstein (1984) and Milne (1984b).

5.2 Staff Training

Advances in nurse training are reflected by the increased sophistication of their use of behavioural approaches over the last 20 years. Initially, nurses were only required to follow simple instructions concerning their reactions to patients, but this developed into lengthy courses of training producing very sophisticated and professionally autonomous 'nurse therapists'. Some indication of the current range of the behaviour-therapy sophistication developed by nurses can be seen from Table 5.1, which distinguishes five levels of proficiency. These distinctions are imposed on the diverse range of studies in order to facilitate discussion.

(a) The Applicator

One of the earliest accounts of nurse involvement in applying a behavioural programme was given by Ayllon and Michael (1959). They provided nurses with simple instructions on how to respond to such psychiatric problems as 'psychotic talk', hoarding rubbish and violence towards other patients. This exploratory study focused on the potential of an application of the triadic model and so did not attempt a precise evaluation of instructions to nurses. In fact, the authors referred to the informal nature of these instructions and to their rather crude presentations of social reinforcement as the way to change these patient behaviours.

Ayllon and Azrin (1964) followed this with a more systematic evaluation of the uses of instructions and reinforcement with another group of chronic psychiatric patients and went on to examine the role of nurses as behaviour therapists in a 'token economy' (Ayllon and Azrin, 1968). This refers to a system in which tokens, such as plastic discs, are given to patients when they have behaved appropriately. These tokens are then exchanged for 'back-up' reinforcers, usually in a special ward shop. The nurses in this scheme had to dispense tokens contingent upon certain patient behaviours. Again, they were not given any formal training, receiving only a detailed written description of their task which included the time, place and type of patient behaviour to attend to, and how to reinforce it with tokens.

A more recent illustration of the 'applicator' level of sophistication was provided by Schnelle *et al.* (1983). They assisted 18 nursing aides working in homes for the elderly to deal with nine incontinent patients. Nurses were asked to check these patients for

Table 5.1: A Classification of Five Levels of Nurse's Sophistication in Behaviour Therapy

	Level of sophistication	Training goals	Example
1.	'Applicator'	Able to apply simple and very specific contingencies within a structured ward environment	Dispensing tokens in token economy ward
2.	'Technician'	Can use a small range of techniques with less structure. Heavily dependent on supervision	Administering specific aspects of a behavioural programme for agoraphobic out-patients, e.g. relaxation training
3.	'Specialist'	Again only trained in a very few techniques but these are relatively well developed and so do not require much supervision or structure	Toilet-training mentally handicapped children in the ward environment
4.	'Generalist'	Will utilise a range of techniques to increase or decrease behaviour in a variety of institutional settings. Supervision and structure minimal	Recording, analysing and intervening in such psychiatric rehabilitation problems as shaving, cooking, budgeting, incontinence, etc.
5.	'Nurse therapist'	Assesses and treats a wide range of complaints, among either long-stay or out-patient groups. No supervision	Carrying out behavioural assessment and treatment for phobias, depression, obsessional-compulsive disorders, etc.

wetness over a 5-day baseline period and also to note whether they requested help with toileting. During the next phase, nurses verbally prompted and toileted the patients, giving them praise or disapproval as appropriate. They found that this simple change in the nurses' behaviour led to a 15 per cent reduction in the frequency of incontinence and a 2 per cent increase in patient requests, with no such changes occurring in a control group.

Faw *et al.* (1981) conducted a similar study, involving six mental handicap nurses and six patients. The aim of the study was to teach these patients to use sign language. The staff attended two group-training sessions which incorporated a description followed by role-played and live demonstrations of the skills they were to use when teaching the patients. The staff then received the supervisor's feedback on their attempts to apply this training to the patient. The results, based on observations of the proportion of correct signs made by patients, indicated an increase of at least 63 per cent over baseline rates. Also, they found that the patients maintained and generalised their use of sign language to different settings and personnel.

This study appeared to have encountered few obstacles, but in the case of most long-stay wards, there are major obstacles, one prominent one being the absence of an 'enriched' (i.e. non-institutional or 'normal') environment (Thomas *et al.*, 1982). We know that nurses can successfully apply therapy skills to such areas of patient handicap as incontinence, providing the ward offers the necessary facilities to sustain these changes, otherwise we may expect both staff and patients to revert to baseline conditions. Staff will simply abandon therapeutic efforts when faced with difficulties in rearranging the ward to support patient change; patients will fail to maintain their improvements as a consequence of both the 'extinction' of the nurses' therapeutic behaviour and the related lack of changes in the ward. To give a specific illustration, consider the difficulty in arranging for the ward to maintain dressing or toileting skills in the mentally handicapped when properly fitting clothes are a rarity and toilet paper is locked away in cupboards (Cullen *et al.*, 1983a). In this case 'institutional constraints' as basic and obstinate, as the laundering arrangements will impede sustained improvements in staff and patients alike, even at the elementary 'applicator' levels of behavioural proficiency.

Horner (1980) has shown that 'enrichments' of the ward allied to simple applicator-level skills are *both* necessary for sustained improvements. He found that providing toys and other play objects did not lead to an increase in the adaptive behaviour (e.g. stacking blocks) or a decrease in the maladaptive behaviour (e.g. throwing objects) of five mentally handicapped children, but when staff attended positively to the former and ignored the latter class of behaviour, a substantial improvement took place. He underlined the need to keep the environment 'rich' by providing new toys from time to time and by maintaining the staff's use of this differential reinforcement of adaptive patient behaviour. Horner concluded by arguing that

> institutional environments should be designed to be rich in

> opportunities for learning adaptive behaviours rather than designed to withstand the maladaptive behaviours assumed to result inevitably from being profoundly retarded.

Horner (1980) did not discuss how these environments might best be achieved in the face of major obstacles, but he did explain how the unit described in the study had been replaced by one specifically designed and programmed to overcome the reported shortcomings. The implication is that the research findings influenced hospital administrators to greatly improve the patients' environment. If this was the case, then Horner achieved a remarkable intervention, influencing several important components in the hospital system so as to promote significant and lasting improvements in the patients' behaviour.

In general, however, research reports concerned with the training of behaviour therapy 'applicators' have not mentioned implementation problems, in keeping with the simple and brief forms of instruction and evaluation.

(b) The Technician

The next level of therapy sophistication is that of 'technician'. As Table 5.1 indicates, the technician may be trained in and apply more than one behavioural technique, but still be dependent on substantial amounts of supervision. For instance, Gardner *et al.* (1970) described a course in which 20 nurses were trained to teach self-help skills to their severely and profoundly mentally handicapped patients. They utilised role-play as their training format, with the supervisors apparently playing the parts of both patient and nurse. Unfortunately, very few details were given of the training procedure, since the paper was primarily concerned with the development of an evaluative measure, the Training Proficiency Scale (TPS). This has already been outlined in Chapter 3 (see Table 3.1). Gardner *et al.* reported that the TPS was a reliable and valid measure of the nurses' skill in the four assessed categories of 'shaping', 'reinforcing', 'communicating' and 'rapport and miscellaneous'. They also reported a high correlation between the TPS scores achieved by nurses and their scores on a knowledge test, but a low correlation with an attitude scale. They regarded this finding as evidence that skills were more related to cognitive factors than to attitudinal variables. They also argued that the TPS allowed supervisors to pinpoint the relevant therapy skills, thus facilitating feedback from the supervisor and improving the nurses' learning of the assessed skills.

Horner *et al.* (1981) provided an illustration of the 'technician' level of sophistication in a single-case study of an 18-year old girl with an obsessional-compulsive disorder. The nursing staff participated in an initial case conference and were then introduced to the relevant behavioural procedures of modelling, flooding and systematic desensitisation. Again, very little information was provided in the research report on this training process, with only one sentence giving the sparse details. It is not clear, therefore, how many nurses were involved, for how long, or what instructional methods were used in this training phase. None the less, the nurses successfully tackled the four problem areas of excessive handwashing, showering, toileting and a germ-contamination phobia. No data were provided on the nurses' behaviour, and reference to the supervisor was restricted to a sentence mentioning that regular consultations took place with the psychologist who devised the therapeutic programme. This lack of information does not help us to understand why the programme was successful. It would have been more useful to know the details of the nurses' and supervisors' behaviour, since these were the novel features of the study.

A similar study by Benjamin and Kincey (1981) evaluated a standardised behaviour treatment with nine agoraphobic in-patients. They had nurses and medical students serve as therapists for these patients. The therapist was provided with a single page of explanation and instructions for the graded *in vivo* exposure procedure. No supervision was arranged, and weekly conferences were restricted to progress reports. The patients received a one-page explanation of the procedure which placed heavy emphasis on their co-operation. They also co-operated in completing records of their outings, including 9-point self-ratings of fear and avoidance, and a task record sheet. Outcome was assessed on the changes in the patients' ratings before and after therapy, with a follow-up period averaging 20 months. The results suggested that they had improved in terms of significantly reduced fear and avoidance, which was maintained at follow-up.

This study is unfortunately also experimentally weak since it lacks a control group, it utilises *ad hoc* self-rating scales and reports no observational data. It also provides scant information on the behaviour of the therapists. In fact, it seems quite plausible from the report that the patients may have actually treated themselves, with the nurses only acting as non-participant observers. Since 'self-help' programmes have been known to produce comparably successful outcomes when rigorously evaluated (e.g. Mathews *et al.*, 1977), the respective contribution of the untrained therapists in this study must remain a matter of speculation.

Hegarty (1980) considered the training of nursing students in assessment skills. Like the nurses in the two preceding studies, the training was limited to relatively brief and focused topics. In this case the students were taught to use Gunzburg's Progress Assessment Charts (PAC) and other structured assessment forms by means of an in-service course. Thirty-four nurses attended the course, starting with a $1\frac{1}{2}$-hour teaching session. During this period the nurses received short handouts describing the PAC, a brief introductory talk and copies of the PAC forms and manual. They were then asked to complete a PAC form from memory for two patients on their ward who were well known to them, one being very dependent and the other as independent as possible. By the next session, 3 months later, the nurses were required to repeat this exercise, but this time to base it on actual observations of the patient. The supervisor provided them with feedback on their completed PAC forms and the implications of this assessment for the care of the patients concerned. The final phase of this intervention was for the supervisor to visit all nurses on their wards and interview them about the assessments and their use of the PAC forms.

Hegarty reported that 20 of these 34 nurses had carried out at least one ward assessment during the course. In interview these nurses gave a favourable account of the course and the assessment procedure, mentioning how it improved their understanding of patients and might also promote patient and staff training. However, the nurses mentioned some implementation problems, including having no opportunity to observe some behaviours because of hospital rules or ward routines, and how difficult it was to find the time to conduct the assessment.

None the less, over the subsequent two years the use of the PAC did increase, from some 30 patients at the outset to 146 two years later. Furthermore, learner nurses were by then receiving a systematic training in its use. Hegarty *et al.* (1978) have also described a course based on audiotaped lectures and a workbook to teach the same assessment skills as the in-service training scheme. This revised course was taught by nurse tutors who were guided by a specially prepared manual and who supervised practical learning assignments. The course consisted of 20 lectures, each 25 minutes in duration. The workbook contained lecture summaries, questions, extra material to refer to and ideas for project work. Both the supervising tutors and the student nurses gave favourable reactions to the audio-tape and workbook courses.

As Hegarty *et al.* concluded, this training package was economical. However, they presented no data on the extent to which it actually influenced the nurses' use of the assessment forms, nor of the changes in their understanding of these procedures that presumably followed from the training process. On the other hand these shortcomings should not obscure the potential value of these and other 'automated' training strategies. The main value of the two Hegarty studies lies in the exploration of instructional media, which he has discussed in a book concerned with audiovisual methods for staff training (Hegarty, 1981).

Felce *et al.* (1984) have developed a very systematic training and management package which also utilises carefully prepared materials. This course starts with six 2-hour training sessions, followed by a co-ordinated approach to assessing the mentally handicapped clients as a basis for planning a sequence of weekly teaching steps. The nurses are helped in this task by a supervisor, who also sets out how they can work with the client so as to achieve the weekly objectives, including the number of teaching sessions per day and the kinds of prompts that may be helpful. The nurses record the results of each teaching session on the client's individual programme chart, and this forms the basis of a weekly staff meeting when supplementary charts are commenced. To their credit, Felce and his colleagues in the Health Care Evaluation Research Team have provided manuals for both supervisor and mediator (Felce *et al.*, 1983; Jenkins *et al.*, 1983). But surprisingly for such a thorough programme, they did not evaluate the effect of their staff training independently of the outcomes achieved with the clients. Thus, when they found little evidence of client progress, they could not be sure whether their disappointing results were due to an ineffective training course or to other salient factors, such as the disorganisation of the ward environments.

More promising results have been reported by Chamberlain and Mullen (1984), who also developed a staff training package revolving around manuals (Chamberlain *et al.*, 1984). Their course consisted of six 1½-hour teaching units taught by the nurse in charge of the unit. Nurses attending the course first read the manual, and then watched a video demonstration of the step before practising it with their handicapped clients under supervision. Again, however, no data were offered on the initial effect of the training package itself, with results being restricted to client programmes and outcomes. These two programmes, therefore, confound the training variable with other organisational factors, leaving us uncertain about whether the better results reported by Chamberlain and Mullen are directly attributable to their comprehensive training programme.

(c) The 'Specialist'

In contrast to the very limited training accorded to 'technician' nurse behaviour therapists, the 'specialist' typically has greater expertise, but shares a similarly restricted range of competence. One of the earliest and most quoted studies falling into this category was described by Gardner (1972). He contrasted the two training methods of educational role-play and lectures in a group of 20 unqualified nurses. The aim of the 14-hour course was to develop the nurses' self-help training skills so that they could teach their mentally handicapped patients to dress or undress, eat with a spoon, and so on. The lecture phase covered the principles of reinforcement, shaping and stimulus control, and the role-play phase was concerned with practising the techniques just learnt. During role-play, a supervisor modelled the skills and then provided feedback to the nurses on their own performances.

In order to assess the relative value of lectures and role-play, the nurses were assigned in random order to each training method. Measures of knowledge and skills were then administered before and after each method of training. The knowledge measure was the Behaviour Modification Test (BMT), a 229-item true-false test. An example is: 'Extinction means removing reinforcement'. The measure of skill was the Training Proficiency Scale (TPS), which we have already described in detail (see Table 3.1 and related text).

Gardner (1972) reported that the nurses scored significantly more highly on the BMT following the lecture, and more highly on the TPS after the educational role-play. This confirmed his prediction that these different training methods would each lead to a very specific outcome.

Panyan and Patterson (1973) described a similar study, also focusing on mentally handicapped patients, but this time comparing the training methods of instructional film and live modelling. Fifteen nurses attended an in-service course, and were randomly assigned to film, modelling or control groups. All three groups received lectures and programmed instruction material on measurement, shaping and reinforcement. Video-tape recordings of the nurses interacting with a mentally handicapped child were made before and after training and were rated by independent assessors who were unaware of the assessment phase. They found that both the live and film-based modelling procedures led to significant pre- to post-test training improvements, with no change in the proficiency of the control group of nurses. They concluded that the 20-minute film or live modelling was a far more effective training tool than 4 hours of lectures with programmed instruction material.

Both Gardner's (1972) and Panyan and Patterson's (1973) results indicated that 'chalk and talk' methods alone were ineffective methods for developing practical skills in reinforcing and shaping behaviour.

The implication for supervisors is to relate the training method to the goals of training: when proficiency in *applying* behaviour therapy is sought, then the onus should be on a role-play or 'enactive' format rather than on lectures.

(d) The 'Generalist'

The research literature contains more accounts of training nurses to the generalist level of therapy sophistication than to any of the other four categories. We shall consider a few examples here to illustrate the wide range of techniques that have been developed. Chapter 6 also provides a detailed account of one particular research programme in which psychiatric nurses were trained to the generalist level.

One of the most comprehensive British programmes of nurse training to the generalist level has been described by Kiernan and Riddick (1973). They combined theoretical and practical units in preparing nurses to teach a wide range of skills to the mentally handicapped, including self-help skills, discrimination learning and eliminating excess or 'problem' behaviours. The ten theoretical units encompassed an introduction to subnormality, the laws of learning, rewards and punishments, shaping new behaviour, time-out and punishment. The practical units corresponded to the theoretical units and were designed to be practised by the nurse when working with a patient. Each unit was planned to last up to 30 minutes and the authors mention using video-tape feedback as well as modelling and role-play to aid the nurses' skill acquisition. The practical units included recording, reward training, generalisation, discrimination and chaining. A list of objectives and contents was provided for each unit. In the case of recording, the objectives included making a baseline observation of the patient's behaviour. A standard objective for all practical units was for nurses to read the theoretical unit, allowing time for any difficulties to be discussed before moving on to the practical phase.

Training was evaluated by report forms (which contained details of the nurses' care-plan objectives), by knowledge questionnaire, by a Behavioural Assessment Form (BAF), and by ratings of the course. The BAF is a seven-category checklist covering such skills as 'presenting task', 'reinforcing performance', 'controlling situation' and 'patient behaviour'. Each category is defined in terms of a series of discrete elements. In the case of 'reinforcing performance' they are 'social-verbal', 'social-physical', 'material' and 'appropriate withhold'. Each element is defined in a manual and rated as 'correct', 'incorrect' or 'does not apply'.

The BAF was administered before and after training using a standard polygon puzzle task in which the nurses were asked to have a mentally handicapped child fit all the pieces of the puzzle together. This was recorded on video tape and coded either trial by trial during the nurses' attempts at training the child or on a time-interval basis. Two independent scorers with high intra- and inter-rater reliability coded the video recordings using the BAF.

The knowledge questionnaire was also administered before and after training. It consists of a series of multiple-choice and programmed learning quizzes, with three short essays to finish. Table 5.2 illustrates an item from each format, in addition to some items from the nurses' questionnaire on the training programme.

The researchers provided no special incentives to the nurses, and noted that the main reinforcement seemed to be success in training the child. For this reason, the supervisors arranged practical tasks so that the nurses had a high probability of effecting change, and also allowed them to continue rehearsing a task beyond the level required to satisfy the supervisor.

In addition to the manual for supervisors described above, the Thomas Coram Research Unit has also produced manuals of programme materials for nurses who had completed the training in operant techniques. These manuals describe steps in teaching a series of skills such as attending to instructions and dressing (Kiernan *et al.*, 1973). Record sheets and training tasks are provided in the

Table 5.2: Sample Items from Kiernan and Riddick's (1973) Evaluations of Nurse Training in Operant Techniques

Evaluation format	Illustrative example
Multiple-choice questionnaire	If a child throws an object whenever he wants adult attention, what do you think the best thing to do would be? (a) Go up and say 'no' each time he does it. (b) Ignore him. (c) Ignore him and give him extra attention at times when he is not throwing. (d) other.
Programmed learning	A response that is rewarded is .... to occur again in the future.
Essay	Say how you would train a child to put a sock on.
Questionnaire on the training programme	Which did you find the most useful: (a) the written units? (b) the practical sessions?

manual to help the nurses in their work with patients.

Hogg *et al.* (1981) used a slightly modified version of Kiernan and Riddick's training programme to evaluate the course in relation to a carefully defined group of profoundly multiply handicapped children. Two multidisciplinary groups, including nurses and teachers, attended the ten-step course. They evaluated the training by use of the Behaviour Assessment Form (BAF), again slightly modified, but unlike Kiernan and Riddick required nurses to work with both 'high' and 'low' functioning children and altered the task to be taught to them. This entailed picking up and shaking a toy for the 'low' functioning children and placing a small coloured beaker on a large beaker of the same colour for the more able ones. In this way, each nurse carried out two pre-test and two post-test training sessions. These were videotaped for 10 minutes and were scored by two independent raters; the scores were converted to an 'Index of Performance' (IP). The IP reflected the nurses' therapy skills over both 'high' and 'low' child functioning sessions. In general, mixed results were obtained, with significantly higher IP scores at the end of training for only 2 of the 6 observed therapy skills, 'physical prompting' and 'reinforcement', the two central techniques of the course. One skill, 'assisting performance', actually earned a lower IP score at post-testing.

No direct assessment of the children's behaviour was made, although Hogg *et al.* noted an indication that there had been some positive behaviour change during the training sessions. Overall, they concluded that their evaluation successfully extended Kiernan and Riddick's course to these very difficult trainees. Following the course, supervisors developed individual behavioural programmes for children selected by nurses. They informally noted that nurses persisted with the behavioural techniques and this seemed to be related to unassessed variables, such as their progress when working with a child, rather than to their post-test level of competence. However, the authors concluded by noting that some children have major learning abnormalities and so are not responsive to behavioural techniques. As a result, careful selection of trainees is necessary so as to avoid extinguishing the nurses' therapy efforts.

A systematic extension of Hogg *et al.*'s (1981) evaluations of nurses' therapy skills in special training session has been reported by Schinke and Wong (1977a). They conducted naturalistic observations of nurse:patient interactions in homes for the mentally handicapped. Thirty nurses received eight 90-minute weekly group-training sessions consisting of a didactic presentation of the principles of behaviour therapy, case examples, and role-playing demonstrations. In-between sessions they read Patterson's book on social learning, *Families* (1971), and also planned, implemented and evaluated a behavioural care plan. These patient training programmes were written into weekly contracts and signed by nurses and supervisors. There were also mid-week telephone calls to encourage nurses in their efforts to implement the care plan. The supervisors (all first- and second-year social-work graduate students) had themselves received careful instructions in how to conduct training: after reading assignments and observations, each supervisor role-played the correct procedures for the training sessions, receiving feedback and coaching over a minimum of 20 hours of practice. Unfortunately, the effect of the supervisors' training programme was not evaluated. It would have been interesting to compare their baseline levels of proficiency with the effects of the training programme, and then to assess its relationship to outcomes achieved with the nurses.

However, Schinke and Wong (1977a) did evaluate carefully the outcomes with the nurses, using measures of knowledge, attitudes, behaviour and a job-satisfaction rating. The first two measures were based on those of Becker (1971), described in Chapter 3. The job-satisfaction rating form consisted of 18 Likert-format items, yielding an indication of the nurses' work satisfaction. Their skills were observed using a 'real-time' measure of the frequency, duration and latency of 29 kinds of resident and staff behaviour (Schinke and Wong, 1977b). This naturalistic observation measure is summarised in Table 5.3 with each of the 29 patient behaviours categorised into 'positive', 'negative', or 'neutral', and the three categories of nurse reaction yield nine interactive sequences.

Nine trained observers gathered data with this measure on two occasions before and after nurse training, focusing on those patients who were likely candidates for the behavioural care plans. The results showed that the trained nurses gave significantly more positive response to positive patient behaviour with less delay and for longer durations than their untrained counterparts in other homes. There were also improvements in five of the other eight interactive sequences as indicated by asterisks in Table 5.3. Schinke and Wong (1977a) also reported improvements in the knowledge, attitude and job-satisfaction measures, as well as increases in the frequency and duration of positive patient behaviour as a function of their nurse training programme.

Carsrud *et al.* (1980/, 1981) developed a more descriptive and detailed measure of therapy skills than that of Schinke and Wong (1977b) in order to assess their two-day nurse training workshops. They particularly stressed the use of their 'Competency Assessment Scale' (CAS) as a means of monitoring the nurses' proficiency *after* training: a 'substandard' performance as defined by the CAS led to additional individual instruction. Their use of an objective skill measure served to both prompt the supervisor when and what to teach, and generated data on the quality of the overall behavioural programme.

The CAS yielded a score for the nurses' quality of training based on a 5-point rating of 36 discrete skills. The rating considered the frequency with which these skills were applied, ranging from 'Does not do it' (score 0) to 'Does it every time' (score 4). Skills included 'Gets client's attention', 'Gives reinforcement within one second', 'Uses short, clear commands', and 'Records appropriate data for each session'. A score of less than 108 (allowing 4 points for non-applicable items) was used to define a nurse as requiring extra training and monitoring. A proficiency score of 75 per cent was required to successfully conclude the initial 2-day phase of training. Monthly monitoring of each staff member was conducted using a

Table 5.3: The Behaviour Categories of Schinke and Wong's (1977b) Resident-Staff Interaction Measure. An asterisk indicates a significant improvement in the trained nurses as compared with their untrained colleagues

Category of patient behaviour	Categories of nurses' reaction	Measures taken
'Positive'	Positive*	Frequency* Latency* Duration*
	Negative*	Frequency* Latency* Duration
	Neutral	Frequency Latency Duration
'Negative'	Positive*	Frequency* Latency* Duration*
	Negative*	Frequency Latency* Duration
	Neutral*	Frequency* Latency Duration
'Neutral'	Positive*	Frequency* Latency Duration
	Negative	Frequency Latency Duration
	Neutral	Frequency Latency Duration

simplified plus or minus CAS scoring system and the results were sent to the programme director.

In addition to these ratings of individual behavioural proficiency, Carsrud *et al.* rated the quality and quantity of patient training and the training environment. Thus, any problems such as those arising from insufficient space or excess noise were also monitored, complementing the assessment of therapy skills.

Paul *et al.* (1973) have described one of the very few other studies of 'generalist' training that match the thoroughness and sophistication of those already reviewed. They trained two groups of staff. The first group ($N = 14$) received academic then practical instruction, and the second group ($N = 14$) had academic input allied to observation and practical training, the latter interestingly given by the first group of nurses. Unlike the three preceding studies, these nurses were working with chronic psychiatric patients who had been hospitalised for an average of 17 years and functioned at extremely low levels, exhibiting bizarre behaviour, muteness, incontinence or nearly total apathy. The training of these nurses was part of a large-scale comparison of social learning and milieu treatments (Paul and Lentz, 1977), involving, for example, up to seven supervisors at any one time.

The practical skills of the nurses were very carefully shaped and continuously observed until errorless performances were demonstrated. Supervision was then reduced gradually over an 18-week period until the nurse was 'certified' to perform a given technique alone. Like Schinke and Wong (1977a), Paul *et al.* (1973) used a measure of nurse-patient interaction in addition to the usual assessments of attitudes and knowledge. Their interaction measure, called the 'Staff-Resident Interaction Chronograph' (SRIC), provided a basis for objective assessments of nurse training and is summarised in Table 5.4. The SRIC involves noting five classes of

Table 5.4: Ten Illustrative Categories of Nurse Behaviour from the 21-category Staff–Resident Interation Chronograph (SRIC: Paul and Lentz, 1977)

Category of nurse behaviour in response to patient	Definition
Positive	Praise, compliments, positive feedback
Negative non-verbal	Frowns, grimaces, negative gestures
Positive non-social	Gives physical or material goods
Negative statement	Statement of negative expectations and prohibitions before the behaviour occurs
Positive prompt	Statement of expectations or requirements
Negative group reference	Statements with negative allusion or reference to a group to which the individual belongs
Reflect/clarify	Statement of problem existence, restatement of problem or opinion
Doing with	Engaging in a specific shared activity
Physical force	Pulls, shoves, drags, pushes, restrains
Attend/record/observe	Attends to patient without interaction, engages in paperwork

patient behaviour, namely 'appropriate', 'inappropriate failure', 'inappropriate crazy', 'request' and 'neutral'. These are related to 21 classes of nurse behaviour, some of which are summarised in Table 5.4. A single SRIC observation would entail ten sequential one-minute periods during which all activities of each nurse in turn were recorded in relationship to the behaviour of the patients who were present. For example, a patient might exhibit an 'inappropriate crazy' behaviour, such as verbalised delusions, to which the nurse might respond with 'ignore/no response', as in turning away from that patient.

Paul *et al.* (1973) reported that, following training, nurses on the social learning ward averaged 230 interactions per hour with patients, 99.7 per cent of them being errorless, as gauged by the SRIC. They found that the integrated academic and practical training format produced the best outcomes on the observational measure, that is, resulted in superior interactions with patients (as defined from a social learning perspective). Like Gardner (1972) and Bailey and Craze (1980) they also found that the nurses they had trained by the integrated format were able to effect improvements in their patients despite an incomplete understanding of behavioural techniques.

In a similar vein, Milne (1982) contrasted 'active' and 'passive' learning formats during 3-day workshops in order to see what their relative effects were on knowledge and skills. The 'active' group of nurses received a course in which the topics were covered by role-play and other enactive behavioural exercises. In contrast, the 'passive' group were not given the opportunity to rehearse the skills covered in each of these topics and received extra 'chalk and talk' and video modelling in lieu of the 'active' groups rehearsal phase. The results indicated that the 'active' group did better on a knowledge test and achieved superior scores on a simulated measure of proficiency. They also reported having conducted more care plans with their mentally handicapped patients than either the 'passive' group or a matched control group.

An alternative to measures that focus on the interactions between nurses and patients or on therapy outcomes are those that pick out and assess specific skills. Two good illustrations of this are the nurses' ability to conduct aspects of a functional analysis and to plan a behavioural programme. Stern and Golden (1977) described a 7-hour course in behaviour modification for 11 nurses which was assessed by means of their descriptions of a video-taped presentation of a child's behaviour. A second measure was their ability to formulate an individual care plan from a one-page case history of a 10-year-old boy who was 'aggressive' and 'disruptive' in the classroom and disobedient at home. Their responses to both measures were scored by independent raters who gave credit for objective descriptions in the case of the video-presented test, and noted the presence of 14 specific programme planning steps in the latter measure. The steps included identifying behavioural problems, and planning treatment steps and reinforcement procedures. Stumphauzer and Davis (1983) reported similar measures and both studies showed significant training effects for these skill measures.

(e) The Nurse Therapist

As far as nurse training is concerned, the fifth and final level of behavioural sophistication is that of 'nurse therapist'. In the UK, nurse therapists receive a post-qualification course of training in behaviour therapy lasting up to 18 months which prepares them to deal with a wide variety of clinical problems from a position of professional autonomy (Marks *et al.*, 1977; Barker, 1980). This may also include co-ordinating other staff in comprehensive therapeutic programmes.

Although a number of different courses exist, our concern here is with two particular illustrations, namely 'short-term therapy' and 'rehabilitation in residential settings'. Both are subsumed under the heading 'adult behavioural psychotherapy' or, for our purposes, that of 'nurse therapist'.

Nurse therapists participating in the short-term therapy course gain clinical experience with at least 12 patients with such problems as phobias, obsessive-compulsive disorders, sexual and marital dysfunction and social maladjustment. Their colleagues on the shorter rehabilitation course focus on a range of long-stay problems including apathy, dependency and various self-help, social and vocational skills. As Hall (1979) has pointed out, this degree of training in behaviour therapy 'puts to shame' that received by many trainee clinical psychologists in the UK.

One of the most researched nurse therapy courses is offered at the Maudsley Hospital in London. Marks *et al.* (1977) have given an extensive account of this course. They described a training format in which behavioural principles were taught by lectures, seminars, group discussions and reviews, live and video-tape modelling and supervised casework. The proportion of teaching time to clinical work was gradually reduced from 50 per cent over the first six months down to 25 per cent in the last six months.

The training was continuously evaluated on the basis of clinical work records, improvements in the patients, number of dropouts and the amount of time spent treating patients. Marks *et al.* went on to provide extensive data on most of these measures, for example, information on the number of patients treated as out-patients (85 per cent), the average number of treatment sessions per patient (12), and the outcomes of training 91 phobic patients, based on patient and therapist ratings. These measures indicated a 'substantial improvement' in patient's conditions, maintained at a 1-year follow-up. As the authors pointed out, such results were at least as good as those obtained by psychiatrists and psychologists using similar techniques. Equally promising outcomes were achieved with the other clinical groups seen by these nurse therapists.

In contrast, very little information was provided regarding the effects of training in terms of specific therapy skills or knowledge; neither was there any attempt to determine the effects of supervision or various training methods. The only apparent baseline measure was an attitude questionnaire which was re-administered during training. This indicated that the nurse therapists came to view themselves as increasingly competent as time went on.

Although one must accept that the main objective in nurse therapy training is that of helping patients, data that *only* illustrate outcomes with patients, without quantifying their own intervention as trainers, do not provide a sound basis for evaluating the training programme as a whole. The sceptic, if not also the rigorous researcher, would want baseline data on the ability of these carefully selected nurses to effect comparable outcomes *without* any training. The supervisor would also wish to measure their therapy strengths and weaknesses prior to training and the change in these as a function of training. As argued in Chapter 1, this would then help them understand more about the training process. Some of these points are also made in a publication by the English and Welsh National Boards entitled 'assessment strategy' (1982).

In keeping with these points Brooker and Wiggins (1983) analysed data from a sample of 251 patients seen by eight nurse therapists attending the Maudsley course and found considerable variability in their clinical success rates. Of those eight therapists, three produced no treatment effect overall, whereas two were highly successful. The authors drew the conclusions that regular assessments are required to determine the effects of training and the development of more adequate selection criteria. One might point out that these are likely to be predictive if they pay greater attention to existing skills and to learning on the course, rather than simply to personal characteristics (Milne, 1984d). In any case, whichever topics are considered worthy of careful study, they require objective measurements during training. Courses such as those at the Maudsley are in a very good position to advance our understanding of training in behaviour therapy, now that initial acceptance of nurse therapists has been achieved by demonstrating the cost-effectiveness of training nurses as behaviour therapists (Grinsberg and Marks, 1977) and the general need to supplement existing behaviour therapy services (Bird *et al.*, 1979).

In this vein, there now exists a 'course evaluation package' (Joint Board of Clinical Nursing Studies, 1978) containing guidelines on various ways of evaluating these courses. The short-term therapy course run at Moorhaven Hospital, Devon, has adopted some aspects of this package and some illustrations now follow (Deakin; personal communication).

To assess casework, both supervisor and trainee nurse therapist completed weekly ratings covering organisational skills such as punctuality, case presentations and clinical discussions. They also rated clinical skills on an 8-point scale, ranging from 'no skill' to 'extremely skilled', bearing in mind what would be feasible with respect to the patient's condition. These ratings were based on direct observation and audio- or video-tape recordings conducted at least four times a month.

In addition to simple 8-point rating scales, the Moorhaven course utilised a series of checklists which enumerated the skills required of their nurse therapists in such situations as interviewing, presenting cases and teaching. Eight-point ratings are made for each item on the checklist. Table 5.5 illustrates one of these checklists.

In addition, trainee nurse therapists were invited to evaluate the course on an 8-point rating scale, ranging from 'very poor' to 'excellent'. These ratings cover the five areas of theoretical instruction, clinical experience, assessments, general course evaluation and, lastly, management and administration.

Such measures of training represent a very valuable progression from the patient-centred evaluations reported by Marks *et al.* (1977). The weekly ratings provide data for supervisor and mediator on their

Table 5.5: An Outline of One of the Interview Checklists Used on the Nurse Therapy Course Based at Moorhaven Hospital

Skills to be assessed	Supervisor's comments	Supervisor's rating (0–8)
(1) Session Orientation		
(a) trainee can define the objectives of the interview?		
(b) greets patient appropriately?		
(c) introduced self, role and role of department?		
(2) Information-gathering skills		
(a) appropriate verbal skills (e.g. fluency)?		
(b) relevant questions?		
(c) were pre-treatment measures collected (e.g. questionnaires)?		
(3) Information-processing		
(a) has trainee identified the patient's main problems?		
(b) has sufficient information been gathered to make a behavioural analysis?		
(c) has treatment been described in outline?		

respective therapy activities and so form a platform for mutual learning that will no doubt be reflected in their measures of patient outcome.

A supplementary step would be to adapt and utilise more objective skill measures, such as the functional analysis, problem formulation and treatment planning tests described earlier (Stern and Golden, 1977; Stumphauzer and Davis, 1983). Adequate checks on the reliability and validity of such measures is not too onerous a task and could legitimately be included in the course objective for trainee nurse therapists. Illustrations of simple but reliable and valid measures of behaviour therapy skills have been described with British mental handicap and psychiatric nurses (Milne, 1982, 1984d). These will be described in detail in the next chapter.

5.3 Training Manuals

One of the major resources available to those who wish to run behaviour therapy training courses are instructional manuals. We have already described one such manual, Kiernan and Riddick's (1973) *Draft Programme for Training in Operant Techniques*. This contains theoretical units which have to be studied by nurses before they rehearse the key skills in the practical units. Whereas there exist plenty of written accounts of behavioural techniques, there are in fact very few manuals providing practical learning exercises for nurses. This is both surprising and unfortunate: the theoretical content of behaviour therapy places so much of its emphasis on actual *behaviour* that one might well expect training for behaviour therapists to include the same principles, i.e. skill acquisition. Furthermore, our behavioural methods suggest that only *skills rehearsal* actually produces therapy proficiency. We have discussed this paradox in detail in the first chapter and elsewhere (Milne, 1983a).

In addition to Kiernan and Riddick's (1973) manual, Yule and Carr (1980) have provided a helpful 'workshop guide'. This is based on educational role-play exercises which give nurses the chance to observe their supervisors demonstrating the skills before they themselves practise them with corrective feedback. The exercises include observation and recording, shaping, prompting, fading and backward chaining. Interestingly, there is also an exercise on 'teaching others'.

Carsrud *et al.* (1981) have produced a very comprehensive manual arising from their research on developing and monitoring staff training programmes. This research will be discussed shortly, in Section 5.4. The manual not only includes a guide for supervisors on nurse training and teaching methods generally but also a literature review and a number of objective measures of nurses' therapeutic behaviour. It does not, however, include practical exercises.

In contrast, the American Psychological Association's *Activities Handbook* (Benjamin and Lowman, 1982) contains a wide range of activities primarily intended for classroom demonstrations, including 'learning and conditioning', 'social psychology' and 'personality'. Each section contains several activities designed to be carried out in classroom settings. For example, activity 25, 'shaping by successive approximation', involves shaping up blackboard teaching in a volunteer member of the class who is unaware of the social reinforcement contingency.

In the next chapter we will describe a programme of nurse training (Milne, 1984c) that was based on a manual, which can be obtained from the British Lending Library at Boston Spa, Yorkshire LS23 7BQ, as supplementary publication SUP 90081. This 'core course' manual contains programmed learning handouts for 12 common topics of behaviour therapy workshops, together with instructions for the supervisor on how to arrange either classroom or ward-based learning exercises ('practicals') for the nurses. The classroom exercises include such tasks as recording behaviour and classical conditioning. The ward-based tasks entail the step-by-step development of a single-subject behavioural care plan with a patient. Evaluative measures and record sheets are also incorporated in the manual. In short, the core course manual provides most of the materials necessary to organise a one-week workshop and offers a number of ideas for developing therapy skills.

5.4 Nurse Management

The main distinction between nurse training and nurse management is that in training it is assumed that nurses lack the necessary skills to conduct behavioural programmes. In contrast, nurse management research has been concerned with motivating nurses to use the behavioural skills they are already assumed to possess (Kissel *et al.*, 1983). Although some studies combine both approaches, the majority of nurse training articles say little about management, and vice-versa. We will therefore treat them separately and consider the research on nurse motivation here as a supplement to the preceding section. In conclusion we will deal with the emerging trend to integrate training and management into what may be termed 'nurse development'.

Approaches to nurse motivation have taken a wide variety of forms. This has followed a widespread recognition that to 'train and hope' is not an adequate approach to institutional change. Rather, we need to ensure the maintenance of skills by arranging cues and consequences that elicit and reinforce them over time (Stokes and Baer, 1977). If we do not do so, there is a very real risk that nurses will fail to use their therapy skills because of institutional constraints, as described in Chapter 2. It follows that supervisors need to look beyond 'pious hope' and towards therapy programming, without which they risk not only failing but also inducing guilt feelings in nurses who are unable to implement what they may believe to be useful ways of helping their patients (Hogg; discussion in Williams and Jackson, 1975).

There are many ways of organising the wide variety of literature on nurse management. One has been to break it down into the four categories of 'antecedent programmes', in which prompts and other cues are used; 'contingency management', which entails the rearrangement of various consequences for using therapy skills; 'self-control' based on recording and praising one's own therapeutic behaviour; and 'multifaceted' approaches, which combine a variety of these procedures (Reid and Whitman, 1983). In order to highlight certain practical and theoretical features of management we will adopt a different categorisation. This involves a crude distinction between management programmes that are based on the introduction of 'extras', that is, which require new resources; and we will contrast this with programmes that place more importance on reanalysing and rearranging existing contingencies. We will refer to this second category as the 'trapping' approach. Self-control management strategies will be tacked on to this latter approach since they do not typically require extra resources.

The studies of natural contingencies that we will discuss suggest that rearranging the immediate environment is in itself sufficient to elicit and reinforce therapy skills with little or no expensive extras. Popular examples include feedback and supervision. This has been referred to as 'trapping' these skills using the 'dormant' contingencies in the ward environment (Stokes and Baer, 1977). The practical significance of such 'trapping' is likely to be considerable in terms of the supervisor's control over reinforcers and their long-term availability. Very few supervisors have access to 'extras'; when they do it is usually only for the often brief duration of a research study (Kiernan and Wright, 1973). As we have seen, these conditions do not provide a basis for permanent institutional change, and we will therefore distinguish them from the more viable 'trapping' contingencies.

(a) Nurse Management by the Use of 'Extras'

Katz *et al.* (1972) were among the first to extend the programming of reinforcement from the trainee to the mediator's behaviour. They investigated the effects of instructions, verbal prompts and money on the therapeutic behaviour of four nurses working in a token-economy scheme. They recorded whether the patients' behaviour was 'task-oriented' or 'inappropriate' (e.g. 'pacing'), and rated the nurses' behaviour as either 'positive', 'negative' or 'neutral' interaction. They discovered that neither instructions nor verbal prompts to the nurses led to improvements in their reinforcement, or 'positive interaction' with patients, but when a $15 reward was offered for using therapy skills, there was a notable increase in the nurses' use of reinforcement and as a consequence an increase in task-oriented behaviour by the patients. This finding is similar to that obtained by Loeber (1971), in which nurses in a simulated situation administered tokens to a head-banging child more accurately when this was made contingent on a monetary reward ($4). In contrast, improvements in the child did not influence their use of tokens. In a less precise study, Quilitch *et al.* (1975) described a similar scheme, interesting in so far as a competitive element, completion of the most successful therapy programme, was added.

A further variation has been to provide nurses with trading stamps contingent upon their application of behaviour therapy. Interestingly, these stamps were used because they overcame union regulations prohibiting the use of extra cash or days off. However, like money, the stamps could be exchanged readily for back-up reinforcers. Hollander and Plutchik (1972) reported that their contingent stamps resulted in a significant increase in the nurses' therapy activities, such as observing, recording and providing tokens for patient behaviour, at a cost of $300 for a 17-week research programme involving 13 nurses. They also pointed out that neither the 6-week nurse-training programme nor such factors as supervisor encouragement or the novelty of a new approach had achieved a comparable effect.

Watson *et al.* (1971a) described the use of three kinds of extras for maintaining therapeutic skills among nurses. These were time off, public recognition and an engraved plaque, awarded monthly to the nurses who achieved the greatest improvements in their mentally handicapped trainees. In addition, they went on to detail the reinforcements that they arranged for the supervisors, the programme director and the hospital superintendent, such as obtaining Federal funding for new clinical programmes and providing favourable publicity for the institution. These latter contingencies begin to blur the somewhat artificial distinction between 'extras' and natural contingencies.

Table 5.6 summarises some of the skills used by supervisors to maintain nurses' therapy skills.

Table 5.6: Some of the Contingencies Used by Supervisors to Maintain Nurses' Therapy Skills

Contingency	Research study
Extra money	Katz *et al.* (1972)
Bingo	Martin (1972)
Lotteries	Iwata *et al.* (1976)
Extra time off	Watson *et al.* (1971b)
Trading stamps	Hollander and Plutchik (1972)
A clear line of responsibility and task assignment	Watson *et al.* (1971b)
Telephone prompts	Stoffelmayer *et al.* (1979)
Random supervision	Carsrud *et al.* (1980)
Feedback	Porterfield and Blunden (1978)
Public posting of results	Greene *et al.* (1978)
Therapeutic success	Kiernan and Riddick (1973)
Participative decision-making	Coles and Blunden (1981)
Peer support	Watson *et al.* (1971b)
Self-monitoring	Burt *et al.* (1979)

Judging that the long-term maintenance of the staff's therapeutic behaviour would not be reinforced simply by improvements in their severely mentally handicapped patients, Martin (1972) utilised additional reinforcers such as staff parties, special favours, or reports of favourable comments from visitors. He also scheduled weekly staff meetings to allow him a regular opportunity to show a great deal of enthusiasm for nurses who had conducted care plans. This was formalised in an 'assignments sheet', which detailed specific training tasks for each nurse. Also, when 100 per cent of assignments were completed, Martin donated £5 to a staff party fund, when greater than 75 per cent were completed he donated £2, and on days when less than 45 per cent were completed he took £2 out of the fund. He reported that the assignment sheets produced an increase from a baseline of approximately 30 per cent to about 60 per cent, further boosted by the money contingency to around 80 per cent. In a subsequent development, Martin described a 'bingo game' in which staff would be able to uncover squares of their cards when they had completed various work assignments, with a jackpot prize of £50 available each month. He saw this incentive as a way of overcoming the preoccupation with minor problems and the cost to nurses of being innovative. It seemed to him that the prevailing contingencies influenced the nurses to 'stay out of trouble and produce lots of minor problems that generate interesting discussions with unit supervisors'. In the longer term he saw the need to develop a more positive form of control, with supervisors reinforcing nurses for conducting activities that helped patients. This could be based on similar principles to those applied to nurses, with clear 'assignments' and consequences.

Watson *et al.* (1971a) also made a special point of tackling implementation problems by introducing 'extras'. They produced an 'itinerant team' of nurses who relieved their colleagues ward by ward, in order to allow them to attend a training course. On returning to their wards they were able to continue the programmes introduced by the itinerant team in their absence. This approach therefore arranged both peer support and prompting for the staff, so increasing the likelihood that the course of training would be utilised.

(b) 'Trapping' Therapy Skills

One of the ways in which Watson *et al.* (1971a) tried to maintain nurses' therapeutic activity crossed the distinction between 'extras' and 'trapping' reinforcers. They defined responsibility and accountability in such a way that if any aspect of therapy was neglected, it was clear who was at fault. This clarification was extended to the supervisors who then knew exactly what to expect from whom, and so on up to the Programme Co-ordinator. Furthermore, this pinpointing of roles allowed each agent in the programme to recognise the achievements of those in their direct line of management.

Because Watson's group employed such a wide range of contingencies, they were unable to judge the relative contribution of any one factor. However, Watson (1972) did provide a list of the stated reinforcement preferences of nurses and found that the most highly rated items were recognition, a letter of commendation and extra salary. Least highly rated were extra time off, promotion and the enthusiasm of subordinates.

Recognition, in the form of feedback to nurses on their use of behaviour therapy has received considerable research attention since then. Porterfield and Blunden (1978), for example, described a 'positive monitoring procedure' in which a supervisor used a checklist to record staff behaviour and then gave the nurses positive and constructive feedback on the basis of these data. They regarded this procedure as an essential part of their 'room management' project. An alternative to this personal form of feedback is to make public the nurses' participation in therapy activities. Greene *et al.*

(1978) found that immediate feedback in the form of supervisors' praise was ineffective in maintaining staff behaviour, but when they conspicuously displayed the proportion of training sessions carried out daily by nursing staff, they found a large and satisfactory increase in the number of sessions conducted on the ward. Not least, these were correlated with an improvement in the patients. However, Greene *et al.* concluded by cautioning against the widespread use of public posting, drawing attention to its potential for humiliating staff for their shortcomings. In contrast, they emphasised the need to recognise publicly both the positive efforts of nurses *and* the achievements of supervisors.

Quilitch (1975) contrasted three methods of maintaining therapeutic behaviour in staff, i.e. memos instructing all staff to engage in therapeutic activities, staff training and scheduling and performance feedback. He reported that only the scheduling and feedback procedure resulted in an improvement in the nurses' engagement of patients in therapeutic activities. There are definite flaws in this piece of research (such as the designation of brief unevaluated talks as 'training' and the confounding of the two variables of scheduling and feedback), but nevertheless it is very interesting to note that following this study the hospital administrators adopted this scheduling and feedback procedure on all wards.

A much more impressive research programme concerned with feedback has been reported by Carsrud *et al.* (1980). They found that by randomly monitoring the nurses' use of behaviour therapy at least twice a month and providing them with feedback on their therapy skills they were able to significantly improve both the training given by nurses and the adaptive behaviours of their mentally handicapped patients.

A comparably sophisticated study by Burg *et al.* (1979) examined whether having the nurses monitor their own therapeutic behaviour was effective in increasing their interactions with patients. A supervisor concurrently recorded the effect of this on the patients. They reported that interactions between the 7 nurses and 15 patients increased from a baseline rate of 13 per cent to 92 per cent during the self-recording contingency. There was a simultaneous decrease in self-stimulating and aggressive or disruptive patient behaviour. In concluding, Burg *et al.* noted that the procedures had been incorporated or 'trapped' into the ward routine and required minimal financial investment or administrative changes.

Burgio *et al.* (1983) have described a very similar study in which goal-setting, self-evaluation and self-reinforcement were added to self-monitoring and supervisor feedback. Nurses were invited to participate actively in the design of this programme. Among the self-control apparatuses used was a wrist response-counter for recording how often they interacted with patients, and a 'self-praise' rating form. This contained nine adjectives describing the number of interactions, ranging from 'lousy' to 'super', and designed to assess indirectly the amount of self-reinforcement given by nurses.

The researchers found that interactions between nurses and patients increased in frequency and appropriateness as a result of this programme, with consequent improvements in patient behaviour. They also reported that nurses ranked this motivational approach as among the most effective and acceptable of a number of management strategies. This kind of approach, with its high social validity, its ease of application and improved staff and patient behaviour, clearly shows considerable promise. The next step would be to tease out the relative effects of such multifaceted interventions, leading to even more effective, precise and economical management.

These studies illustrate some of the options 'naturally' available to supervisors in maintaining not only the mediators' behaviour but also their own and that of important others, such as administrators and programme directors. From this research we can see how therapeutic innovations can be successful by virtue not only of obvious but ephemeral extras, but also by careful manipulations of existing contingencies. Some of these entail increasing facilitating factors, as in the case of feedback; whereas others involve decreasing or removing obstacles, such as the resistance engendered by excluding staff from decision-making meetings. Indeed, the range of already exisiting contingencies that have been used span the four types of consequences in operant conditioning, as illustrated in Table 5.7.

From Table 5.7 we can see how management strategies fall into four types of operant conditioning. Those that are manipulated to promote and maintain skills involve either giving away something positive, such as extra money, or removing something aversive, such as resentment at the lack of involvement in decision-making. Equally, we might say that therapy skills and the involvement of nurses generally in care programmes are reduced by removing pleasant consequences, such as peer support, or by administering

Table 5.7: Examples of the Four Types of Consequences that Influence Therapy Skills and Activities among Nurses

	Pleasant stimulus	Aversive stimulus
Stimulus given	• Extra time-off or money • Supervision • Feedback (positive reinforcement)	• Reprimands • Delayed promotion • Transfers to other wards or hospitals • Peer hostility (punishment)
Stimulus removed	• Peer support (extinction)	• Participative decision-making • Therapy success (escape)

aversive consequences, such as public reprimands. It should be noted as a backdrop that aversive consequences tend to be the predominant management strategy (Mayhew, 1979).

Of course, as always it is crucial to define these four consequences *empirically*, that is, on the basis of observing their actual *effects*. For instance, if administering feedback leads to a reduction in therapeutic effort, then it must be defined as a punishment, and so on. As Greene *et al.* (1978) have cautioned, we cannot assume that feedback, or any other consequence of using therapy skills, will necessary result in the effect we are expecting.

Similarly, there is a need to attend to the actual effects of different prompts on the nurses' use of therapy skills. There is no guarantee that telephone calls or random supervision will lead to the desired behaviour: what we need to look at are the more pervasive setting events, such as hospital routines. These have been found to be a major impediment to therapeutic innovations, but are amenable to change along with other institutional constraints (Cullen *et al.*, 1983a). For instance, Barker (1980) followed up 20 nurse therapists who had completed the course based at the Royal Dundee Liff Hospital, in order to ascertain the contingencies operating on them. He approvingly quoted from Tizard *et al.* (1975), who stated that 'training programmes will be wasted if they concentrate upon the wrong staff and send them out with the wrong skills to an inappropriate and unsupportive organization'. Nineteen of these 20 nurses filled in questionnaires for Barker within 6 months of course completion. The findings from this survey included the following:

(a) only five of the group were still working in 'standard' (i.e. non-behavioural) wards;
(b) only one nurse stated being 'hardly ever' allowed to practice behaviour therapy;
(c) nine of the group had been promoted since completing the course, and seven of them believed this was largely due to obtaining the new qualification;
(d) 14 had been accorded 'specialist' status.

However, the nurses had encountered great difficulties in applying and disseminating their behavioural skills. In their own personal work with patients they reported problems with lack of time and with routine duties that made incompatible demands, as did staff turnover and poor control by their Nursing Officers. In their role as supervisors the nurse therapists had problems with lack of facilities (such as no quiet area in ward), lack of interest among junior staff, and 'hostile attitudes' of senior staff, including open scepticism about the value of behaviour therapy. Many experienced a general sense of 'being on trial' when they returned from training and a cynical regard from colleagues for their 'specialist' status.

Barker (1980) concluded by emphasising the need to revise the ward environment and not simply to train the nurse. Organisational support appeared to be the main determinant of continued nurse therapy, as indicated by the attitudes of senior hospital managers (especially nursing), the role delineated for nurse therapists and the moral and physical support made available to them. Barker (1982) had provided a helpful introduction to these and other implementation issues, particularly those concerned with the management of any stress associated with change.

In short, the foregoing studies indicate that nurse management calls for as much analysis as any other intervention. It is no more likely to succeed by adopting a given approach than is the individual therapist who applies a preferred technique without careful assessment of each new case. How can such an analysis be conducted? One option is to ask nurses about the factors that influence their use of therapy skills. Burdett and Milne (1985) did this by carrying out lengthy individual interviews with nurses and other members of a rehabilitation unit's multidisciplinary team. Their replies indicated that specialised training and Nursing Officer support were the most helpful factors, and that inadequate feedback was the major obstacle. Traditional complaints about insufficient time or staff were *not* regarded as problems. These replies may help managers to decide where to start their intervention, and could be supplemented by relevant questionnaires referring to work environments. For example, Milne *et al.* (1985) reported that nurses on two psychiatric wards, designated as 'unstressed' by their low absenteeism/sickness records, differed markedly from two 'stressed' wards on such questionnaire items as being encouraged to use initiative, having clear rules and regulations and not having constant pressure to keep working. Like the interview replies, these findings provide a helpful pointer as to where one might intervene in a system. None the less, the most appropriate level at which to begin an analysis of the nurses' use of behaviour therapy skills must surely be by observation. As discussed in Chapter 2, all those researchers who have observed the consequences for staff of applying therapy skills have agreed that powerful counter-control is exerted over them by *patients*. The result is that staff have few therapeutic opportunities and when these do arise the patients typically punish them for attempting to introduce change (e.g. Sanson-Fisher and Jenkins, 1978).

Latterly, studies of nurse training in behaviour therapy skills have taken greater note of the need to supplement training with the kind of management that would allow it to be utilised and reinforced. These studies, which conclude this chapter, will be referred to as 'nurse development'.

5.5 Nurse Development

In general, studies of nurse development have assumed that it is necessary to provide nurses with both skills and motivation if they are to act successfully as therapists. This contrasts with the nurse-training and nurse-management literatures, which tend to emphasise just one of these factors in isolation.

This distinction has been made by Kissel *et al.* (1983) who investigated whether four nurses who had received a very brief training (4 hours) based on instruction, modelling, rehearsal and feedback were able to teach self-help skills to their patients. They reported that the brief training resulted in substantial improvements in their use of three targeted skills, namely 'instruct', 'guide' and 'reward'. These were skills that had been used inappropriately and less frequently prior to training and maintenance. For example, in the case of 'toothbrushing' they found that nurses used prompts and instructions on less than half of the possible occasions. Following training and feedback these skills increased in frequency to an average of 84 per cent of trials, with a comparable improvement in proficiency. In turn, this led to improvements in patients' self-help skills. The researchers also established that the nurses generalised their skills to other self-help areas. In addition, they examined the effectiveness of a self-monitoring procedure in maintaining these newly acquired skills. To do this they asked nurses to record and graph both their own application of the teaching procedure and the response of their trainee. Feedback was provided to nurses on these records which were returned to the supervisor each day. The supervisor directly observed the nurses carrying out both training and recording exercises at least once a week and if satisfied with their progress gave a $25 gift, a certificate of participation and a memo documenting their training experience for their personal file. In short, a number of potentially effective consequences were used to encourage nurses to apply their therapy skills, although it appears from the research report that self- and supervisor-monitoring were the main contingencies during the maintenance phase, with the remainder being added at the close of the project. It also appeared that the nurses' self-recording was the most important factor, since fading out of supervisor monitoring did not produce a drop in their use of therapy skills.

The confounding of several maintenance variables and the brevity of the intervention (6 months in total) limit the confidence one can place in self-control procedures on the basis of this novel piece of research. None the less, they do indicate the potential that such 'trapping' contingencies have for maintaining staff behaviour. Ivancic *et al.* (1981) carried out a similar investigation into the value of supervisor monitoring in maintaining language training skills among nurses. Having taught the nurses to use prompts, praise and imitation systematically in their verbal interactions with residents, the researchers then arranged for three kinds of supervision. The first was a meeting in which different kinds of language-training methods were taught, using discussion, modelling and feedback. This was followed by further feedback and prompts in the form of public displays and a weekly ward round by the supervisor as a maintenance strategy. These included graphic recognition of exceptional language-training skills by the nurses and improvements in their profoundly handicapped trainees. Ivancic *et al.* reported improvements in nurse behaviours as a function of this supervision and maintenance approach. They emphasised the relative ease with which this kind of strategy could be utilised, entailing no new activities for nurses (since the language training occurred during the routine bathing of patients), and minimal additional demands on the supervisor. However, there were no overall improvements in the trainee's use of language as a result of this 5-month programme. The researchers attributed this to the severity of the child's handicap and the ineffectiveness of the training procedure, concluding with a somewhat leading remark on the need to train supervisors. As their own study utilised an inexperienced psychologist who was completing a Master's degree as the staff supervisor, it does raise the possibility that the supervision was indeed ineffective. Data on supervisory behaviour would have allayed this doubt and perhaps also clarified where the difficulty lay in developing the trainee's language skills.

One of the very few studies to provide information on supervisors' behaviour did in fact report improvements in patients who were multiply handicapped and had no functional speech (Page *et al.*, 1982). This was a large-scale comprehensive investigation which examined the functional relationship between the training of supervisors, mediators and trainees. They began by training the existing supervisors to discriminate correct teaching behaviours on the part of their staff and to instruct in and prompt and praise these behaviours when they occurred, None of the supervisors had any prior experience of behaviour therapy, but with less than 2 hours of training they had influenced 45 staff to improve substantially their use of instructions, prompts and consequences. For example, in the communication training programme, correct instructions among the mediators rose from a baseline figure of 30 per cent correct to 77 per cent correct following supervisor training. The researchers also introduced a maintenance procedure, involving brief feedback sessions with the supervisors on the training behaviour of their staff. This shaped the behaviours to which the supervisors attended, and was based on precise observational data.

Page *et al.* concluded that the improvements in mediators' use of therapy skills were a function of the training and feedback provided to supervisors and could be related to improvements noted in the trainees 'attending' and 'correct' responses. They pointed out that this 'pyramid' approach was very economical, involving the training of only three supervisors in order to influence the therapy skills of 45 staff. Other advantages included the lack of disruption entailed by scheduling large numbers to attend training courses, and utilising existing supervisory personnel. This study is particularly important in emphasising the training relationship between supervisor, mediator and trainee: it showed that existing supervisory skills were inadequate, that they could be improved with simple, brief instruction and feedback, and that these changes led in turn to improvements in the behaviour of mediators and trainees. This underlines the need to provide data on all three agents in the therapeutic triad, and emphasises the *reflexivity* of training methods. Feedback, for instance, is as essential for the effective supervision of mediators as it is for the successful training of patients.

The three foregoing studies are useful explorations of natural or 'trapping' contingencies for behaviour therapy skills. An equally practical but quite different approach has been described by MacKrell (1983). He utilised Keller's Personalized System of Instruction (PSI) to train nurses how to carry out a functional analysis of patients' behaviour.

The PSI is characterised by active learner responding, such as completing reading units and assignments, mastering earlier units before progressing on to new material, self-pacing, and reinforcement for work completed. Interestingly, reinforcements included contingent attendance at all lectures, films and demonstrations, and written targets specifying the amount of work most nurses should be able to complete.

MacKrell hypothesised that, in contrast to traditional teaching methods, the PSI method would give nurses a better grasp of the principles or 'rules' governing operant conditioning techniques. These rules could then control their use of techniques in the ward. Contrasting the PSI with conventional lecture/discussion methods, he reported that the former did indeed lead to improved learning of the relevant principles. Subsequent studies then indicated that considerably more effective ward programmes occurred with those nurses who had attended a 5-day in-service training course based on the PSI format, as contrasted with an untrained group of nurses.

These studies by MacKrell are important in highlighting the role played by the *training* format in the acquisition and maintenance of therapy skills. They also raise the possibility that systematic training in *principles* can lead to changes in *behaviour*, under some conditions. They may also lead to nurses applying the rules to new problems, for instance when they carry out a functional analysis of the contingencies in the ward that control their own use of therapy skills with patients, the original focus. Furthermore, MacKrell's research requires us to re-examine some of the unsubstantiated generalisations about training and motivation. One recurring belief is that training provides only skills, and that a motivational system is then necessary to make them operative. However, MacKrell's work indicates that training is a more complex variable than one might assume from the preceding discussion and so, for instance, a sound introduction to the behavioural rules may also possess motivational and skill-acquisition properties.

Milne (1984e) also found that variations in the training process influenced both motivation and skills: an initial 5-day in-service course in behaviour therapy resulted in satisfactorily high levels of knowledge and skills but low levels of implementation (27 per cent). When the training format was revised so that the nurses rehearsed the course content in the ward with patients, the knowledge and skill results were comparable to the earlier 'classroom'-based course, but with greatly increased levels of implementation (75 per cent), in the form of single-subject programmes with patients. These studies are discussed in detail in the next chapter.

On the basis of these studies it is apparent that the training process can have an important bearing on both skills and motivation. Nurse-development research would benefit from a careful analysis of the ways in which such training interventions *interact* with motivational variables to produce institutional change, rather than dealing with one or the other in isolation.

5.6 Summary and Conclusions

In this chapter we have discussed three broad approaches to nurse therapy. In the first of these, 'nurse training', we described five levels of therapy sophistication, ranging from the 'applicator', who receives almost no training, through to the autonomous and highly trained 'nurse therapist'. These levels represented points on continua associated with more thorough training and evaluation. Among the other generalisations that apply to nurse training it may be worth emphasising the overwhelming conclusion of researchers that enactive or *behavioural rehearsal* methods of learning were necessary for the acquisition of therapy *skills*: traditional 'chalk and talk' methods may improve the understanding of principles but do not typically promote proficiency. It therefore follows that if nurse training is intended to develop practical skills, then enactive methods of instruction are required. Illustrations of these methods were drawn from training manuals. Other general conclusions arising from this literature are the paradoxical under-utilisation of skill measures to assess whether training is indeed promoting targeted skills; the lack of detail provided on the actual training procedure which is used to develop these skills; the lack of a systematic analysis of relationships between supervisor, mediator and trainee behaviours during training; and at best only a small emphasis on the implementation difficulties encountered by researchers.

The second broad approach we considered was that of 'nurse management'. This focuses on ways of motivating nurses to use the therapy skills that they already possess. Two general strategies were distinguished, the provision of 'extras' such as more money or time off; and the rearrangement of existing or inexpensive contingencies such as supervisor feedback. This distinction was drawn so as to highlight the different degrees of feasibility and sophistication between these two approaches. Natural contingencies that 'trap' the nurses' therapy skills were regarded as the more effective, acceptable and durable option. They also maintained a greater emphasis on an analysis of the existing contingencies, which was more in keeping with the principles underlying the intervention. However, the majority of researchers have tended to combine a number of variables together into a management 'package', with the result that we do not know how much each one contributes to the generally successful outcomes. Future research that isolates these variables should lead to more precise, economical and effective management. In the meantime, it appears that management strategies based on feedback and self-control show most promise, perhaps due to their greater acceptability and the amount of control that nurses are given. The implication of this view is that social validity and self-control are elements of nurse management that should now receive particular attention. By increasing the acceptability and control that nurses have over their own therapeutic behaviour we also reduce the probability of nurses using 'counter-control' or resistance (Skinner, 1953), one of the greatest obstacles to improved psychological services in hospitals.

The third broad approach we considered was the incorporation of 'training' and 'management' interventions into 'nurse development'.

This topic has been the most recent extension of research into nurse therapy skills and so as yet there are few systematic studies. However, some promising dimensions are indicated already, such as self-management and pyramid training. Nurse-development research also explicitly highlights the *interactive* nature of important variables in large institutions, in contrast to the somewhat idealised and simplistic cause-effect models of change that abound in the nurse training literature. In this context we discussed how variables that often pass unmentioned in research reports, such as the participation of nurses in the initial planning of change, can have a considerable bearing on the subsequent success of the change process. We elaborated on this and other 'setting events' in the second chapter and will provide further illustrations in the next.

In contrast to the parent training literature, which focused largely on the trainee, the research on nurses as behaviour therapists has tended to give most of its attention to the behaviour of the mediator. Only one study was found which actually analysed the training relationship between supervisor, mediator and trainee. Furthermore, the nurse training literature has only latterly begun to provide data on the effect of this exercise on trainees. There is, therefore, a considerable gulf between the research involving parents and nurses as therapy mediators. This includes the amount of data provided, the experimental rigour and the sheer number of studies, all of which indicate the greater sophistication of parent training at this stage. However, both fields should give more details of the fundamental training variable and illustrate its influence within the therapeutic triad, as Isaacs *et al.* (1982) and Page *et al.* (1982) have done. We also need to look outside the confines of training, management and development towards a broader range of implementation problems. These could be described in research reports. For instance, Carsrud *et al.* (1980) were prevented from directly measuring the effects of their nurse training programme because of a hostile reaction from staff to the possible observation of their behaviour. They decided to forego these data so as to avoid jeopardising the whole study. Could this have been avoided by participative management? In another rare illustration of this dimension, Watson (1979) described how his attempts to observe nurses and their elderly patients ran up against attempts by staff to prevent the observations from taking place. This included de-focusing the camera lenses and turning the angle away from the planned focus on the nursing stations. It is to the great credit of these researchers that they have conducted their work in natural environments, but it would be misleading if we were made to believe that such settings are closely akin to laboratories. To do so reduces the social validity of these reports among potential users and creates a false sense of precision and control. Ultimately we need to present a balanced account of the complex range of variables in hospitals and to incorporate these into our analysis alongside a detailed description of the actual training intervention. This will provide a sounder basis for developing and disseminating effective technologies that justify the triadic model in terms of helping trainees by helping nurses.

6 NURSES AS THERAPISTS: THE 'CORE COURSE' ILLUSTRATION

6.1 Introduction

The literature review in the preceding chapter highlighted a number of fundamental weaknesses in nurse therapy research. Prominent among these were the lack of specification of the training process, the paucity of skill evaluations, and the simplistic, 'cause-effect' accounts of training. In the following summary of one research programme we will try to provide information that partially rectifies those weaknesses, and we will be particularly concerned to provide an account that considers training as an intervention into a system. This 'ecological' perspective, introduced in the second chapter, deals with some of the more complex and far-reaching dimensions of nurse training, such as generalisation and institutional change. As we have seen, this is an unusual perspective, but one that may ultimately be necessary for a satisfactory account of the development of nurses as behaviour therapists (Kiernan *et al.*, 1975; Bernstein, 1982).

The research programme took place at Carlton Hayes, a psychiatric hospital in Leicester, England, during 1980–83. It evolved from earlier work on nurse training in a neighbouring mental handicap hospital (Milne, 1982) and was concluded by the presentation of a doctoral thesis. In this chapter we will be attempting to provide a comprehensive and replicable account of the training programme. This will afford readers the necessary information, materials and procedures to conduct similar programmes, or to develop their own variations. It should also help to point out some of the implementation difficulties attendant upon such a programme, and some of the options for resolving these. Reference to detailed journal articles derived from this research will be cited as we proceed, and readers can consult these if they wish for further details of the programme.

6.2 Evaluative Measures

It is traditional to consider thoughts (understanding), feelings (attitudes) and behaviour (skills or proficiency) when evaluating training, and we observed this tradition in our programme. But because the main focus in behaviour therapy training must ultimately be on behavioural skills, we will spend most of this section considering these measures. Following this section we will describe the two versions of the core course, so as to facilitate discussion of their respective outcomes.

(a) Understanding

The nurses' grasp of the ideas covered in the core course was measured with a modified version of O'Dell *et al.*'s (1979b) 'Knowledge of Behavioural Principles as Applied to Children' (KBPAC). This was adopted since it was the most psychometrically sound measure of the few that were available.

Because of its exclusive focus on the parent-child relationship, it was necessary for face-validity reasons to alter the wording to refer to nurse-patient relationships. The modified measure was then christened the 'Knowledge of Behavioural Principles Questionnaire' (KBPQ). The test-retest reliability of the KBPQ was assessed by administering it to a control group of 18 psychiatric nurses, with a 4-day interval in-between testings. The validity was determined by the 'known groups' method, in which eight clinical psychologists (who made at least a 'great deal' of use of behaviour therapy) completed the KBPQ. Their scores were then contrasted with a behaviourally naïve group of nurses, and were found to be significantly higher than the scores achieved by the nurses (means: 78 per cent; 34 per cent, respectively). Following training, nurses scored an average of 56 per cent, a significant increase and one that also bestowed 'empirical validity' on the KBPQ.

The KBPQ consists of 50 multiple-choice questions, as illustrated earlier in Table 3.3, and because of high split-half reliability it can be administered as two equivalent 25-item measures. This reduces testing time and provides an alternative version for retesting. A mean percentage score is calculated by multiplying the number of correct answers by 4. A copy of both 25-item versions of the KBPQ is given in the core course manual (a copy of the manual can be obtained from the British Lending Library at Boston Spa, Yorkshire LS23 7BQ, as supplementary publication SUP 90081).

(b) Attitudes

We used two attitudinal measures. The first was Wilson and

Patterson's 'Conservatism Scale' ('C-scale'; 1968) which was considered to measure the flexible, non-authoritarian approach regarded as essential to novel practices such as behaviour therapy. The C-scale consists of 100 items, which nurses are asked to state whether they believe in or favour them with a yes, a no, or don't know/in-between. The items include straightjackets, divorce, royalty and patriotism. A mean percentage conservatism score is derived by giving a score of 2 to all disagreements with liberal items (e.g. mixed marriage) and 2 to all agreements with conservative items, as illustrated above, with undecided replies scoring 1. The raw total is then divided by 2 to give the mean percentage score.

The second measure of attitudes used was the 'Attitude to Treatment Questionnaire' (ATQ; Caine and Smail, 1968). The original version consisted of 40 items with which nurses rated their agreement from strongly agree to strongly disagree. Items include 'Nurse-patient relationships can be just as effective in treatment as doctor-patient relationships'; and 'By and large, psychotherapy is a waste of time.' Because the ATQ was developed for use in a traditional psychotherapeutic setting, there were a number of items with little obvious relevance to our programme. We therefore carried out a factor analysis and retained those behaviourally orientated items that contributed most to the variance. As a result, we had a revised 24-item Attitudes to Behaviour Therapy Questionnaire (ABTQ).

The factor structure of the ABTQ was very similar to the original in terms of the variance accounted for by the main three factors (27.2 per cent for Caine and Smail's ATQ; 32.9 per cent for the ABTQ) but equally importantly the ABTQ's main factors now incorporated a 'behavioural psychology' component accounting for 11.1 per cent of the variance. There was, therefore, a change in the statistical structure which mirrored the shift in the proportion of items from the original 'milieu' ATQ to the ABTQ, and which made the revised version more likely to be sensitive to our programme. The ABTQ is also in the manual. It is scored by crediting up to 5 points for strong disagreement with an 'anti-behavioural' item (e.g. 'suggesting to patients the underlying reasons for what they say and do') or strong agreement with a pro-behavioural item (e.g. 'physical treatments are a means of getting through to patients but not a cure in themselves'). A mean percentage score is derived by dividing the raw total by 120 and multiplying the result by 100.

(c) Behaviour Therapy Skills: 'Classroom' Tests

We developed three measures of behaviour therapy skills which were intended for video-presented administration in the classroom. They were a 'Functional Analysis Test' (FA), leading to a Formulation and Treatment Plan (FTP), and a Simulated Proficiency Test (SPT). A further two skill measures were created for use in the ward and they will be described shortly.

The Functional Analysis Test (FA) is a brief video-tape recording of an interaction between two psychiatric patients, role-played by actors. As Figure 6.1 illustrates, one patient is joined at the mealtime table by a second. This leads to some cynical exchanges, finger-pointing and table-banging before the second patient gets up and leaves the table at the first patient's suggestion.

The nurses' task was to carry out a functional analysis of this interaction, selecting any behaviour they wished to regard as 'the problem'. To help them to do this, the video was shown three times. On the first showing they were asked to choose a behaviour to observe. This was followed by the second run-through, during which they were to count the number of times this behaviour occurred. On the final showing they were asked to record the antecedents and consequences of the behaviour they had selected. The assessed skills were thus the ability to pick out and clearly describe a behaviour, to note its frequency, and to record the events that triggered it off and followed it. A record sheet (see manual), gave an outline of the task and the relevant headings of 'behaviour', 'how often', 'before' and 'after'. Two minutes were allowed for any additional writing once the video had stopped.

The Formulation and Treatment Plan Task (FTP) was a simple extension of the FA. Nurses were presented with a new answer sheet and asked to say 'what made the patient behave as he did'; and 'what could be done to help the patient' in response to a fourth showing of the FA video. Both the FA and the FTP scoring manuals allowed for a range of possible answers to score, but the best marks were credited to those replies that focused on the more problematic behaviours in the FA (i.e. table-banging, finger-pointing and other 'aggressive' acts); and which offered behavioural answers to the two FTP questions. (These manuals, as well as those for all the other skill measures described in this section, are available on request from the author.)

The third and last classroom-based assessment of skill was the

Figure 6.1: An Illustration of the Contents of a Functional Analysis Test. Drawings by Tim Burton

Simulated Proficiency Test (SPT). As its title implies, this video-presented task was intended to approximate to real demonstrations of proficiency in the ward. It consisted of ten episodes or 'vignettes' which covered a wide range of nurse-patient interactions, including patients who were unable to dress, talking 'psychotically', and stealing food. The video stopped at critical points in these interactions. Some of the scenes from these episodes are illustrated in Figure 6.2

The answer sheet contained an introductory statement on the nature of each interaction and asked the nurses to select one of the four listed responses once the video stopped. Emphasis was placed in the instructions on choosing the answer that best described how they would react if they were actually in the depicted situation. *An example from the SPT is:*

> This piece of film shows a patient setting a table, but she is clearly having difficulty with the task. When she has finally completed placing the forks would you:
> (a) encourage her to work more rapidly;
> (b) use a physical prompt to help her gain confidence;
> (c) praise her as soon as possible after she finishes; or
> (d) ask her to stop smoking so she can concentrate on the task.

(d) Subsequent Analysis of Classroom Measures

In addition to the studies of test reliability and validity referred to above, all the measures administered immediately before and after the course were subjected to four further analyses.

The first was a step-wise discriminant analysis, intended to disclose which of the six measures most clearly identified those nurses who implemented the course by carrying out behavioural care plans. This revealed the Functional Analysis (FA) to be by far the best discriminator, accounting for 74 per cent of the variance when all six measures together accounted for 86 per cent of the total variance. The FTP and SPT added little information to the FA above, either before or after training (Milne, 1984b).

A second analysis looked at the relationship between scores achieved before and after the course and the personal characteristics of the nurses. To do this, seven demographic variables were correlated with the nurses' learning. The amount of learning was calculated by taking the difference between the nurses' scores at the

Figure 6.2: Artist's Impressions of Four Critical Incidents in the Simulated Proficiency Test (SPT). Drawn by Tim Burton

baseline and immediately after training. These demographic variables were age, sex, nursing grade, nursing qualifications, academic qualifications, duration of employment as nurse, and prior knowledge and experience of behaviour therapy. Each one was then correlated with the nurses' learning on each of the six course tests. Correlations ranged from −0.25 to +0.22, with seven associations being significant, indicating that overall there was only a very modest relationship between demographic variables and learning. One prominent finding was that younger nurses were more likely to show flexible and behavioural attitudes towards the treatment of patients, as a consequence of exposure to training in behaviour therapy (Milne, 1984d).

A third analysis of the six course measures involved retrospectively examining the demographic variables which were most strongly associated with implementing the training. To do this, 55 trained nurses were divided into two groups according to whether or not they had implemented the single-subject behavioural care plans which were the course goal. The result was 29 'implementers' and 26 'resisters'. However, only one of the 25 variables distinguished these two groups, namely a higher score on the knowledge questionnaire (KBPQ) at the baseline assessment

Table 6.1: The Correlation Matrix for the Six Course Measures, Based on the Scores of 55 Nurses at Baseline and Post-training Assessments. Pearson's statistic was applied and an asterisk indicates a significant correlation at the 5% level

Measures, in order of administration	1 'C-scale'	2 SPT	3 KBPQ	4 ABTQ	5 FA	6 FTP
1. Conservatism Scale ('C-scale')	—	−0.13	−0.15	−0.15	0.05	0.00
2. Simulated Proficiency Scale (SPT)		—	0.18	0.00	0.32*	0.18
3. Knowledge of Behavioural Principles Questionnaire (KBPQ)			—	0.04	0.02	0.09
4. Attitude to Behaviour Therapy Questionnaire (ABTQ)				—	−0.05	0.04
5. Functional Analysis Test (FA)					—	−0.04
6. Formulation and Treatment Plan (FTP)						—

(Milne, 1985b). Taken together with the first analysis (discussed above), this indicates that higher FA and KBPQ scores at the baseline assessment were predictive of implementation. In general, though, the foregoing analyses suggest only a weak relationship between demographic characteristics, test scores and implementation. This raises the question as to which other variables determine whether or not nurses make use of their behavioural training. We will return to this point in Section 6.7.

The fourth and final analysis of the six course measures correlated test scores with one another, in order to see the extent to which they appeared to measure similar or different aspects of learning. The correlations are listed in Table 6.1. It will be seen from this table that there is only one significant correlation between any two measures. This analysis indicated that the measures were therefore assessing distinct things, so that each one provided novel information about the learning that was taking place and hence justified the use of multiple measures.

(e) Ward-based Tests of Behaviour-therapy skills

Two further measures of skill were developed to assess the impact of training on the nurses' use of behaviour therapy with individual patients on their wards. These were the Written Nursing Care Plan (Plan) and the Behaviour Therapy Proficiency Scale (BTPS).

Both these and the preceding three classroom measures are described in an article which provides details of their construction, reliability and validity (Milne, 1985b).

The Written Nursing Care Plan (Plan)

The goal of the course was to enable nurses to conduct behaviour therapy care plans with individual patients. This entailed setting out a proposed course of action and following it through in a proficient manner. In order to assess their ability to do this, nurses were provided with a 'care plan sheet' which had seven headings indicating the kind of information required. This included details of the problem, its history and possible determinants, together with the therapy goal and procedure. Their replies were first scored by a supervising clinical psychologist according to a manual, following which the nurse and psychologist discussed and modified the plan as appropriate. As with all measures used in this research, the total raw score was converted to a mean percentage score. Inter-rater reliability on the plans was comparatively poor (67 per cent perfect agreement; weighted κ = 0.5), apparently reflecting some differences in the two raters' orientation.

The Behaviour Therapy Proficiency Scale (BTPS)

The BTPS was based on two existing but unsuitable measures, Gardner *et al.*'s (1970) 'Trainer Proficiency Scale' (TPS; described in Chapter 5) and McBrien's (1978) 'Trainee Assessment Form' (TAF; described in Chapter 8). The BTPS consisted of five categories which are listed in Table 6.2, together with the three key rating criteria for each category. These categories were broad enough to encompass both 'excess' and 'deficit' behaviour problems and the criteria were simple enough to allow rapid ratings to be made. In the event of any difficulty in making ratings, a general qualitative rating scale was used, ranging from 'incorrect' to 'excellent'.

The inter-rater reliability of the BTPS was satisfactory (77 per cent perfect agreement; weighted κ = 0.8) and had adequate concurrent validity with the TPS. Its empirical validity was also indicated by the significantly higher scores achieved by nurses who had completed the course, as compared with a control group made up of their colleagues. The BTPS was scored by crediting one point for each correctly applied and applicable criterion, giving a total possible raw score of 15. A mean score was calculated when (as was usually the

Table 6.2: The Behaviour Therapy Proficiency Scale (BTPS) with Categories and Key Criteria

Skill category		Key rating criteria
1. Presenting the session	(a)	obtains patient's attention
	(b)	starts at an appropriate level
	(c)	uses the proper sequence of steps
2. Providing prompts	(a)	prompts used in the correct order
	(b)	given in the correct manner
	(c)	at the correct time
3. Applying contingencies	(a)	consistent use of a consequence (i.e. contingent)
	(b)	immediate consequence (contiguous)
	(c)	appropriate
4. Ending the session	(a)	removes cues
	(b)	stops contingencies
	(c)	reinstates or arranges activities for the patient
5. Data collection	(a)	accurate records
	(b)	complete records
	(c)	summary of data (e.g. graph)

case) less than five categories were applicable. This was then converted to a final percentage score. The BTPS manual and record sheet are in the appendix.

(f) Other Evaluative Measures

Once nurses had completed the course, we asked them to complete anonymous ratings of the teaching methods and invited them to air their feelings about the course in interviews with a third party. We also carried out observations on the wards where they worked, and this will be described in Section 6.5.

Rating of Teaching Methods

Nurses rated the 10 listed methods in terms of their usefulness and their theoretical value. The methods listed were: lecture, question and answer, discussion, role-play, practising (behavioural rehearsal), written exercises, programmed learning handouts, video modelling, video feedback and the overall course. A 5-point rating scale was used, ranging from 'very unhelpful' to 'very helpful'.

Interview

In the weeks following the course, nurses were contacted and interviewed individually and anonymously, either by a psychiatrist or a nursing officer working in the hospital. The interview consisted of 14 questions, covering their willingness to attend, the effects of the course on their work and the quality and usefulness of the course.

6.3 A Classroom-based Course in Behaviour Therapy

(a) Introduction

The measures described in the preceding section were applied to both versions of the 'core course' in behaviour therapy. Both courses were run at the same hospital for successive groups of five to ten nurses until all were trained. The Nursing Officers made these allocations and, as it turned out, there were no differences on seven demographic variables or baseline scores between the 41 nurses assigned to the initial 'classroom' course and the 24 who attended the subsequent 'patient-centred' course. The different outcomes were therefore not readily attributable to any apparent selection bias.

Both versions of the 'core course' ran for 5 successive days. As the manual shows, a total of 25 hours of teaching took place during this period, including evaluations, with additional time later on for nurses to carry out the behavioural care plans on the ward.

The focus in this and the next section is on teaching and learning methods and the main results they achieved in terms of the measures just discussed. A more detailed account has been published elsewhere (Milne, 1984c). We will also consider some of the more immediate implementation problems, although reserving a more thorough discussion for Section 6.7.

(b) The Structured Learning Format

The teaching method we adopted employed a number of techniques, combined systematically into a package called the 'structured learning format' (SLF; Bouchard *et al.*, 1980; Wright *et al.*, 1981). The SLF begins with a definition and description of the learning step to be covered, followed by a reading assignment. At each step the basic principle was presented in the form of a programmed learning script which required the reader to provide some key missing words. We ensured that these scripts were quite readable by analysing their complexity and reducing them to an easy level wherever possible. This written and spoken (or 'symbolic') introduction occupied about 30 per cent of the teaching time spent on each step. The remaining time would be allocated to teaching methods which we believed to be more useful in developing the practical skills we sought.

The next phase of the SLF consisted of 'iconic' modes of learning, including viewing videotaped or live demonstrations of the skill covered in each step. Finally, students took part in a practical or 'enactive' phase of behavioural rehearsal, based on role-plays or

Table 6.3: A Breakdown of the Teaching Methods Used in the Structured Learning Format (SLF)

Order	Teaching method	Approximate proportion of time (%)
1.	Lecture	10
2.	Question, answers and discussion	10
3.	Programmed learning scripts	10
4.	Live or video-presented modelling of skill	20
5.	'Practical': role-play or other behavioural rehearsal tasks with ongoing feedback	40
6.	Group feedback and discussion	10

practical exercises. More precise details of these are given in the manual, but an example may help to give the general idea at this stage. The classical conditioning step, for example, required nurses to try to condition the eye-blink reflex by means of an air puff (utilising a drinking straw) and a noise. Nurses took turns to be trainer and trainee. The course supervisor helped the trainer by providing reinforcement and prompting. Once the practical phase was over, the group were invited to discuss any issues or problems that had arisen during the exercises. Further information on this teaching and learning format can be obtained from Bruner (1966) or Foxen (1978).

(c) The Course Content

As already mentioned, each part of the course was regarded as a learning step, the final goal of which was the ability to plan and conduct a behavioural care plan. The initial (classroom) course had 16 learning steps. These were: defining behaviour; recording behaviour; baseline records and graphing; observational techniques; behaviour therapy (introduction to the approach); learning modalities; classical conditioning; operant conditioning; applications of learning principles; the use of contingencies; shaping, prompting and fading; chaining; modelling; extinction and time-out; maintenance and generalisation; planning programmes. The timetable in the manual indicates how these steps were arranged. Each step took about 90 minutes to complete.

(d) Results and Discussion

All six course tests were scored by volunteers (psychology students) who were unaware of whether the answer sheets came from control or experimental groups of nurses. The results, when analysed statistically, indicated that all 41 nurses from the 'classroom' core course had shown a significant amount of learning during the week. Improvements were found for two skill measures (the Functional Analysis test, FA; the Formulation and Treatment Plan, FTP) and for the knowledge questionnaire (KBPQ). No changes were found on either of the attitude scales or the SPT. Neither were there any significant changes in the control group's scores: they were retested over the same period without receiving the course. Comparisons between the control and trained groups supported these findings, with significant differences being found at post-training on all three skill measures (FA, FTP, SPT) and the knowledge test (KBPQ).

A one-year follow-up assessment indicated that the course-trained nurses had maintained these improvements and had developed significantly more pro-behavioural attitudes, as gauged by the ABTQ Favourable results were also obtained from the ward-based assessments, in which nurses continued to prove their competence at both planning and conducting behavioural care plans. Mean scores of 83 per cent and 86 per cent were obtained, respectively, based on the 'Plan' and Behaviour Therapy Proficiency Scale (BTPS) measures described in the preceding section. Both of these scores were significantly greater than those achieved by a control group of nurses (20 per cent and 18 per cent, respectively), indicating that the course succeeded in markedly raising the behavioural proficiency of the nurses who attended. These high scores were also associated with clinically successful care plans: reductions in excess behaviours (e.g. incontinence) and increases in deficit skills (e.g. shaving) had been achieved quite rapidly with chronic psychiatric patients.

However, only a minority of these 41 nurses had actually carried out nursing care plans in their wards. In total, only 11 (26 per cent) concluded the course in this way, although there was every indication that the course had given all nurses the necessary skills to conduct a care plan. For some reason these skills were not being applied outside the classroom setting. This represented a major failure of the course, since it meant that we were not actually achieving the kind of therapeutic impact that we had hoped for in our nurse training. There was consolation, though, in the clinical successes which nurses achieved when they did carry out their care plans, giving support to our emphasis on behaviour therapy. A revised, 'patient-centred' course was therefore developed in an attempt to increase the proportion of care plans that were conducted, while maintaining the good results achieved in learning the necessary behaviour therapy skills.

6.4 A Patient-centred Course in Behaviour Therapy

(a) Introduction

The prompt for us to revise the course came from the nurses themselves, who voiced dissatisfaction in interviews and during courses with the way in which the classroom course had kept the teaching of behaviour therapy separate from the patients to whom it was intended to apply. Thus, while retaining the structured learning format as the instructional procedure, we modified the practical phase so that as far as possible each step could be practised with a patient on the ward. The revised course, based on the nurses' comments and criticisms, is now described. Again, there is an article that provides an account of the patient-centred course (Milne, 1984e).

(b) The Revised Structured Learning Format

As just mentioned, the only change to the course format was to focus as many of the learning steps as practicable on direct work with a patient. For this reason the nurses were asked to select at least one patient with whom they could work over the week of the course and preferably also thereafter. This made the learning more practical and required nurses to return to their wards during most steps. (Alternative timetabling arrangements have subsequently been attempted, however, and these are referred to in Section 6.6.) It also meant that the care plans could be planned and tried out during the week of the course.

The revised course, however, brought with it some practical problems as well, such as choosing or locating suitable patients and finding extra time to go off to wards and get organised. This in turn limited the supervisor's ability to observe the nurses and provide feedback. None the less, the main criticisms of the 'classroom' course had been overcome and the problem-centred approach fitted well with the nursing process, thus improving motivation and interest generally.

(c) The Revised Course Content

Partly because of the extra time demands of adopting a patient and ward-centred approach, and partly because of nurse dissatisfaction with the earlier syllabus, four learning steps were either dropped altogether or incorporated into other steps. The new course now contained the following 12 topics: applications of learning principles; defining and describing behaviour; recording behaviour; observational techniques; baseline records and graphs; classical conditioning; operant conditioning; types and uses of consequences; prompting learning; chaining; maintenance and generalisation; and, lastly, planning programmes of care. The manual (see p. 158) is based on this revised content and method rather than the original. It contains 'trainer's notes' which suggest what topics to cover during the introductory talk, the programmed learning scripts, one or two practical exercises for each step (except the first), answer sheets for some of the measures and other record sheets and introductory remarks.

(d) Results and Discussion

We again obtained good results in terms of the amount of learning demonstrated by nurses over the week of the course. The nurses' (*N* = 24) post-course scores were significantly higher on all three skill measures (FA, FTP and SPT) and the knowledge test (KBPQ). Again, though, there were no changes on the attitudinal measures. A comparison between the results of the 'classroom' and 'patient-centred' course indicated that the latter group of nurses had a lower baseline score than the classroom group on the FA. Overall, the revised course achieved better results on both the FA and the FTP.

Table 6.4 presents the scores of both the trained groups and the control group. A 9-month follow-up assessment of the patient-centred group of nurses indicated that they had maintained their

Table 6.4: The Mean Percentage Scores Achieved by Both Trained Groups of Nurses and by an Untrained Control Group over a 5-day Period and at Follow-up

Measure	Assessment phase	'Classroom group' (*N* = 41)	'Patient-centred' group (*N* = 24)	Control group (*N* = 18)
1. Conservatism Scale (C-scale)	Baseline	43	46	40
	Post-test	43	46	39
	Follow-up	—	—	—
2. Simulated Proficiency Test (SPT)	Baseline	48	44	46
	Post-test	61	60	48
	Follow-up	—	—	—
3. Knowledge of Behavioural Principles Questionnaire (KBPQ)	Baseline	34	39	40
	Post-test	56	58	45
	Follow-up	49	50	44
4. Attitude to Behaviour Therapy Questionnaire (ABTQ)	Baseline	74	71	83
	Post-test	76	73	83
	Follow-up	77	63	72
5. Functional Analysis Test (FA)	Baseline	26	11	26
	Post-test	58	55	31
	Follow-up	50	50	38
6. Formulation and Treatment Plan (FTP)	Baseline	23	17	24
	Post-test	26	47	23
	Follow-up	—	—	—

post-test results, but, unlike their predecessors, did not alter their scores on the attitude scale (ABTQ).

Most crucial of all, in addition to the improved learning demonstrated over the 5-day course by the patient-centred group, they carried out more behavioural care plans. As this was the major reason for altering the core course, it justified the changes that were made in response to the nurses' suggestions.

In contrast to the earlier course, 75 per cent of the 'patient-centred' group conducted care plans and did so with comparable skill in planning and application (81 per cent and 76 per cent, respectively). They also achieved very similar levels of clinical success with patients as a consequence of these care plans.

We can now consider the nurses' rating of the teaching methods and their interview replies from both courses. Table 6.5 presents their evaluation of the teaching methods, showing a marked preference for the revised course. In particular, we can see from Table 6.5 that the practical discussions and programmed scripts were rated favourably. The second, patient-centred group were therefore

Table 6.5: A Summary of the Results of the Teaching Methods Evaluation for the 'Classroom' and 'Patient-centred' Versions of the Core Course. The figures represent the percentage of nurses who rated the methods as being either 'to a large extent helpful' (4/5) or as 'very helpful' (5/5) on the 5-point rating scale

	The 'classroom' course (*N* = 41)		The 'patient-centred' course (*N* = 24)	
Teaching method	Useful, of practical value	Informative, of theoretical value	Useful of practical value	Informative, of theoretical value
1. Lecture	72	84	100	100
2. Questions, Answers	82	85	93	93
3. Discussion	82	85	100	86
4. Role-play	58	65	67	66
5. Practicals (behavioural rehearsal)	70	65	93	100
6. Programmed learning scripts	89	80	93	100
7. Video-presented modelling of skills	81	85	79	64
8. Video feedback	78	85	75	75
9. Overall course	75	90	100	100

Table 6.6: The Results of the Anonymous Interviews with Nurses Following the Course. The figures represent the percentage of nurses responding in the affirmative

Interview Question	'Classroom' Course ($N=41$)	'Patient-centred' Course ($N=24$)
Did you want to attend the course?	87	100
Are you glad you did?	87	100
Did the course:		
(a) Make work more interesting?	66	100
(b) Lead to your feeling more competent?	50	87
(c) Lead to improved work skills?	70	87
(d) Improve your chances of job advancement	25	47
(e) Improve your understanding of patients?	62	100
Were there any ways in which you think the course was unhelpful?	25	0
In what ways do you think the course could be improved:		
(a) Changed content?	45	13
(b) Changed teaching methods?	41	20
(c) Shorter?	9	0
(d) Longer?	37	69
Do you think the course improved your attitudes?	29	80
In terms of helping your patients, how important do you think behaviour therapy is?		
(a) Unimportant	0	0
(b) Quite useful	41	20
(c) Very useful	54	67
(d) Best available treatment	4	13

confirming the views expressed by their colleagues on the teaching methods and general course organisation.

An equally positive response was received during the interviews with the second group of nurses. All of those available for interview ($N = 15$) gave their approval to the revised course, regarding it as improving their knowledge, skills and attitudes. They also rated behaviour therapy as more important than did their colleagues.

The revised, patient-centred course was therefore more valid, both socially and clinically, more acceptable to the nurses, and more often applied. As the second group of nurses did not differ from the first on demographic or baseline variables, the results cannot be attributed to having 'better' students. Furthermore, there were no other obvious concurrent changes in the hospital wards which might have accounted for the findings, leaving the revised training approach as the most likely explanation.

It is very interesting to find that the training process itself is influencing the establishment of a new approach, since the variables in the ward are usually regarded as primary; but it is perhaps a mistake to regard training and ward as though they were separate entities, and more realistic to view them as *interactional*, as argued in Chapter 2. This is especially the case when the training process is explicitly designed to alter ward factors so that implementation is facilitated. To pick out two illustrations, nurses on the 'classroom' course regarded lack of time as a major obstacle to preparing and carrying out a care plan. In the 'patient-centred' version we allocated extra time for this during the course. Another 'interactional' event was the increased motivation nurses had for a problem-orientated approach, particularly one chosen by themselves.

It would be difficult to imagine any course of training that did not possess some potential for favourably influencing implementation, but, in the case of our 'classroom-centred' course, either this was not developed (as in improving its social validity), or it did occur but was not picked up by the evaluation.

We turn next to a so-called ecological approach to evaluation which illustrates some of the less obvious dimensions along which changes may occur following training.

6.5 An 'Ecological' Evaluation of the Core Course

(a) Introduction

Thus far we have been concerned with the more immediate learning effects of nurse training in behaviour therapy. However, in considering the hospital as a *system*, we need to anticipate cause-effect relationships which are not always straightforward or readily predictable, and hence we need to study the wider consequences of our intervention. This orientation, referred to as 'ecological' after Willems (1973, 1974), is an exceedingly rare one in nurse training, not to mention the rest of behavioural psychology. The striking feature of an ecological orientation is that it assigns great importance to the unexpected 'side-effects' of new technologies, since these are often the best way to develop our understanding of the system we wish to change (Holman, 1977). This makes it distinct from the usual behavioural orientation and requires a number of related tests to determine the effect of the intervention on various components of the system (Campbell *et al.*, 1982; Milne, 1984a).

One of the central problems in validating nurse training in an ecological manner is that of measuring and promoting generalisation (Bernstein, 1982). In this section we will consider three kinds of generalisation: that occurring between people; across behaviours; and across settings (Drabman *et al.*, 1979). We have already considered the fourth basic kind of generalisation, that which occurs over time, in discussing the maintenance of the nurses' learning over follow-up periods of up to one year post-training.

(b) Generalisation between People

One problem that has concerned the political opponents of 'giving psychology away' has been the danger of disseminating a 'mindless technology' (Berger, 1979), especially to those who may abuse it (Stein, 1975). The short-term risk is that courses such as ours will only develop an incomplete understanding of behaviour therapy in nurses. We have illustrated how a moderately thorough programme of training and evaluation can allay this concern, but there remains a very real possibility that short-term good may lead to long-term harm. This leads to an additional need to conduct evaluations of the effect of training on untrained colleagues, in addition to the other measures of generalisation.

In our case this meant looking at the effect of training on student nurses, since the hospital did not employ nursing assistants and we had trained all the available qualified nursing staff. These students were, therefore, the only accessible test of generalisation across staff that we could find.

The students were assigned by routine rotation to different sectors of the hospital (the acute, rehabilitation and psychogeriatric wards) for periods of 3 months. On the hypothesis that they would be influenced to differing extents by their qualified colleagues on these sectors, we carried out a before-and-after assessment of their knowledge (KBPQ), attitudes (ABTQ) and skills (FA). The scores of the students assigned to the rehabilitation sector were compared with those of their colleagues who were concurrently allocated to the acute wards. We expected that students in both areas would have comparable baseline scores, but that those who were based in the rehabilitation wards would do better at the post-testing, because of their association with the course-trained senior nurses.

The results confirmed this expectation, with students on the rehabilitation wards scoring significantly more highly on the functional analysis test (FA) and the knowledge of behavioural principles measure (KBPQ) at post-testing, with no change in the control group's (acute wards) scores over the same 3-month period.

A fourth measure was also administered, namely a rating of how much use the students made of behaviour therapy. This indicated that both groups judged themselves to be making a 'fair amount' of use at baseline and somewhat more by the post-test assessment. Given the very modest scores that these groups achieved at the baseline assessment on measures of their understanding and proficiency, this adds credence to the view that 'new' approaches to patient care need to be monitored carefully. We had already measured the competence of the qualified nurses whom we had trained and this represented one form of monitoring; but had there not been a course, the students might not have received any monitoring whatsoever by competent behaviour therapists. This lends irony to the arguments about 'giving psychology away': it is usually 'given away' willy-nilly.

This point is similar to the arguments about training in behaviour therapy with respect to the quality of nurse/patient interaction. According to social learning theory a 'behavioural' component is inescapably present in these interactions and will surely influence them (see, for instance, Gelfand *et al.*, 1967; and Solomon and Wahler, 1973). In this sense it is meaningless to talk of withholding training in relevant psychology: it already goes on, at least at some 'common-sense' level, and already influences the quality of care. The options are surely either to allow students and others to continue making considerable use of what they incorrectly regard as behaviour therapy, or to correct and develop their skills via training. This small study of learners shows how such training can be moderately successful even when conducted indirectly and without any special programming or support. Further details of this study can be found in Milne (1985c).

A second, observationally based assessment of generalisation between people was also conducted, in order to see whether the training of nurses had any indirect effects on the patients. Again, this was not an organized part of the rehabilitation programme and so had an unobtrusive, ecological flavour to it. For this study we used the Behaviour Observation Instrument (BOI; Alevizos *et al.*, 1978), which consists of 30 behaviours subsumed within six broad categories of patient behaviour, such as 'social participation' and 'unusual or maladaptive behaviour'.

The results of these observations were equivocal, since patients in the presence of our course-trained nurses exhibited more inappropriate (e.g. a 'social activity') and more appropriate (e.g. social participation) behaviour. The only clear finding was that the trained nurses, in contrast to their as yet untrained colleagues, were associated with an overall increase in patient activity.

These two studies therefore indicated some of the side-effects of training, including a considerable and desirable impact on students, but no clear effect on the appropriateness of patients' behaviour.

(c) Generalisation across Behaviours

An equally important dimension of change in a system is that of *response generalisation*: to what extent did the trained nurses develop new behavioural skills after the course? We evaluated this by means of two further studies. The first was concerned with the written records nurses kept of their patient's behaviour, which we will refer to as the nursing notes.

We retrospectively examined these notes over a 6-month period before and after behaviour therapy training, for both the nurses we had trained and for a control group, again drawn from the 'acute' wards of the same hospital. We were especially interested in the effects of our training on their use of subjective, inferential or 'fuzzy' accounts of patient behaviour, and in the alternative, more objective and descriptive accounts.

It again transpired that there was an improvement in the nurses' notes following training, with a pre- to post-training reduction in subjective entries and an increase in objective ones. There were no such changes in the entries made by the control group over the same period, ruling out the possibility that other ongoing changes in the hospital were responsible for the findings. A more complete account of this study is to be found in Milne (1985c).

A second study of generalisation across behaviours was concerned with some of the issues in nurse-patient interaction introduced above. We utilised naturalistic observation, the preferred ecological tool, to see whether our training had had any effect on the *quality* of interactions between nurses and patients. Using a 'cross-sectional' research design, we contrasted those nurses who had received the core course with a group of their colleagues who were yet to attend the course. We made use of Gelfand *et al.*'s (1967) 'Social Reinforcement Rating Scale' (SRRS), which allows the observer to time-sample interactions in the ward in terms of whether the patients' behaviour was 'appropriate', 'inappropriate' or 'neutral'. This class of behaviour is then coded in relation to the nurses' reaction to it, classified as either 'reward', 'punish' or 'ignore'.

Again, we expected that the nurses who had received training in behaviour therapy would be 'better' at interacting (i.e. react more appropriately, as for example in ignoring the patients' 'psychotic talk'). However, we found that the 'trained' nurses made significantly less use of reward and interacted less frequently with patients than their colleagues who had not yet attended the core course (Milne, 1985d). This surprising result was interpreted in terms of an active 'coercion' process by the patients, of the kind discussed in Chapter 2. This effectively reduced the number of opportunities available to staff to apply their new techniques.

Both these studies illustrate the ecological nature of hospitals, as they suggest that an *interaction* took place between the intervention and the system. In our case, this occurred in different components of the system and with quite different consequences. Furthermore, the observational study suggested a major problem for the training intervention that was *not* apparent at the other levels of evaluation, and which might ultimately have led to its failure. In turn, this meant considering new solutions, or at least better approximations to the problem, which we will discuss further in Section 6.7.

(d) Generalisation across Settings

In this fourth and final dimension of generalisation we will again consider findings from naturalistic observations and look at the unexpected side-effects of our intervention. (Incidentally, readers may be reassured to know that we were careful to check whether these observations were valid. To do this we applied both the 'habituation' and 'obtrusion' methods of assessing the reactivity of nurses and patients to our observations, but found only minimal effects, which were of no significance to the intervention. This reactivity study is described in Milne and Hodd, 1984.)

The observational system we used to determine the extent of generalisation across settings was the Attendant Behaviour Checklist (ABCL; Gardner and Giampa, 1971). We thought that training might lead to a re-allocation of nurses' time towards more therapeutic activities and away from 'housekeeping' duties, as found by Watson *et al.* (1971). However, there was no significant increase in the frequency with which the behaviourally trained nurses engaged in therapeutic activities after the course, as contrasted with colleagues who had yet to receive this training. Nor was there any reduction in other duties, which were unrelated to direct patient contact (see Milne, 1985d, for details).

Here again, then, there was conflicting evidence on the 'success' or 'impact' of the training programme and again this was only disclosed by an ecological assessment. This assessment offered some clear and practical implications for any future interventions. In contrast, when we looked at another parameter of generalisation across settings we found fairly good evidence that it had occurred. This was a more precise and direct analysis than the observations and involved a comparison of the nurses' ability to write care plans in the classroom and the ward. We found that they did slightly better in the ward, scoring more highly on the three assessed categories of defining the problem, formulating it in behavioural terms and planning a behavioural programme.

These two studies, like the preceding assessments of generalisation, provide conflicting evidence. Some of it suggests that there has been a successful transfer of training to new places, people and behaviours, whereas other studies indicate that there was no transfer at all, or even that training had undesirable 'side-effects'.

Interestingly, some more sweeping and subjective assessments which we conducted tended to furnish us with equally conflicting outcomes. For instance, the Nursing Officers regarded the rehabilitation programme and the core course as valuable in improving staff morale. They described instances where nurses had broken with past trends and asked to stay or be allocated to the rehabilitation wards because 'they were doing something there'. This was substantiated by evidence from absenteeism/sickness records, which showed improvement in the rehabilitation wards over the period of innovation (Milne *et al.*, 1985a). On the other hand, patient discharges from the unit to the community actually declined over the same period, an apparently negative consequence of the changes we introduced. Although these may be unwanted consequences, they are inevitable in such work with systems, as Willems has indicated (1973). Furthermore, although they are undesirable in the short-term, they may in fact be useful in the development of longer-term programmes of care, since they pinpoint problems that might otherwise destroy it. Indeed, this is the logic underlying the ecological approach within behaviour therapy: to look far and wide in the hope of discovering irregularities. Paradoxical as it might sound, we only learn from our mistakes, or 'falsifications'. According to Popper (1976), who promotes this view of the growth of knowledge, 'science begins with problems and ends with problems'. However, this does not imply that science is static, but rather that it progresses by systematic trial-and-error elimination towards better theories.

It would seem then that behavioural ecology could provide us with a much more useful test of our training intervention than any short-term, focused assessments, such as the commonly used measures of 'understanding' or 'attitudes'. The result is that we become aware of errors and problems, and knowing these we can start to consider how to eliminate them.

6.6 Replications of the Core Course

There was another way in which we could expose our training programme to the 'falsification' test. This involved encouraging others to use it, since this inevitably entailed changing a number of the factors that may have made it effective in its original form. These included the fact that the course was incorporated within a major rehabilitation scheme, involving the systematic behavioural assessment and regrouping of the 300 or so patients within the whole rehabilitation unit (Burdett, 1981, 1982).

Following the initial phase of research, as described above, there were seven attempted replications of the course within 2 years, each of which represented a change in at least one of the original variables. For example, the course was run by one trainer rather than two, by nurse therapists, tutors and psychiatrists as well as psychologists, with different grades of nursing staff, in geographically dispersed hospitals, without large-scale rehabilitation programmes and in a one step per week timetable. Table 6.7 summarises these studies (see Milne *et al.*, 1985b, for details).

Although not all these replications repeated all six course measures outlined earlier in Section 6.2, they all obtained comparable results on the measures that were applied. The sole exception to this was a version of the core course which severely reduced enactive learning opportunities so as to finish within 3 days. In keeping with the predictions and findings presented in Chapter 1 and earlier in this chapter, this resulted in comparable knowledge outcomes but no significant skill development. This represented an attempted but failed falsification of one of the basic tenets of training, namely that skills develop through systematised *practice*. In turn, this strengthens our confidence in this principle.

It is rare to encounter replications of any kind in applied clinical research and so the present ones must be considered as an uncommonly stringent test.

This is not to belittle some important remaining risks, which have not yet been subjected to systematic test. They include the problems of implementation, such as achieving high proportions of care plans, leading to more routine behaviour therapy for the patients; and the related difficulty of not enough comparably large-scale applications of the course or its derivatives. Surely one dimension of replication is that the supervisors are reinforced for running the course, to ensure they continue to run it in the future. With one exception, Table 6.7 indicates that this has not yet occurred. Of course, there are undoubtedly many determinants of a supervisor's behaviour (see Chapter 2) and so it is quite possible that the potentially reinforcing properties of the course are being counterbalanced by pervasive institutional constraints. This remains a crucial area for research, one in which we have only conducted an incomplete 'single-subject' case study in one hospital. Additional hospitals will have to be subjected to the same kind of analyses if we are to learn more about our errors and progress towards their elimination.

Table 6.7: A Summary of the Seven Replications of the Core Course. An asterisk indicates a significant improvement by the post-training assessment ($P<0.05$)

Location and Trainers	Nurses	Modifications to original two courses	Results of all tests administered (mean percentage) Measure	Baseline	Post-training
Middlewood Hospital, Sheffield (Paul Conway)	*N*=5: 2 Charge Nurses/Sisters, 1 SEN, 2 Staff Nurses	Only one trainer instead of two. Nurse therapist rather than Psychologist as trainer	C-scale SPT KBPQ ABTQ FA FTP	23 48 45 70 28 37	24 70* 66* 71 87* 63*
Stanley Royd Day Hospital, Wakefield (Derek Milne)	*N*=7: 2 Charge Nurses/Sisters, 1 SEN, 4 Nursing Assistants	Course taught in two 1-hour sessions per week over a 3-month period. One Psychologist trainer instead of two. Not all nurses qualified	KBPQ ABTQ FA	34 72 18	47* 71 43*
St. David's Hospital, Carmarthen (Charles Burdett and Tim Hooper)	*N*=44: 30 Nurses 2 CPNs 1 Clinical Teacher 10 OT Aides, 1 Medical Assistant	5 Courses taught by Psychologist and Senior Nurse Tutor	KBPQ ABTQ FA	43 84 42	59* 86 75*
Carlton Hayes Hospital, Leicester (Cath Burley and Giotto Bonomally)	*N*=8: 4 Staff Nurses 4 Sister/Charge Nurses	Course taught by Psychologist and Nurse Tutor	KBPQ	36	57*
Kingsway Hospital Derby (Robert Wojciechowski and Cahil Daley)	*N*=7: 3 Sisters 2 Staff Nurses 1 SEN 1 Nursing Officer	Course taught by Psychologist and Nurse Therapist	KBPQ ABTQ FA FTF	31 70 0	52* 73 33*
Carlton Hayes Hospital, Leicester	*N*=7: 5 Qualified Nurses 1 Psychiatrist	Course taught by Psychiatrist	KBPQ ABTQ FA	45 69 52	63* 74 67

We concluded the analysis at our hospital, Carlton Hayes, by examining the extent to which the training innovation had been maintained and generalised following the end of our active involvement. This was a test of the 'hero-innovator' hypothesis (Georgiades and Phillimore, 1975), as well as an enumeration of institutional constraints. It is described in the next section.

6.7 Implementation Problems

We have already discussed in some detail the problem of achieving a high proportion of behavioural care plans from the nurses who attended the core course. It will be recalled that a revised, patient-centred course substantially improved implementation at this level and so overcame that problem. In this section we will consider a subsequent problem of implementation, namely how to maintain the routine use of behaviour therapy by nurses once they have carried out their supervised care plans.

We investigated this question by means of interviews, questionnaires and archival data. Again, a more elaborate account is available (Burdett and Milne, 1985), but for present purposes we will simply provide an outline of the study.

There are some quite elementary questions one can ask about the problems of establishing an innovative programme. One of these is whether the continued presence of the innovator, the so-called 'hero-innovator', is necessary as many believe (Georgiades and Phillimore, 1975). We found evidence that heroes may not be essential. A random sample of seven nurses reported that they had carried out an average of over five behavioural programmes each. This was 6 months after the end of our 'hero-innovator's' active involvement and so suggested that it was not simply our presence and participation that was maintaining the innovation. It should perhaps be emphasised that we did have other sources of information (e.g. Nursing Officers, psychiatrists) regarding the nurses' continued use of behaviour therapy, and that this corroborated their self-reports.

The second question we might ask is whether the nurses' maintenance of the new routines was related to their disposition towards change in general and specifically to behavioural approaches. We assessed this 'personality' view of innovation by administering three relevant questionnaires. They were Kirton's Adaption Innovation Inventory (1976), the Work Environment

Scale (Moos, 1974) and the Attitude to Behaviour Therapy Questionnaire (adapted from Caine and Smail, 1968). Overall, the results from these questionnaires did not sustain a 'personality' basis for the nurses' maintenance of the innovation. This was also consistent with the results of the retrospective analysis of 'implementers' and 'rejectors', outlined at the start of this chapter (Milne, 1985b).

We therefore asked nurses during extensive interviews to offer their own reasons for their continued use of behaviour therapy. They came up with some surprising opinions: low staffing levels, lack of time and work routines were *not* regarded as inhibiting their use of behaviour therapy. In contrast, the support of their Nursing Officers, the rewards they obtained in terms of patients' improvements and the support of the psychologists were regarded as facilitating factors. They all regarded the core course as important, but criticised the lack of feedback on their own efforts and those of their colleagues in other wards within the unit.

These replies are inconsistent with the prevailing views on institutional resistance to change, which regard such factors as work routines and patient change as highly important determinants of the use of therapy skills (Cullen *et al.*, 1983a; Woods and Cullen, 1983). These differences may be due to their respective roots in psychiatric rehabilitation as opposed to mental handicap settings, or to the different methods of gathering information used in these studies, among other possibilities.

Another question that was raised concerned the proportion of nurses remaining within the rehabilitation unit following their training in behaviour therapy. Like many hospitals, Carlton Hayes had a policy of periodically rotating staff to different units of the hospital, so creating a considerable pressure on the programme to continue training newly allocated nurses to replace their rotated colleagues. When we looked at the records a year after the last course, we found that only 25 per cent of the nurses we had trained over a 3-year period were still on the unit. This represents a very real implementation problem, as it creates an endless demand on supervisors to provide training, rather than focusing their attention on other innovation problems. It also means that there is a low level of continuity in staffing within the unit, which may undermine involvement in behavioural programmes. However, the nurses we interviewed did not seem to regard this as an obstacle, so it may be more of a problem for supervisors.

This small-scale pilot study was therefore useful in suggesting ways in which the new scheme could be facilitated (i.e. by feedback and support). It also indicated that the programme had made a lasting impact on the quality of patient care. This was a remarkably successful outcome, bearing in mind the previous research on institutional change, and especially since it was achieved without recourse to the kind of special 'extras' described in Chapter 5. Rather, it seemed that the kind of 'natural contingencies' we considered earlier were 'trapping' the nurses' use of behaviour therapy in such a way that it was maintained without 'hero-innovators' or other special factors. Furthermore, in the interview the nurses themselves indicated some inexpensive ways of boosting this effect.

6.8 Summary

This chapter provided an outline of one programme of nurse-therapy research. In it we attempted to ameliorate some of the shortcomings identified in Chapter 5, particularly the need for detailed specifications of the training process, and objective, ecological evaluations of training.

The major theme emerging from this programme has been the potential of nurse training in behaviour therapy to introduce important changes in the hospital system, for the benefit of both nurses and patients. These benefits include obvious changes such as the nurses' enhanced skills and clinical effectiveness, and less apparent improvements in morale as measured by absenteeism/ sickness records. These could not have been disclosed without a systematic approach to programme evaluation. It was argued that this approach leads to a clearer specification of the inevitable problems that arise when a system is asked to change, and this then provides the basis for better understanding and a more informed process of institutional change. This process may be counter-intuitive, as illustrated by the success of the revised, patient-centred course in improving the implementation of behaviour therapy. Perhaps this is surprising because current generalisations about training are somewhat simplistic and prematurely pessimistic (Milne, 1985a). This has arisen partly because of the paucity of hard data on training in hospitals, and partly because research has tended to view staff training as a barely necessary condition for institutional change. The present programme provides some evidence that training is indeed a necessary condition for change. Furthermore, it may interact with institutional variables in such a way as to become a sufficient condition for improvements in the quality of patient care. Clearly this depends on the existing work environment and in particular on its capacity to 'trap' behavioural skills as they emerge.

Hopefully, this programme and the analysis of training that it presents will promote a more ecological view of change, one that does not simply assume direct cause-effect relationships. Not all hospital wards may prove equally amenable to change or respond in similar ways, but there is considerable scope under the rubric of 'training' to adjust it, as determined by sensitive analyses and process evaluations. It may then become more widely accepted as a truly economical and effective vehicle to institutional change.

7 TEACHERS AS THERAPISTS: A REVIEW OF RESEARCH

7.1 Introduction

The aim of this chapter is to look critically at some of the illustrative research done on training teachers as behaviour modifiers. Once again we will be particularly concerned with training methods, evaluation and implementation. We will attempt to relate this literature to nurse and parent training, although this will be undertaken more thoroughly in the final chapter. This chapter should also provide a backdrop for the following one, which illustrates in detail one teacher training programme. As with previous chapters, the intention is not to try to provide an exhaustive review of the literature on teacher training in behaviour modification, but rather to introduce and develop some of the issues raised by previous researchers which are of concern to us in this book. Other reviews and discussions are available in Clark *et al.* (1972), O'Leary (1972), Madsen and Madsen (1973), Ulrich *et al.* (1974), Litow and Pumroy (1975), Sloane (1976), Kazdin and Moyer (1976), O'Leary and O'Leary (1977), Merrett (1981), and Merrett and Wheldall (1984).

In considering teachers as behaviour modifiers we highlight a theme which has recurred throughout this book, namely the *reflexivity* of teaching and learning (see Chapter 1, particularly). Since teaching is essentially the task of arranging suitable conditions for learning (Stones, 1979), and since behaviour modification is based on learning principles, one might expect that the literature on teacher training would reveal an interesting interaction of theories, experiences and techniques.

Behaviour modification and teaching also share a common purpose in trying to identify and manipulate factors that influence learning. Traditionally, educational researchers have long been interested in the characteristics of teachers which appear to facilitate pupils' learning, such as their teaching methods and personality (see, for example, Gagé, 1963). The question of what made a 'good' teacher typically concerned factors such as authoritarianism and experience. This is not to say that there was not a degree of interest in the teacher's *behaviour*. Gilchrist (1916), for instance, studied the effects of praise and reproof on pupils' work, and the educational establishment offered general guidelines on behavioural methods of maintaining control and discipline in the classroom (Board of Education, 1937).

Behaviour therapists with an interest in education have addressed the same questions but from a more rigorous standpoint. Their research history followed the familiar pattern of initially demonstrating the relevance of a behavioural analysis in the classroom before proceeding to large-scale interventions. We will now consider this development.

The early behavioural projects tended to be individual case studies where the teacher served as experimenter. Zimmerman and Zimmerman (1962), for instance, showed how temper tantrums and other 'unproductive classroom behaviours' could be reduced when the teacher systematically ignored them and attended to more appropriate behaviour. The next research phase was to introduce teachers to the active role of behaviour modifier through training programmes. Ward and Baker (1968), for example, trained teachers to use attention and praise to reduce disruptive behaviour. This supported the view that 'teachers with various "personalities" and backgrounds can be trained systematically to control their own behaviour in ways which will improve the behaviour of the children they are teaching' (Madsen *et al.*, 1968). Summaries of these early studies can be found in Becker (1971) and Guerney (1969). Their flavour is caught neatly in B. F. Skinner's book *The Technology of Teaching* (1968), which draws out some of the many connections between teaching and learning, before arguing the need for behavioural analysis and then intervention.

The behavioural approach has been particularly attractive to teachers because of its attention to the classroom factors that control behaviour. This makes it possible for them to influence pupils in a way that would be impossible with other psychotherapeutic approaches (Clarizio and Yelon, 1967). There is also the fact that schools are one of the few primary socialisation systems that involve virtually all children, who spend there an average of 30 hours a week (Suckerman *et al.*, 1982). As part of this system, teachers are in a crucial position to influence academic and social development. Also, they have a good chance of a successful intervention before any behaviours become engrained problems.

Behavioural researchers have responded to the mutual appeal of classroom interventions by studying a wide range of educational issues, including teaching methods (Becker and Cornine, 1980), teacher control over class behaviour (Speltz *et al.*, 1979), self-control over classroom behaviour (Whitman *et al.*, 1982), self-instruction (Bryant and Budd, 1982), self-assessment (Hallahan *et al.*, 1982), playground aggression (Murphy *et al.*, 1983) and disruption on school buses (Greene *et al.*, 1981), to mention only a few recent themes.

Because of the obvious appeal of behaviour modification for teachers (and teachers for behaviour modifiers), there has been considerable interest in training them to act as 'therapists' for their pupils. We now turn to consider in detail some of the issues arising from this development, in particular the research on training, evaluating and implementing behaviour modification in the classroom.

7.2 Teacher Training Methods

One way of considering the research literature on teacher training is by the amount of time and effort invested in training and evaluating teachers in behavioural techniques. This parallels the levels of sophistication drawn up for nurses in Chapter 5 (see Table 5.1). Thus there have been some very brief and 'lightweight' training programmes for teachers, and some very extensive and thorough ones. We shall utilise this framework in discussing teacher training, since the amount and quality of training are clearly important variables.

(a) 'Brief' Training Programmes

Like the research concerned with training parents and nurses, the early studies of teacher training have relied on simple brief instructions to alter mediator behaviour. One illustration of this is provided by Robinson *et al.* (1981) who had the teacher administer tokens and record the pupils' progress on a wall chart. Once the pupils had earned enough tokens, they could leave the classroom to play a pinball machine for 15 minutes. Tokens were awarded for learning words, a response which was arranged so as to be incompatible with the original behaviour of the pupils who were repeatedly out-of-seat and fighting. Word learning assignments increased nine-fold during the token system, and standard school test scores also improved for the class of 18 hyperactive and underachieving children. The authors concluded that the token system was an inexpensive and effective approach to problem behaviours and could be operated by one teacher.

Burland and Burland (1979) were also concerned with the question of how to make behavioural techniques practicable. They found that one teacher with a class of 11 maladjusted boys was able to observe, formulate, implement and evaluate a behavioural programme and still teach. They set up a system which entailed peer reporting and management, with group discussion and selection of reinforcers in exchange for reducing disruptive classroom behaviours such as stamping, kicking and nudging. They found that this programme was extremely successful in changing the pupils' individual problem behaviours, and managed to incorporate into it powerful group contingencies rather than depending solely on the teacher to provide them.

Tsoi and Yule (1976) described a similar group study in which reinforcement depended upon either the behaviour of the whole class or that of one individual member, as chosen by the teacher. The teacher's training for this intervention was some $4\frac{1}{2}$ hours of 'discussions' on the principles of behaviour modification and their application to classroom management. Then the teacher was informed of the general research procedure and was provided with an instruction sheet prior to each practical session. For instance, while administering group reinforcement for group behaviour the teacher was instructed to give extra break time (reinforcement) only if the group total for 'off-task' behaviour (e.g. out of seat or non-attending) fell below a certain level. The authors reported that this contingency produced desirable changes in the behaviour of the children by reducing off-task behaviour and promoting work towards a common goal.

A different approach to training has been to provide frequent feedback to teachers on the appropriateness of their attention to pupils. Parsonson *et al.* (1974) observed two teachers of institutionalised, mentally handicapped children and gave them summaries of the percentages of attention they had given to appropriate behaviours (e.g. following instructions) and inappropriate behaviour (e.g. self-destructive acts). They reported that prior to training both teachers were giving attention to appropriate pupil behaviours an average 67 per cent of the time. Instructions to one teacher to improve her attentional skills by her own efforts (i.e. without feedback) did not produce any improvement over baseline. Once feedback was introduced, both teachers rapidly increased the proportion of attention given to appropriate child behaviour to a mean of 83 per cent. The authors regarded such an increase as important for modifying the pupils' behaviour.

A variation on this is to have pupils record their own problematic behaviour, since this kind of feedback often brings about improvement. McNamara (1979) described a small study in which teachers were instructed to have 13- to 14-year-old pupils self-record such activities as temper tantrums and low work output. Observers concurrently recorded the pupils' behaviour in the classroom and this information was supplied to the pupils at the end of each class as a secondary form of feedback. These procedures were successful in improving behaviour in the three case studies presented, and again illustrated a simple yet feasible and effective approach.

These studies illustrate the nature and effects of brief teacher training programmes. They illustrate the applicability and effectiveness of behaviour modification in the classroom. Their weaknesses as pieces of research are quite considerable, since none provides any data on the joint behaviours of teachers *and* pupils, nor do they specify the details of training. In fact, Parsonson *et al.* (1974) were the first researchers reviewed here to measure *teacher* behaviour at all. As this was the independent variable in all the studies, it makes the interpretation of results rather difficult: in the triadic model of supervisor (trainer), mediator (teacher) and trainee (pupil) it is necessary to show a *functional* relationship between changes in the mediator and the trainee. That is, which of the trained teacher behaviours actually influence pupils, to what extent and in what way?

Unfortunately, this weakness is also a characteristic of brief training programmes with nurses and parents as therapy mediators. As we shall see, more comprehensive programmes tend to introduce more careful assessments of the teacher's behaviour following training, before relating this to changes in the pupil's behaviour.

(b) 'Intermediate' Training Programmes

We have just looked at some examples of feedback as a means of improving teaching behaviour. There are many studies in which other kinds of prompts are used for this same purpose, including graphic and video-tape feedback, and the use of a wireless receiver, placed in the teacher's ear in order to give verbal prompts, known as the 'bug-in-the-ear'. Bowles and Nelson (1976) described a course given to teachers working in a variety of school settings. The 'bug-in-the-ear' device was worn by the teachers during normal classroom activities and the supervisor gave instructions from behind a one-way mirror on five categories of the teachers' behaviour. These were 'prompt', 'contingency statement' (e.g. do this, then that), 'praise', 'appropriate verbalisations' (speech correctly directed at inappropriate pupil behaviour), and finally 'inappropriate verbalisations' (teacher's speech which could increase the pupil's inappropriate behaviour). Two hours of 'bug-in-the-ear' training were given to some of the teachers in addition to a 16-hour, in-service training workshop attended by all teachers. The workshop covered behaviour management in the classroom and learning disabilities. Training methods included lectures, discussions, behavioural rehearsal (e.g. viewing a video tape of some inappropriate pupil behaviours, then counting their frequency), films and a case-study assignment in the classroom. Bowles and Nelson found that only those teachers who had received 'bug-in-the-ear' training actually improved their behaviour in the classroom under routine conditions (more praise and contingency statements), although all teachers improved their behaviour with respect to their case studies. As they pointed out, for the training to have real benefit the behavioural techniques needed more generalised practice and so the 'bug-in-the-ear' was a more effective method of instruction. As it only required an additional 2 hours of training per teacher, it would also be expected to prove cost-effective.

The Bowles and Nelson study represents an evaluation of a training 'package', since the separate effects of 'bug-in-the-ear' and training workshop were not determined. Similarly, Speidel and Tharp (1978) developed a 3-day training package based on a variety of instructional techniques, assessed as a whole. They offered lectures, discrimination training, modelling, guided practice, video-tape feedback and group discussion. 'Discrimination training' entailed independently observing and recording videotaped examples of 'on-task' and 'off-task' pupil behaviours, followed by discussions about the different recordings made of these two behaviour categories. The aim of this exercise was to improve the teachers' ability to discriminate praiseworthy pupil behaviour. 'Guided practice' involved individual supervision of teachers in the classroom, in which the supervisor first modelled how to praise children before the teacher tried to imitate, with supervisor feedback. These interactions were recorded and provided additional video-tape feedback.

The whole workshop was evaluated by means of further video-tape recordings which analysed the frequency of six categories of teacher behaviour. It was found that the behaviours trained ('academic praise' and 'management praise') increased significantly in frequency as a function of training, whereas the remaining four categories which were not trained (such as 'scolds' and 'delivery of tokens') did not show any change. A 5-month follow-up assessment indicated that these results had been maintained.

This study illustrates the success of a workshop 'package' in transferring and maintaining important teaching skills to the classroom. However, neither of the preceding studies directly related the changes in teachers' behaviour to changes in their pupils' behaviour. In complete contrast, Weinrott *et al.* (1979) reported a study which provided some data on pupils but none on teachers. They trained teachers to increase the frequency of 'pro-social' pupil behaviours, using 'problems exercises' (identifying antecedents and consequences; selecting reinforcers), and instruction in such topics as modelling, defining objectives and contingent reinforcement. The research design included an initial baseline phase during which no alterations of any kind were made. There followed a 'demand' condition in which the teachers were asked to choose a particular child and try to make him appear as outgoing as possible. Next came training and finally a 5-week follow-up. This design allowed the researchers to conclude that training had produced significant improvements in the selected pupils, with reductions in 'social withdrawal' and increases in 'appropriate interaction with peers'. A control group of children showed no such improvement overall.

One study which did consider the effect of training on both teachers and pupils was conducted by Hundert (1982). This study was also original in training teachers to plan as well as execute behavioural programmes. Training was again offered as a 'package', with an 82-page manual at its centre and supplemented by corrective tutoring from a supervisor on completed exercises from the manual. The teachers first learned to write behavioural programmes for a pupil they had selected for this study from their class of 'multihandicapped' pupils (i.e. with behavioural, sensory, emotional and learning problems). They did this by working through the manual and receiving tutoring. Following training there was an increase of up to 100 per cent in the scores they received for these plans. Furthermore, before training, the teachers rarely used behavioural methods and their pupils showed very low levels of appropriate behaviour (e.g. 'on-task' and 'writing'), but after training the teachers used behavioural methods an average of 76 per cent of observed occasions and there were commensurate improvements in pupil performance. For example, the children's 'on-task' behaviour increased from a mean of 33 per cent during the baseline to 96 per cent after training. Hundert also reported that the teachers had acquired a general problem-solving approach through this training programme, and had extended their application of behaviour therapy to other pupils and behaviours in the classroom. He also established that merely training the teachers how to observe and measure their pupils' behaviour did not produce a 'baseline cure' effect, in which the heightened awareness of problems can lead to improved teacher and pupil behaviour.

Hundert's study is one of the very few to have simultaneously considered the 'therapeutic triad' of supervisor, mediator (teacher) and trainee (pupil) in the whole literature on teachers, nurses and parents. Such studies are especially valuable since they shed light on the relationship between the behaviour of each member of the triad. The other studies we have considered say little or nothing about two of the three agents. This obscures potentially important variables in the training process and hence limits our learning about training. As a consequence, supervisors never know exactly what makes the difference between effective and ineffective training practices and may develop 'superstitious' behaviours; that is, persistent training activities which actually have no real effect on the teachers' learning (Milne, 1984f). However, what we know about the supervisor's behaviour in Hundert's study is based solely on the manual, which means that we do not know much about the remainder of the trainer's behaviour (i.e. the corrective tutoring) and its relative effect on the *teachers'* learning. This is acknowledged by Hundert, who also urges researchers to study larger samples and different groups of pupils. On the other hand, the availability of a manual is a huge increment on most training research, where even the most detailed accounts may only indicate the broad title of an educational technique used, such as 'modelling' or 'role-play'. A manual can thus greatly enhance the replicability and utility of a training programme. Future research in which training is the independent variable should make manuals available.

(c) 'Extensive' Training Programmes

A step up from using manuals only is the 'minicourse' (Borg *et al.*, 1970), which is a self-contained, self-instructional package, supplemented by videotaped material, practice and self-evaluation. Jones and Robson (1983) described a minicourse designed to educate teachers of the severely mentally handicapped in order to improve their use of prompts and encouragement for their pupils' speech. Nine teachers attended a 5-week course, which covered setting behavioural objectives, modelling, reinforcement and the opportunity to practise these skills with individuals and then groups of children. Each teacher was given a teacher's handbook which described these skills and incorporated self-evaluation checklists. They also watched a video-tape model of the skills in action before preparing a language lesson for one of their class. This lesson was videotaped and played back to the teacher, who self-evaluated using the appropriate checklist from the handbook. The teachers then repeated the lesson on the basis of this feedback, and this was again videotaped and self-evaluated.

In addition to indicating the overall effectiveness of the course (Robson, 1983), Jones and Robson (1983) tried to determine how the course results were affected by the different elements of the training package. To do this they utilised the data from each week of training and related this to the different contents. They found that each week's score, based on the number of pupil utterances obtained during individual lessons, exceeded that of the previous week, with the sole exception of the modelling skill. They also reported that teachers appeared to have imitated a range of supervisor skills from the video tapes, rather than just acquiring the specific skill that was targeted for that session. This led to 'premature' training effects, which may have influenced the subsequent results of the different instructional methods. In general, though, these findings suggested that each method made a contribution to the overall improvements in the teachers' skills and so the authors concluded that a combination of methods received qualified support.

Madsen and Madsen (1973) have also assessed the effects of different training methods. They regarded their workshop for teachers as having three main components: reading or hearing about principles and concepts of behavioural analysis; role-playing with feedback; and working as teachers in the classroom with feedback from supervisors. The key skills they considered were those of developing teachers' 'approving' and 'disapproving' behaviours. They contrasted the above sequence of training, which is the traditional order, with two other sequences.

First the researchers observed the 16 teachers in their classrooms prior to training, then they received either:

(a) four hours each of self-analysed video-tape feedback, discussion on the principles of applied behaviour analysis, then role-playing and practice; or
(b) role-playing, then video-tape feedback, then discussion; or
(c) the traditional order (discussion, role-playing, then feedback).

These variations, each involving four teachers, were contrasted with a 'no-training' control group of six teachers. The results of observations maintained during and after training indicated that the largest gains in the teachers' appropriate use of 'approving' and 'disapproving' were achieved by those receiving sequence (a) above, with (b) the second most successful and the traditional approach (c) least effective of all. All trained groups did better than the control group.

This surprising finding highlights the need for more evaluations, which unpack 'packages' and so begin the difficult task of determining the relative value of different training contents, orders and methods. Such studies will allow us to make packages more streamlined, since they raise the question of whether equivalent effects can be achieved by shorter, different or less complex courses (Applebee, 1976).

There is, however, a definite limit to our interest in unpacking training packages since the systematic appraisal of each single and joint contribution of variables represents a large number of studies. For example, a package with three main components, A, B and C (such as Madsen's) would require seven studies to determine the respective contributions of each component (i.e. A,B,C; A,B; A,C; B,C; A; B; C). A four-component package would require 14 combinations of studies, a five-component one 30 studies, and so on. In view of the fact that packages typically involve more than five variables, it must be accepted that the likelihood of anyone ever unpacking all of them is remote. A second and equally important determinant of the researcher's behaviour is the low return for this laborious effort, when contrasted with the alternative of developing new packages for new problems. That is particularly the case when the old package has resolved the old problem. Thus, it is improbable that the 'intervention researchers' who specialise in packages will ever get round to the kind of elegant, unconfounded research typified in basic (laboratory) research (Baer, 1981).

Madsen and Madsen (1973) have also described a longer course of teacher training where the method of instruction was a 2-week introductory workshop followed by graphic feedback based on observations in the classroom. This study involved 32 teachers and covered behavioural principles, making observations, and reinforcement. They were observed on an average of three times a week for a year and were provided with a graph showing weekly summaries of their percentage approval to appropriate behaviour, disapproval to inappropriate behaviour and mistakes of approval and disapproval reinforcement. Pupils' 'off-task' behaviour was also recorded throughout the year. The results indicated that teachers receiving this workshop plus graphic feedback maintained an approval ratio of 84 per cent and made less than 1 per cent mistakes of reinforcement. This contrasted favourably with a lower approval ratio (23 per cent) and more mistakes of reinforcement (5 per cent) in a comparison group of untrained teachers. The off-task behaviour of pupils was 24 per cent, which Madsen and Madsen regarded as an acceptable level for a newly integrated school.

These studies are clearly very thorough in their assessment of training methods, incorporating observational data on the behaviour of both teacher and pupil as indices of effectiveness. A comparably systematic programme of research has been conducted at the Hester Adrian Research Centre in Manchester, England, called the 'Education of the Developmentally Young' project (EDY). The overall aim of the EDY project was to enhance the learning of mentally handicapped children, as a result of being taught by specialist methods. This was linked to a strategy of 'pyramid training', as a means of disseminating specialised teaching methods nationally (Foxen, 1978).

A course package was developed to train teachers and other agents (such as nurses) working with mentally handicapped children. This consisted of a teacher's manual and workbook, a video demonstration tape and a workshop training format similar to Madsen and Madsen's (1973) 'traditional' sequence of discussion, modelling, role-playing and simulated practice. Foxen argued that this sequence of instructional methods was compatible with a learning theory analysis of training (Bruner, 1966), in which the representation of information occurs at three levels, the symbolic (cognitive), iconic (perceptual) and enactive (behavioural). The EDY workshop utilised these three modalities for each of its ten, 1-hour practical units in order to develop teachers' skills in recording behaviour, task analysis, shaping and reinforcement. These practical sessions were linked to a theoretical text contained in the teacher's manual. Before attending a practical session the teacher must read the appropriate unit in the manual and answer the study questions in the workbook. They then select a child with whom to work during the practical unit. Any problems can be discussed at the start of the practical session, which then entails watching the demonstration video tape of the given technique and unit. There follows a role-play, with the supervisor and teacher taking turns as trainer, before the teacher has an opportunity to practise the technique with the selected child. This phase is the largest single component (20 minutes) in the practical unit. It is concluded by a feedback discussion with the supervisor.

The progress of the teacher through the EDY course is evaluated unit by unit in terms of both understanding of the principles and being proficient in their execution. Special measures were developed for both areas, and these are described later, in sections (c) and (d). A score of at least 50 per cent on these measures is required at the end of the course for certification.

Evaluations of the EDY course have included the short-term learning of participating teachers. Farrell (1982) reported a study in which ten school staff (five teachers and five classroom attendants) received the EDY package. The teachers showed significant improvements on both proficiency and knowledge after training, and this was maintained at a 7-week follow-up. The classroom assistants, however, did not produce such improvements on the proficiency measure, and their knowledge scores, although higher than baseline, were significantly lower than those achieved by the teachers. Farrell concluded that the EDY course had been an effective method of training teachers in behavioural techniques, but otherwise had been unsuccessful. He suggested that this may have been due to the assistants' difficulty in reading the manual and workbook, or perhaps the unusually intense 2-week 'crash course', which replaced the usual 10-week training period. This relatively slow progress of the classroom assistants was confirmed in a subsequent study by Farrell and Sugden (1984), even though they achieved significant gains on a measure of proficiency in behaviour therapy and maintained this at a 10-week follow-up. A more detailed account of his work involving the EDY package is provided by Farrell in the next chapter.

Farrell also investigated how far individuals had disseminated what they had learnt from attending the EDY course. Eighty educational psychologists and 20 special education advisers attended from 46 local education authorities (LEAs), representing 44 per cent of the total number of possible LEAs. Seven successfully completed EDY courses had been run by trainees on return to their own LEA, with 14 currently running and 32 proposed at the time of Foxen's 1978 report. Since then many more courses have been run in schools, as described in the following chapter.

The EDY project represents an unusually vigorous attempt to integrate training with implementation. This is all the more welcome since both are linked to a systematic approach and careful evaluation. As we will now see, many other self-instructional packages have been developed with the same aim of influencing as many teachers as possible to develop their behavioural skills, although many lack a comparable emphasis on objective evaluation of learning.

In addition to being more systematic as training packages, the 'extensive' programmes discussed above illustrate some other welcome characteristics. One of these is the emergence of evaluations in which the behaviours trained in the teachers are strictly related to changes in pupils. We have bemoaned the inattention to this relationship in the 'brief' and 'intermediate' levels of training and have argued that it is necessary for a better understanding of both training and learning processes.

Another improvement has been the dissecting of training packages. Clearly these consist of a number of training methods, any one of which may be responsible for the majority of learning that occurs. Similarly, the traditional order in which these methods are introduced has come to receive careful attention. Taken together these dissections pave the way to more streamlined courses of training, giving us a package of enhanced efficiency. With supervisor and mediator time at such a premium, these developments are especially valuable, particularly since there is little likelihood that packages will receive more than this preliminary amount of research attention.

(c) Self-instructional Manuals

'Manuals' can be distinguished from introductory texts by the onus they place on behaviour change rather than on improving understanding. Whereas a text typically offers an introduction to the basic *concepts* of behaviour therapy, a manual attempts to develop practical *skills*. Of course, some manuals attempt to develop understanding as well, but their overriding goal remains that of skill enhancement. As Becker *et al.* (1971) have pointed out, the primary goal is to improve the practice of teaching rather than to teach the student to talk about various theories of learning. We will be concerned here, then, with manuals rather than texts since the main concern of this book is that of skill enhancement. Those who wish to focus on concepts and principles are referred to texts such as those by Madsen and Madsen (1970), Carter (1972), Jeffree *et al.* (1977), Kiernan *et al.* (1978), and Fontana (1982).

Manuals themselves vary considerably in their emphasis on skill development. At one end of the continuum are those that utilise the 'programmed learning' format, where one reads an account of a principle, then completes a sentence, then checks to see whether the inserted word was correct (e.g. Buckley and Walker, 1970). More behaviourally taxing formats include 'exercises', which require the teacher to complete quizzes (e.g. Westmacott and Cameron, 1981), or write out aspects of assessment or therapy relating to their own pupils (e.g. Sheppard *et al.*, 1972). Still more enactive tasks were set out by Sulzer and Mayer (1972) who asked their readers to select and observe the behaviour of an animal, their own behaviour, or that of a friend.

Becker *et al.* (1971) provided a comprehensive manual which formed the basis of a course in the applied behavioural psychology for teachers, designed to run without lectures. A variety of instructional procedures were suggested including individual and group formats. The essence was to first read a unit, to do the exercise for that unit, check the result and then proceed to discussion and questions. Exercises included programmed learning passages and projects. The first project included data collection and attempting to increase a pupil's 'on-task' behaviour. Record sheets were provided as additional prompts to the teachers, illustrating the emphasis on their actually trying out the principles.

A further progression in this respect has been the development of elaborate curricula for teaching. Bender and Valletutti (1976) have prepared a lengthy series of skills analyses which provide a step-by-step breakdown of how to teach a moderately or severely mentally handicapped person. This is preceded by guidelines for teachers using these 'task analyses', including points on reinforcement, prompting, feedback, goal-planning and so on. This is followed by suggested readings for each skill section (e.g. self-care skills). Madsen and Madsen (1973) also provided detailed written prompts, in the form of record sheets and a series of learning assignments which can occupy up to a total of 50 hours. These are intended to enhance the classroom applications of behavioural principles and include role-play exercises, work with pupils in classrooms and self-recording. Another variation is for manuals to attempt to shape up routine teaching practice in such areas as revising pupil progress and planning individual educational programmes, for instance by emphasising the value of a task analysis (Valett, 1970).

These manuals seek to prompt and provide feedback to the reader in a way that is intended to facilitate learning of both principles and practice. As such, they are the behavioural counterparts of textbooks and, as we have already seen, can serve a valuable 'supervisory' function. One of the key supervisory elements which manuals tend to omit, however, is an independent or more objective form of feedback. We will now review some ways of arranging for this feedback.

7.3 Evaluation Methods

(a) Introduction

Several evaluative procedures can be self-administered and indeed some of the early observational methods were based on developing means of coding one's own teaching behaviour (e.g. Flanders, 1970). As we have seen from the preceding examples, however, it is quite feasible to develop these skills from self-instructional manuals, although some supervision from an independent 'expert' may still be helpful and necessary.

In this section we essentially progress from self-observation techniques to more objective forms of evaluation. These include attempts to measure changes in the teacher's attitudes, knowledge or skills as a function of behavioural training, and different approaches to assessing the effects of this intervention on the pupils. Other important areas for evaluation are the maintenance and generalisation of training, for instance in its effect on a teacher's colleagues who have not received any behavioural training.

(b) Evaluations of Teachers' Attitudes

Madsen and Madsen (1973) described an in-service training course for 16 teachers in which they administered the Minnesota Teacher Attitude Inventory (MTAI) before, during and following the course. The MTAI is a 150-item measure of the teachers' permissive and child-centred orientation. Although it was not in fact the main focus of the Madsens' behavioural training, the MTAI reflected the teachers' somewhat antagonistic perspective, from which behaviour modification was regarded at best as a poor educational strategy, if not actually 'downright inhuman and controlling'. However, the Madsens reported that following behavioural training there were significant improvements in the teachers' attitudes, whereas those of an untrained control group actually declined. These findings were interpreted as evidence that attitude change is most speedily accomplished by initiating behaviour change, and that the discrepancy between responses to MTAI items and actual classroom behaviour was reduced by this form of training. This was in contrast to the control group, who became less satisfied with their own teaching results during this study through exposure to their trained colleagues. Sloane *et al.* (1976) reported a similar study in which behaviour therapists who were in general caricatured as being controlling and lacking in empathy were actually experienced by their clients as more warm and approachable than their psychoanalytic counterparts. Both these studies, therefore, suggest that the practice of behaviour modification may be considerably *more* congenial to its practitioners and clients than may appear at first acquaintance. This is an important issue, since the acceptability or 'social validity' of any intervention is crucial if we wish teachers and pupils to conform willingly to its requirements. As we have already seen in the case of parents, their 'attitude' towards behaviour modification is one of the major determinants of their clinic attendance and subsequent use of the recommended techniques with their children, so this clearly merits attention when we are considering teacher training and pupil 'receptiveness' to the new approach. One illustration of this has been provided by Hundert (1982). He assessed two teachers' attitudes towards their pupils' behaviour and found that they became more favourable after behavioural training. He also assessed their satisfaction with the training, using ratings of its applicability to their own classrooms, the time cost, its effect on their enjoyment of teaching and the benefits for the pupils. Both teachers participating in this study gave high ratings on all these counts (a mean of 4.5 out of 5).

(c) Evaluation of Teacher Knowledge

Like attitudes, teachers' understanding of behaviour therapy has not been assessed as often as their behaviour. Examples of knowledge measures have been provided by Bowles and Nelson (1976) and by the EDY project. Bowles and Nelson used a 20-item multiple choice questionnaire on behaviour modification and reported that the teachers achieved significantly higher scores by post-training. Like the many other studies we have reviewed (e.g. Gardner, 1972; Milne, 1982) they found that improved understanding did not result in any change in their teaching behaviour.

The Education of the Developmentally Young Project (EDY) described earlier utilised a 25-item quiz to assess teachers' knowledge. This required respondents to place missing words in sentences (e.g. 'Behaviour modification is concerned with .... observable voluntary behaviour') and to define and describe terms or procedures. Examples included 'Define a reward'; 'What is meant by task analysis?'; and 'Describe briefly three ways of assessing a reward for any given child.' These 25 items covered the main points of the EDY course and it was estimated that pre-test scores would average about 20 per cent correct and post-training scores about 60 per cent correct. A score of less than 50 per cent led to further practical assessments before a certificate was issued (Foxen, 1978). Farrell (1982) found that his group of teachers and classroom assistants improved significantly with post-training, with classroom assistants averaging 14 per cent before and 60 per cent after training, compared with 33 per cent and 80 per cent for the teachers. Farrell's study also offered data on the relationship between knowledge scores and proficiency in behavioural methods, indicating a comparable gain. Again, the classroom assistants did less well as a group than the teachers, and in the case of proficiency showed only a very small and non-significant improvement. This led Farrell to conclude that the training of the assistants had not been successful. We will discuss the related proficiency measure shortly (the Trainee Assessment Form; TAF).

(d) Evaluations of Teachers' Behaviour

As a complement to measuring changes occurring 'inside' the teacher (i.e. attitudes and knowledge), one could try to assess the effects of training on the behaviour of teachers and pupils. Ideally, the behaviour of teacher, pupil *and* supervisor should all be evaluated in order to determine the relationships between the various training and learning events. We start by considering the teachers' behaviour.

Jones and Robson (1983) recorded the frequency with which nine teachers, trained by the 'minicourse' method, used basic behavioural techniques to elicit language from severely mentally handicapped children. They recorded the teachers' use of such things as verbal modelling and prompts, requesting information and providing encouragement before, during and after their course. Substantial increases were recorded in the latter two assessment phases. In addition, some of these responses were related to pupil behaviour, and this could be measured as a percentage of children's vocalisations receiving encouragement, so providing a valuable contextual evaluation of the teachers' behaviour too.

In a similar way the EDY project utilised a measure of the teachers' practical skills during a training session with a child. This was the Trainee Assessment Form (TAF), an instrument with six categories of teacher behaviour, each of which is rated for quality on a 5-point scale. The categories include 'presents task', 'physical prompt' and 'verbal feedback'.

The rating scale used for judging the quality of these teacher behaviours ranges from 0 (lack of response) to 4 (excellent response). Each rating is defined carefully for each category, so reducing the likelihood of inter-rater unreliability. The TAF was used to monitor the teachers' progress during the ten-unit course and so afforded supervisors with a valuable means of structuring their feedback to teachers, as well as evaluating the success of training. The inclusion of a pupil behaviour category (child's response) also permitted the supervisors and mediators to judge the training in terms of its effects on the pupil. This could have the valuable role of 'face-validating' the behavioural techniques for the teachers and of minimising the development of irrelevant methods of training.

Hundert (1982) has described a third approach to evaluating teacher behaviour following training. It consists of assessing a subset of the relevant skills, in this case writing behaviour modification programmes. Teachers were supplied with a response sheet with nine headings: objectives, measurement, curriculum, instructional materials, consequences for correct responses, consequences for errors, prompts, instructions and handling disruptions. They completed this sheet in about 20 minutes at a baseline assessment and then at two post-training phases. Their programmes were scored as 'correct', 'incorrect' or 'not applicable', each of which was defined for each category. An example of the scoring in the case of the first 'objectives' response category was that it clearly specified the pupils' goals, the conditions under which these would be achieved and a specific mastery criterion.

Hundert also assessed the teachers' behaviour in the classroom in terms of their use of 'approval', 'prompt', 'instructions' and 'correction', as well as the related frequencies of pupil behaviours as selected and outlined in the teachers' written programmes. He reported that the programme score averaged 0 per cent at the baseline assessment but rose to 89 per cent after the manual-based training, with a comparable improvement in the actual implementation of their behaviour-modification programmes in the classroom.

This study comes closest of the ones we have considered to evaluating the behaviour of all three agents in the therapeutic triad, in so far as the training was largely based on a self-instructional manual and hence provided a clear account of the behaviours expected from the supervisor during training. This was then related to two parameters of teacher behaviour (written and implemented programmes) and several measures of the related child behaviour. However, Hundert pointed out that his own role in providing corrective feedback was not specified objectively, and so his way of dealing with the teachers' questions (concerning the manual material) may have contributed as much to the successful outcomes as did the manuals themselves. None the less, this is an uncommonly thorough evaluation and points the way for future research.

(e) Evaluation of Pupils' Behaviour

Much more common than assessments of teachers are those that focus on the pupil. This bias has been present from the outset, with Zimmerman and Zimmerman (1962), for instance, only reporting general changes in the frequency of the child's behaviour as a result of teacher training. Since that time, evaluations have become increasingly wide ranging and sophisticated, following the trend set by parent training studies.

One illustration of this has been the development of broad behaviour rating instruments which incorporate some teacher behaviour as well. Becker *et al.* (1967), for example, produced a 'Classroom Behaviour Rating Schedule' (CBRS) which is summarised in Table 7.1. The CBRS includes eight pupil behaviours and four teacher responses and was completed by observers seated at the rear of the classroom using a time-sampling procedure.

A second illustration of observing both pupils' and teachers' behaviour has been provided by Parsonson *et al.* (1974). They used a 10-category instrument covering all classes of child behaviour attended to by the teachers. The categories included 'activity', 'bizarre', 'compliance', 'language', 'self-help' and 'social' behaviours, and most were classified in 'appropriate' and 'inappropriate' forms. For example, a child-appropriate form of compliance is to follow instructions within 10 seconds, whereas an inappropriate form would not occur within this period. Similarly, there was a two-form code for the teachers' behaviour, namely 'negative teacher attention' (e.g. expressions of disapproval such as head-shaking) and 'positive teacher attention' (e.g. praise).

Table 7.1: A Summary of the Becker *et al.* (1967) Classroom Behaviour Rating Schedule (CBRS)

Behaviour Category	Examples
Pupils:	
1. Motor behaviours (at seat)	Rocking in chair
2. Gross motor behaviours (not at desk)	Running
3. Aggression	Hitting
4. Deviant talking	Carrying on conversation with other children
5. Non-attending and disobeying	Does something different from that which he has been directed to do
6. Thumb-sucking	Sucking finger or pencil
7. Relevant behaviour	Time on-task; answering questions
8. Hand raising	Raises hand to answer question
Teachers:	
9. Teacher attention	Attends during observation interval
10. Positive commands	'Good'; 'Fine'
11. General reprimand	Telling off class or group of pupils
12. Negative comments	'Shut up'; 'Sit in your seat'

Whenever the teacher attended to an individual child, this was coded as 'negative' or 'positive' and then the child's behaviour that had preceded attention was coded into one of the ten categories, together with an 'appropriate' or 'inappropriate' designation. This procedure allowed the researchers to determine the effects of training on the teachers' selective attention to different child behaviours and on the quality of this attention, although unfortunately, it did not include an evaluation of the effects of this attention on pupil behaviour.

An alternative to these two coding systems is to simply record the frequency of one or two child behaviours. This can range from simple 'on-task' or 'off-task' counts for individual pupils or the whole class (e.g. Tsoi and Yule, 1976), to recording the frequency of question-asking (Speltz *et al.*, 1979), number of fulfilled assignments (Robinson *et al.*, 1981) per cent correct arithmetical answers (Whitman and Johnston, 1983), or out-of-seat and driver coercion counts in the school bus (Greene *et al.*, 1981). These counts are made before and during the various intervention strategies so as to provide a baseline to intervention comparison of the same behaviour under the different conditions. These are then examined visually or reported as percentage change.

A variation of this form of evaluation is to utilise self-recording of targeted behaviours by the pupils themselves. As this can be inaccurate (Thomas, 1976), it is useful to monitor and feedback independent recordings to the pupils. McNamara (1979), for example, provided self-recording slips to secondary-school pupils aged between 12 and 14 as part of a self-control study of inappropriate vocalisations. An example of a recording form is given in Table 7.2, illustrating that the teachers also recorded the pupils' behaviour and that the pupils knew this in advance and could see their respective totals. McNamara's (1979) three case studies indicated that self-recording could produce accurate data and reduce problem behaviours with minimal teacher effort. This finding was also obtained by Hallahan *et al.* (1982), who found that self-assessment and recording substantially increased on-task behaviour and academic productivity. The self-assessment entailed pupils asking themselves 'Was I paying attention or not?' and then recording the answer every time they were cued by a tone given at irregular intervals. The authors regarded their findings as supporting the view that self-monitoring can motivate behaviour change, which could also explain McNamara's (1979) results. The other practical

Table 7.2: A Pupil Self-recording Form (McNamara, 1979)

Pupil's Name ....

Date .... *Teacher* ....

Lesson 1 2 3 4 5 6 7 8 (circle)

Please make a mark every time you talk when you are not supposed to.

My Total ....

Teacher's Total ....

This is an honest record of my behaviour.

Signed ....
(Pupil's signature)

advantages of self-recording reported by Hallahan *et al.* (1982) were the maintenance of high levels of 'on-task' behaviour and academic productivity, even when the audio cues and record slips were speedily faded out.

Compared with the broader-based evaluations, these examples of simple frequency measures of pupil behaviour have the advantage of being easy to administer, highly specific and potentially motivational to both teacher and pupil. However, their use is restricted to assessing problem behaviours, and they could not, therefore, provide a good baseline assessment of the wide range of individual or group activities that occur in classrooms. The 'cost' of this breadth is borne by observer time, since only very crude records can be sustained by teachers or pupils themselves, such as 'on' or 'off' task behaviour. This will severely limit the utility of such measures and favour the development of simple, discrete and self-administered recordings.

7.4 Implementation Issues

(a) Introduction

We have just considered some of the problems in introducing and sustaining novel recording procedures in the classroom. We can expect them to be part and parcel of any innovation, always assuming that the accompanying analysis is adequate enough to disclose them. Douglas (1981) has discussed some of the more common examples of 'bugs' in the system, including the different expectations of teacher and supervisor and the need for staff support for any planned change. Minimising these problems entails careful 'entry' into the system, a point already elaborated in Chapter 2.

Martin (1977), in his article on 'implementing the engineered classroom', offers the teacher a systematic plan for assigning educational tasks to individual pupils, for giving immediate and effective reinforcement for any on-task learning activity and for maintaining classroom behaviour within well-defined limits. His concern is that the 'engineered classroom', like many other innovations, demands organisational, procedural and interactional skills which teachers may not already possess. In addition there is the

Table 7.3: An Outline of Martin's (1977) Steps in Implementing the 'Engineered Classroom'

Step	Content
1. Observational training	Train teachers to observe pupil behaviours and specify learning objectives for them
2. Interactional training	Developing teachers' contingent use of attention, praise and so on as reinforcers for on-task and off-task pupil behaviour
3. Checkmark system	Introduction of the token incentive system which begins with one pupils' assigned tasks and gradually includes the whole class
4. Introduction of learning centres	Once the checkmark system has been implemented, pupils can exchange tokens for 'free time' in a sub-unit of the classroom containing relevant learning materials
5. Interest centres	These units provide concrete manipulative materials which develop the learning objectives. Examples include art, science and communication centres. Like the learning centres, access is contingent on tokens
6. The daily schedule	Attention is given to structuring the class's routine so as to maximise access to the centres and to promote learning

implicit departure from classroom routine, and, as Martin points out, changes in routines and skills do not take place automatically, simply by deciding that they should occur. To facilitate this transition he outlines six steps which gradually shape up the engineered classroom. These steps are outlined in Table 7.3 and effectively bridge the often large and unmentioned gap between theory and practice.

Elias *et al.* (1982) have also discussed general implementation issues for the supervisor. They advise researchers to tread carefully in entering the school system (e.g. meeting *all* groups concerned with the proposed changes) and to build up a consultation team incorporating school personnel before proceeding to the intervention and evaluation phases.

Nevertheless, implementation difficulties are so widespread that many researchers have become sceptical about the utility of traditional behavioural approaches in schools (e.g. Ward, 1976). This has led to a growing emphasis on linking home and school, which allows an extended analysis of the child's behaviour and can help to explain otherwise 'senseless' acts by indicating antecedents at home which serve as 'setting events' for subsequent problems in the classroom (Aponte, 1976). This is just one aspect of the very broad issue of implementing behavioural approaches in schools, but it serves to highlight the need to 'take our blinkers off', as Douglas put it (1981), when trying to promote change. We will now briefly consider some examples of this analysis, beginning with the home and school as linked systems.

(b) Home and School

One of the basic reasons for studying home and school jointly is the major role played by the family background in educational attainment (Jencks, 1972). Blechman *et al.* (1981), for instance, assessed the value of having parents and teachers co-operate in a behavioural approach to improving pupils' mathematics and reading. This entailed having parents prepare contingency contracts for their children in which academic goals were set and which, when achieved, were reinforced by the parents. The teachers collaborated in setting goals by providing daily 'good news' notes, which informed parents of their child's progress with classwork. If there had been no progress that day, then no note was sent home and the parents made no reference to schoolwork. A total of almost 200 children were included in this study, which resulted in improved accuracy of classwork among the inconsistent performers as well as raised ratings of themselves as students. A control group excluded the possibility that this favourable outcome was simply due to enhanced motivation.

A broader intervention has been described by Suckerman *et al.* (1982), who trained both parents and teachers to define, observe and modify problem behaviours using Hall and Copeland's (1972) responsive teaching programme. This common approach was intended to increase the consistency between the child-management approaches used at home and in school and to foster improved parent-teacher communication. Over the course of a 3-year intervention, 15 children and 8 families took part, with a resulting improvement in academic achievement. Other examples of this kind of collaboration are presented in Atkeson and Forehand (1979).

(c) Peer Tutoring

Another facet of the school system which has received attention from behaviour therapists has been the use of pupils as teachers for their peers, called 'peer tutoring'. This approach is far from new, having a history dating back to the 'monitor' system of the eighteenth century in which one schoolmaster was able to teach hundreds of children by proxy (Henderson, 1978).

This apparent efficiency in the use of professional time contrasts with the considerable extra cost to teachers of directly assessing, recording and modifying pupil behaviour themselves. Such practical advantages have led to token-based systems in which pupils monitor and tutor their underachieving peers (Willis *et al.*, 1972; Richardson and Harlick, 1975).

Trovato and Bucher (1980) have combined a study of peer tutoring with home-based reinforcement, nicely illustrating co-operation between school and home. Tutoring involved a pupil helping a peer to read on a one-to-one basis by pointing out errors, allowing self-correction, and dispensing tokens and praise for improved reading. The tokens earned were then exchanged for back-up reinforcers already agreed between parent and child, such as desirable activities and preferred foods. Trovato and Bucher reported that peer tutoring had improved both reading and comprehension in relation to a control group, and that the home-based reinforcement doubled this effect. Furthermore, all parties rated themselves as satisfied with the programme, and compliance remained high.

(d) Peer versus Teacher Control

The peer tutoring and home-school links described above represent constructive responses to the complex nature of educational systems. However, both of these also represent facets of pupil control in which the teacher is reduced to a secondary controlling agent. This underlines a traditional problem in which the pupil's peers or parents utilise more powerful contingencies than the teachers and so gain the ultimate control over pupil behaviour. Solomon and Wahler (1973) carried out a classic study of this by conducting a careful observation of peer control. They found that pupils reinforced one another for disruptive classroom behaviours by giving contingent attention. At the same time they ignored their peers' pro-social behaviour. Solomon and Wahler were able to alter this state of affairs completely by having peers ignore disruptive behaviour and attend to pro-social activities, leading them to anticipate the value of 'peer therapists' as teacher-aides. Peer-administered tokens could be used to achieve this, in which individual pupils earn back-up reinforcement for the whole class, such as field trips. This increases the maintenance and generalisation of appropriate peer control (Walker and Buckley, 1972; Stokes *et al.*, 1978). Such studies have the important ingredient of offering continuing 'social support' for the changes introduced. This seems to be a crucial determinant of the long-term outcome. Greer and Polirstok (1982), for instance, found evidence that only peer tutors who had acquired the ability to recruit reinforcement from the rest of the class managed to maintain this behaviour. In a similar vein, Kistner *et al.* (1982) reported that pupils in a classroom token economy controlled the *teacher's* use of tokens by reducing her popularity until she finally 'conformed' with the behaviour of her peers and started to administer tokens! One solution to such dilemmas has been to give pupils the task of dispensing tokens. Carden-Smith and Fowler (1984) showed that this kind of peer control could be just as effective as teacher monitoring and did not depend on a prior demonstration of the token system by a teacher. However, one longer-term problem they uncovered was that if the pupil 'monitors' were not given corrective feedback by the teacher on their use of tokens, they would frequently award tokens which were not earned, for instance by not withholding tokens for disruptive peer behaviour.

(e) Self-control

Other attempts at gaining effective and lasting classroom control have been to develop the pupil's self-control. Bolstad and Johnson (1972) contrasted teacher versus pupil control over disruptive behaviour and found evidence that pupil self-control was the most successful. Glynn *et al.* (1973) illustrated some of the key elements of such an approach. This began with 'self-assessment', in which pupils were taught to identify their own on-task behaviour and carry out self-recording. If the data so recorded represented an increase in on-task behaviour, the pupils administered themselves a reinforcer of their own choosing. In addition to developing the pupils' responsibility for learning, this approach has the advantage of being easy on the teacher's time and energy, thus allowing more room for individualised attention. There is also evidence that self-control can have desirable generalisation effects. Stevenson and Fantuzzo (1984) found that a self-control procedure similar to Glynn *et al.*'s (1973) resulted in improvements in the initial focus of self-control (mathematics), as well as decreasing disruptiveness in the classroom. Both effects were also obtained at home and extended equally favourably to 'untreated' peers' behaviour in both settings. Reviews of self-control training have been presented by O'Leary and Dubly (1979) and by Gross and Drabman (1982).

These selected examples begin to illustrate the complex nature of the classroom and the value of comparably subtle evaluations of behavioural interventions. They can highlight the 'bugs' in the system and indicate more effective ways of promoting social and academic gains. They also draw attention to some of the problems in introducing behavioural techniques in the classroom. It is important that we attend to these, since they ultimately determine the success of the intervention.

7.5 Summary and Discussion

(a) Summary

In this chapter we have reviewed some of the developments in training teachers to use behavioural approaches. At the outset we anticipated a productive interaction between traditional educational practices and behaviour modification, resulting from some of their shared principles and objectives. This symbiotic relationship was confirmed by the research, which indicated a very broad range of promising developments.

Our main concern lay with those schemes that enabled teachers to plan and implement their own behavioural approaches in the classroom, and so we focused on the relevant issues of training methods, evaluative procedures and implementation issues. We distinguished between training courses that were 'brief', 'intermediate' or 'extensive' in their duration, comprehensiveness and sophistication. In this way it was possible to describe a progression from elementary training methods such as verbal instructions through to complex 'packages' of multi-media learning devices incorporating manuals, videos, auditory prompting and supervisory feedback.

These variations in training were accompanied by comparable degrees of attention to evaluation. The 'brief' programmes tended towards limited changes in related pupil activity, for instance in out-of-seat or attending behaviour. There was also a general lack of specificity regarding the actual training process, making the outcome difficult to judge and the programme impossible to replicate. 'Intermediate' programmes were presented with a more systematic attempt to evaluate processes and results, as illustrated by the attention to the relationship between teacher *and* pupil behaviours and the availability of detailed training manuals. In the 'extensive' courses many evaluations attempted to dissect the training packages, in order to tease out the most efficient and effective procedures. Likewise there was an increase in the measurement of teacher and pupil behaviour, as well as some interest in the effects of training on their attitudes and knowledge concerning behaviour modification. Observations of behaviour included scales for recording the teachers' and pupils' classroom behaviour, either jointly or separately. The former have the advantage of pinpointing which teacher responses have most influence on the pupil's behaviour. An interesting development was the introduction of self-evaluation procedures for both pupils and teachers, which again could be linked or separate. This has the practical advantage of easing the teacher's task in implementing behavioural techniques. The emphasis on cognitive processes involved in such self-monitoring procedures may also promote its acceptance among teachers.

We concluded the chapter by outlining some of the other implementation issues and problems, beginning with Martin's

(1977) guidelines on how to institute the 'engineered classroom'. This was a useful step-by-step approach to the much-neglected question of *how* to procure change, based on behavioural principles. Such internal consistency between theory and practice indicates a rare but desirable degree of reflexivity in our analyses and interventions. We then proceeded to look at four examples of how research had attempted to overcome implementation problems. They were to link the home and school in order to provide consistent use of contingencies between parent and teacher; to examine the use of pupils as peer tutors; to assess ways of controlling the peer culture as a determinant of pupil behaviour (e.g. peer monitoring); and lastly to look at pupil self-monitoring and self-control. What these four examples share is a concern with contingencies other than those exclusively administered by the teacher, namely those relating to home and peer 'subcultures'. This is a valuable extension of the earlier focus on the teacher, since it raises the possibility of successfully implementing and maintaining adaptive behaviour change in the classroom.

Variables such as peer and self-control have been found to be important in these respects in the research on parent and nurse training, and one can discern an emerging consensus on the significance of these in carefully developed mediator training packages which are linked to sensitive implementation and support. However, the impression one gets is that so far the respective research on training parents, teachers and nurses has not made much reference to one another's potentially valuable developments or perspectives. None the less, they do seem to have evolved in remarkably similar ways, perhaps as a result of developments in the 'parent' discipline of behaviour analysis and modification. Self-control, token systems, social validity, objective measurement, prevention, efficiency and relative effectiveness are some of the examples of shared development.

(b) Discussion

During this development of mediator training, some major obstacles have been confronted. They have included the traditional view of pupils' behaviour as being controlled by deeply ingrained personality characteristics, which makes manipulations of the classroom environment seem irrelevant and inconsequential; the presence of intransigent disciplinarian attitudes which view behaviour modification as a soft option or rooted in bribery; and the disproportionate attention to one or two children at the expense of the rest of the class (Macmillan and Kelvin, 1977). To these obstacles can be added the debatable goals of procuring 'still, quiet and docile' pupils (Winnett and Winkler, 1972); and the extent to which any goals are achieved in an acceptable sense (such as 'normalising' behaviour), rather than in a purely statistical sense (Abikoff and Gittelman, 1984). Such evaluations may lend an intervention more credibility and hence maintenance than purely academic achievements (Macmillan *et al.*, 1978).

If these individual perspectives were not a sufficient deterrent to researchers, then the numerous organisational and administrative obstacles might have been expected to prevent the development of a behavioural approach in teaching. For even if the teacher has no objection to behaviour modification and rapidly acquires the relevant skills, factors such as obtaining 'extras' for reinforcement purposes and the problem of uncooperative pupils may curtail the development. Presland (1977), for example, contrasted two schools in which behavioural programmes had been introduced, although successfully in only one. In this school the programme had evolved in consultation with all staff and so the teacher involved received support and encouragement, in contrast to the social isolation experienced by the teacher in the unsuccessful programme. Burland and Burland (1979) have a further example of the importance of social contingencies in recounting how staff shortages deprived one teacher of her reinforcement (a day off). This appeared to be compensated for by the pupils who took pity and shared their own reinforcement of sweets and biscuits with her!

Merely acknowledging obstacles of this kind indicates that the development of a behavioural approach within the teacher's repertoire has indeed made a step forward. This is confirmed in a review by Merrett (1981), but there remains a glaring and unacceptable tendency to omit any serious discussion of these obstacles and their relationship to the more prominently displayed outcomes. This omission is not consistent with a full behavioural analysis. To do this properly requires consideration of the broader *exchange* between environment and behaviour, for instance in the way that researchers or teachers are themselves controlled for introducing new forms of control. Such data, perhaps only of a descriptive and 'soft' self-report nature to begin with, are necessary for the longer-term development of behaviour modification in the classroom. Another dimension is the relationship between behavioural and other classroom approaches, and again the literature tends to present an over-simple picture of the naive teacher, devoid of any sort of baseline repertoire or learning history. To develop further, behaviour modification must openly negotiate its place alongside the existing and well-honed skills of teachers. For instance, adherence to a particularly authoritarian teaching approach only encourages resistance to change and is not a characteristic of successful educational innovations (Gilbert, 1982).

There is another reason for making behaviour modification as acceptable to teachers as possible, and this is the need to develop our mutual awareness of the implications of the behavioural model. One criticism is that it has become an instrument which unquestioningly serves to maintain a system 'thriving on a petty reign of law and order to the apparent detriment of the educational process itself' (Winnett and Winkler, 1972). To the extent that behaviour modification is effective, it can clearly perpetuate tyranny or transform education, depending on the goals of the modifiers. However, value judgements concerning educational objectives or procedures are by no means limited to this model. One consistent way of responding to this criticism is to examine the goals which behaviour modifiers have actually pursued. O'Leary (1972) reviewed the relevant literature and reported that a wide range of traditional academic and social behaviours were sought, such as the use of descriptive adjectives in spontaneous speech, pro-social interactions and following teachers' instructions. He also drew attention to the research concerned with training pupils to control teacher behaviour, that is, to acquire *self-control* by operating on their own environment. This is surely an important educational and social goal, and furthermore a process that minimises tyranny or the necessary persistence of the *status quo*. However, even if the work of behaviour modifiers is compatible with most teachers' goals, as O'Leary asserts, it is crucial for teachers themselves to participate fully in the selection of such behavioural goals and procedures. This is not just because of its consequences for implementation, but also because this degree of collaboration will promote a mutual understanding of behaviour modification, with potential benefits for all concerned.

In contrast, it does not seem helpful to shrug off behaviour modification as the latest fad or as some kind of accessory which can be added at a later date if desired. The behavioural perspective implies an active participation between teacher and pupil whether 'unconsciously' or not, as some of the studies reviewed above and in

Chapter 2 have demonstrated. It is, therefore, essential that the teacher considers these processes, since they are an important and ever-present influence in the classroom. To ignore this fact and the evidence supporting it is to risk perpetuating the very tyranny that some teachers ascribe to behaviour modification. This may be a difficult implication to accept, since many may hold the view that teaching is an art and not a scientific process. As Skinner (1954) has pointed out, there is a science of learning *and* an art of teaching, and the two can be combined efficiently. Far from mechanising education, this science creates the basis for setting the teacher free from irrelevant, tedious or harmful behaviours and engaging in more rewarding teaching. Thirty years on, Skinner (1984) has attacked educationalists for their continued failure to incorporate this science into routine teaching practice. He refers to the conspiracy of silence about teaching as a skill and the contingencies on educationalists to seek solutions in other areas. Teaching and learning variables have meantime declined very far down their list of possible solutions to poor pupil attainment, leading Skinner to reiterate the need to teach teachers both how to teach and the behavioural means by which this can be achieved.

Clearly there remain some major and unyielding obstacles to implementing the 'engineered classroom', despite hard evidence of the advantages of this approach. Perhaps Cunningham (1983) has put his finger on one reason for the rejection of a behavioural approach in his discussion of the dangerous condition of 'expertosis'. Like myxomatosis, this involves a swelling head and blindness, leading to much-reduced collaboration between supervisor and potential mediators.

8 TEACHERS AS THERAPISTS: AN ACCOUNT OF THE EDY PROJECT

Peter Farrell

8.1 Introduction

The Education of the Developmentally Young (EDY) project represents the first attempt in the UK to systematically train school staff who work with mentally handicapped children in behavioural teaching techniques. The project was fully operational from October 1976 until September 1980 and was based at the Hester Adrian Research Centre (HARC) in Manchester. Since that time the EDY workshop materials have been published (Foxen and McBrien, 1981; McBrien and Foxen, 1981) and are being used extensively throughout the United Kingdom. Initially the Project Directors were Tom Foxen and Judith McBrien, and they were joined by Maria Thomas in 1979. Full details about the project can be obtained by consulting the materials themselves, by reading McBrien (1981), Farrell (1983) or McBrien and Foxen (in press), or by consulting the project's Annual Reports, which are available from HARC (Foxen, 1977, 1978; McBrien, 1980, 1982; McBrien and Thomas, 1981). In addition Boucher and Feiler (1982) describe in detail how they ran an EDY course, and Cocks and Gardner (1978) describe briefly how EDY has been used in Walsall. Furthermore, Farrell (1981) gives an account of how EDY has been adapted for use on the Manchester training course for educational psychologists. Finally, the proceedings of two National EDY Users' Conferences which were held in Manchester in 1979 and 1983 provide extensive examples of different applications of EDY throughout the United Kingdom (HARC, 1980; Farrell, 1985).

Initially the Project Team developed a workshop package which covered the essential features of the behavioural approach to teaching mentally handicapped children. This is described in detail later in the chapter. Having developed the workshop, a pyramid dissemination model was employed whereby each Local Education Authority in the country was invited to send an educational psychologist or an adviser in special education to attend an intensive one-week workshop, as a result of which they were 'qualified' to run

EDY workshops as instructors in their own LEAs. Eighty educational psychologists and twenty advisers attended these workshops which took place between 1976 and 1980. In addition to running EDY workshops in schools, many instructors have trained additional colleagues, either educational psychologists or senior teachers, as instructors, hence ensuring the continued dissemination of the training. Furthermore, the publication of the materials in self-instructional form (Foxen and McBrien, 1981; McBrien and Foxen, 1981) has enabled this process to continue. Judging from the extent to which the materials are selling, the course is still being used extensively. Indeed, the publishers, Manchester University Press, have embarked on a third reprint and a second revised and improved edition of the EDY materials is being prepared.

8.2 The EDY Course

The EDY course was designed to train all staff who work with mentally handicapped children — teachers and non-teaching assistants — in behavioural techniques. It is divided into four phases. Phase 1 is the workshop phase, Phases 2 and 3 are concerned with permanent implementation of the techniques, and Phase 4 considers wider issues to do with incorporating behavioural teaching in the context of the classroom. Phase 1 has been the most extensively developed and researched and is dealt with fully in this section; Phases 2 and 3 are also described and discussed and Phase 4 is considered briefly later in this chapter.

8.2.1 Phase 1: The Workshop

In Phase 1, staff who attend the workshop (trainees)*, receive training in ten separate units, each one relating to a different feature of behavioural teaching. The theoretical background to the units and details of the practical work that accompanies them are contained in the *Trainee Workbook* (Foxen and McBrien, 1981). The workshop instructor also has an *Instructors' Handbook* (McBrien and Foxen, 1981), which contains guidelines as to how to run Phase 1 as a whole and also specific suggestions pertaining to the training on each unit. The demonstration video tape shows staff working with mentally handicapped children using the techniques relevant to each of the units. The units cover the following areas.

* The EDY convention is to refer to supervisors as 'instructors', mediators as 'trainees' and trainees as 'children'.

Unit 1 — Operant Behaviour. This is an introductory unit in which trainees are introduced to behavioural principles, with particular emphasis on the effect that changing the setting condition (the antecedents) can have on children's behaviour. For the practical work the trainees observe a predetermined aspect of a child's behaviour, e.g. 'on-task', 'out of seat', under a variety of different setting conditions, for example when the child is alone, with an adult, or with different equipment.

Unit 2 — Reward Assessment. This unit introduces trainees to the importance of rewards when working with children who are mentally handicapped, and stresses the need for them to be strong, consistent and immediate, particularly when teaching children new tasks. The use of different types of rewards (social praise, food, physical contact, toys and music) is discussed. For the practical work the trainee uses multiple choice and/or sequential sampling to assess which rewards a child will work for.

Unit 3 — Reward Training. This unit introduces the concept of pairing known but 'difficult to give' rewards (e.g. food), with unlearned but 'easy to give' rewards (e.g. social praise) in order to teach a child to respond to the easier reward. This technique is practised with a child in the practical session. In addition the unit covers certain key features of the behavioural approach to teaching mentally handicapped children, which are central to EDY and which are used in each of these subsequent units. These key features are:

(a) trial by trial teaching;
(b) recording children's progress on each trial using a standard record form known as the Qualitative Behaviour Record Sheet (QBRS);
(c) setting precise target behaviours;
(d) taking baseline measures; and
(e) setting criteria of success.

A detailed example of training in one EDY unit is given later in this chapter and illustrates these features.

Unit 4 — Prompting. This unit describes the use of physical, gestural and verbal prompts, and discusses fading techniques, all of which are practised in the practical session.

Unit 5 — Task Analysis. The importance of task analysis when working with mentally handicapped children is stressed, and examples of task analyses are provided in the workbook. Trainees are encouraged to think of different ways of task-analysing similar tasks and, in the practical session, a task is broken down into small steps and the trainee attempts to teach the child to complete it.

Unit 6 — Shaping. This unit covers shaping a child to complete a task by rewarding successive approximations to the target behaviour. The merits of forward and backward training are also discussed. In the practical work a child and task are chosen to illustrate one or other of these approaches.

Unit 7 — Imitation. This unit defines imitation as a 'learning to learn' skill as the child's ability to imitate forms the basis for learning a whole range of skills. If a child is unable to imitate simple gross movements, then he or she will not be able to learn more complex skills which can only be taught through imitation (e.g. speech, language, signing and more complex forms of play). In the practical work the trainees attempt to teach the child to imitate or they use imitation training to extend the range of actions or words that he or she can already imitate.

Unit 8 — Time-out. This unit covers the form of time-out in which the trainee and materials are removed from the child. Consequently only relatively minor misbehaviours are dealt with in the practical session, for example, too much talking, giggling, or 'messing' with the materials. Placing a child in a 'time-out' room contingent on the occurrence of more severe behaviours is not discussed in this unit.

Unit 9 — Overcorrection. This is the only unit which does not necessitate using a child for the practical work. It covers restitutional and positive practice overcorrection. Restitutional overcorrection can be used when a child throws objects around the room and is made to tidy them up and the rest of the classroom as well. In positive practice overcorrection, the child is 'trained' to practise physical actions which are incompatible with the undesirable behaviour, for example, folding one's arms instead of head-slapping. The training in this unit is done using role-play.

Unit 10 — Discrimination and Generalisation. In this unit the theory behind children's ability to develop discrimination and generalisation is discussed at some length and the importance of these skills for mentally handicapped children is stressed. For the practical work a trainee attempts to teach a child an aspect of discrimination and generalisation.

Although each unit covers a different feature of behavioural teaching, there is a considerable overlap between them, and consequently trainees rehearse skills learned on previous units as they proceed through the workshop. For example, rewards are considered on every unit, and prompting and task analysis are dealt with on every unit after unit 3. However, the choice of the child and the task to use on a given training session is made with a particular unit in mind. In fact the choice of an appropriate child and selection of a suitable task, that is, one which is not too easy or too difficult for the child to do, are very important considerations and have a direct bearing on the success of each unit and therefore of the workshop as a whole.

From the preceding description of the units it is also clear that the workshop is mainly concerned with using behavioural teaching techniques to build up new behaviours in mentally handicapped children. Units 8 and 9, time-out and overcorrection, are the only ones concerned with the removal of undesirable behaviours. EDY is therefore mainly a positive and constructive behavioural training course, a feature which is not always evident in other behavioural training packages, many of which deal exclusively with overcoming problem behaviour.

Units 7 (Imitation) and 10 (Discrimination and Generalisation). The subjects of these units are not aspects of learning in the mentally handicapped which are tied to behavioural methods. Clearly both these skills are vital for all children's development, but are particularly crucial for children with severe learning difficulties as they find them difficult to acquire; it is for this reason that these units are included in the EDY package.

8.2.2 The Training Format

A central feature of EDY is the practical nature of the course. The Project Directors examined Bruner's (1966) model of learning, the symbolic, iconic and enactive, and considered how this might be applied to EDY. Learning in the symbolic mode consists of reading books or listening to lectures. In the iconic mode one learns through watching a film or a video tape or by observing others at work, for example, children or teachers. In the enactive mode one learns by practising new skills in as natural an environment as possible. For a course such as EDY with its emphasis on training staff in new skills, it is important to make the training as practical as possible, and consequently a great deal of the training on each unit is done in the enactive mode. Indeed Bruner's three modes of learning, the symbolic, iconic and enactive, correspond with the oft-used phrase 'I listen and I forget' (symbolic), 'I see and I remember' (iconic), 'I do and I understand' (enactive).

The training format in each unit (see Figure 8.1) illustrates the extent of the enactive learning employed in an EDY workshop. From this it can be seen that it takes a minimum of one hour to complete a unit. More time may be needed, particularly if the practical sessions are filmed and played back to the trainees.

During the first 15 minutes the trainees observe a video tape of a

Figure 8.1: EDY Course. Structure of one-hour training sessions on each unit

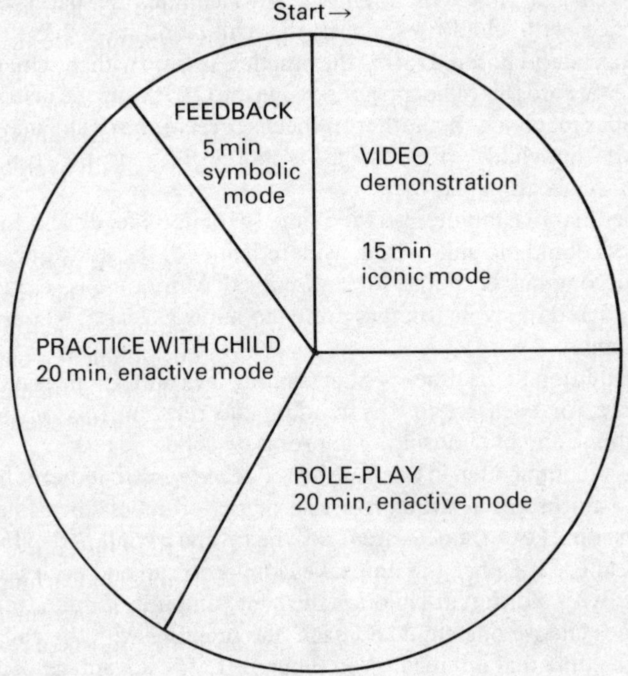

teacher working with a child using the particular behavioural teaching technique pertinent to the unit. Trainees record the child's progress using the Qualitative Behaviour Record Sheet (QBRS) (see Figure 8.3) and later in the course they may also be introduced to the Trainee Assessment Form (TAF), which is a recording device designed to rate different features of trainees' teaching techniques. Although introducing the TAF to the trainees is not an essential part of the training, it adds extra insight into behavioural teaching. (A full description of the TAF and how it is used by instructors to assess trainees' progress is given later in the chapter, Section 8.2.4.)

Following the video demonstration the trainee discusses the child and task with the instructor and role-plays the training session, either using another trainee as the child or by taking the part of the trainee and the trainee being the child. This role may be reversed in order to give the trainee practice in role-playing what is entailed in working with the child using the particular behavioural technique for a unit. Role-play is a vitally important part of each unit as it provides opportunities to ensure that such detailed features as the seating arrangements, the materials, the recording sheets and the rewards are all carefully positioned. This greatly facilitates the success of the 'practice with child' session if the child and task have been appropriately chosen. During the practical session with the child, the trainee records his or her progress using the QBRS and the instructor provides feedback. If another trainee is present, he or she may also record the child's progress using the QBRS or the trainee's performance using the TAF.

The final five minutes provide time for general feedback, for the theory behind the unit to be considered, and for the study questions that accompany each unit to be discussed. More time is frequently needed and many instructors prefer to allow at least $1\frac{1}{4}$ hours for each unit.

In addition to the time spent in training on a unit, trainees have to prepare for each session by reading the relevant section in the workbook and by choosing an appropriate child and task.

It is recommended in the *Instructors' Handbook* that there should be a ratio of one instructor to one or two trainees for a Phase 1 workshop. If two trainees are used, the format as outlined in Figure 8.1 is altered. Either the unit takes longer to run and each trainee works with a different child for the same amount of time, or both trainees choose one child and each one practises with the child for half the time that is indicated on Figure 8.1. The advantage of using

Figure 8.2: EDY Course. The Birches School Spring Term, 1982

Course Instructors: Peter Farrell, Barbara Smith

The Course will run on Monday and Friday mornings from 22 February until 26 March

Instructor	*Trainees* *Group A: 9.00–10.15 a.m.*	*Group B: 10.15–11.30 a.m.*
Barbara Smith	Jeni Clarke Jane Price	Gill Bean Carol Price
Peter Farrell	Chris Hughes June Wright	Mary Stanley Maria Tomlinson

Notes on the Course

1. At the initial meeting at 2.00 p.m. on Friday 12 February, the workbooks will be distributed and trainees will complete a 'quiz' on theoretical aspects.
2. For the practical work on each unit, trainees will work in pairs under the supervision of Barbara Smith or Peter Farrell.
3. We will discuss in general terms the child and task selection in the session prior to each unit being run. However, it is most important to plan in detail before each unit how you intend to work with your selected child in the practical sessions.
4. We intend to film trainees on units 4, 5, 6 and 7. In order to discuss the playback adequately, it will be necessary to find time during the dinner break. We will discuss details of this nearer the time.

two trainees per instructor are first that it is more economic on instructors' time, and secondly that the two trainees can provide mutual support to each other during the workshop. It is not feasible to run an EDY course successfully with more than two trainees per instructor as this cuts into the vitally important 'practice with child' time.

From the above it is clear that care needs to be taken when organising an EDY workshop. As children are required, it has to take place in school time and this means that adequate cover in the classroom has to be made for absent trainees. Figure 8.2 is an example of a timetable for an EDY course in which there were eight trainees and two instructors, namely an educational psychologist and a deputy headteacher.

In the workshop outlined in Figure 8.2, two units were covered each week over a five-week period. Boucher and Feiler (1982), who also provide a detailed timetable outlining how they trained their staff, ran their workshop completing one unit a day for two weeks. Many others have run workshops covering a unit a week for ten weeks. At the moment instructors appear to be divided as to the most successful way to run a workshop. The advantages of running units on a weekly basis are that this helps to keep the anxiety levels of the trainees down and that the materials can be assimilated adequately, particularly as it is possible for the trainees to have time to discuss aspects of the course between units and hence prepare adequately for them. The disadvantages of running units on a weekly basis are that the gap between them is too long and hence the momentum and interest in the Course can be lost. Arguments in favour of intensive EDY Courses with units being run once or twice a day over a short period are that they are much easier to organise, particularly if a large number of trainees are going through at the same time, as the disruption to the school routine is relatively short-lived.

8.2.3 Example of Training on One EDY Unit

The following is a detailed example of how training on one EDY unit (Unit 5) was run during a Phase 1 workshop.

Child — Samantha
Trainees — Chris and Jane
Instructor — Peter
Unit 5 — Task analysis
Task — To lay the table
Target behaviour — Samantha will lay one place setting (knife, fork, spoon, plate and glass)

Task analysis

Step 1. Put fork on table after demonstration
Step 2. Put fork on table, no demonstration
Step 3. Put fork and knife on table, no demonstration
Step 4. Put fork, knife and spoon on table, no demonstration
Step 5. Put fork, knife, spoon and glass on table, no demonstration
Step 6. Put fork, knife, spoon, glass and plate on table, no demonstration

(NB For all these steps the materials had to be put in the correct place on the table in relation to each other.)

Criterion of Success — Three out of three correct trials on each step
Reward — Social praise

After watching the demonstration video, the practical session was planned in detail. In the role-play Chris and Jane each had a turn at being trainee and child. This enabled them to plan the seating arrangements, to organise the materials properly and to practise teaching and recording in the most realistic way possible. A form of backward training was decided upon where the last step of the task was taught first. Therefore in Step 1 of the task analysis all the materials were arranged in the correct place except for the fork, so that when Step 1 was completed the table was set properly. In Step 2 the fork and the knife had to be placed correctly with the remaining materials being in the proper position. This process continued until Step 6, when the materials were placed at random on an adjacent tray and Samantha had to arrange them correctly on the table. Behavioural purists will have spotted that this is not in fact the correct application of the backward-training technique as this usually requires the trainee to start at the beginning of the task on each trial and the instructor demonstrates each step until the step is reached at which the child is asked to complete the task. In this case the child was presented with the partially completed task and was asked to finish it.

When the child was brought in for the start of the practice-with-child session, a baseline trial was conducted when she was asked to lay the table with the materials placed at random on the adjoining tray and no help was given by the trainees. (The baseline is of course identical to Step 6, the target behaviour.) The baseline procedure is standard practice in behavioural teaching, as from this an objective measure of how the child progresses through training can be obtained. In addition a baseline trial may reveal that the child knows all or some of the task and this can result in the task analysis being altered.

Samantha's progress during the practice-with-child session is shown on the QBRS (see Figure 8.3) which was completed by the trainees during the practice session. From the QBRS it can be seen that recording is done on a trial-by-trial basis. A score of 1 indicates that the child has failed the trial completely, a 2 shows that it was completed with a physical prompt from the trainee, a 3 indicates that a gestural or verbal prompt was needed, and a 4 shows that the trainee successfully completed the trial without any prompts. On this session three 4s are required before the child can move on to the next step.

The completed QBRS shows that:

(1) On the baseline trial Samantha could not do the task. In fact the video of this session showed that Samantha just idly fiddled with the material.
(2) Chris was the trainee for the start of the session and Jane took over on trial 19.
(3) Samantha made rapid progress until the final step when she needed eight trials before reaching criterion.

Although in this session Samantha was trained to lay the table, it has to be remembered that in Phase 1 the training is done out of context and there would be no guarantee that learning would be generalised to other settings. Secondly the criterion of success (three out of three successful trials) is not very demanding and a much stricter criterion would need to be set in the context of the school or home, in order to be sure that learning had been established. These two points apply to all the Units and it is therefore important for instructors to discuss the application of EDY techniques in the classroom and in other contexts.

8.2.4 The Assessment of Trainees

In order to pass Phase 1 of the course and therefore qualify for a certificate from the University of Manchester, trainees must have taken part in each unit and have practised the techniques with children on all of them except for Unit 9. In addition they complete a quiz, the pre-test, on theoretical aspects of the course before reading the materials and they do this again after Unit 10, the post-test. They are also assessed by their instructor on the Trainee Assessment Form (TAF) on Unit 3 and on Unit 10.

The TAF is a scaled-down version of a rating scale known as the Behaviour Assessment Form for Learning Evaluation (BAFFLE: Kiernan and Riddick, 1973). It is designed to measure the following features of behavioural teaching which are central to the EDY Course: 'prepares child', 'presents task', 'prompting', and 'rewards'. 'Prepares child' refers to the trainee's ability to ensure that the child is attending prior to each trial of the training session. 'Presents task' refers to the clarity with which the child is asked to complete a task,

Figure 8.3: Completed QBRS

Date Feb, 1983 Unit 5

QUALITATIVE BEHAVIOUR RECORD SHEET

Child: Samantha Trainee: Chris/Jane

Behaviour: Samantha will lay one place setting

STEP		TRIALS (Chris: 1–18; Jane: 19–30)																													
No.	Steps - Description	1	2	3	4	5	6	7	8	9	10	11	12	13	14	15	16	17	18	19	20	21	22	23	24	25	26	27	28	29	30
–	BASELINE	1																													
1	Fork in place (Demonstration)		2	2	4	4	4																								
2	Fork in place							4	4	4																					
3	Fork + Knife in place										3	3	4	4	4																
4	Fork, Knife and spoon in place															3	4	4	4												
5	Fork, Knife, spoon and glass in place																			3	4	4	4								
6	Fork, Knife, spoon glass + plate in place																							3	1	4	4	2	4	4	4

Score Key:
- 0 – No response
- 1 – Incorrect response
- 2 – Poor approximation
- 3 – Good approximation
- 4 – Excellent approximation

Comments:
1. Use Backward Training
2. Criterion of Success

3/3 unprompted trials on each step

Figure 8.4: Trainee Assessment Form

TRAINEE. Chris/Jane .... DATE. Feb. 1983.
RATER. P.T.F. .... V.T. NO. ——........
CHILD. Samantha ...... UNIT. 5 ....

TASK
To lay one place setting
STEPS
1. Fork (Demo.)
2. Fork
3. Fork + knife
4. Fork, knife + spoon
5. Fork, knife, spoon + cup
6. Fork, knife, spoon, cup + plate

SCORING
4 = Excellent Response
3 = Good Response
2 = Approximately Correct
1 = Incorrect Response
0 = No Response
– = Irrelevant

REWARDS/PROMPTS/CRITERION/ETC. .... Social Rewards, criterion 3/3 ....

Chris | Jane

RATING CATEGORIES	1	2	3	4	5	6	7	8	9	10	11	12	13	14	15	16	17	18	19	20	21	22	23	24	25	26	27	28	29	30	No. of Trials	Score	%
(Baseline/Steps — Trials)																															(Data Summary)		
A. PREPARES CHILD FOR TASK	0	–	–	–	–	–	–	–	–	4	–	–	–	–	4	–	–	–	4	–	–	–	4	–	–	–	–	–	–	–	5	16	60
B. PRESENTS TASK (demo, instruction, step)	3	4	4	4	4	4	4	3	3	4	4	4	4	4	4	4	4	4	4	4	4	4	4	4	4	4	4	4	4	4	30	117	97.5
C. PROMPTS (physical, gestural, verbal)	–	3	4	–	–	–	–	–	–	4	4	–	–	–	4	–	–	–	4	–	–	–	4	0	–	–	3	–	–	–	9	30	83.3
D. CHILD'S RESPONSE (30 | 107 | 89.1)	1	2	2	4	4	4	4	4	4	3	3	4	4	4	3	4	4	4	3	4	4	4	3	1	4	4	2	4	4	4			
E. REWARDS	2	3	2	3	4	4	4	2	3	4	3	4	4	3	4	4	4	4	4	3	4	3	4	1	4	4	4	4	4	4	30	100	83.3

'prompting' refers to the trainee's ability to use physical, gestural and verbal prompts appropriately, and 'rewarding' refers to the trainee's ability to use rewards appropriately on each trial. In addition to these categories there is space on the TAF to record the child's response on each trial. All TAF categories are rated on a four-point scale, and detailed guidelines as to its use are provided in the *Instructors' Handbook* (McBrien and Foxen, 1981). Figure 8.4 is an example of the completed TAF for the session that was described in Section 8.2.3. Inspection of this reveals the following points. First, the 'prepares child' category was only needed at the start of each new step of the task, indicating that Samantha co-operated well during the session. Secondly, the trainees presented the task well to the child on each trial. Thirdly the prompting category was hardly needed, but on trial 24 the trainee should have prompted but didn't. Fourthly the trainees rewarded Samantha well but Jane's scores were slightly better than Chris's for this category.

In order to pass Phase 1 and hence qualify for a certificate from the University of Manchester, trainees have to obtain a score of at least 50 per cent on the quiz post-test and an average TAF score of 65 per cent or more on Unit 10. Typically trainees do much better than this, nursery nurses achieving an average pre-test score on the quiz of 10 per cent and an average post-test score of 70 per cent, whereas for teachers these figures are 25 per cent and 82 per cent, respectively. On the TAF on Unit 3 the mean score for both groups of trainees is 80 per cent and on Unit 10 it is 95 per cent, for all categories taken together. As instructors only request certificates from trainees who pass Phase 1, no figures exist concerning those who fail, but it is likely that this number is extremely small. So far nearly 3000 certificates have been issued and this number is increasing all the time.

8.2.5 Phases 2 and 3

In Phase 1, staff who worked with mentally handicapped children are trained to improve their behavioural teaching techniques in unfamiliar surroundings, e.g. a resource room, and in the presence of an instructor and possibly a video camera. In Phases 2 and 3 staff have to apply these techniques in the context of a classroom.

Planning for Phase 2 normally begins on completion of Unit 10 and guidelines are included in the trainee workbook. In this Phase the trainee selects a child in his or her class and plans a detailed teaching programme under the supervision of the instructor. This programme should be relevant to the child's overall curricular needs and should therefore be an important aspect of his or her education. All the techniques that the trainee acquired in Phase 1 are brought together and used in planning and running the programme. Hence in Phase 2 the trainee will set target behaviours accurately, carry out baseline assessments, plan a task analysis, set a criterion of success, use prompting and rewards, and record the child's progress on the QBRS. In addition, time-out, imitation, discrimination and generalisation may also be used depending on the child and on the precise programme. Having planned the programme carefully the trainee carries it out daily in his or her classroom. The instructor will supervise the programme regularly and hopefully observe the trainee working with the child at least once a week.

In Phase 3, trainees plan and carry out detailed teaching programmes with little or no support from their instructor, and indeed at this stage it is hoped that the techniques will become adopted permanently by the trainees.

As mentioned previously, Phase 2 and 3 programmes employ a much stricter criterion of success than is used in Phase 1; for example, a criterion of five out of five successful trials every day for a week on each step is not uncommon. In addition it is strongly suggested that trainees set target behaviours which should be attainable within about four weeks. Programmes which take longer than this to complete can result in the child and trainee becoming disheartened.

The detailed way in which Phases 2 and 3 are implemented is to some extent dependent on the number and availability of instructors in a school, on their ability to supervise the programmes properly and on the number of other staff in the school who have already completed EDY training. These and other issues related to the long-term implementation of EDY techniques in a school are discussed later in the chapter.

8.2.6 The Skills of EDY-trained Staff

Trainees who have successfully completed Phases 1, 2 and 3 should regularly use the following techniques as part of their teaching.

(1) They should have a commitment to, and actually carry out, individual teaching sessions on a regular basis on key areas from the curriculum with all children in their care.
(2) Target behaviours should be stated clearly as behavioural objectives and criteria of success should be set.
(3) Task analyses should be carried out on the target behaviours that

are appropriate, both for the task and for the children.

(4) The individual teaching should be carried out on a trial-by-trial basis.

(5) Children's progress should be recorded on each trial on the QBRS or on something similar.

(6) Staff should prepare children, present tasks, prompt and reward correctly. Therefore, if rated on the Trainee Assessment Form (TAF) by an instructor, their scores would be well over 65 per cent, the minimum level for passing Phase 1.

(7) Shaping, imitation training, discrimination and generalisation should be used appropriately when planning for and carrying out individual teaching.

(8) Similarly, time-out, as practised on Unit 8, should be used as and when needed.

Although one might hope that EDY-trained staff will generalise some of the skills to group teaching, as EDY Phases 1, 2 and 3 do not cover this area one can hardly judge the implementation of the techniques on whether they are used when staff are working with a group of children. In addition, as overcorrection has come in for some criticism, its use in managing difficult children should not be viewed as something EDY-trained staff would automatically want to do.

8.3 Evaluations of EDY

8.3.1 Phase 1

The previous chapter considered issues in the evaluation of behavioural training packages in some detail, and it also referred to the formal evaluation of EDY. In this section EDY evaluation studies are briefly described and their implications considered.

Although the method by which trainees can qualify for certificates, namely a score of at least 50 per cent on the quiz post-test and cf over 65 per cent on the TAF on Unit 10, provides a measure of the evaluation of their performance, from the empirical standpoint there are weaknesses in this approach, even if in addition (as occurs in most EDY courses) the trainees complete a questionnaire concerning their views on different features of the course. These weaknesses exist firstly because the TAF ratings on Units 3 and 10 are almost invariably completed by the instructors who may well have a vested interest in seeing that their trainees do well. Secondly, although data from the quiz provide objective evidence about what the trainees have learned on a course, there is conflicting evidence as to whether they apply their newly acquired knowledge in their practical work. Carr (1980) found a positive correlation between scores on theoretical tests and practical performance, whereas Watson and Uzzell (1980) found no such relationship. Thirdly, as Carr (1980) points out, completed questionnaires about a course frequently contain positive remarks, and although this is pleasing for the course organisers, it does not necessarily mean that the trainees have learned anything or that they will use the behavioural techniques in their work.

In the light of these limitations to the standard evaluation of EDY, four formal studies have been conducted, each one employing the following methodology with minor modifications (see Barrowclough, 1981; Farrell, 1982; Farrell and Sugden, 1984; and McBrien and Edmonds, in press).

Prior to trainees attending a workshop, they were filmed working with a child on an unfamiliar task. This was repeated immediately after the course and between 7 weeks and 14 months later. They were filmed in a quiet room for between 5 and 10 minutes. The video tapes were randomly arranged and shown to trained independent raters who therefore did not know whether the trainees were classroom teachers or classroom assistants, nor which occasion they were rating. The rating scale used was a modified version of the TAF in that 'presents task', 'prompts' and 'rewards' were retained, and a further TAF score was given for 'task analysis' — the raters scoring this on completion of each separate tape. In addition to this procedure the trainees on all of the workshops that were evaluated completed the quiz and a questionnaire about the course.

In Farrell's study, where five classroom teachers and five nursery nurses were trained over a 2-week period by an educational psychologist and a deputy headteacher, teachers made significant gains in their behavioural teaching skills which were maintained after a 7-week follow-up whereas the nursery nurses made small and insignificant gains which were not maintained. Barrowclough evaluated the performance of four class teachers who were trained by a different educational psychologist and deputy headteacher over 5 weeks, and found that as a group they made significant gains which were maintained after 10 weeks. Farrell and Sugden evaluated an EDY course in which eight nursery nurses were trained by a deputy headteacher and an educational psychologist over a 5-week period, and in this case the trainees made significant gains which were maintained and enhanced after a 10-week period. McBrien and Edmonds evaluated an EDY course in which four class teachers were trained over a ten-week period by a clinical psychologist, and in this case the trainees made significant gains in their behavioural teaching which were maintained after 14 months. This study also contained a control group which received no EDY training but which was filmed at the same time as the experimental group, and their behavioural teaching skills remained the same. At the follow-up stage the experimental group, as well as being filmed working on their own with a child, were also filmed working with a child in the classroom and their scores on the TAF in this setting were much higher than on all other occasions.

Although there were some minor differences between studies in the way the rating was carried out and in the way inter-rater reliabilities were calculated, these reliabilities were consistently high and demonstrated that the TAF is a reliable rating instrument.

In the studies of Farrell, Barrowclough, and Farrell and Sugden, two instructors (an educational psychologist and a deputy headteacher) were used. The results showed that there was no difference in the trainees' scores between those trained by the psychologist and those trained by the deputy headteacher. In all of these studies the trainees' scores on the quiz immediately following the EDY course were all well above 50 per cent and consistent with scores obtained by trainees trained on other courses. It was interesting that in Farrell and Sugden's study, as well as completing the quiz immediately following the EDY course, the trainees also completed it after 10 weeks, when the final filming session took place, and their scores fell off significantly from an average of 84.25 per cent to 59.12 per cent. However, there was no corresponding fall off in their practical skills, hence confirming the findings of Watson and Uzzell (1980) in respect of the tenuous link between theoretical knowledge and practical skills.

The study of McBrien and Edmonds is the only one that filmed class teachers in the classroom, albeit on the final occasion — the 14-month follow-up. However, the fact that the trainees did far better in this setting suggests that all the studies may have underestimated the trainees' skills by always filming them in unfamiliar surroundings. But the small number of trainees used in the studies and the fact that McBrien and Edmonds did not film the staff in the classroom on the other occasions makes conclusions of this kind extremely tenuous.

Although the number of trainees used in these studies is comparatively small, the findings as regard class teachers are reasonably consistent and strongly indicate that their behavioural teaching skills do improve as a result of EDY training, and that these skills are maintained on follow-up. The fact that the teachers in Edmonds' study maintained their skills after 14 months is particularly encouraging, especially as this group had not completed Phase 2.

Classroom assistants appear not to be quite so successful. There were only five classroom assistants in Farrell's study and they received an intensive two-week EDY course which many reported was quite stressful. In addition, all the staff in the school were trained in that fortnight. Consequently the trainees did not volunteer for the course and hence their motivation to succeed may not have been so high as for other trainees. In Farrell and Sugden's study the trainees were all volunteers and the training took place over a five-week period. These factors may have contributed to the classroom assistants doing better in that study. Even so, the degree of significance only reached the 0.5 level as compared with 0.01 for teachers. Therefore teachers do appear to improve their practical skills to a greater extent than classroom assistants after undergoing Phase 1. Informal feedback gathered from EDY instructors has suggested that classroom assistants find the theoretical component of the course difficult to assimilate, and, furthermore, in-service training of staff is traditionally reserved for teachers and consequently classroom assistants may find the whole process rather daunting. However, more research is needed before one can arrive at more definitive conclusions, as the number of classroom assistants involved in these studies is quite small.

8.3.2 Phase 2

In regard to the evaluation of Phase 2, accounts from instructors around the country consistently report successful outcomes in terms of children learning new skills (see Farrell 1985). Although this is heartening, it has to be said that these accounts by no means correspond to a formal evaluation of Phase 2 as there has been little or no objective and independent verification of the success of the programmes. To date, a study by Davies (1983) represents the first formal attempt to evaluate Phase 2.

Davies's study took place in a hostel for children who are mentally handicapped. This was the first time that any of its staff had been trained in EDY techniques. Four staff, the experimental group, received a standard Phase 1 course and then embarked on their Phase 2. At the same time four further staff, the control group, also ran a Phase 2 programme. The children and tasks in both groups were selected by the staff under the guidance of the instructor. Both groups were helped to pick a task that was appropriate for the child and that he or she might be expected to learn in approximately 5 weeks. However, the control group were given no further assistance whereas the experimental group were given regular support from the instructor along the lines suggested in the workbook.

Both groups were filmed on two occasions, once at the start of the programme and once at the end. It was therefore possible to gain an objective assessment of how each child performed on their Phase 2 programme and to see how this was related to the trainees' skills. As in previous studies, the video tapes were randomly arranged and shown to two independent and trained raters.

The results of this study were not very clear cut and it is hard to draw firm conclusions from them. One quite unforeseen difficulty occurred when one of the trainees in the experimental group had to abandon her Phase 2 programme owing to the sudden and tragic death of the client with whom she was working. This made the findings somewhat unbalanced and rendered it meaningless to apply formal statistical procedures to them.

However, broadly speaking as regards the trainees' practical skills, the experimental group performed better than the control group on the TAF. This confirms the results of the previous studies. In regard to the progress that children had made when filmed on the second occasion, of the three children in the experimental group who completed Phase 2, one child completed the task, another child was about halfway through and the third child did not complete it. In the control group, one child completed the task and the remaining three children failed to do so, although one trainee was convinced that her child had learned the task but had an 'off day' when he was filmed.

There are clearly considerable methodological weaknesses with this study, which Davies (1983) explores fully. The central problems concern the near impossibility of selecting equally appropriate tasks for all the children. It was never entirely fair to expect to find eight tasks which the children could reasonably learn within the 5-week duration of the Phase 2 programme. Another major problem was the fact that the staff were not working in a school, and, as residential workers, had other pressing duties to perform. Consequently some of them found it difficult to find time to work with the child and this was exacerbated by the staff shift system and a certain amount of staff absenteeism in the hostel. Consequently the children received different amounts of instruction during their Phase 2 programmes. Finally, the logistic arrangements within the hostel made it impossible to match the two groups of staff and as a result there was an imbalance as two staff in the control group had recently attended a course on individual programme planning with handicapped children whereas none of the other staff had received training of this sort.

There is no doubt that there are considerable methodological factors to take into account when embarking on formal evaluations of Phase 2. However, the status of the EDY training package would be greatly enhanced if these could be conducted and hence accompany the anecdotal accounts of the success of Phase 2 that already exist (see Farrell, 1985).

8.4 EDY in the United Kingdom

8.4.1 Factors Affecting Implementation

Judging from the number of EDY workshops that are being run, from the way the materials are selling, and from the number of certificates that have been and still are being requested, EDY has had a great impact in the UK. However, this may not be a sufficient criterion on which to judge whether or not the techniques have been successfully applied in schools. Nevertheless, the chapters in the book of the 1983 Conference (Farrell, 1985) contain the results of formal surveys and more informal accounts of the application of EDY throughout the UK. In addition the participants at the Conference completed a questionnaire on this topic, and Project Impact, based at HARC, has started to conduct a more thorough nationwide survey. Consequently a lot is already known about the factors within schools that affect the successful long-term implementation of EDY techniques, and some of these are now discussed.

(a) EDY is School-focused. A great many in-service training (INSET) courses for teachers are run in teachers' centres, colleges or universities. Usually only a few teachers from a school attend, and

consequently it is difficult for them to return to their school and use their new-found knowledge and skills to substantially change the way they work or the work of their colleagues. The fact that EDY courses are run in schools and in school time and that all staff, teachers and nursery nurses are involved are factors that affect the successful long-term implementation of the techniques. Indeed other courses have now adopted a school-focused model, for example BAT-PACK (Wheldall *et al.*, 1982) and SNAP (Ainscow and Muncey, 1984).

Furthermore, the active support of the headteacher in encouraging staff to be EDY trained, in facilitating the organisation of workshops, and in ensuring that Phase 2 programmes are carried out adequately is also crucial in ensuring EDY's success.

(b) The Course Itself. Since the inception of the project, trainees have consistently reported that several features of the EDY package are related to its successful implementation. These are, first, the practical emphasis of the course which involves live supervision of trainees during Phases 1 and 2; secondly, the intensive nature of the training, which necessitates a ratio of one instructor to only one or two trainees; thirdly, the obvious relevance of the course to teaching children who are mentally handicapped; and, finally, the planned opportunity to maintain and generalise techniques through Phases 2 and 3.

(c) Senior Staff as Instructors. Although the initial aim of the project was to train educational psychologists and advisers as instructors, in view of the limited time that they could give to schools for children with severe learning difficulties (for educational psychologists usually no more than one visit a week, and for advisers much less than this), it was not possible for all staff in schools to be trained within a short space of time. In addition, educational psychologists in particular have other roles to perform when they visit schools for children with severe learning difficulties (Farrell, in press) and running EDY courses is only one of them. These roles include the formal assessment of children prior to their placement, and reviewing their progress when they are 13 years old: these functions are mandated under the terms of the 1981 Special Education Act. In addition they assess children just before they leave school and they give advice to parents and teachers concerning the management of children who may present particular problems of learning and/or

behaviour. They may be involved in discussions about the curriculum or about the setting up of special facilities in schools, e.g. behavioural units, and finally by their regular presence in a school they can give general support and encouragement to all staff who work there.

In view of these other important roles for educational psychologists who visit schools for children with severe learning difficulties, many have now 'given away' their EDY instructor skills by training senior teachers as instructors, and they in turn have trained other staff. Consequently in some schools there exists a pool of two or three senior staff who are EDY instructors and who run the EDY courses for the staff in the school. EDY training therefore becomes an ongoing feature of staff development and the psychologists may only be used in a consultative capacity.

A further consequence of this development is that it enables senior staff to supervise and support their junior colleagues on professional issues, and hence they are using their acknowledged expertise as skilled practitioners to good effect and their role becomes much more than one of checking on staff absences, on equipment and on timetable matters. Therefore the training of senior staff as EDY instructors has been one of the most promising results of the EDY project.

(d) EDY and the Curriculum. EDY is concerned with training staff to develop behavioural teaching techniques when working with children who have severe learning difficulties, that is, with *how* to teach them. It does not consider any aspects of the curriculum that children should receive, that is, *what* to teach them. Obviously questions relating to how and what to teach children with severe learning difficulties are equally important when planning for their total education. Alongside the development of EDY in the UK a great deal has been written about the development of the curriculum for children with special educational needs (Burman *et al.*, 1983; Gardner *et al.*, 1983; Coupe and Porter, 1985) and EDY users have consistently stated that unless the school has developed a clearly defined objectives-based curriculum, then it is virtually impossible to consistently apply EDY techniques. Conversely, it is very difficult to teach an objectives-based curriculum if the staff are not EDY trained. EDY and the curriculum are thus complementary and both are needed for a school to run satisfactorily.

(e) Classroom Management. In addition to EDY being unrelated to the curriculum, Phases 1, 2 and 3 are also unrelated to aspects of classroom management as these Phases of the course deal exclusively with using behavioural teaching techniques in one-to-one teaching. Obviously, as there are about eight to ten children per class in a school for children with severe learning difficulties, even with the aid of a nursery nurse, only two children can receive one-to-one teaching at any given moment. Indeed the remainder of the children will need supervision, and hence it is likely that only one member of staff will be able to do one-to-one teaching. Consequently staff in a classroom need to plan their teaching very carefully to ensure that the children receive sufficient one-to-one instruction in the basic areas of the curriculum; that they are usefully employed when they are not being taught individually; and that sufficient out-of-class experiences, for example educational visits, are offered to meet the children's needs in these areas. With ten children in a class, and with a teacher and a nursery nurse, it takes a relatively simple calculation to work out the amount of one-to-one teaching each child can possibly receive in a day. In one school, when all the additional timetabling considerations were accounted for, it was calculated that each child could receive a maximum of 15 minutes a day of individual work (Boucher, 1985). The need to make most use of the time when children are not in individual teaching sessions is therefore obvious, and classroom management techniques attempt to achieve this.

Classroom management, Phase 4 of EDY, is based on the early work of Porterfield and Blunden (1978) and is widely used in some schools. Staff are allocated the following specific clearly defined roles. One member undertakes to do individual teaching, another (the mover) deals with interruptions and accidents that may occur in the classroom, and the third (the manager) ensures that the remainder of the children are productively engaged in useful tasks. The manager therefore has the key role in reinforcing children who are on task and in prompting those who are not. In addition, the manager needs to ensure that sufficient materials are available to keep the children occupied during the classroom management period. Thomas (1985) provides a detailed account of how to run classroom management sessions. Many EDY instructors now include a session on classroom management in their Phase 1 workshops, as the successful use of this approach may directly affect the implementation of Phases 2 and 3, in addition to the long-term permanent implementation of EDY techniques in schools.

In summary, therefore, EDY has to be seen in the wider educational context of a school for severe learning difficulties. A carefully organised objectives-based curriculum and regular implementation of classroom management techniques are also vital ingredients for the successful education of these children. However, the process is greatly facilitated if senior staff are trained as EDY instructors and if EDY is given active support from the headteacher.

8.4.2 Future Developments

Although EDY users have consistently made favourable comments about the training package and have provided valuable insights concerning factors that affect the implementation of EDY techniques, they have also made suggestions for improvements. These suggestions refer almost exclusively to Phase 1, and although a great many different and overlapping ideas have been put forward, the following are most commonly stated. First, some instructors have complained that the theory in the *Trainee Workbook* is too complicated, particularly for Units 1 and 10, and that nursery nurses find this difficult to digest and anxiety-invoking. Secondly, Unit 8 (time-out) and especially Unit 9 (overcorrection) have attracted considerable criticism, partly because they are 'punishment' units and hence are out of keeping with the rest of the workshop, and partly because the techniques, particularly overcorrection, are poorly researched and evaluated and may be of little use in the classroom. Thirdly, some instructors have criticised the demonstration video tape, partly because the teachers do not record and hence provide an inappropriate model, and also because the TAF ratings of the video that are included in the *Instructors' Handbook* are thought to be too generous.

As a result of these criticisms a new and revised edition is being prepared which should be available in 1986. This will include an adult version, as EDY is being increasingly used in adult settings — in particular in hospitals: see, for example, Knight *et al.* (1985) — and the existing materials and video were only designed to be used in schools. Perhaps it is a measure of the success of EDY that instructors have found the existing materials to be of some use in adult contexts.

Although formal evaluations of EDY have been carried out (Barrowclough, 1981; Farrell, 1982; Farrell and Sugden, 1984; McBrien and Edmonds, 1985) and some of these are referred to in the previous chapter, there is still a need for more work to be done. Indeed, Project Impact based at HARC and referred to earlier has begun this process by asking instructors and trainees to complete a more detailed questionnaire. From this, more extensive knowledge related to the relevant school factors that affect the implementation of EDY will be obtained. In addition it is hoped that more research into specific areas of Phase 1 can be conducted, particularly on the relative success of intensive EDY courses, where the units were covered in two weeks, compared with courses where the training is completed over a 10-week period (one unit a week). In addition it would be valuable to compare the success of courses that are run by instructors who were trained by senior teachers and those who were trained by psychologists. There is also a need for additional formal evaluations of Phase 2.

When the materials were published in self-instructional form (Foxen and McBrien, 1981; McBrien and Foxen, 1981), this signalled the end of formal instructor courses being run at HARC. Of course many existing instructors have trained further staff as instructors, and others have trained themselves (although no exact figures are available concerning the number of self-trained instructors). However, considering the number of enquiries that are still sent to HARC, it seems that there is a demand for more instructor courses to be run and it is likely that one or two will take place every year.

8.5 Conclusion

EDY has been a great success in the United Kingdom, and the fact that requests for Certificates are still coming at the rate of 12 a week, that there is pressure for more instructor courses and that a revised edition is being planned is evidence of this success. Furthermore, the surveys and accounts of the implementation of EDY which are reported in the book of the 1983 Conference (Farrell, 1985a), and other reports from instructors and trainees are in general very positive about the training and about the long-term impact that EDY has had in schools. The formal evaluations of EDY which are referred to briefly in this chapter and also in the previous one suggest that class teachers and, to a lesser extent, classroom assistants can improve their behavioural teaching following EDY training, although more research is still needed to reinforce this finding, particularly in regard to the long-term maintenance of the techniques in the classroom.

EDY may also have had other spin-offs in terms of the way education is planned for children with severe learning difficulties in addition to the intended effect of systematically training staff in behavioural teaching methods. First, the inclusion of nursery nurses as trainees has greatly enhanced their status in schools and has taken them beyond a 'caring' role. This has had other repercussions in the way teachers and nursery nurses define their respective roles, since, if both are trained and experienced users of behavioural teaching methods, why do teachers deserve the greater salary and better conditions of service? Although there are some indications that this can be a problem in a few schools, in many others, teachers can justify their superior status as they generally take on responsibility for the overall management of the class, for choosing teaching objectives for the children and in planning the overall curriculum, often in consultation with other teachers. Secondly, as has been mentioned earlier, in those schools where senior teachers have become instructors, school-based INSET is now a permanent feature of the way a school is run and this ensures that senior staff pass on their skills by being supportive to more junior staff. Thirdly, for those schools whose curriculum is poorly developed, EDY has acted as an impetus for staff to make progress in this direction, as it quickly became apparent that it is not possible to apply newly acquired individual teaching techniques to an absent curriculum. Fourthly, EDY has sparked off a general debate on the most effective way to organise schools and classrooms so that behavioural teaching can become a fully integrated part of school life. Finally, EDY, especially at the start of the project, has had an effect on the role of educational psychologists in schools as it provided a ready-made INSET package which gave them a more varied, and possibly more valued, role. This also was a starting point for senior staff being trained as instructors.

It is likely that, with the onset of the revised edition (which will probably correspond with further instructor courses being run), EDY will become a permanent feature of the school-focused training of all staff who work with children with severe learning difficulties. Furthermore, it is probable that similar large-scale developments will take place in the adult sector. The next few years may therefore see exciting developments and improvements in the EDY training package.

9 SUMMARY AND DISCUSSION: 'GIVING PSYCHOLOGY AWAY' — AN INTEGRATION

9.1 Introduction

This concluding chapter brings together the research we have considered in order to highlight some of the main issues in training behaviour therapists. Broadly speaking, these include instructional methods, evaluative procedures and the implementation problems entailed by training. So far we have discussed them with respect to parents, nurses and teachers. We will now integrate the research to offer an overview of mediator training. This is a relatively rare perspective, since supervisors have tended to refer to the literature within their own areas rather than drawing on the potentially relevant work of their colleagues in others. One might equally well add that the research on mediator training has itself been somewhat isolated from more general issues, such as the instruction of supervisors and the experimental status of the work in relation to the general field of behaviour therapy.

It is consistent with the emphasis which we have placed on the *context* of events to relate therapist training to some of these broader professional issues. This may help us to understand the relative status of the research and some of the problems it faces. We will begin by discussing a theme that has recurred throughout the book, namely the role of the supervisor in the triadic or 'consultative' model of service development. This leads us to consider training methods reflexively, that is, as a basis for the learning of both supervisor and mediator. An integral element in such a development is the corrective feedback which such an evaluation can provide. This perspective remains valid in the 'quadratic model', where the supervisor influences the mediator through a 'programme designer', 'behavioural engineer' or similarly titled professional aid. The only important distinction lies in the additional evaluation made necessary by the fourth agent (Bernstein, 1982).

All the consultative models share a risk of 'superstitious supervision', namely the development of supervisor activities that are irrelevant to training but which, because of inadequate feedback, remain in use. We begin by considering this problem.

In the following section we will consider some of the major mediator problems, as encountered by those applying the triadic model in complex environments. This is clearly a topic worthy of greater research attention and one that will tax our current methodology. Some promising ideas are reviewed which may develop the mediator's role. Next we consider issues affecting the trainee, such as needs assessments, before proceeding to discuss all those agents in terms of the requirements for future research.

9.2 'Superstitious Supervision'

Psychotherapy has a long and undistinguished scientific history, notable for the passing fads and fancies of various quacks and therapists. The results of their efforts owed more to such non-specific factors as the effects of invoking gods and evicting demons than to any specific therapeutic procedure. Often, both the therapist's and client's imaginations were actively involved. Lawrence (1910) refers to the 'many professional healers . . . of whom some were honest and believed themselves to be endowed with supernatural powers like certain magnetisers, and who used suggestion without knowing it'. For the client's part, Lawrence pointed out that 'if a verbal charm is to cure a physical ailment, the patient must first form a mental conception of the cure, and believe in the charm's efficacy'. However, Lawrence goes on to conclude that 'faith in healing spells of human devising is sometimes cruelly misplaced'.

We may be amused in retrospect by the gullibility of clients and the beliefs of therapists. In fact there exist numerous contemporary parallels for this state of affairs. These may be observed in many walks of life, where the same conditions of ignorance and time-honoured custom prevail, usually because of insufficient information or motivation to change. For instance, one of the most traditional and popular means of achieving a therapeutic effect is to consume alcohol. Indeed, the process of preparing alcoholic drinks can itself illustrate just how superstitious we can become in our attempts to develop therapeutic devices. Champagne, for example, has been prepared following principles evolved over hundreds of years, involving bottling the wine before the second fermentation is finished, so that some of the natural carbon dioxide given off during fermentation is trapped in the bottle. This basic process is accompanied by ritual activities that were thought to be essential to the process, such as having expert *remeurs* who turned the bottles a fraction of an inch each day during the wine's maturation to encourage the sediment to move to the top of the bottle for later removal. Furthermore, these *remeurs* were regarded as acquiring their special touch by heredity, so that training became a secondary issue. But on scientific analysis, introduced by the American technological revolution in wine-making, such activities were found to be either irrelevant or replaceable by more efficient mechanical procedures. In short, the behaviour of the traditional wine producers was partly 'superstitious' — the behaviours they regarded as crucial to the sparkling outcome were subsequently shown to be functionally unrelated. (During my own training I usually gave my supervisors a bottle of champagne in recognition of all their help, although at the time the symbolism of this gesture had not yet occurred to me!)

Though it may be harsh to regard these beliefs as 'cruelly misplaced', in the sense that Lawrence refers to primitive psychotherapy, readers may like to consider how much of our own behaviour is as superstitious as that of the *remeur*. We are particularly concerned here with the extent to which therapist training is amenable to this parallel: how much time do supervisors spend engaged in 'superstitious' behaviour which they mistakenly believe is an important part of the training process? Let us now consider this question in more detail.

In Skinner's classic experiment (1948) a pigeon was reinforced without being required to emit a given response, such as the customary pecking of coloured discs. As a result, the pigeon developed a number of apparently bizarre or ritualistic behaviours, such as turning round in circles and wing-flapping. These activities were designated as 'superstitious' by Skinner because they were not related to reinforcement, although one might conjecture that the pigeon believed they were important. This superstition was developed and sustained by 'accidental' relationship between behaviours and outcomes which directly parallels the circumstances surrounding the behaviours of primitive psychotherapists or those of traditional champagne producers. The circumstances include one key factor, namely the weak relationship between process and outcome. This is an understandable state of affairs, since on the one hand the processes are complex and on the other the 'goods' still seem to be produced. Under these circumstances it is not surprising that we leave traditional practices well alone. However, as the American champagne producers have shown, we *can* improve our efficiency without jeopardising the end-product.

The process of training also involves a number of traditional and poorly researched variables, including the subjects, the supervisor, the training methods and the content of training. Furthermore, the triadic model involves these variables in the relationships between supervisor and mediator, as well as between mediator and trainee. A comprehensive account of the training process would incorporate information on these variables and relate them to the obtained effects of training. At the very least we need to specify the relevant basic information in research reports. Failing this, we invite those who attempt to replicate our work to engage in superstitious behaviour, free-associating their attempts with general terms such as 'role-play', 'staff' and 'reinforcement principles'. The problem is that the vagueness of these terms does not prevent trainers from earning their reinforcement, usually in the form of a 'thank you' from grateful mediators. This is a problem because such expressions of gratitude may be better explained by reference to the escape experienced by nurses, teachers or parents from their respective settings. That is, they are not necessarily attributable to the training process itself, but, made to feel good, the superstitious supervisors may continue to do what they've always done.

An amusing perspective on this issue has been presented by Potter (1981), who enumerated several ploys and strategems relevant to the part of the mediator in order to divert the supervisor from recognising that his training skills are ineffective and that no work is being done. Although Potter's article referred to academic supervision, the lessons are germane to training. For one thing, they make us consider the mediator's contribution to superstitious supervision. Potter's mockery of the supervisee-supervisor relationship included 'BBCmanship', which meant blinding the supervisor with science, and 'Graphmanship', which referred to the rule that no matter how much you have written during a rare burst of effort, make sure you only show half of it to your supervisor at any one time. Potter concluded by urging the pioneers of superviseeship to continue developing efficient counterploys or else suffer the terrible fate of having to work flat out every week!

No doubt behaviour therapy mediators have also developed ploys to camouflage their true activities. One common example is the use of self-report as the preferred form of feedback to supervisors. This can lead to errors in reporting the events occurring between mediator and trainee: Muslin *et al.* (1981) reported errors of the order of 40 per cent in terms of both the omissions and commissions reported by mediators, in contrast to an objective video tape recording. Thus, supervisors who base their supervision on self-report data are falling for a bit of Potter's 'superviseeship'.

One solution to this 'superstition trap' is to develop through objective evaluation clearly specified training programmes, of which the outstanding example is the supervisor's manual. This can provide details of how supervisors conduct training programmes, thereby increasing the consistency between supervisors. Unfortunately, manuals accompanying research reports are very much the exception rather than the rule. A complementary and more rigorous solution is to observe the behaviour of supervisors and relate this to the outcomes. For instance, teachers' personality variables have long been regarded as important and have led to precise observational procedures, such as the one developed by Flanders (1970). Using techniques such as 'micro-teaching', the teacher can improve the effective elements in their repertoire and eliminate the superstitious ones.

Let us now consider the superstition issue in terms of the main considerations of the supervisors, mediators, training methods and course contents.

(a) 'Supervisor Supervision'

This kind of analysis has rarely been extended to the training of supervisors, since research has traditionally focused on the behaviour of either mediator or trainee. Such a narrow perspective is a further prop to superstitious beliefs, allowing us to assume that a 'Ph.D. level' or 'graduate student' status automatically bestows supervision skills. One of the few empirical studies ever conducted indicated that representative supervisors who had not themselves received specialised training were largely ineffective (Isaacs *et al.*, 1982). This is supported by systematic comparisons of the relative effectiveness of teacher trainers as a function of their level of attainments. It was found that BA level graduates were as effective as their Ph.D. counterparts and were in fact preferred by their students (Kent and O'Leary, 1977). Schortinghuis and Frohman (1974) also indicated that, following a 1-week pre-service training, para-professionals were as effective as a group of graduate professionals in teaching parents to train their children. These findings illustrate how misleading some designations can be, and suggest that clear specifications of supervisor training and experience (i.e. their relevant learning history) would be more valuable to our understanding of training outcomes. Indeed, Patterson and Fleischman (1979) have reported higher success rates for their more experienced parent supervisors.

Presumably this point also holds for those operating a 'quadratic' model, in which students or other professional intermediaries serve as the contact point between mediator and supervisor. In such cases the learning histories of both student and supervisor could have an important bearing on the training process and hence should be studied carefully.

Increasing the specification and control which we exercise over such factors as the training skills of the supervisor and mediator may very well help us to improve our efficiency substantially. Problems presented by the trainee are often less frequent than those brought about through trying to supervise mediators: Bernstein (1979) interviewed 26 agents involved in a quadratic approach and found that they regarded over half of the difficulties which they encountered as those of mediator supervision. (This finding may have a familiar ring to those who work in institutions. A recurring viewpoint there is that it is not the clients but the staff who are the 'problem'.)

(b) Mediators

The research literature also seems to assume that mediators, like supervisors, are some form of invariant 'blobs' that require no specification of their individual differences. As well as flying in the face of the traditional emphasis on these subject variables within psychotherapy generally, this vagueness obscures what may well be an important variable in training. Bernal (1984) reviews a number of potent subject variables in parent training, including marital conflict, colour, class, child-rearing philosophies, social isolation and single parenthood. Any of these can control the ability and willingness of parents to acquire and utilise therapy skills.

Some nurse training research has also substantiated the variability of mediators. Brooker and Wiggins (1983) examined the outcomes achieved by a group of eight nurse therapists with a total of 251 patients treated by behaviour therapy. They found that three of these nurses did not significantly improve the condition of their patients, whereas their colleagues, who had received the same course of training, had achieved clinical improvements. Brooker and Wiggins did not consider any specific demographic variables in order to account for their findings. In another study certain personal characteristics such as the age, sex and academic qualifications of nurses were found to have only a weak association with learning behaviour therapy (Milne, 1984d). A similarly weak relationship was found between these characteristics and their implementation of training on the wards (Milne, 1985b), leading to the view that system variables, such as peer support and feedback, were more important determinants of therapeutic behaviour than were the nurses' demographic backgrounds.

None the less, it may well transpire that such findings were mediated by the kind of training format which is adopted. O'Dell *et al.* (1982), for instance, found that parents who achieved the best results with behavioural training were generally those with better education and higher socio-economic status. However, they suggested that these parent characteristics were also related to the training method, in that the more educated and motivated parents were less affected by variations in the instructional procedures. It follows that some training processes may actually minimise subject differences. This illustrates an interaction between subjects and training and highlights another potential snare for the superstitious supervisor — that of assuming that subject variables are either unimportant or account for most of the obtained training effect.

(c) Training Methods

Another problematic aspect of the training process is the relative value of different learning formats. This is a rich source of 'accidental reinforcement' for the supervisor, since a range of successive methods can be introduced and intertwined, making it very difficult to identify the contributions each has made to the outcome. This may explain why the consistent finding that verbal methods of training only produce verbal proficiency has not reduced the dependence of supervisors on 'chalk and talk' when they seek to promote skills. One must assume that one variable sustaining the practice of such 'lullaby lectures' is the confusion of the effects that are due to different methods. Other variables may include the respective escapes of supervisor and mediator from the more taxing and potentially embarrassing demands of enactive learning; the virtual absence of any kind of sensitive evaluation which might indicate the true value of certain training activities; and the supervisors' often limited repertoire, which may force them to imitate academic teaching behaviours, even though they may regard them as inappropriate to the goals of training (Milne, 1984f).

In addition to comparing different methods of training, it seems self-evident that there are major variations *within* each method. In this sense we may develop skills by merely listening to a brilliant lecturer or fail to develop them because of the misuse of a generally powerful enactive method. Again, the preference for 'fuzzy' labels in lieu of a precise account of the teaching method as utilised encourages a superstitious belief in their guaranteed effects. Thus the supervisor may maintain that 'role-play' is enhancing skills by reference to the literature. However, that literature does not typically say what took place under the rubric of 'role-play', so there is every possibility that the supervisor mistakenly believes that they are imitating a well-tried procedure. The same applies to any other method. 'Modelling', for instance, involves the dimensions of the message, the valence, the model and the medium (Ford, 1980). 'Feedback' can be immediate or delayed, group or individual, public or private, personal or mechanical, accurate or inaccurate, and so on (Hutchinson *et al.*, 1980). As Bernstein (1982) rightly says, research is needed which systematically determines the effects of these 'within-method' variables.

This point has been made in the general behaviour therapy literature, where a survey of articles revealed that the majority did not use any assessment of the actual occurrence of the independent variable and a sizeable minority did not even provide an operational definition (Peterson *et al.*, 1982). As we will discuss shortly, this shortcoming may obscure the functional relationship between a change in the environment and a change in the problematic behaviour, the fundamental purpose of behavioural research. Peterson *et al.* offer the illustration of a parent or teacher who has been inadvertently reinforcing a maladaptive behaviour at baseline and who then ignored this during treatment. They point out that it would be useful to have a permanent record of the mediator's reinforcing and ignoring of the problem behaviour, in addition to data on the effects of these contingencies, for otherwise we cannot say with any precision which mediator behaviour's affected which trainee behaviours. The risk that accompanies this imprecision is as great for supervisors as it is for mediators.

(d) The Content of Training Programmes

Similar arguments could be advanced regarding the content of training programmes. These also consist of a number of variables which are usually considered as a unified package, such as 'behaviour therapy course'. Baer (1981) has indicated one reason for the unquestioning acceptance of such packages, namely that they would require a great deal of research effort to 'unpack'. A five-component package, for instance, yields thirty possible combinations of the course contents for evaluation. Each of these combinations may yield slightly different results, some inevitably being more efficient than others. But it is a characteristic of mediator training that the content is accepted as it stands, even when it is only approximately right, that is, on the basis of the first approximation. Subsequent experimental refinements of course contents are a rarity since, along with the magnitude of the task, there is always another pressing practical problem begging for a first approximation. None the less, the contents of courses clearly merit research attention alongside training methods and implementation problems, as they have an important place in the overall package.

Those few studies which have manipulated course contents have tended to conclude that some elements were unnecessary, such as the emphasis on theoretical aspects of behaviour therapy. Hudson (1982), for instance, found that teaching parents behavioural principles did not improve the outcome in terms of their skills. Interestingly, another group of parents who did not receive this theoretical input still seemed to show a grasp of the underlying principles from their skills-based version of the course. In nurse training we have obtained a similar finding (Milne, 1984e): we were able to drop four of the sixteen learning steps in our introductory course without any loss in knowledge of behavioural principles or skills. A very valuable study by Isaacs *et al.* (1982) also documented the largely unreflexive methods of intervention used by supervisors, prior to specialised training. These methods include an unhelpful tendency to inform the parents about aspects of child development which were irrelevant to the task in hand. But once the supervisors themselves received training, they reduced the information on these topics and increased relevant instructions and information.

This kind of 'pruning' exercise can be based on a number of considerations other than the one of systematic comparison. One is the judgement of the mediators in terms of the perceived relevance of the various course contents for their behavioural work; and a second is to observe this work and to successively adjust the course content so that it only teaches skills and knowledge that are clearly relevant, provided of course that the programme's goals are still being achieved. A similar 'shaping' process could also be applied to each individual course component, with elements being omitted or elaborated as required and the effects being assessed at each step. This might be most worthwhile when the components so studied are crucial to the package.

Koegel *et al.* (1978) have illustrated from their parent training work that broad evaluations may be necessary to determine accurately the relative effects of different course contents. They reported that specific elements presented individually produced differential effects in both parent and child. This suggests that multiple measures of outcome would be most appropriate in future studies bearing on this issue.

(e) Minimising Superstitious 'Supervision'

Given the various difficulties faced by supervisors in providing efficient training, it may be useful to consider some ways of improving matters. To this end there appear to be two principal and related options: either to receive proper training in supervision; or to structure and evaluate one's own experience as a supervisor.

Unfortunately, supervision is rarely taught as a discrete skill and so supervisors usually find themselves imitating the 'symbolic' learning procedures prevalent in their own higher education and supervision. This is a rather inadequate preparation for a very difficult task and is particularly ironic in view of the relevance of the very subject they teach for their own learning. That is, behaviour therapy is admirably reflexive, with the same principles of learning being applicable to mediator, trainee or supervisor.

A number of studies exist in which this reflexivity has been demonstrated. One illustration was Levine and Tilker's (1974) use of modelling, rehearsal, direct feedback and audio-visual equipment to shape up clinical skills in the mediator, followed by a graded fading of supervision as the student took on a more active role in therapy. However, it was Bernard (1981) who applied the model reflexively to supervisor training. She utilised a variety of therapeutic models, including counselling and problem-solving, in a behavioural rehearsal format contained in a two-day 'training laboratory'. The laboratory began with a baseline study of the supervisors' existing perspectives and roles, before proceeding to experiential learning exercises. Finally, supervisors had an opportunity to contrast their subjective evaluations of their students against objective data and also to practise giving evaluative feedback. Unfortunately, Bernard presented no objective, evaluative data on the laboratory's success, although she indicated that it had received a 'positive reaction'.

The main value of her approach therefore lies in the attention paid to experiential learning exercises for supervisors. She has written a manual (Bernard, 1982) describing eight exercises, such as obtaining baseline data, discriminating between different supervisory approaches and micro-training. In the latter case the group views a video tape of a counselling session, then divides into smaller groups. Each group then decides on two or three clearly observable skills which could be taught to the counsellor on the video tape so as to improve the counselling session. They then re-group and a volunteer acts as supervisor to the counsellor. Modelling and rehearsal are used and a video-tape recording is made of this and of the subsequent attempt of the counsellor to apply the new skill to a client (role-played by another group member). The whole group then watch the video tape, and provide feedback to 'supervisor' and counsellor on both the former's skill and clarity in teaching and the latter's ability to translate this into more effective counselling. If any problems arise, the sequence is repeated, taking into account the feedback received. Bernard regarded the ability of the counsellor to apply the supervisor's teaching as the best form of feedback.

This 'training laboratory' has a number of prominent advantages over traditional practices. Foremost among these must rank the sharing of objective feedback by both mediator and supervisor. This integrates their related learning tasks and makes a refreshing contrast to the traditional practice of having only the supervisors give feedback to the mediator, typically in the absence of data. It also answers the call by a group of psychologists for improved training within the profession, incorporating more emphasis on supervised clinical experience and a greater balance between theory and practice (Garfield and Kurtz, 1976). A good example of this in an educational setting has been provided by Shearer and Loftin (1984). They utilised a systematic format for providing monitoring and feedback to home teachers in their Portage project. These teachers liaised between supervisor and mediator, carrying out all the parent training but drawing on the supervisor's expertise as necessary. The supervisor ensured that each home teacher received an initial training and monthly home-based monitoring linked to an individual 'conference'. This included reviewing the teacher's documentation and the establishment of performance objectives for the next month.

As Bernard stressed in her manual, the major value of this kind of training approach is that it gives supervisors objective feedback on the effects of their training. In terms of our present concern, this would appear to be an excellent means of eliminating superstitious components from the supervisor's repertoire. Such data would be extremely valuable, both in terms of the short-term learning of supervisors and the generalisation of these skills to routine conditions. The emergence of successful semi-automated (or 'supervisor-free') training packages (e.g. Koegel *et al.*, 1978; Jones and Robson, 1983) creates a growing need for these data.

To turn to the second major option, supervisors who do not receive adequate preparation for their role can still minimise superstitious training behaviour by a careful evaluation of their own work. This can focus on the relationship between issues such as the content or methods of their training procedures and the mediators' learning. This serves as feedback for both supervisors and mediators: the mediators know how much they have learnt and the supervisors know how far they have facilitated learning. The result is that successive and informed approximations can be made to the goals of training. Provided these evaluations are precise and objective, and not simply broad 'appreciative' data (such as the mediator's expressed satisfaction with training), then supervisory behaviour is 'tested out'. This learning strategy therefore reduces the probability of irrelevant supervisory behaviours because it allows us to become aware of and eliminate those which are found to be functionally unrelated to mediator learning.

A major impediment in pursuing this 'feedback' option can be the shortage of suitable objective measures of mediator learning. Nurse training, for instance, has generated strikingly few instruments which are widely available and applicable (Milne, 1984b). Under these circumstances the supervisor is placed in the even more taxing position of having to develop appropriate measures prior to an evaluation. Such demands may account for the relative preponderance of measures of trainee behaviours, since these will often be available from other interventions and a professional history steeped in client assessments. Unfortunately, simply treating changes in the client or trainee as a measure of the mediator's skill is problematic (although it does have the advantages of minimising fruitless debates on what constitutes 'good' clinical behaviour). The basic problem is that trainees will vary in their response to even the most excellent therapy, or may improve without receiving any systematic help. To some extent, studies of groups of trainees can overcome this difficulty, although those conducted in natural settings are often subject to other intervening variables which may affect all subjects and so confound the findings (e.g. changes in staff or medication).

These considerations tend to favour a careful 'across-the-board' evaluation, in which all members of the triad are studied in turn. A diagram indicating the steps in such an evaluation is to be found on page 283, but, as we have seen, such studies are extremely rare in any therapeutic approach. In this vein Fischer (1975) pointed out that no training programme in social work had demonstrated that students had actually learned what was taught. He went on to stress the view that 'years of intellectual, cognitively oriented educational programmes as a preparation for professional practice may be an elaborate mythology', since these qualities may either be weakly related or even opposed to the qualities of effective helpers.

(f) Summary

This survey of some aspects of supervising mediators indicates the widespread practice of so-called 'superstitious supervision'. Difficulties in developing relevant supervisory behaviours were evident in our discussions of the main areas of supervisors, mediators, training methods and course contents. Each of these presented a recurring theme, namely the potential irrelevance of much supervisory behaviour to the actual learning of mediators (and trainees).

Two compatible courses of action seem relevant to this problem. One is to conduct careful evaluations of our own supervision. These could reveal the true value of a number of suspect activities, such as including a large proportion of theory in courses or excluding consideration of subject variables. In this way we can test out the relative contributions of each variable and relate them to outcomes in the original and subsequent training courses.

Perhaps the first step, however, is to provide structured training for supervisors. We considered one example in which supervisors could learn key skills by microtraining methods. This incorporated practising training the mediator followed by observing the effect of this training on the mediator's behaviour with a trainee. As this approach builds in immediate, relevant and objective feedback to the supervisor, it promises to eliminate superstitious components. Research on both training programmes and self-evaluation are sorely needed if we are to improve the efficiency of the triadic model. The supervisors have been the least considered agents in this approach, and yet they clearly cannot advantageously be omitted from our evaluations of therapist training. These points apply with equal strength to the 'quadratic model', in which graduate students typically serve as the supervisors with direct mediator contact.

9.3 Training Tactics

(a) Introduction

We have just discussed how the content and methods of training may play a significant role in influencing supervisor's behaviour without their full awareness. The discussion that follows emphasises the more deliberate aspects of that role, as developed in parent, nurse and teacher training research. The aim is to integrate some of the more promising training procedures that emerge from these studies so as to facilitate further research and practice in these areas.

In the reviews and illustrations we have considered so far, there have been a very wide range of training methods. We have discriminated broadly between 'symbolic' (reading, writing, lectures, discussion, etc.), 'iconic' (e.g. modelling) and 'enactive' methods (e.g. rehearsal, role-play and performance feedback). We have also recounted strikingly consistent findings regarding their relative effect on mediators' knowledge and skills, with symbolic training methods most effective in promoting the former and enactive methods best at developing proficiency. However, there was also compelling evidence to suggest that training 'packages' consisting of a combination of methods were more effective than those using a more limited range of methods. The structured learning format (SLF, Bouchard *et al.*, 1980) was one illustration of a complementary use of several popular training methods, with each one 'setting the occasion' for the next. Gagné (1970) has discussed how necessary this careful progression is to successful 'learning by discovery'. For instance, a basic knowledge of principles, followed by some prompting and modelling, pave the way to efficient performances. In contrast, Gagné pointed out that asking the student to either 'discover' the principles or succeed in the practice makes poor educational sense. The right balance of 'training' and 'education' are required for true learning, and, as Skinner (1968) has pointed out, the student should learn without being taught.

There have been a number of interesting developments stemming from these principles of training and learning within the research on behaviour therapy mediators. Felce *et al.* (1984), for instance, have evolved the 'Bereweeke system' which promotes discovery learning by gradually taking the nurse through a series of structured therapy sessions with trainees. The first step entails a behavioural assessment of the skills of a mentally handicapped client by the nurses, leading to the selection of a realistic training goal. A programme is then written by the supervisor which includes a sequence of weekly training steps, taking the client from the initial baseline by small learning increments to the selected goal. In addition, the supervisor writes out an activity chart for each week's step, specifying the number of learning trials, the objective, and the means to achieve it. This includes how staff can prepare for the training session, what to ask the client to do, and how to give help and reinforcement as necessary. The staff record the results of each session at the bottom of the activity chart. The supervisor bases the staff training around six 2-hour sessions.

Another promising new direction has been in the area of 'incidental training'. This refers to training programmes for trainees that are incorporated into existing routines, so minimising the many obstacles to additional training sessions. Successful studies have been conducted with pre-school children (Hart and Risley, 1975) as well as with nursing staff working with the mentally handicapped (Ivancic *et al.*, 1981). In this second study a series of very brief (i.e. 10 to 40 minutes) staff training sessions were held prior to their incidental language training of trainees. These were supplemented by various prompts to staff (e.g. public postings, supervisor modelling) and individual feedback and praise. The effect of these procedures was to increase verbal interactions between the staff mediators and the trainees at the cost of minimal supervisor time and effort.

A related development in the efficient use of supervisor time is the pyramid training strategy. This has the advantage of reducing the number of staff the supervisor needs to train, and overcomes staff scheduling problems. The pyramid approach has been an integral feature of the EDY teacher-training project described in Chapter 8. It has also been applied in hospitals by Page *et al.* (1982), who trained an initial group of three staff to act as 'supervisors' to a further 45 nurses, with satisfactory results. Interestingly, an incidental training strategy was in effect during the pyramid phase, so that once again the existing routines could continue with minimal disruption. This promotes the possibility of effective maintenance and generalisation of mediator training. For instance, in hospitals it reduces the problem of programme continuity brought about by staff rotation to other units, as well as the more pervasive institutional problem of absenteeism and sickness.

Summary

These examples of training tactics share two important characteristics. First, they systematically build experiential learning into the mediator's existing work routine. Secondly, they link this to 'natural' work contingencies, such as the monitoring duties undertaken by managers. Both characteristics have great potential for improving the motivation of mediators as well as for promoting the learning of mediator and trainee alike. This former problem of motivation is really the major one facing supervisors, since they commonly experience much more success in promoting the mediator's initial learning of behavioural skills. Any approach that simultaneously facilitates learning and motivation is particularly worthy of research attention. Unfortunately, studies have tended to deal with them separately, that is, as problems of either 'training' or 'management'. We will now consider the management issue, before considering the combination of management and training approaches, that is, 'mediator development'.

9.4 Mediator Development

(a) Mediator Management

It seems clear from the many studies we have reviewed of training nurses, parents and teachers that training is a necessary but insufficient condition for the successful use of behaviour therapy skills. An additional condition which is equally necessary is to provide incentives to mediators, contingent on the appropriate application of these skills. We refer to this motivational emphasis as '*mediator management*'.

There are a number of approaches to mediator management.

Broadly speaking we can distinguish antecedent and consequent events. Antecedents include such things as the initial negotiation of the training intervention, sometimes referred to as the 'port of entry' problem (Repucci, 1977). At the other end of the intervention are the consequences that affect mediator behaviour, such as the response of the trainee or the reactions of colleagues.

'*Setting Events*'. Antecedents that occur some time in advance of training or overlap with it have been called 'setting events'. This refers to stimulus-response interactions which then affect subsequent interactions (Wahler and Fox, 1981). They include such phenomena as the effect of playtime events during school break on classroom interactions; or the effect of parental isolation on their interactions with their child; or the effect of staffing levels on nurse-patient interactions in hospitals. These illustrations share an emphasis on antecedents more complex and often further removed in time than the ones customarily considered in behavioural research.

Examples from teacher training in behaviour modification have included such setting events as the teacher's lack of necessary organisational skills to initiate programmes (Martin, 1977) and the pupils' control over one another's behaviour at the expense of teacher control (Solomon and Wahler, 1973).

Some setting events for nurse training include comparable interactions among patients which appear to coerce the staff into abandoning their therapy skills (Sanson-Fisher and Jenkins, 1978). In addition, there are often severe obstacles in the availability of equipment and even the most basic materials needed to start training (Thomas *et al.*, 1982). Wahler (1980) has provided a clear indication of how parental isolation and the quality of interactions with other adults affect parenting skills. Forehand *et al.* (1984) demonstrated how the same skills are affected by 'maternal distress', a setting event incorporating such factors as parental relations and depression. To these examples can be added the more general social-psychological variables inherent in the implementation of any behavioural programme, such as the inflexibility to compromise (Repucci and Saunders, 1974) or the innovatory zeal of the supervisor (Georgiades and Phillimore, 1975).

These setting events are the kinds of factor that very few supervisors can have failed to notice, yet their representation in the literature is infrequent. Not uncommonly, reports of mediator training omit any mention of setting events at all, encouraging a mistaken belief that we have achieved rigorous scientific control.

Consequences Affecting Motivation. This point seems less valid when applied to the longer-term consequences of our training interventions. For some time now there has been a definite interest in the maintenance and generalisation of therapy skills by the manipulation of consequences. Even so, it remains an under-represented topic in the literature, in terms of its theoretical and applied importance. Bernstein (1982) noted how little research existed on the effects of training across time (maintenance), settings, behaviours and subjects. She pointed out that these are vital to effective programming and cited some of the few studies. They included those in which nurses had generalised their training to new clients (Schinke, 1979), parents who had generalised a workshop training to the home setting (O'Dell *et al.*, 1977), and teachers who had trained other teachers in behaviour modification skills (Jones *et al.*, 1977).

To these studies can be added the interesting work of Koegel *et al.* (1978), who compared the generalisation of two parent training packages. They found that a course covering general behaviour modification procedures was more effective than a highly specific one in generalising the parents' training to a variety of their children's problem behaviours. A related comparison of training methods was conducted by Sanders and Glynn (1981), but in this instance parental 'self-management' was found to be more effective to an approach involving instructions plus feedback. The self-management training consisted of the parents doing their own goal-setting, planning and monitoring, and resulted in generalisation from home to community for both parents and children. Similarly, we have already discussed some studies in teacher training (Chapter 7) in which self-control played a part in promoting maintenance and generalisation. Stevenson and Fantuzzo (1984), for example, reported that improvements in the pupils' mathematics generalised to decreased classroom disruption.

In nurse training there has also been a dearth of generalisation studies. One review concluded that staff training results in small changes in staff behaviour immediately after training, and only for certain skills (Ziarnik and Bernstein, 1982). Although this conclusion must be regarded as premature, owing to the shortage of systematic studies in nurse training (Milne, 1985a), it is wholly justified on the basis of the studies reviewed by these authors. Subsequent research, reviewed in Chapter 6, indicates that a thorough course of training can lead to maintenance of skills and knowledge for as long as a year, as well as generalisation across settings, behaviours and subjects. The 'ecological' approach to evaluation illustrated in these recent studies utilised a variety of research designs and 'probes' to assess the effects of training on various components of a system, following the preferred strategy (Campbell *et al.*, 1982). They included the nurses' case notes (archival data), the generalisation of training across subjects (paper and pencil assessments) and the generalisation of training to new settings (naturalistic observation). Some supervisors have also extended the training nationally to other hospitals and subjects (Milne *et al.*, 1985b).

These studies of nurse training, like the ecological studies of parents and teachers, lead to a more complex view of generalisation than that based purely on the provision of 'extras'. This view suggests that the ecological approach advocated by Willems (1973) becomes a necessary basis for understanding the process and outcomes of mediator training. It extends our awareness to the competing variables which often account for the failure of programmes (Holman, 1977) and so provides a fresh impetus to research and practice. Wahler and Dumas (1984) have illustrated this broadened analysis and the competing variables in their review of setting events in parent training. They focused on processes of coercion between the parents and their extended social environment, such as aversive exchanges with the family and the wider community. It led the authors to consider an alternative view of training in which the attentional deficits of certain parents (as opposed to the traditional skills deficits) were regarded as central to problems in maintenance and generalisation. This made child monitoring a crucial determinant of parental behaviour, in that the parents' failure to note these events set them up to act towards the child in ways likely to exacerbate the problem. On this basis it became appropriate to focus parent training efforts on their haphazard attending to and coding of child behaviour. Wahler and Dumas regarded these additions to the more traditional approach as particularly valuable in maintaining good parenting among parents experiencing coercion from a number of sources.

Interestingly, in terms of our earlier discussion of superstitious supervision, Wahler and Dumas also regarded some parents as being under superstitious stimulus control. This control developed, they believed, because the coercion they experienced made the parents very inconsistent in attending and responding to their children. It would appear that the same conceptualisation could also apply to supervisors and hence prove fruitful in understanding their superstitious behaviour. Although this would result in our requiring a very broad analysis, the payoffs in terms of understanding mediator motivation would probably be very considerable.

(b) Mediator Development

The synthesis of training and management strategies as illustrated above is known as *mediator development*. There are some helpful examples of this combined approach, including the Bereweeke system just mentioned. In this programme a supervisor's manual provides rare guidance on monitoring and implementing training (Felce *et al.*, 1983b) and includes tips on providing appropriate recognition of the mediators' efforts, such as encouraging them to advise other staff. The authors also suggest that supervisors make a special point of dealing with equipment or administrative obstacles. As regards implementation, they list a number of ways of determining the quantity and quality of mediators' work. This includes the proportion of teaching sessions being carried out as well as more specific factors, such as assigning individual mediators to conduct each scheduled training session.

Another promising development in this approach has been to transfer some supervisory functions over to the mediator. Burgio *et al.* (1983) studied the effects of having nursing staff monitor, evaluate and reinforce their own use of therapy skills in their interactions with trainees. This form of 'participative management' or self-control was effective in increasing the number of interactions, leading in turn to improvements in the trainees. We have already discussed similar strategies that have been utilised in school classrooms, with the pupil responsible for self-monitoring (see Chapter 7). In both settings this self-control method has been successful in reducing the amount of supervisor time and effort required to implement training. It has also been found to have advantages in improving the quality of the mediator's performance, their monitoring and their general motivation to utilise training skills (e.g. Gladstone and Sherman, 1975; Hundert, 1982). In addition to the success in promoting mediator development, Burgio *et al.* (1983) obtained their mediators' opinions about this approach. Self-control was rated above a variety of popular alternatives, such as supervisor praise and public feedback. The relationship between the acceptability of this kind of mediator development and its implementation is a little-researched but interesting perspective. As described in Chapter 6, a training approach which was adapted to overcome the mediators' criticisms was much more fully implemented than an approach with lower acceptability (Milne, 1984e). As Bernstein (1982) has stressed, the 'social validity' of mediator development is a very relevant concern and should be pursued systematically in future studies. It would appear to have the status of a setting event and, as discussed in the previous section, these factors can have a powerful effect on training and so merit our attention.

(c) Conclusion

The studies we have discussed in this section underline the potential of mediator training as the basis for successful interventions with trainees. Some of the more traditional obstacles to this approach, for example low staff motivation in institutions or poor monitoring in domestic settings, can be lessened by procedures such as self-control. The major implication, therefore, is that training *can* be effective provided it is linked to a facilitating system. These studies show how this can be achieved in an integrated approach which we referred to as 'mediator development'. This is surely one of the major training problems and hence one that should now receive most research attention. In contrast, studies that consider training in isolation from management factors are of less interest, although there is undoubtedly valuable work to be done in which training packages and motivational procedures are considered independently. Indeed, some of these studies may only be feasible when constructed in such an independent way, as in the assessment of setting events or the analysis of some long-term generalisation effects. However, the long-term objective must be to integrate the findings from these studies into a coherent explanation of mediator development. Only in this way can we anticipate less superstitious supervision, more successful mediators and more responsive trainees.

9.5 The Trainee

(a) Introduction

Of the many objections raised against behavioural approaches, one of the most frequent concerns the client or 'trainee'. Common examples include the deterministic philosophy which is viewed by some as treating the trainee like a robot; and the use of reinforcement as a form of bribery which may corrupt. The proponents of these perspectives advocate a trainee-centred approach in which the needs of the trainee are regarded as paramount. Winnett and Winkler (1972) highlighted this point in distinguishing between the needs of the educational system for 'still, quiet and docile' pupils, and the antagonistic needs of the children for freedom, exploration and informality. In this sense, behavioural approaches are seen as a means of achieving 'law and order', where trainees are encouraged to adjust more appropriately to the system in which they live, rather than with actualising their potential.

This perspective merits discussion, since it bears on such important issues as the needs of trainees, their self-control and the ethics of behavioural interventions. We shall now discuss these issues, with regard to the literature on nurses, parents and teachers as behaviour therapists.

(b) Needs of Trainees

Broadly speaking, both mediators and trainees have needs that have often been sacrificed for those of the supervisor or the system. This may have been especially true during what Mittler and Mittler (1983) referred to as the early 'transplant' phase of behavioural consultancy. This was characterised by a tendency for the 'professionals' to assume that they already understood the needs of mediators and trainees and could therefore impose solutions upon them without negotiation. This was often difficult for the mediators to accept, but it was particularly problematic for the trainees, since typically they had even less direct influence on these programmes. As a consequence, both agents may have resorted to practices of indirect 'counter-control', with the effect of annulling the intervention. Such resistance clearly undermines their motivation to achieve the goals selected by supervisors.

One way of dealing with this difficulty has been for the supervisors to seek guidance from other colleagues. Sulzer-Azaroff *et al.* (1975) attempted this by surveying editors and contributors to behavioural journals so as to clarify their perceptions of mediators' needs. An alternative approach has been to have the mediators themselves rate the effectiveness of different therapeutic approaches. Medway and Forman (1980) had teachers viewing video tapes of two different approaches to classroom control, leading to their selection of one as the more effective. This process could then lead to training, based on informed mediator choice.

The Mittlers' 'partnership' approach extends this process by stressing the identification and sharing of decisions about goals with parents *and* their children. The emphasis is on individuality rather than stereotyping, since the latter can lead to misidentification of problems: for example, parents' individual child-rearing practices can be regarded by professionals as 'overprotective' or 'rejecting' and their children as 'hyperactive' or 'autistic'. This can then lead to interventions which may not be perceived by parent or child as necessary or desirable. Meanwhile, those needs which they would regard as meriting intervention go unheeded, such as home teaching and home visiting, family support centres, accurate information, marital counselling and psychotherapy for the parents (Russell, 1983).

However, it is worth pointing out that the 'partnership' approach to needs assessment is only one way of sampling *options*. As Bernstein (1984) has stated, this approach may lead to the identification of mediator needs that are only superstitiously related to effective training, rather than being functionally important. The same may apply to trainees. One way of providing a more objective basis for assessing needs is to observe mediator behaviour in relation to that of the trainees. Fredericks *et al.* (1977) did this by comparing teachers whose severely handicapped trainees made large gains with a second group of teachers whose trainees made less progress. The more effective teachers were observed to use more carefully analysed training programmes and more appropriate consequences than the less successful teachers.

Regardless of the method of needs assessment, it should be noted that there is often considerable overlap between those needs traditionally highlighted by supervisors for the trainees and those identified by other methods, such as training programmes in self-help skills. Other trainee needs have taken more time to gain acceptance, as with the sexual needs of the mentally handicapped and more generally their need to understand relationships and emotions, or to have privacy and independence (Fairbrother, 1983).

These points also apply to the residents of psychiatric hospitals and compel us to review the stereotyped approach to institutional care which still prevails. One recent attempt to break away from the stereotype is the 'normalisation' of psychiatric and mentally handicapped hospital residents by placing them in the community. This scheme is forging ahead in the UK on the assumption that it meets the needs of patients, even though it is often impossible to determine what their own perceptions of their needs are.

A recurring feature of normalisation and most other definitions of trainees' needs is the ill-defined way in which they are specified. This perhaps has its roots in traditional psychometric assessment of 'personality' and 'intelligence', and has fostered the identification of such client needs as 'achievement', 'affiliation', 'aggression', 'deference' and 'dominance' (see Anastasi, 1976). To some extent the specification of needs has remained 'fuzzy', as illustrated by such vague objectives as 'resocialisation' and 'instrumental role performance'. But more recent and systematic programmes have begun to define these in precise and objective terms (e.g. Paul and Lentz, 1977). However, these still appear to be the goals of supervisors, meeting the needs of the time rather than necessarily those of the individuals.

Perhaps this is inevitable, since many trainees cannot articulate their needs at all. In these instances it is vital that others set specific objectives on their behalf, ones that are likely to be acceptable to those at the receiving end. A literature review found that such goal-setting improved trainee performance by such means as focusing attention and mobilising effort (Locke *et al.*, 1981).

(c) Self-control

One further way of determining the needs of trainees is by promoting their use of self-control. We have already considered examples of school pupils who were taught to identify, record and reinforce key aspects of their own classroom behaviour (e.g. 'on-task' behaviour), but research with other populations has tended to focus on the self-control of mediators. Burgio *et al.* (1983) illustrated this approach by providing nurses with wrist counters to monitor their own interactions with residents and by their use of 'self-praise' rating forms.

Although there is a risk that some self-control procedures may simply transfer the responsibility for achieving the supervisors' goals on to the trainee or mediator, at least the strength of their response may indicate the extent to which these are shared needs. This could possibly be regarded as an empirical assessment in cases where the trainees are unable to state their needs, or as corroborative evidence where they can.

(d) Ethical Issues

One of the major fears expressed about training parents, nurses and teachers as behaviour therapists is that their inevitably partial understanding of the principles involved may lead to misapplication of the approach, to the detriment of all concerned (Stein, 1975). Others have argued that it is misleading to discuss behavioural training as if it were entirely novel and hence introducing a new ethical dilemma. It is rather a case of having increased awareness, understanding and skill in applying techniques which we all routinely use, knowingly or unknowingly (Hawkins, 1972). From this point of view, it would be unethical *not* to offer training, even if this was only minimal.

As regards the trainees, concern has long been expressed about the capacity of behavioural techniques to dehumanise or to exert 'mind control'. Behaviour therapists have shared this concern, but argued that relative to some alternatives (e.g. psychosurgery and ECT) their approach involves minor ethical issues. Only socially valued changes tend to be introduced, and even then these are often reversible. There being so little data on the relative risks entailed by different therapies, evaluations often provoke only prejudice and polemic. Furthermore, there are no scientifically precise criteria for deciding what ought to be done in a given situation, leading to a 'rubber yardstick' in which even the standards and criteria of individuals often vary, especially when applied to the behaviour of others. For this reason Eilbert and Eilbert (1982) argued for detached decision-makers and for training that sensitised individuals to ethical dilemmas. To this we can add the need for evaluations of the clinical outcomes of behavioural programmes and their acceptability to trainees and to society generally. Similarly, behavioural goals and procedures could be subjected to social validation prior to an intervention, if regarded as necessary. Other relevant considerations include the importance of careful assessments of supervisor and mediator competence, and the need for individuals to recognise their own limitations and seek advice or assistance if required.

A different kind of ethical issue concerns the consequences that may be experienced by mediators and trainees when training is introduced. From the perspective of the trainee we have just mentioned the risk that new mediator skills will be applied so as to alter their behaviour in line with the mediators' (or system) needs, rather than their own. From the mediators' perspective there is a comparable problem, in that the system (and the trainee) may make it aversive for them to use their new skills. This means that the supervisors have effectively placed the mediators in a difficult and unpleasant position. An ethical requirement which follows from this dilemma is to provide supervisor support to the mediator which addresses the problems of aversive control over newly trained skills and builds in some positive reinforcement for their use.

One theme permeating this section has been the exploitation of the trainee. Supervisors, mediators and systems may sometimes be regarded as promoting their own interests at the expense of their often silent clients. This suggestion may be made about many other aspects of the health services, but the behavioural model and its 'dehumanising' technology attract particular concern. This has focused on the devaluation of clients' needs and the ethics of behavioural interventions. Both of these subjects remain elusive aspects of much of our work, as they depend on highly subjective criteria. Some of the programmes and evaluations themselves may act as safeguards, such as those involving self-control or social validation, but we also need an awareness of and a willingness to tackle the issues, as in the case of trainees who are unable to articulate their needs and require supervisors who can specify clear goals which are public and socially acceptable. More generally, the risk of unethical interventions can be reduced by careful evaluations of both their process and outcomes. This enables us to monitor and adjust our programmes in terms of socially accepted criteria as well as our own professional standards.

9.6 Research Requirements

(a) Introduction

Time and again throughout this book we have highlighted the strengths and weaknesses of various research projects. In this section we bring together the main points as they relate to nurse, parent and teacher training. The aim is to clarify the major requirements of systematic research in this area, so as to facilitate its continued development.

In a sense, the central problem is simply one of inadequate reporting: the bulk of our requirements could be satisfied by more detailed accounts and evaluations of training. Since it is impossible to achieve the ideal and directly observe the supervisor behaviour implicit in all these reports, we must rely on their descriptions of training. For this to be a useful exercise we require objective specifications of all the important variables, namely the subjects, settings, training procedures and content, and the evaluative measures applied. Each of these is discussed below and suggestions are made about their specification in future research.

(b) Subject Variables

Training involves a number of agents in a relationship which is expected to result in systematic forms of influence. This is equally true of dyadic, triadic or quadratic versions of training, and provides the basic rationale for consultancy. Paradoxically we are only rarely allowed to glimpse the behaviour of all agents at any one time. Instead, we are typically offered reports with a disproportionate emphasis on the trainee, with little said about the mediator and nothing at all about the supervisor. The impression is that parent training research generally achieves the best balance in representing the activities of mediator and trainee (child), with nurse training research at the other extreme being preoccupied with the mediator and often ignoring both supervisor and trainee.

Callias (1980) concluded her review of teacher, parent and nurse training by noting that 'methodological problems abound'. She drew attention to a number of potentially important mediator variables (such as socio-economic and educational status), trainee variables (such as degree and type of handicap) and supervisor variables (experience and professional discipline). Clark and Baker (1983) were able to predict parents' proficiency and application of training skills based on such characteristics as their amount of previous child training and their expectations of training outcomes. O'Dell *et al.* (1982) have gone on to examine the interaction between parent characteristics and training methods, one of the several practical implications of assessing subject variables. Indeed, the relationship between these kind of factors and either the initial learning or the subsequent application of training does seem to call for this kind of careful analysis. Simple, direct relationships between subject variables did not appear to influence learning or application in two studies involving nurses, even though a large number of variables were considered (Milne, 1984d, 1985b). On the other hand, Brooker and Wiggins (1983) reported considerable variability in the clinical success of nurse therapists, who all apparently received the same kind of training and clients and presumably differed on subject variables. With teachers as subjects Farrell (1982) found that classroom assistants achieved lower baseline and post-training knowledge scores than qualified teachers. Only the teachers achieved a significantly higher proficiency score at the post-training assessment.

A first step in clarifying the role of subject variables is to specify and quantify them. Previous experience with formal behavioural training (e.g. as student psychiatric nurse or student teachers) or more informal experience (e.g. being a parent of or having a handicapped sibling) are obvious variables to consider first. Others include indicators of previous academic or applied learning, such as school or university qualifications and apprenticeships served. In addition, it might prove valuable to consider the relationship between more traditional variables such as mediator attitudes and motivation, and training outcome.

These factors are rarely studied, as revealed by a systematic review of 17 research studies concerned with nurse training: only one study had reported information on their subjects' relevant past experiences, and only two referred to their academic and four to their nursing qualifications (Milne, 1984b). One can't help noting that it is precisely these kinds of variable that determine the career developments of teachers and nurses! This is not to suggest that the conventions for selection and promotion are therefore correct, but to fly in the face of such received wisdom requires more empirical data. Since this is, with the co-operation of the subjects, a relatively simple task, researchers can readily address this issue. An equally straightforward but rarely undertaken task is to detail how subjects (mediators or trainees) were recruited. Bernstein (1984) reviewed over 700 relevant studies and found that in over three-quarters of these there was no indication of how selection occurred.

If we make a more concerted effort to study subject and selection variables, we can expect to further improve the efficiency of our training endeavours by matching mediators and trainees. The generality of training for various subjects may also be determined and lead to refined courses. We can also approximate more closely to the status of an applied science, which requires us to answer Paul's (1969) question: 'What treatment, by whom, is most effective for this individual with that specific problem, under which set of circumstances, and how does it come about?'

(c) Settings

We have just considered the theoretical inconsistency of behaviourists in ignoring people's earlier learning while busy promoting their current and future learning. A second theoretical paradox that arises from research reports is how these people appear to learn their behavioural skills in a vacuum. Even more than prior learning or current motivation, behaviour therapy traditionally places its emphasis on the *context* in which behaviour occurs: behaviour is to be understood in terms of the interactions between the individual and his environment. To some extent this simply refers to the content and procedures of training, being a series of stimuli and responses. We will discuss these shortly. The context of training also includes any other variables that may be less obvious but more powerful determinants of mediator or supervisor behaviour. We have already considered one range of these variables known as 'setting events' in Section 9.4. We saw there how apparently unimportant and typically unconsidered variables (such as parental insularity) could influence the mediator's application of training.

Setting events include the social and physical properties of the training location. For instance, they include the negotiation of the training interventions (Repucci, 1977) and the mediator's prior experiences of such events. As Ziarnik and Bernstein (1982) point out, this can include mistaken assumptions on the part of the supervisor that training is the most appropriate form of intervention. This may imply to nurses, teachers or parents that they cannot perform the key skills without training, an assumption that can be both incorrect and bad for mediator motivation. In terms of the latter, Mittler and Mittler's (1983) 'partnership' orientation aims to augment mediators' present skills, rather than trying to change them into some kind of preconceived professional. They regard this orientation as the latest in a series of developments in behavioural training which began with occasional advice and then proceeded through the co-therapist or 'transplant' phase to partnership. In their view, the advantage of the partnership approach is that it limits the mediators' rejection of their supervisors. Traditional assumptions are challenged, such as the supervisor knows best what the trainee should learn and, therefore, what the mediator should do. The emphasis is on understanding, quality and respect for mediators and trainees in their settings, rather than applying an educational technology to meet institutional or community needs (McConachie, 1983). Since this is a consumer-oriented approach, one can expect much greater co-operation and success. It is exemplified in a law passed in the USA in 1975 (P.L. 94–142), which extended the right to parents of handicapped children to assume the role of educational decision-maker. Individualized Education Programs (IEPs) were at the heart of this law, and meetings between parents and teachers were expected to promote IEPs through their equal participation. Unfortunately, in a survey of over 2000 parents and 400 school districts, over half the parents reported that their child's IEP had been completed before the first meeting (Turnbull and Turnbull, 1982). They also reviewed other evidence indicating that teachers monopolised the conversation when parents were 'involved' in planning meetings. This led them to question the assumptions of policy makers and to suggest (like the Mittlers) a graduated, parent-determined degree of involvement in IEPs.

So far we have discussed particularly subjective and difficult-to-quantify variables such as the assumptions of supervisors and mediators. There are other social factors within the training context that have received more systematic attention, although again this has only very rarely been correlated with a training intervention. One such factor is the 'baseline' behaviour of trainees and mediators. For example, psychiatric patients who spend substantial proportions of their day dozing or being inaccessible in other ways limit the therapeutic options available to nurses. Milne and Hodd (1985) found such patients sitting with their eyes closed (apparently sleeping) during 25 per cent of baseline observations between the hours of 5 and 6 p.m. Another factor that has been studied in this setting is the quality and quantity of nurse-patient interactions. Both Sanson-Fisher and Jenkins (1978) and Milne (1985d) found indications of a subtle coercion process in which the trainees appeared to restrict the mediators' use of behaviour therapy. Solomon and Wahler (1973) have demonstrated how peer reinforcement in the classroom played a similar role in controlling problematic behaviour. In turn, Gelfand *et al.* (1967) have shown that such behaviours were more likely to receive mediator attention than appropriate acts.

These findings, based on 'hard' observational data, agree with the essential implication of the subjective views recounted earlier and point to a 'real life' context which is far from being a vacuum. This being so, we should relate our training to potentially relevant contextual variables. For instance, the content of training should be linked to the actual and perceived needs of trainees, perhaps in terms of the 'partnership' approach.

To conclude this section, let us turn briefly to another dimension of the training context, the physical setting. The behaviour of trainees, mediators and supervisors can be studied in terms of the settings in which they occur. This 'behaviour settings' approach has a lengthy history, going back to Barker and Wright's (1955) findings on the strong relationships between where people are and how they behave. Willems (1972) has extended Barker's community work to hospital settings, with similar results. Willems found that 90 per cent of all patient behaviour in a psychiatric rehabilitation hospital occurred in only 4 per cent of the hospital's 122 physical contexts, such as the wards, cafeteria, and so on. Cullen *et al.* (1983b) conducted observations in a mental handicap hospital, reporting that 'inappropriate behaviour' occurred more frequently in the hall than in the ward, although the reverse was true for appropriate behaviour. In a similar way, Thomas *et al.* (1982) described how the physical organisation of wards for the mentally handicapped limited the behaviour of trainees, and hence concluded that structure factors should be incorporated into trainee assessments. These factors included communal washing and sleeping facilities, the absence of locks on toilet doors and clothing fixed by 'Velcro' rather than zips or buttons. Clearly, such environments place constraints on training mediators or trainees and make reorganisation of the setting the first priority.

It is obviously impossible for articles to convey all this information in addition to detailing the training process, although some books (e.g. Paul and Lentz, 1977) manage to provide both. The point is rather that we must openly acknowledge in our research reports the possible contributions made by the social and physical context. We can then study these factors in a more systematic fashion. One approach has been to conduct structured interviews with mediators after an intervention, in order to list and rank the many contextual factors they perceive as important (Burdett and Milne, 1985). Another approach is to utilise questionnaires which tap opinions about the 'atmosphere' of settings (Moos, 1976). In practice, these are quite complementary to the more traditional focus on distinct behaviours and individuals, allowing us to effectively monitor the context in which mediators utilise their behavioural skills.

(d) Training Variables

It has been suggested that independent variables such as 'training' have lacked integrity in the behavioural literature generally (Peterson *et al.*, 1982). Based on a review of articles, these authors found that the majority did not use any assessment of the actual occurrence of the independent variable at all and a sizeable minority did not even provide an operational definition. They stress that this contrasts with the considerable attention accorded to dependent variables (i.e. measures of outcome) and undermines our attempts to establish a functional relationship between the two. They go on to suggest that this lack of specificity is a likely reason for poor replication, a common feature of management research (Reid and Whitman, 1983).

Baer *et al.* (1968) used the term 'technological' to refer to independent variables which were completely identified and described. Thus, 'social reinforcement' does not qualify as 'technological' until all important ingredients are specified (stimuli, contingency, schedule and effect). They suggest that a rule of thumb for determining whether an independent variable is 'technological' is when an adequately trained reader could replicate the procedure well enough to produce the same results. Reviewing parent training research, Johnson and Katz (1973) pointed out that this standard was not met by the majority of studies, with 65 per cent providing little or no descriptions of the experimental procedure. Bijou (1984) has urged that this 'glossing over' be replaced with a specific account of the training procedure.

Such accounts are essential if we are to achieve one of the hallmarks of good science, namely replicability. As Baer *et al.* (1968) remarked, 'replication is the essence of believability'. Replication is furthermore the essence of generalising a course of training to new supervisors and settings, which is a hallmark of effectiveness. Given that research accounts are necessarily condensed, it would seem that manuals are the cheapest solution to the problem of replication. These can be made available on request or deposited in central sources, such as the British Lending Library. They provide enough space for supervisors to specify the process of training up to Baer's 'technological' standard. The empirical test, however, is whether other supervisors can 'replicate' the course by use of the manual and its related materials. There are examples of successful replications, such as the Portage model involving parents (Shearer and Loftin, 1984), the 'core course' for nurses (Milne *et al.*, 1985b), and the EDY course for teachers (Foxen, 1978). They are, however, rare events, as indeed are attempts to replicate that fail to yield the same results. Such 'falsifications' are arguably more important for our understanding of training and for the elimination of errors than endless verifications (Popper, 1976). Thus, although we had repeated our core course for psychiatric nurses ten times in one setting and other supervisors had done so in different settings (see Chapter 6), the predicted outcome was always verified. Then one supervisor omitted the 'enactive' phase (which we regarded as crucial to the development of skills) and was the first not to obtain any significant degree of learning, as gauged by the key skill measure. Logically, this represented an unusually severe test or attempted falsification of our structured learning format approach. But since it had failed to falsify our model we could place greater confidence in it that we might have done had it continued to receive unthreatening replications.

This finding indicated how important enactive learning is for skill acquisition, a point already made by many researchers through the verification strategy. It also leads us on to the question of the functional importance of other components of training packages. In terms of the present discussion, researchers must specify these components in sufficient detail to permit 'true' falsification, as opposed to the apparently 'false falsification' that occurs simply because we believe we are replicating a procedure when we quite plausibly are not. Consider the report by Quilitch (1975) in which he concluded, unlike some other researchers, that a 'workshop' was an ineffective approach to staff management. This conclusion was based on half a day's training in which trainees listened to lectures on how to maintain good contact with the environment, the importance of social relationships and 'simple activities'. A short film described a procedure for passing from one activity area to another and a slide presentation illustrated the learning potential of profoundly retarded residents. No indication exists in this report that the mediators rehearsed or the supervisors modelled any aspects of the course, making the term 'workshop' wholly inappropriate.

Although one might question Quilitch's use of the word 'workshop' simply in terms of its proper meaning (i.e. a place where *practical* work is done) it should be said that such vagueness is a recurring characteristic of training reports, and frequently includes many other commonly used terms, such as 'feedback' or 'role-playing', which adorn their smaller recesses. Perhaps, then, it is not surprising when a supervisor presumably free-associates with such terms and fails to replicate a reported programme. In fact, in the absence of manuals it is probably only the effect of a combined package of training methods and contents that produces what consistency we do have from one study to the next.

Even in cases where manuals are utilised, there remain many other unidentified variables which may contribute to the overall training effect. Hundert (1982) has pointed out that his use of corrective tutoring as specified by the manual may still leave some variables uncontrolled, such as the way in which the teacher's questions are answered. Live or video-based observation can rectify this kind of shortfall, but is often quite impractical. The minicourse approach, on the other hand, can overcome the difficulty because it bases its supervisor behaviour on video and written material which remains constant. This provides a sound basis for assessing other variables, such as subjects or course content. It also permits others to see exactly what took place under the rubric of 'training'. However, this approach has its limitations, e.g. in the preparation time required or the need for video facilities. For these kinds of reasons, and maybe also because some supervisors actually enjoy face-to-face teaching, we may have to fall back on the manual for our specifications of training. This should be clear and detailed enough to allow supervisors to replicate the training procedure. It will hopefully come to pass that future research reports include access to such a manual as a condition of publication.

Training interventions also involve other salient variables we have not yet mentioned, such as the supervisor's interpretation of a manual. In addition to describing how supervisors and mediators are expected to behave during training, it is every bit as important to determine the effect of what these agents do, whether specified by a manual or not. This is a different kind of independent variable problem. It asks about the relationship between supervisor and mediator behaviours and training outcomes, and so refers us back to the problem of 'superstitious superstition' discussed at the start of this chapter. As emphasised there, the way to minimise irrelevant training activities is to evaluate their functional value. We must not overlook this large research task if we wish our training to have integrity.

A related requirement is for research describing supervisors' behaviour in relation to the system in which they train mediators. This is a different level of analysis from the customary one and yet is undoubtedly worthy of comparable attention. Fairweather *et al.* (1974) are among the very few researchers to have carefully evaluated alternative initiatives in entering systems, although many others have referred to a number of potent variables in a retrospective fashion. We should now consider such examples as the system's learning history with respect to training, the initial contact and the negotiation of entry. Such supervisor and system behaviours will vary in terms of the kind of quantification and manipulation that is feasible, but a broader perspective and an extended application of our methodology make substantial progress in this area quite attainable and very enticing.

(e) Training Outcomes

The outcomes of training interventions are generally far more carefully specified than is the process of training, even though the process is adjudged to have produced the changes. We have described many carefully prepared and administered measures of outcome in the preceding chapters, many of them illustrating a fine-grained analysis of the behaviour of mediators and trainees.

Although the research literature can be seen to vary in its respective attention to either mediator or trainee, they all share a reluctance to concurrently assess the outcome for both groups. This is a logical requisite of the consultative model, which emphasises training the mediator to train the trainee. It therefore follows that an interpretation of an outcome with either agent must be related to the outcome with the other. Thus, before we can attribute an improvement in trainee behaviour to training the mediator, we have to demonstrate that the mediator actually benefited from the training first.

This preliminary step is not a common feature of training interventions, and yet is crucial to our interpretation of the final outcome. Furthermore, even if we have this evidence, there are still at least three remaining problems. One is the need to demonstrate that the skills were actually *applied* as intended, which refers us back to the preceding section on the 'integrity' of the training variable. Secondly we need to show that those trained skills are in fact *relevant* to the needs of trainees and mediators; and thirdly that the training effect was *sufficient* to provide mediators with the necessary level of behavioural proficiency.

It is clear that these three aspects of training are independent and logically necessary conditions for producing and demonstrating a training effect. They are not, however, a prominent feature of research reports, and hence obscure our understanding and efficiency. For example, when Quilitch (1975) suggested that 'workshops' are ineffective, he failed to offer any data either on this or on the three issues of application, relevance and sufficiency. As this 'workshop' appeared to be closer to an introductory 'appreciation' of behavioural techniques, one might legitimately expect only a small increase in the mediators' knowledge, a dimension we know from other studies to be an inadequate springboard for developing practical skills. In this sense, then, the 'workshop' may or may not have influenced those attending, and, if it did, we would predict from the available information that the learning was relevant but insufficient. Similarly, Bailey and Craze (1980) described a training programme in which the only outcomes presented were changes in the trainees. Since other institutional variables may have accounted for the obtained improvements, they can only very tentatively attribute the outcomes to the training course itself.

In addition to the logical requirement to determine the effects of training at each stage, there is another important reason to be thorough in our evaluations. This is to promote the supervisor's learning about training, as we have discussed in terms of the 'superstition trap' at the start of this chapter. In many cases the failure to assess the specific contribution made by training forces us to persist with existing approaches, or to make random changes. To make matters worse, we cannot even exclude the possibility of a simple 'Hawthorn effect', which motivates mediators to use dormant but relevant skills with a real but general training effect.

A comprehensive evaluation of training would appear to require careful measurement of outcomes at six levels, as schematised in Figure 9.1. It must be noted that this kind of evaluative breakdown is largely concerned with determining the effects of training as they proceed *down* the therapeutic triad. Though this is undoubtedly of prime concern, we should not dismiss the relevance of the potential of such a framework for promoting learning among mediators and supervisors as well. This is represented by the upward arrows and can tell us a great deal about some training outcomes. These include the

Figure 9.1: An Outline for Determining the Effects of Training within the Triadic or Similar Consultancy Models

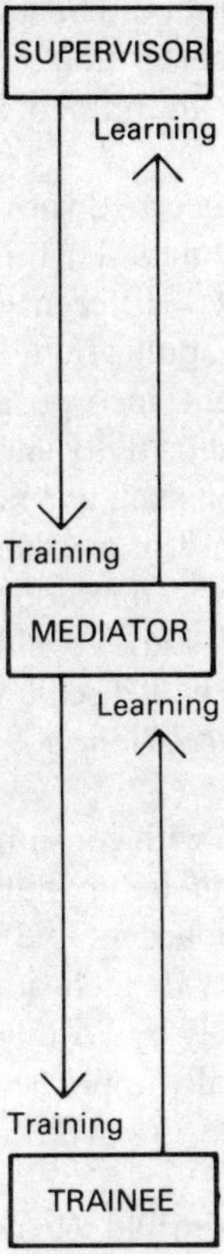

BASELINE

(1) Information on the supervisors' existing training repertoire (e.g. relevance and proficiency)

Implication: supervision skills are subject to the same general laws of learning as are those of mediators

(3) Base rates, existing skills, and needs can be determined and used to adapt training as appropriate to the subjects and setting

Implication: a given training process can be selected that is 'socially valid' and provides relevant, sufficient skills. These factors enhance the effectiveness of the intervention

(5) Similar to (3): needs, strengths, weaknesses can be assessed so that the training is appropriate

Implication: increases the probability of a successful intervention and permits a much more confident interpretation of outcome

POST-TRAINING

(2) The effects of any training or preparation for supervision can be quantified, and some objective description of the supervisor and the supervision process can be generated

Implication: we can begin to specify and manipulate a functional relationship between one major variable and the two that follow

(4) The outcome of training can be measured in terms of the amount of learning and the value of this can be judged for the problem at hand.

Implication: This can reduce 'superstitious supervision' and allows for a logical interpretation of the contribution of mediator training to trainee change

(6) Finally, improvements in the problem behaviours can be judged against (5) and related to the other levels of evaluation

Implication: the overall intervention can be evaluated by its ultimate criterion of success: ameliorating problems. The amount of improvement (and its cost) should also be considered and may justify continuing the whole strategy

supervisor's learning about the relevance or sufficiency of the training; and the mediator's learning about the value of different approaches to trainee management which they have developed through training. Clearly, these kinds of training outcomes are potentially important and should be noted. The essential feature of the framework in this respect is that it provides corrective feedback and thus paves the way to refined and more efficient training procedures.

So far we have been concerned with a conceptual framework for evaluating training outcomes. To this can be added a range of measures which tap its different aspects and some basic requirements for their application. These are clearly related dimensions of measurement, incorporating traditional criteria such as instrument reliability, sensitivity and validity, in association with the focus of the evaluation such as knowledge or skill acquisition. Although these two dimensions overlap, we shall only be concerned here with the different kinds of measures that have been applied in mediator training and with some considerations about their relative value. The measures we will discuss are those relating to *social validity*, *efficiency* and *generalisation*.

Social Validity. A concern with consumer satisfaction has appeared only relatively recently in behaviour therapy and is only now beginning to emerge as an acceptable form of outcome in training research. The rationale for its inclusion in the evaluation 'battery' has been stated persuasively by Wolf (1978). He pointed out that if we wished to achieve socially important interventions, then society would need to validate our work in terms of its goals, procedures and outcomes.

Several authors before him had suggested that the social validity of an intervention was likely to be a factor in its ultimate effectiveness (e.g. Margolis *et al.*, 1977; Yates, 1978). This led to the development and application of several instruments. McMahon and Forehand (1984), for instance, used a questionnaire to assess parents' satisfaction with their training programme, the teaching format and the supervision. Looking back to Chapter 6, we saw how nurses' perceptions of the social validity of a course of training were associated with its subsequent adoption. Social validity may therefore be one way of determining the shape of successive courses. It may simultaneously improve the effectiveness of training, presumably through a closer approximation to the mediators' needs and by facilitating their 'psychological ownership' of the course.

For these reasons social validity becomes an important measure of outcome. It is easily assessed, in terms of the supervisors' time and effort, and adds 'subjective' evidence to the more objective observational data. The only hazard is when these two forms of data conflict in their indications for future courses, and this may place supervisors in a dilemma. For instance, mediators may prefer shorter courses or ones with more reading and videos, and less rehearsal. The objective data may suggest that targeted skills are not sufficiently developed in such courses. In this situation a 'negotiated settlement' might be sought, such as the supervisor breaking down the course into two shorter units while attempting to develop appropriate proficiency levels for each one so that the targeted skills still emerge.

Efficiency. Perhaps the ultimate value of mediator training is the amount of change achieved in relation to the effort required to achieve it. Patterson *et al.* (1970), among others, have stressed the utility of such data as the amount of supervisor time devoted to training, and one could readily add to this other considerations such as the cost in mediator time when they undertake in-service training, or the more straightforward costs of equipment and facilities. These costs must be balanced against the obtained outcomes, of which there are several varieties. The obvious one is improvement in the trainee's problem and in such cases one might contrast a short course with a longer one to see if the shorter, less expensive one produced equivalent results.

To give an illustration, Milne (1982) compared an 'inexpensive' course (heavily based on minimal supervision methods such as reading and video presentations) with a more supervisor-intensive alternative. In terms of social validity, learning and utilisation, it was the latter version that produced superior results. Thus, although this course was more 'expensive' (in both supervisor time and effort), it achieved outcomes that justified the additional investment. The data presented in this study included the amount of supervisor time taken to prepare and execute the training, the learning of the mediators, and the number of trainees (mentally handicapped children) with whom this was applied. Such information is relatively easy to gather, as are other data such as the reduced cost of time to other helping agencies and less use of their resources such as medication (Ginsberg and Marks, 1977).

Of course, it is essential that these outcomes be tied to intervention procedures that produce large enough effects for practical value, that is, for them to be judged socially important (Baer *et al.*, 1968). Even inexpensive procedures are valueless if they produce statistically significant but socially and practically invalid outcomes. Baer cites the illustration of a new classroom procedure which only raises the grade-level achievements of culturally deprived children from D− to D: hardly a sufficient result to merit the effort involved. Such an improvement *might* tell us something valuable about instructional methods, and this may in due course reap more impressive dividends; but it does not yet meet the criterion that the change was sufficient to overcome the given problem. That is, the intervention was ineffective by a practical rather than scientific yardstick (see Abikoff and Gittelman, 1984). In contrast, good practical and scientific outcomes have been reported in parent training ventures using various procedures. They have included manuals and videos as sizeable chunks of the training input and have also used group formats (e.g Christensen *et al.*, 1980). Efficiency may well be boosted further by matching mediator characteristics such as educational background to the training process (O'Dell *et al.*, 1982).

There are thus secondary or 'ecological' outcomes which may none the less justify the continuation of initially ineffective interventions. For example, in large institutions there are very often major organisational problems resulting in low staff morale, high absenteeism/sickness and deteriorated performance. In the midst of this forbidding context a training programme may only achieve modest outcomes in terms of its immediate focus. However, it may have compensatory, secondary effects such as raising morale and reducing absenteeism and sickness, as we found in one study (Milne *et al.*, 1985a). It may also improve the training of students and the records made of patients' behaviour, as we found in another study (Milne, 1985c). Such 'indirect' outcomes may encourage us to sustain our interventions in the face of initially poor clinical outcomes and suggest the potential of wide-ranging or 'ecological' evaluations.

Another 'indirect' dimension concerns the nature of the training input. This also holds promise of improving our efficiency, as in peer tutoring and pyramid training. In addition to reducing the supervisor's involvement in repeated training exercises, these approaches seem likely to promote generalisation and encourage evaluations at a variety of 'ecological' levels. For instance, peer tutoring may promote both learning and motivation in the natural environment while simultaneously reducing implementation problems because of high mediator participation in management.

Generalisation. The 'ecological' dimensions picked out above can readily be construed as an extension of the traditional concern of behaviour therapists with the generality of change to other situations, behaviours and people. If our procedures yield socially valid and effective short-term results in an efficient manner, we must then ask whether these outcomes persist over time (maintenance) and whether they affect any behaviours apart from the targeted ones (generalisation). These issues are very critical to the successful development of mediator training, since the extension of training effects over time, persons, settings and problems is necessary for its ultimate effectiveness and acceptance.

Unfortunately, the research results bearing on these issues do not suggest that training has much generality, reminding us of what Baer *et al.* (1968) have stated: 'generalization should be programmed rather than expected or lamented'. Furthermore, a review of parent training indicated that the more rigorous the assessment, the less evidence there was for any generalisation (Forehand and Atkeson, 1977). Bernstein (1982) also regretted the paucity of research, finding only three studies of generalisation. Burg *et al.* (1979) have also pointed out that although staff training interventions have been successful in the short term, factors such as economic infeasibility (e.g. maintaining a lottery) and administrative reluctance to adopt procedures have frequently curtailed them. Stolz (1981) has examined the generality of four famous and successful behavioural programmes and lamented their demise: 'few of these technologies enjoy widespread adoption by our society.'

Generalisation is much more difficult to evaluate than outcomes such as mediator or trainee learning. It requires effort over and above the basic intervention, and other contingencies, such as brief funding periods and editorial criteria, may militate against it as a widespread research topic. However, generalisation data are necessary before we can fully justify our training interventions. There are several promising topics that could successfully be linked to evaluations of generalisation. These include social support networks for both mediator and supervisor, self-control programmes for mediator or trainee, setting events in the mediator's environment, 'mediator development' packages, and the 'trapping' of a mediator's use of behaviour therapy by existing contingencies within their own environment.

9.7 Conclusion

This book began by acknowledging the potential of the triadic or consultancy model for addressing behavioural problems in health care and education. In the intervening chapters we have reviewed a large number of studies which provided compelling evidence that this potential has largely been realised. We also considered in detail the system or context in which these studies took place. This necessary backdrop to the initial demonstration of mediator learning has given rise to the most serious question marks, with issues of maintenance and particularly generalisation still begging for further systematic study.

A large question mark must also be placed alongside the training relationship: whereas we have a great deal of information on trainee and to a lesser extent mediator behaviour, we know surprisingly little about the role of various supervisor behaviours in facilitating change in either of these two agents. This led us to consider the risk of 'superstitious supervision' and the potential of feedback and supervisor training as antidotes. The 'training laboratory' described by Bernard (1981) appeared particularly promising in developing supervision skills, since the supervisors could immediately observe the effects of their work with mediators in terms of their subsequent efforts with trainees. However, the particulars of supervisor preparation should not obscure from us the great uncharted contribution they make to consultation. Future research reports should not only detail this contribution, but also might advantageously manipulate supervision variables in order to assess their effect on both mediator and trainee: it's high time we overcame our superstition!

None the less, research has successfully addressed an impressive variety of issues. They include promising procedures such as pyramid and incidental training, participative management, mediator and trainee self-control, and 'partnership' between mediator and supervisor. These have the advantage of considering system variables alongside the training technology and so usher in a more fitting analysis of our interventions into complex environments. Setting events are one outstanding illustration of this expanded analysis and merits greater research investment.

Evaluative procedures have also expanded over the last decade to include new variables, such as social validity. It may transpire that this training parameter is highly sensitive to generalisation, particularly if it taps the needs of mediators and trainees. These have been much neglected to date and would complement data on subject variables. We have a long way to go in terms of matching mediators and trainees to training interventions, although to date parent training has been an exception.

In sum, given a growing commitment to these issues within the very framework of the behavioural principles we teach, we can look forward to fulfilling the original promise of the consultancy models and to reaping a little more of what we give away.

APPENDIX: BEHAVIOUR THERAPY PROFICIENCY SCALE (BTPS)

INTRODUCTION

The BTPS is intended to provide a relatively brief yet reliable and valid measure of the application of behaviour therapy suitable for use in the ward context. Users of the scale (supervisors) must first obtain satisfactorily high levels of inter-rater agreement before evaluating mediators.

The scale consists of five categories:

(1) Presenting the session
(2) Providing prompts
(3) Applying contingencies
(4) Ending the session
(5) Data collection

These categories are expected to cover most forms of mediator applied behavioural programmes. However, few programmes will involve all five categories. In this circumstance a mean score is calculated.

The scoring criteria for each category are first broadly outlined, and then more specific guidelines are provided. The scoring system is as follows.

General Scoring System (Quantitative)

– = Irrelevant to score; no opportunity to observe
0 = Lack of trainer response, or totally incorrect response
1 = 'Poor' trainer response; neither good nor bad, intermediate
2 = 'Good' trainer response
3 = 'Excellent' trainer response

NB: It is important to relate these ratings to the prevailing conditions rather than to an absolute standard.

Detailed Scoring System (Qualitative)

Category One — Presenting Session. Broadly: a consistent and appropriate start to the session. Important factors are that:

(1) the mediator obtains the trainee's attention;
(2) the mediator begins at a level appropriate to the trainee's progress (correct step in chain);
(3) the mediator uses the proper sequence of steps and only proceeds to the next step if the trainee is successful.

Specifically:

Score	*Mediator activity*
Score –	Not applicable (e.g. in 'excess' programmes, if there is no occurrence of the target response for reasons beyond the scope of the programme)
Score 0	If the mediator is inconsistent, fails to initiate (cue), or begins at an inappropriate level
Score 1	One of above, OR two poorly introduced (one or two minor errors)
Score 2	Two of the broad factors, OR all three with up to two small errors
Score 3	All three broad factors observed, OR does as well as possible ('excellent'), given the constraints of the programme or situation

Category Two — Providing Prompts. Broadly: The key factors are:

(1) Prompts given in the correct order, i.e. verbal, gestural, physical (if no previous trial);
(2) prompts given in the correct manner, i.e. as minimal as is necessary to enable the trainee to start to respond (NB rate first prompt only);
(3) prompts at the correct time, i.e. as soon as the trainee appears to be unable to respond.

Specifically:

Score	*Mediator activity*
Score –	If prompting is irrelevant or inappropriate
Score 0	If no prompt of any kind is given when the trainee fails to respond
Score 1	When the mediator does one of the key things, i.e. correct order, correct time, correct manner

Score 2	When the mediator does two key things, OR all three factors, with up to two minor errors
Score 3	When the mediator provides all three factors, OR does as well as possible, given the constraints of the programme

Category Three — Applying Contingencies. Broadly:

(1) Mediator consistently uses the same consequence for a given response. i.e. *contingent*. Does not reward inappropriate behaviour.
(2) Mediator provides immediate consequence, i.e. *contiguous*.
(3) Mediator uses appropriate consequences, (i.e. decelerators for excess responses and rewards for deficit responses).

Specifically:

Score	*Mediator activity*
Score –	If the use of consequences is irrelevant
Score 0	When the mediator fails to provide any consequences appropriately
Score 1	Mediator adheres to one of above, or two (max.) poorly administered
Score 2	Mediator does two of the broad factors, OR all three, with up to two minor errors
Score 3	Mediator does all three of above, OR does as well as possible, given the constraints of the programme and situation

Category Four — Ending the Training Session. Broadly:

(1) Removal of the important cue/s for the session.
(2) Cessation of the programme's consequences where appropriate.
(3) Reinstating or arranging other activities for trainee/s.

Specifically:

Score	*Mediator activity*
Score –	Where contingency is continued across more than the training setting

Score 0	Mediator provides no distinction between session and other periods
Score 1	One of the broad factors present, OR two present, but with minor errors
Score 2	Two factors present, correctly administered, OR all three, with up to two minimal errors
Score 3	All three factors employed, OR best possible end, given the programme and situation

Category Five — Data Collection. Broadly:

(1) Mediator maintains accurate records, i.e. involving reliable, appropriately measured data, using correctly labelled and completed record sheets (e.g. trainer's name, date, etc.)
(2) Trainer keeps complete records (i.e. no missing data).
(3) Summary of data prepared (e.g. graph of mean scores).

Specifically:

Score	*Mediator activity*
Score –	(Very improbable)
Score 0	Mediator fails to maintain any form of record.
Score 1	Mediator does one of the broad factors, OR two elements present, but with up to two minor errors, (e.g. graph poorly labeled, 10% of data missing)
Score 2	Two of the above observed, OR all three, with minor errors
Score 3	All three of the factors present and correct, OR records as excellent as possible, given the programme and situation

BTPS: RECORD SHEET

MEDIATOR'S NAME .... WARD ....
SUPERVISOR'S NAME ....
TRAINEE'S NAME .... TARGET RESPONSE ....
GOAL OF PROGRAMME: ....
SUMMARY OF PLAN: ....
....

CATEGORY NUMBER	CATEGORY TITLE	THREE KEY FACTORS	DATES AND RATINGS					F-UP	MEAN SCORE FOR ALL OBSERVATIONS
1.	Presenting the session	• gains attention • Apt. level • Sequence	Date						
			Score						
2.	Providing prompts	• Order • Timing • Manner	Date						
			Score						
3.	Applying contingencies	• Contingent • Appropriate • Contiguous	Date						
			Score						
4.	Ending the training session	• Cues • Consequences • Activity	Date						
			Score						
5.	Data collection	• Complete • Accurate • Summarised	Date						
			Score						

OVERALL MEAN SCORE: ....
COMMENTS: ....
....
....
....

REFERENCES

Abidin, R. R. (1971) 'What's Wrong with Behaviour Modification', *Journal of School Psychology, 9*, 38–42

Abikoff, H. and Gittelman, R. (1984) 'Does Behaviour Therapy Normalize the Classroom Behaviour of Hyperactive Children?', *Archives of General Psychiatry, 41*, 449–54

Ackoff, R. L. (1969) 'Systems Organizations and Inter-disciplinary Research', in F. E. Emery (ed.), *Systems Thinking*, Penguin, Harmondsworth

Adesso, V. J. and Lipson, J. W. (1981) 'Group Training of Parents as Therapists for their Children', *Behaviour Therapy, 12*, 625–33

Adubato, S. A., Adams, M. K. and Budd, K. J. (1981) 'Teaching a Parent to Train a Spouse in Child Management Techniques', *Journal of Applied Behaviour Analysis, 14*, 193–205

Agras, W. S. and Berkowitz, C. (1980) 'Clinical Research in Behaviour Therapy Halfway There?', *Behaviour Therapy, 11*, 472–87

Ainscow, M. and Muncey, J. (1984) *Special Needs Action Programme (SNAP)*, Drake Education Associates, Coventry Local Education Authority

Alevizos, P., Derisi, W., Liberman, R., Eckman, T. and Callahan, E. (1978) 'The Behaviour Observation Instrument: a Method for Direct Observation for Programme Evaluation', *Journal of Applied Behaviour Analysis, 11*, 243–57

Allport, G. W. (1954) 'The Historical Background of Modern Social Psychology', in G. Lindzey (ed.), *Handbook of Social Psychology, Vol. 1, Theory and Method*, Addison-Wesley, Cambridge, Mass.

Ambrose, S. A. and Baker, B. L. (1979, September) *Training Parents of Developmentally Disabled Children: Follow-up Outcome*. Paper presented at the American Psychological Association 87th Annual Convention, New York

Anastasi, A. (1976) *Psychological Testing*, Collier-MacMillan, London

Aponte, H. J. (1976) 'The Family-School interview: an Ecostructural Approach', *Family Process, 15*, 303–13

Applebee, A. N. (1976) 'Microteaching, Component Skills, and the Training of Teachers: an Evaluation of an R & D Project', *British Journal of Educational Technology, 7*, 35–44

Atkeson, B. M. and Forehand, R. (1979) 'Home-based Reinforcement Programmes Designed to Modify Classroom Behaviours a Review and Methodological Evaluation', *Psychological Bulletin, 86*, 1298–1308

Ayllon, T. and Azrin, N. H. (1964) 'Reinforcement and Instructions with Mental Patients', *Journal of Experimental Analysis of Behaviour, 7*, 327–31

Ayllon, T. and Azrin, N. (1968) *The Token Economy*, Appleton-Century-Crofts, New York

Ayllon, T. and Michael, J. (1959) 'The Psychiatric Nurse as a Behavioural Engineer', *Journal of Applied Behaviour Analysis, 2*, 323–34

Baer, D. M. (1981) 'The Nature of Intervention Research', in R. L. Schiebelbusch and D. D. Bricker (eds), *Early Language: Acquisition and Intervention*, University Park Press, Baltimore

Baer, D. M., Wolf, M. M. and Risley, T. R. (1968) 'Some Current Dimensions of Applied Behaviour Analysis', *Journal of Applied Behaviour Analysis, 1*, 91–7

Bailey, R. D. and Craze, A. (1980) 'Nursing Assistants as Co-therapists', *Child Care, Health and Development, 6*, 17–24

Baker, B. L. (1980) 'Training Parents as Teachers of their Developmentally Disabled Children', in S. Salzinger, J. Antrobus and J. Glick (eds), *The Eco-system of the 'Sick' Child*, Academic Press, New York

Baker, B. L. (1983) 'Parents as Teachers: Issues in Training', in J. A. Mulick and S. M. Pueschel (eds), *Parent-Professional Participation in Developmental Disability Services: Foundations and Prospects*, Ware Press, Cambridge, Mass.

Baker, B. L. (1984) 'Intervention with Families with Severely Retarded Children', in J. Blacher (ed.), *Young Severely Handicapped Children and their Families: Research in Review*, Academic Press, New York

Baker, B. L. and Brightman, R. P. (1984) 'Training Parents of Retarded Children: Program-specific Outcomes', *Journal of Behaviour Therapy and Experimental Psychiatry, 15*, 255–60

Baker, B. L. and Heifetz, L. J. (1976) 'The READ Project: Teaching Manuals for Parents of Retarded Children', in T. D. Tjossem (ed.), *Intervention Strategies for High Risk Infants and Young Children*, University Park Press, Baltimore, MD

Baker, B. L. and McCurry, M. C. (1984, December). 'School-based Parent Training: An Alternative for Parents Predicted to Demonstrate Low Teaching Proficiency Following Group Training', *Education and Training of the Mentally Retarded*, December, 261–7

Baker, B. L., Brightman, A. J. and Blatt, J. (1976). *Parents as Teachers Videotapes*, Educational Projects Inc., Cambridge, Mass.

Baker, B. L., Brightman, A. J., Heifetz, L. J. and Murphy, D. (1976–77) *Steps to Independence Series: Behavior Problems*, 1976; *Early Self-help Skills*, 1976; *Intermediate Self-help Skills*, 1976; *Advanced Self-help Skills*, 1976; *Toilet Training*, 1977. Research Press Co., Champaign, Ill.

Baker, B. L., Brightman, A. J., Carroll, N. B., Heifetz, B. B. and Hinshaw, S. P. (1978). *Steps to Independence Series: Speech and Language: Levels 1 & 2*, Research Press, Champaign, Ill.

Baker, B. L., Heifetz, L. J. and Murphy, D. (1980) 'Behavioural Training for Parents of Retarded Children: One-year Follow-up', *American Journal of Mental Deficiency, 85*, 31–8

Baker, B. L., Brightman, A. J. and Heifetz, L. J. (1981a) *Steps to Independence Series: Toward Independent Living*, Research Press, Champaign, Ill.

Baker, B. L., Clark, D. B. and Yasuda, P. M. (1981b) 'Predictors of Success in Parent Training', in P. Mittler (ed.), *Frontiers of Knowledge in Mental Retardation, Vol. I, Social, Educational, and Behavioral Aspects*, University Park Press, Baltimore, MD

Baker, B. L., Brightman, A. J. and Blacher, J. B. (1983). *Steps to Independence Series: Play Skills*, Research Press Co., Champaign, Ill.

Balch, P. and Solomon, R. (1976) 'The Training of Para-professionals as Behaviour Modifiers: a Review', *American Journal of Community Psychology, 4*, 167–79

Balint, M. (1964) *The Doctor, his Patient and the Illness*, London, Pitman

Barker, P. J. (1980) 'Behaviour Therapy in Psychiatric and Mental Handicap Nursing', *Journal of Advanced Nursing, 5*, 55–69

Barker, P. J. (1982) *Behaviour Therapy Nursing*, Croom-Helm, London

Barker, R. G. and Wright, H. F. (1955) *Midwest and its Children: the Psychological Ecology of an American Town*, Harper & Row, New York

Barrowclough, C. (1981) 'An Evaluation of a Staff Training Course in the Use of Behaviour Modification Techniques with the Mentally Retarded', unpublished M.Sc. Thesis, University of Manchester

Baum, C. G. and Forehand, R. (1981) 'Long-term Follow-up Assessment of Parent Training by Use of Multiple Outcome Measures', *Behaviour Therapy, 12*, 643–52

Bauman, K. E., Reiss, M. L., Rogers, R. W. and Bailey, J. S. (1983) 'Dining Out with Children: Effectiveness of a Parent Advice Package on Pre-meal Appropriate

Behaviour', *Journal of Applied Behaviour Analysis, 16*, 55–68

Becker, W. C. (1960) 'The Relationship of Factors in Parental Ratings of Self and Each Other to the Behaviour of Kindergarten Children as Rated by Mothers, Fathers and Teachers', *Journal of Consulting Psychology, 24*, 507–27

Becker, W. C. (1971a) *An Empirical Basis for Change in Education*, Science Research Associates, Chicago

Becker, W. C. (1971b) *Parents are Teachers: a Child Management Programme*, Research Press, Champaign, Ill.

Becker, W. C. and Cornine, D. W. (1980) 'Direct Instruction: an Effective Approach to Educational Intervention with the Disadvantaged and Low Performers', in B. B. Lahey and A. E. Kazdin, *Advances in Clinical Child Psychology, Vol. 3*, Plenum, New York

Becker, W. C., Madsen, C. H., Arnold, C. and Thomas, D. R. (1967) 'The Contingent Use of Teacher Attention and Praise in Reducing Classroom Behaviour Problems', *Journal of Special Education, 1*, 287–307

Becker, W. C., Engelmann, S. and Thomas, D. R. (1971) *Instructor's Manual: Teaching: a Course in Applied Psychology*, Science Research Associates, Henley on Thames

Beckman, D. (1977) *The Mechanical Baby: A Popular History of the Theory and Practice of Child Raising*, Lawrence Hill, Westport, CT

Bender, M. and Valletutti, P. J. (1976) *Teaching the Moderately and Severely Handicapped*, University Park Press, Baltimore, MD

Benjamin, L. T. and Lowman, K. D. (eds) (1982) *Activities Handbook for the Teaching of Psychology*, American Psychological Association, Washington

Benjamin, S. and Kincey, J. (1981) 'Evaluation of Standardized Behavioural Treatment for Agoraphobic In-patients Administered by Untrained Therapists', *British Journal of Psychiatry, 138*, 423–8

Bennis, W. G., Berne, K. D., Ghin, L. and Corey, K. E. (1976) *The Planning of Change*, Holt, Rinehart & Winston, London

Berger, M. (1975) 'Commentary', in C. C. Kiernan and F. P. Woodford (eds), *Behaviour Modification with the Severely Retarded*, Associated Scientific Publishers, Oxford

Berger, M. (1979) 'Behaviour Modification in Educational and Professional Practice: the Dangers of a Mindless Technology', *Bulletin of the British Psychological Society, 32*, 418–19

Berkowitz, B. P. and Graziano, A. M. (1972) 'Training Parents as Behaviour Therapists: a Review', *Behaviour Research and Therapy, 10*, 297–317

Berlin, P. H. and Baker, B. L. (1983) 'Role Conflict and Organizational Climate as Predictors to Implementation of a Parent Training Program', Unpublished manuscript, UCLA

Bernal, M. E. (1969) 'Behavioural Feedback in the Modification of Brat Behaviours', *Journal of Nervous and Mental Disease, 148*, 375–85

Bernal, M. E. (1984) 'Consumer Issues in Parent Training', in, *Parent Training: Foundations of Research and Practice*, R. F. Dangel and R. A. Polster (eds), Guildford Press, London

Bernal, M. E. and North, J. A. (1978) 'A Survey of Parent Training Manuals', *Journal of Applied Behaviour Analysis, 11*, 533–44

Bernal, M. E., Klinnert, M. D. and Schultz, L. A. (1980) 'Outcome Evaluation of Behavioural Parent Training and Client-centred Parent Counselling for Children with Conduct Problems', *Journal of Applied Behaviour Analysis, 13*, 677–91

Bernard, J. M. (1981) 'In Service Training for Clinical Supervisors', *Professional Psychology, 12*, 740–8

Bernard, J. M. (1982) *A Training Laboratory in Clinical Supervision*, Unpublished Manual, Counselling and Guidance Centre, Purdue University

Bernstein, G. S. (1977) 'Training, Modifying and Maintaining Behaviour Managers: a Comprehensive Bibliography', *Psychological Reports, 40*, 182

Bernstein, G. S. (1979) 'Development and Evaluation of an Instrument Designed to Assess the Competence of Behaviour Managers' (Doctoral dissertation University of Wisconsin, 1978), *Dissertation Abstracts International, 39*, 4567–8

Bernstein, G. S. (1982) 'Training Behaviour Change Agents. A Conceptual Review', *Behaviour Therapy, 13*, 1–23

Bernstein, G. S. (1984) 'Training of Behaviour Change Agents', in R. M. Eisler and P. M. Miller (eds), *Progress in Behaviour Modification*, Vol. 17, Academic Press, New York

Berry, I. and Woods, J. (1981) 'The Evaluations of Parent Interventions with Young Handicapped Children', *Behavioural Psychotherapy, 9*, 358–68

Bijou, S. W. (1984) 'Parent Training: Actualizing the Critical Conditions of Early Childhood Development', in: R. F. Dangel and R. A. Polster (eds), *Parent Training: Foundations of Research and Practice,* Guildford Press, London

Bird, J., Marks, I. M. and Lindley, P. (1979) 'Nurse Therapists in Psychiatry: Developments, Controversies and Implications', *British Journal of Psychiatry, 135*, 321–9

Blacher, J. (Ed.) (1984) *Severely Handicapped Young Children and their Families: Research in Review*, Academic Press, New York

Blechman, E. A., Kotanchik, N. L. and Taylor, C. J. (1981) 'Families and Schools Together: Early Behavioural Intervention with High Risk Children', *Behaviour Therapy, 12*, 308–19

Bluna, S., Shearer, M., Frohman, A. and Hilliard, J. (1976) *Portage Guide to Early Education: Checklist*, Portage Project, CESA 12, Box 564, Portage, Wisconsin 53901, USA

Board of Education (1937) *Handbook of Suggestions for the Consideration of Teachers*, HMSO, London

Boardman, W. K. (1962) 'Rusty: a Brief Behaviour Disorder', *Journal of Consulting Psychology, 26*, 293–7

Bolstad, O. D. and Johnson, S. M. (1972) 'Self-regulation in the Modification of Disruptive Classroom Behaviour', *Journal of Applied Behaviour Analysis, 5*, 443–54

Bolton, F. E. (1910) *Principles of Education*, Charles Scribners Sons, New York

Borg, W. R., Kelley, M. L., Langer, P. and Gall, M. (1970) *The Minicourse: a Microteaching Approach to Teacher Education*, Macmillan, London

Bouchard, M. A., Wright, J., Mathieu, M., Laloude, F., Bergeron, G. and Tompin, J. (1980) 'Structured Learning in Teaching Therapists Social Skills: Training, Maintenance and Impact on Client Outcome', *Journal of Consulting and Clinical Psychology, 48*, 491–502

Boucher, J. and Feiler, A. (1982) 'Training Teachers of Children with Severe Learning Difficulties', *Journal of the Association of Educational Psychologists, 8*, 37–40

Boucher, J. (1985) 'Consequences', in: Farrell, P. T. (ed), *E.D.Y.: Its Impact on Staff Training in Mental Handicap*, Manchester University Press, Manchester

Bowles, P. E. and Nelson, R. O. (1976) 'Training Teachers as Mediators: Efficacy of a Workshop versus the Bug-in-the-ear Technique', *Journal of School Psychology, 14*, 15–26

Bragg, L. A. and Wagner, M. K. (1968) 'Issues and Implications of Operant Conditioning: Can Deprivations be Justified?', *Hospital and Community Psychiatry, 19*, 229–30

Braukmann, C. J., Ramp, K. K., Tigner, D. M. and Wolf, M. M. (1984) 'The Teaching Family Approach to Training Group — Home Parents: Training Procedures, Validation Research and Outcome Findings', in R. F. Dangel and R.

A. Polster (eds), *Parent Training: Foundations of Research and Practice*, Guildford Press, London

Brightman, R. P. (1984) 'Training Parents as Advocates for their Developmentally Disabled Children', in J. M. Berg (ed.), *Perspectives and Progress in Mental Retardation. Vol. I, Social, Psychological and Educational Aspects*, University Park Press, Baltimore, MD

Brightman, R. P., Ambrose, S. A. and Baker, B. L. (1980) 'Parent Training: A School-based Model for Enhancing Teaching Performance, *Child Behavior Therapy, 2*, 35–47

Brightman, R. P., Baker, B. L., Clark, D. B. and Ambrose, S. A. (1982) 'Effectiveness of Alternative Parent Training Formats', *Journal of Behavior Therapy and Experimental Psychiatry, 13*, 113–17

Brooker, C. and Wiggins, R. D. (1983) 'Nurse Therapist Trainee Variability: the Implications for Selection and Training', *Journal of Advanced Nursing, 8*, 321–8

Bruner, J. S. (1966) *Toward a Theory of Instruction*, Norton, New York

Bryant, L. E. and Budd, K. S. (1982) 'Self-instructional Training to Increase Independent Work Performance in Pre-schoolers', *Journal of Applied Behaviour Analysis, 15*, 259–71

Buckley, N. K. and Walker, H. M. (1970) *Modifying Classroom Behaviour: a Manual of Procedure for Classroom Teachers*, Research Press, Champaign, Ill.

Budd, K. S. and Fabry, P. L. (1984) 'Behaviour Assessment in Applied Parent Training: Use of a Structured Observation System', in R. F. Dangel and R. A. Polster (eds), *Parent Training: Foundations of Research and Practice*, Guildford Press, London

Buehler, N. E., Patterson, G. K. and Furness, A. M. (1966) 'The Reinforcement of Behaviour in Institutional Settings', *Behaviour Research and Therapy, 4*, 157–67

Burdett, C. (1981) 'The Development of a Ward-based Rehabilitation Scheme for Long-stay Patients: Reorganisation', paper presented at the Annual Conference of the British Association for Behavioural Psychotherapy, Bristol

Burdett, C. (1982) 'Some Practical Aspects and Data on an Innovative Psychiatric Rehabilitation Scheme', paper presented at the Annual Conference of the British Association for Behavioural Psychotherapy, Brighton

Burdett, C. and Milne, D. L. (1985) '"Setting Events" as Determinants of Staff Behaviour: an Exploratory Study', *Behavioural Psychotherapy* (*13*,300-8)

Burg, M. M., Reid, D. H. and Lattimore, J. (1979) 'Use of a Self-recording and Supervision Programme to Change Institutional Staff Behaviour', *Journal of Applied Behaviour Analysis, 12*, 363–75

Burgio, L. D., Whitman, T. L. and Reid, D. H. (1983) 'A Participative Management Approach for Improving Direct Care Staff Performance in an Institutional Setting', *Journal of Applied Behaviour Analysis, 16*, 37–54

Burkhart, B. R., Behles, M. N. and Stumphauzer, J. S. (1976) 'Training Juvenile Probation Officers in Behaviour Modification: Knowledge, Attitude Change or Behavioural Competence?', *Behaviour Therapy, 7*, 47–53

Burland, P. M. and Burland, J. R. (1979) '. . . And Teacher Came Too!' *Behavioural Psychotherapy, 7*, 11–18

Burman, L., Farrell, P. T., Feiler, A., Meffernan, M., Mittler, H. and Reason, R. (1983) 'Redesigning the School Curriculum', *Special Education: Forward Trends, 10 (2)*, 33–6

Buttrum, S. M. (1976) 'So Now I'm a Psychologist: A Critique of Graduate Training in Clinical Psychology by a Recent Graduate', *Ontario Psychologist, 8*, 14–21

Cahoon, O. D. (1968) 'Issues and Implications of Operant Conditioning: Balancing Procedures against Outcomes', *Hospital and Community Psychiatry, 19*, 228–9

Caine, T. M. and Smail, D. J. (1968) 'Attitudes of Psychiatric Nurses to their Role in Treatment', *British Journal of Medial Psychology, 41*, 193–7

Callias, M. (1980) Teaching Parents, Teachers and Nurses, in W. Yule and J. Carr (eds), *Behaviour Modification for the Mentally Handicapped*, Croom-Helm, London

Campbell, D. E., Steenbarger, B. N., Smith, T. W. and Stucky, R. J. (1982) 'An Ecological Systems Approach to Evaluation', *Evaluation Review, 6*, 625–48

Carden-Smith, L. K. and Fowler, S. A. (1984) 'Positive Peer Pressure: the Effects of Peer Monitoring on Children's Disruptive Behaviour', *Journal of Applied Behaviour Analysis, 17*, 213–27

Carr, J. (1980) 'The Organisation of Short Courses', in W. Yule and J. Carr (eds), *Behaviour Modification for the Mentally Handicapped*, Croom-Helm, London

Carsrud, A. L., Carsrud, K. B. and Dodd, B. G. (1980) 'Randomly Monitored Staff Utilization of Behaviour Modification Techniques: Long-term Effects on Clients', *Journal of Consulting and Clinical Psychology, 48*, 704–10

Carsrud, A. L., Carsrud, K. B., Dodd, B. G. and Edwards, V. J. (1981) '*A Behaviour Modification Training Manual and Monitoring/Feedback System for Staff Working with the Mentally Retarded*', University of Texas, Austin, Texas

Carter, R. (1972) *Help! These Kids are Driving me Crazy*, Research Press, Champaign, Ill.

Casey, W. F. (1984) 'Cardio-pulmonary Resuscitation: a Survey of Standards among Junior Hospital Doctors', *Journal of the Royal Society of Medicine, 77*, 921–4

Chamberlain, P. and Mullen, M. (1981) 'Teaching Skills to Severely Mentally Handicapped Adults in Residential Settings', in S. Simpson, P. Higson, R. Holland, J. McBrien, J. Williams and L. Henneman, (eds), *Facing the Challenge*, British Association for Behavioural Psychotherapy, Rossendale, Lancashire

Chamberlain, P., Eysenck, A., Hill, P. and Wallis, J. (1984) *Skills Teaching Education Programme Planning*: Staff Training Package, Psychology Dept, Coldeast Hospital, Southampton SO3 62D

Cherniss, C. (1980) *Staff Burnout*, Sage Publications, London

Christensen, A. (1979) 'Naturalistic Observation of Families: A System for Random Audio Recordings in the Home', *Behaviour Therapy, 10*, 418–22

Christensen, A., Johnson, S. M., Phillips, S. and Glasgow, R. E. (1980) 'Cost-effectiveness in Behavioural Family Therapy', *Behaviour Therapy, 11*, 208–26

Christopherson, E. G. (1977) *Little People*, H & H Enterprises Inc., Lawrence, Kansas

Clarizio, H. F. and Yelon, S. L. (1967) 'Learning Theory Approaches to Classroom Management: Rationale and Intervention Techniques', *Journal of Special Education, 1*, 267–74

Clark, D. B. and Baker, B. L. (1982) *The Teaching Proficiency Test: A Measure of Skill in Applying Behavior Modification Techniques for Parents of Retarded Children*, Unpublished manuscript, UCLA

Clark, D. B. and Baker, B. L. (1983) 'Predicting Outcome in Parent Training', *Journal of Consulting and Clinical Psychology, 51*, 309–11

Clark, D. B., Baker, B. L. and Heifetz, L. J. (1982) 'Behavioural Training for Parents of Mentally Retarded Children: Prediction of Outcome', *American Journal of Mental Deficiency, 87*, 14–19

Clark, F. W., Evans, D. R. and Hamerlynck, L. A. (eds) (1972) *Implementing Behavioural Programmes for Schools and Clinics*, Research Press, Champaign, Ill

Clements, J., Evans, C., Jones, C., Osborne, K. and Upton, G. (1982) 'Evaluation of a Homebased Language Training Programme with Severely Mentally Handicapped Children' *Behaviour Research and Therapy, 20*, 243–9

Cocks, R. P. and Gardner, J. M. (1978) 'The Role of the Educational Psychologist in the Education of Severely Subnormal Children', *Journal of the Association of Educational Psychologists, 2*, 13–20

Coles, E. and Blunden, R. (1981) 'Maintaining New Procedures Using Feedback to

Staff, a Hierarchical Reporting System, and a Multidisciplinary Management Group', *Journal of Organizational Behaviour Management, 3*, 19–33

Cotter, L. H. (1967) 'Operant Conditioning in a Vietnamese Mental Hospital', *American Journal of Psychiatry, 124*, 23–8

Coupe, J. and Porter, J. (in press) *Educating Children with Severe Learning Difficulties — Bridging the Credibility Gap*, Croom Helm, London

Cowen, E. L., Huser, J., Beach, D. R. and Rappaport, J. (1970) 'Parental Perceptions of Young Children and their Relation to Indexes of Adjustment', *Journal of Consulting and Clinical Psychology, 34*, 97–103

Cullen, C., Burton, M., Thomas, M. and Watts, S. (1983a) 'Residents Development Project', Hester Adrian Research Centre, University of Manchester, UK

Cullen, C., Burton, M., Watts, S. and Thomas, M. (1983b) 'A Preliminary Report on the Nature of Interactions in a Mental Handicap Institution', *Behaviour Research and Therapy, 21*, 579–83

Cunningham, C. (1983) 'Early Support and Intervention: the HARC Infant Programme', in P. Mittler and H. McConachie (eds), *Parents, Professionals and Mentally Handicapped People*, Croom Helm, London

Dangel, R. F. and Polster, R. A. (1984a) *Parent Training: Foundations of Research and Practice*, Guildford Press, London

Dangel, R. F. and Polster, R. A. (1984b) 'WINNING! a Systematic, Empirical Approach to Parent Training', in R. F. Dangel and R. A. Polster (eds), *Parent Training: Foundations of Research and Practice*, Guildford Press, London

Davidson, A. F. (1977) 'Clinical Psychology and General Practice: A Preliminary Enquiry', *Bulletin of the British Psychological Society, 30*, 337–8

Davies, K. (1983) 'An Evaluation of Phase 2 of an EDY Course for Residential Social Workers in a Hostel for Mentally Handicapped Children', unpublished M.Sc. Thesis. University of Manchester

DeFleur, M. L. and Westie, F. R. (1963) 'Attitude as a Scientific Concept', *Social Forces, 42*, 17–31

Delfini, L. F., Bernal, M. E. and Rosen, R. M. (1976) 'Comparison of Deviant and Normal Boys in Natural Settings', in E. J. Mash, L. A. Hamerlynck and L. C. Handy (eds), *Behaviour Modification and Families*, Bruner-Mazel, New York

Denicola, J. and Sandler, J. (1980) 'Training Abusive Parents in Child Management and Self-control Skills', *Behaviour Therapy, 11*, 263–70

Doleys, D. M., Cartelli, L. M. and Doster, J. (1976) 'Comparison of Patterns of Mother-Child Interactions', *Journal of Learning Disabilities, 9*, 42–6

Douglas, J. (1981) 'Behaviour Therapy in a Systems Framework', *Bulletin of the British Psychological Society, 34*, 64–7

Drabman, R. S., Hammer, D. and Rosenbaum, M. A. (1979) 'Assessing Generalisation with Children: the Generalisation Map', *Behaviour Assessment, 1*, 203–19

Durlak, J. A. (1979) 'Comparative Effectiveness of Para-professional and Professional Helpers', *Psychological Bulletin, 86*, 80–92

Eilbert, L. R. and Eilbert, H. (1982) 'A Structural Framework for Conceptualizing Ethical Issues in Behavioural-Ecological Practice', in A. M. Jeger and R. S. Slotnick (eds), *Community Mental Health and Behavioural Ecology*, Plenum Press, London

Elias, M. J., Chinsky, J. M., Larcen, S. W. and Allan, G. J. (1982) 'A Multi-level Behavioural Preventive School Programme: Process Problems and Potential', in A. M. Jeger and R. S. Slotnick (eds), *Community Mental Health and Behavioural Ecology*, Plenum Press, London

Embry, L. H. (1980) 'Analysis, Assessment and Development of Family Support for Handicapped Pre-school Children at Risk for Abuse', in J. J. Gallagher (ed.), *New Directions for Exceptional Children*, Jossey-Bass, San Francisco

English and Welsh National Boards for Midwifery and Health Visiting (undated) *Outline Curriculum in Adult Behavioural Psychotherapy*, 178–202 Great Portland Street, London

English and Welsh National Boards for Midwifery and Health Visiting (1982) *Assessment Strategy: Guidance for Staff Involved in Post-basic Clinical Studies Courses* (PBCS Occasional Publication 4), Victory House, 170 Tottenham Court Road, London W1P 0HA

Eyberg, S. M. and Johnson, S. M. (1974) 'Multiple Assessment of Behaviour Modification with Families: Effects of Contingency Contracting and Order of Treated Problems', *Journal of Consulting and Clinical Psychology, 42*, 594–606

Eysenck, H. J. (1957) *Sense and Nonsense in Psychology*, Penguin, London

Fairbrother, P. (1983) 'Needs of Parents of Adults', in P. Mittler and H. McConachie (eds), *Parents, Professionals and Mentally Handicapped People*, Croom Helm, London

Fairweather, G. W. (1967) *Methods for Experimental Social Innovation*, Wiley, London

Fairweather, G. W., Sanders, D., Cressler, D. L. and Maynard, H. (1969) *Community Life for the Mentally Ill: An Alternative to Institutional Care*, Aldine, Chicago

Fairweather, G. W., Sanders, D. H. and Tornatzky, L. G. (1974) *Creating Change in Mental Health Organizations*, Pergamon Press, New York

Farrell, P. T. (1981) 'Training Educational Psychologists to Train Teachers in Behaviour Modification Techniques', *Journal of the Association of Educational Psychologists, 5*, (6) 31–3

Farrell, P. T. (1982) 'An Evaluation of an EDY Course in Behaviour Modification Techniques for Teachers and Care Staff in an ESN (S) School', *Special Education: Forward Trends, 9*, 21–5

Farrell, P. T. (1983) 'Staff Training in Mental Handicap — the E.D.Y. Course', *Newsletter of the Association for Child Psychiatry, 15*, 16–18

Farrell, P. T. (ed.) (1985a) *EDY: Its Impact on Staff Training in Mental Handicap*, Manchester University Press, Manchester

Farrell, P. T. (1985b) 'The Role of Linked Agencies — Educational Psychologists', in J. Coupe and J. Porter (eds), *Educating Children with Severe Learning Difficulties — Bridging the Credibility Gap*, Croom Helm, London

Farrell, P. and Sugden, M. (1984) 'An Evaluation of an EDY Course in Behavioural Techniques for Classroom Assistants in a School for Children with Severe Learning Difficulties', *Educational Psychology, 4*, 185–98

Faw, G. D., Reid, D. H., Schopis, M. M., Fitzgerald, J. R. and Welty, P. A. (1981) 'Involving Institutional Staff in the Development and Maintenance of Sign Language Skills with Profoundly Retarded Persons', *Journal of Applied Behaviour Analysis, 14*, 411–23

Fawcett, S. B. and Fletcher, R. K. (1977) 'Community Applications of Instructional Technology: Training Writers of Instructional Packages', *Journal of Applied Behaviour Analysis, 10*, 739–46

Fawcett, S. B., Mathews, A. M. and Fletcher, L. K. (1980) 'Some Promising Dimensions for Behavioural Community Technology', *Journal of Applied Behaviour Analysis, 13*, 505–78

Felce, D., Jenkins, J., de Koch, V. and Mansell, J. (1983a) *The Bereweeke Skill Teaching System: Training Workshop Workbook*, Health Care Evaluation Research Team, 45/47 Salisbury Road, Southampton SO9 5NH

Felce, D., Jenkins, J., Dell, D., Flight, C. and Mansell, J. (1983b) *The Bereweeke Skill Teaching System: System Administrator's Handbook*, NFER-Nelson, Windsor, Berks

Felce, D., de Koch, V., Mansell, J. and Jenkins, J. (1984) 'Providing Systematic

Individual Teaching for Severely Disturbed and Profoundly Mentally Handicapped Adults in Residential Care', *Behaviour Research Therapy, 22*, 299–309

Feldman, W. S., Manella, K. J., Apodaca, L. and Varni, J. W. (1982) 'Behavioural Group Parent Training in Spina Bifida', *Journal of Clinical Child Psychology, 11*, 144–50

Feldman, W. S., Manella, K. J. and Varni, J. W. (1983) 'A Behavioural Parent Training Program for Single Mothers of Physically Handicapped Children', *Child: Care, Health, and Development, 9*, 157–68

Ferser, H., Keely, S. M. and Shemberg, K. M. (1974) 'Training Parents in Behaviour Modification Outcome and Problems Encountered in a Programme after Patterson's Work', *Behaviour Therapy, 5*, 415–19

Fichter, M. M. and Wittchen, H. U. (1980) 'Clinical Psychology and Psychotherapy: a Survey of the Present State of Professionalization in 23 Countries', *American Psychologist, 35*, 16–25

Fischer, J. (1975) 'Training for Effective Therapeutic Practice', *Psychotherapy: Theory, Research and Practice, 12*, 118–23

Fisher, E. B., Winkler, N. C., Krasner, L., Kagah, J., Battalio, K. C. and Basnum, N. L. (1978) 'Economic Perspectives in Behaviour Therapy: Complex Interdependencies in Token Economies', *Behaviour Therapy, 9*, 391–403

Flanagan, S., Adams, H. E. and Forehand, R. (1979) 'A Comparison of Four Instructional Techniques for Teaching Parents to Use Time-out', *Behaviour Therapy, 10*, 94–102

Flanders, N. (1970) *Analyzing Teacher Behaviour*, Addison-Wesley, New York

Fleischman, M. J. (1981) 'A Replication of Patterson's "Intervention for boys with conduct problems"', *Journal of Consulting and Clinical Psychology, 49*, 342–51

Fleischman, M. J. and Szyhula, S. A. (1981) 'A Community Setting Replication of a Social Learning Treatment for Aggressive Children', *Behaviour Therapy, 12*, 115–22

Fontana, D. (1982) Class Control and Management, in Fontana, D. (ed.) *Psychology for Teachers*, Macmillan Press, London

Ford, J. E. (1980) 'A Classification System for Feedback Procedures', *Journal of Organizational Behaviour Management, 2*, 183–91

Forehand, R. and Atkeson, B. M. (1977) 'Generality of Treatment Effects with Parents as Therapists: a Review of Assessment and Implementation Procedures', *Behaviour Therapy, 8*, 575–93

Forehand, R. Griest, D. L. and Wells, K. C. (1979) 'Parent Behaviour Training: an Analysis of the Relationship among Multiple Outcome Measures', *Journal of Abnormal Child Psychology, 7*, 229–42

Forehand, R., Wells, K. C. and Griest, D. L. (1980) 'An Examination of the Social Validity of a Parent Training Programme', *Behaviour Therapy, 11*, 488–502

Forehand, R., Breiner, J., McMahon, R. J. and Davies, G. (1981) 'Predictors of Cross Setting Behaviour Change in the Treatment of Child Problems', *Journal of Behaviour Therapy and Experimental Psychiatry, 12*, 311–13

Forehand, R., Furey, W. M. and McMahon, R. J. (1984) 'The Role of Maternal Distress in a Parent Training Programme to Modify Child Non-compliance', *Behavioural Psychotherapy, 12*, 93–108

Foxen, T. (1977) *Education of the Developmentally Young Mentally Handicapped Child: A Programme of Evaluated Dissemination and Research* (first report to the Department of Education and Science), Hester Adrian Research Centre, University of Manchester

Foxen, T. (1978) 'Education of the Developmentally Young Mentally Handicapped Child: a Programme of Evaluated Dissemination and Research', (Second Annual Report to the Department of Education and Science), Hester Adrian Research

Centre, University of Manchester
Foxen, T. and McBrien, J. (1981) *Trainee Workbook*, Manchester University Press, Manchester
Franzini, L. R. and Tilker, H. A. (1972) 'On the Terminological Confusion between Behaviour Therapy and Behaviour Modification', *Behaviour Therapy, 3*, 279–82
Fredericks, H. D. B., Anderson, R. B., Baldwin, V. L., Grove, D., Moore, W. G., Moore, M. and Beaird, J. H. (1977) *The Identification of Competencies of Teachers of the Severely Handicapped*, Oregon State Systems of Higher Education, Monmouth, Oregon
Freud, S. (1909) 'Analysis of a Phobia in a 5-year-old Boy', *Collected Papers, Vol. 3*, Basic Books (1959), New York
Freud, S. (1927) 'The Question of Lay Analysis', *Two Short Accounts of Psychoanalysis*, Penguin (1972), Middlesex
Furnham, A. (1983) 'Social Psychology as Common Sense', *Bulletin of the British Psychological Society, 36*, 105–9
Gagé, N. L. (ed.) (1973) *Handbook of Research on Teaching*, Rand McNally, Chicago
Gagné, R. M. (1970) *The Conditions of Learning*, Holt, Rinehart & Winston, London
Gardner, J., Murphy, J. and Crawford, N. (1983) *The Skills Analysis Model*, British Institute of Mental Handicap, Kidderminster
Gardner, J. M. (1972) 'Teaching Behaviour Modification to Non-professionals', *Journal of Applied Behaviour Analysis, 5*, 517–21
Gardner, J. M. (1973) 'Training the Trainer: a Review of Research on Teaching Behaviour Modification', in Rubin *et al.* (eds), *Advances in Behaviour Therapy*, Academic Press, New York
Gardner, J. M. and Giampa, F. L. (1971) 'The Attendant Behaviour Checklist: Measuring On-the-ward Behaviour of Institutional Attendants', *American Journal of Mental Deficiency, 75*, 617–22
Gardner, J. M., Brust, D. J. and Watson, L. S. (1970) 'A Scale to Measure Skill in Applying Behaviour Modification Techniques to the Mentally Handicapped', *American Journal of Mental Deficiency, 74*, 633–6
Garfield, S. L. and Kurtz, R. (1976) 'Clinical Psychologists in the 1970s', *American Psychologist, 31*, 1–9
Gelfand, D. M., Gelfand, S. and Dobson, W. R. (1967) 'Unprogrammed Reinforcement of Patients Behaviour in a Mental Hospital', *Behaviour Research and Therapy, 5*, 201–7
Georgiades, N. J. and Phillimore, L. (1975) 'The Myth of the Hero-innovator and Alternative Strategies for Organisational Change', C. C. Kiernan and F. P. Woodford (eds), *Behaviour Modification with the Severely Retarded*, Associated Scientific Publishers, New York
Gibran, K. (1926) *The Prophet*, Heinemann, London
Gilbert, T. F. (1982) 'Human Incompetence: the Autobiography of an Educational Revolutionist', *Journal of Organizational Behaviour Management, 3*, 55–67
Gilchrist, E. (1916) 'The Extent to Which Praise and Reproof Affect a Pupil's Work', *School and Society, 4*, 372–4
Ginsberg, G. and Marks, I. (1977) 'Costs and Benefits of Behavioural Psychotherapy: a Pilot Study of Neurotics Treated by Nurse-therapists', *Psychological Medicine*, 7, 685–700
Gladstone, B. W. and Sherman, J. A. (1975) 'Developing Generalized Behaviour Modification Skills in High School Students Working with Retarded Children', *Journal of Applied Behaviour Analysis, 8*, 169–80
Glen, F. (1975) *The Social Psychology of Organisations*, Methuen, London
Glogower, F. and Sloop, E. W. (1976) 'Two Strategies of Group Training of Parents as Effective Behaviour Modifiers', *Behaviour Therapy, 7*, 177–84

Glynn, E. L., Thomas, J. D. and Shee, S. M. (1973) 'Behavioural Self-control of On-task Behaviour in an Elementary Classroom', *Journal of Applied Behaviour Analysis, 6*, 105–13

Goffman, E. (1961) *Asylums*, Pelican, Middlesex

Graziano, A. M. (1977) 'Parents as Behaviour Therapists', in M. Hersen, R. M. Eisler and P. M. Miller (eds), *Progress in Behaviour Modification*, Academic Press, New York

Greene, B. F., Willis, B. S., Levy, R. and Bailey, J. S. (1978) 'Measuring Client Gains from Staff-implemented Programmes', *Journal of Applied Behaviour Analysis, 11*, 395–412

Greene, B. F., Bailey, J. S. and Barber, F. (1981) 'An Analysis and Reduction of Disruptive Behaviour on School Buses', *Journal of Applied Behaviour Analysis, 14*, 177–92

Greer, R. D. and Polirstok, S. R. (1982) 'Collateral Gains and Short-term Maintenance in Reading and On-task Responses by Inner-city Adolescents as a Function of their Use of Social Reinforcement while Tutoring', *Journal of Applied Behaviour Analysis, 15*, 123–39

Griest, D. L. and Wells, K. C. (1983) 'Behavioural Family Therapy with Conduct Disorders in Children', *Behaviour Therapy, 14*, 37–53

Gross, A. M. and Drabman, R. S. (1982) 'Teaching Self-recording, Self-evaluation and Self-reward to Non-clinic Children and Adolescents', in P. Karoly and F. H. Kanfer (eds), *Self-management and Behaviour Change: from Theory to Practice*, pp. 285–314, Pergamon, New York

Gruver, G. (1971) 'College Students as Therapeutic Agents', *Psychological Bulletins, 76*, 111–27

Guerney, B. G. (1969) *Psychotherapeutic Agents*, Holt, Rinehart & Winston, London

Hall, J. N. (1973) 'Ward Behaviour Modification Projects in Great Britain', *Bulletin of the British Psychological Society, 26*, 199–201

Hall, J. N. (1974) 'Training Nurses in Behaviour Modification. An Analysis of Current British Practice', *Behaviour Modification Newsletter, 6*, 17–24

Hall, J. N. (1979) 'Nurse Therapy and Role Change in the Health Care Professions', *Bulletin of the British Psychological Society, 32*, 71–3

Hall, J. N. and Baker, N. (1973) 'Token Economy Systems: Breakdown and Control', *Behaviour Research and Therapy, 11*, 253–63

Hall, J. N. and Brooks, K. M. (1976) 'Teaching Psychologists to Teach Psychology: the Improvement of Teaching Skills in Health Service Professions', *Medical Education, 10*, 183–8

Hall, M. C. (1984) 'Responsive Parenting: a Large-scale Training Programme for School Districts, Hospitals and Mental Health Centres', in R. F. Dangel and R. A. Polster (eds), *Parent Training: Foundations of Research and Practice*, Guildford Press, London

Hall, R. V. (1971) *Managing Behaviour 2*, H & H Enterprises, Lawrence

Hall, R. V. and Copeland, R. E. (1972) 'The Responsive Teaching Model: a First Step in Shaping School Personnel as Behaviour Modification Specialists', in F. W. Clark, D. R. Evans and L. A. Hamerlynck (eds), *Implementing Behavioural Programmes for Schools and Clinics*, Research Press, Champaign, Ill.

Hallahan, D. P., Lloyd, J. W., Kneedler, R. D. and Marshall, K. J. (1982) 'A Comparison of the Effects of Self versus Teacher Assessment of On-task Behaviour', *Behaviour Therapy, 13*, 715–23

Hallam, R. S. (1975) 'The Training of Nurses as Therapists: Outcomes and Implications', *Bulletin of the British Psychological Society, 28*, 331–6

Harris, S. L., Wolchik, S. A. and Weitz, S. (1981) 'The Acquisition of Language Skills by Autistic Children: Can Parents do the Job?', *Journal of Autism and*

Developmental Disorders, 11, 373–84

Hart, B. nd Risley, T. R. (1975) 'Incidental Teaching of Language in the Pre-school Child', *Journal of Applied Behaviour Analysis, 8*, 411–20

Hawkins, N. P. (1972) 'It's Time we Taught the Young how to Be Good Parents', *Psychology Today, 6*, 28

Hawkins, R. P., Peterson, R. F., Schweid, E. and Bijou, S. W. (1966) 'Behaviour Therapy in the Home: Amelioration of Problem Parent-Child Relations with the Parent in a Therapeutic Role', *Journal of Experimental Child Psychology, 4*, 99–107

Hawks, D. (1981) 'The Dilemma of Clinical Practice: Surviving as a Clinical Psychologist', in I. McPherson and A. Sutton (eds), *Reconstructing Psychological Practice*, Croom Helm, London

Hattie, J. A., Sharpley, C. F. and Rogers, H. J. (1984) 'Comparative Effectiveness of Professional and Paraprofessional Helpers', *Psychological Bulletin, 95*, 534–41

Hegarty, J. R. (1980) 'Teaching Assessment Skills to Care Staff', Paper presented at the British Institute of Mental Handicap, Lincoln

Hegarty, J. R. (1981) *Audio-visual Methods for Staff Training*, Graves Medical Audio-visual Library, Chelmsford, Essex

Hegarty, J. R., Winter, S. P. and Lawson, S. D. (1978) 'The Use of Audiotaped Lectures during Staff Training in Mental Handicap', in P. Williams (ed.), *Progress in Practice*, APMH, London

Heider, F. (1958) *The Psychology of Interpersonal Relations*, Wiley, New York

Heifetz, L. J. (1977) 'Behavioural Training for Parents of Retarded Children: Alternative Formats Based on Instructional Manuals', *American Journal of Mental Deficiency, 82*, 194–203

Heinrich, R. L. (1981) 'AABT's Continuing Education Committee: 1977–1980', *The Behaviour Therapist, 4*, 11–13

Henderson, E. S. (1978) *The Evaluation of In-service Teacher Training*, Croom Helm, London

Herbert, E. W. and Baer, D. M. (1972) 'Training Parents as Behaviour Modifiers: Self-recording Contingent Attention', *Journal of Applied Behaviour Analysis, 5*, 139–49

Herbert, M. (1981) *Behavioural Treatment of Problem Children: a Practice Manual*, Academic Press, London

Herbert, M. and Ivaniec, D. (1981) 'Behavioural Psychotherapy in Natural Home-settings: an Empirical Study Applied to Conduct Disordered and Incontinent Children', *Behavioural Psychotherapy, 9*, 55–76

Hereford, C. F. (1963) *Changing Parental Attitudes through Group Discussion*, University of Texas Press, Austin

Hersen, M. (1979) 'Limitations and Problems in the Clinical Application of Behavioural Techniques in Psychiatric Settings', *Behaviour Therapy, 10*, 65–80

Hersen, M. (1981) 'Complex Problems Require Complex Solutions', *Behaviour Therapy, 12*, 15–29

Hester Adrian Research Centre (HARC) (1980) *Proceedings of the EDY Instructors' Conference*, University of Manchester, Manchester

Hogg, J., Foxen, T. and McBrien, J. (1981) 'Issues in the Training and Evaluation of Behaviour Modification Skills for Staff Working with Profoundly Retarded Multiply Handicapped Children', *Behavioural Psychotherapy, 9*, 345–57

Hokanson, J. E. (1983) *Introduction to the Therapeutic Process*, Addison-Wesley, London

Hollander, M. A. and Plutchik, R. (1972) 'A Reinforcement Programme for Psychiatric Attendants', *Journal of Behaviour Therapy and Experimental Psychiatry, 3*, 297–300

Holman, J. (1977) 'The Moral Risk and High Cost of Ecological Concern in Applied

Behaviour Analysis', in A. Rogers-Warren and S. F. Warren (eds), *Ecological Perspectives in Behaviour Analysis*, University Park Press, Baltimore

Hopkinson, D. and Hurley, S. J. (1976) 'Helper Ethics and the Professional-Paraprofessional Gap', *Professional Psychologist, 7*, 319–22

Horne, D. de L., McTiernan, G. and Strauss, N. H. M. (1981) 'A Case of Severe Obsessive-Compulsive Behaviour Treated by Nurse-therapists in an In-patient Unit', *Behavioural Psychotherapy, 9*, 46–54

Horner, R. D. (1973) 'Three Years of Attendant Application of Behaviour Modification', Rubin *et al.* (eds), *Advances in Behaviour Therapy*, Academic Press, New York

Horner, R. D. (1980) 'The Effects of an Environmental "Enrichment" Programme on the Behaviour of Institutionalised Profoundly Retarded Children', *Journal of Applied Behaviour Analysis, 13*, 473–91

Hosford, R. E. and Mills, M. E. (1983) 'Video in Social Skills Training', in P. W. Dowrick and S. J. Biggs (eds), *Using Video*, pp. 125–150, Wiley, New York

Hudson, A. M. (1982) 'Training Parents of Developed Mentally Handicapped Children: a Component Analysis', *Behaviour Therapy, 13*, 325–33

Hundert, J. (1982) 'Training Teachers in Generalized Writing of Behaviour Modification Programmes for Multi-handicapped Deaf Children', *Journal of Applied Behaviour Analysis, 15*, 111–23

Hutchinson, J. M., Jarman, P. H. and Bailey, J. S. (1980) 'Public Posting with a Rehabilitation Team: Effects on Attendance and Performance', *Behaviour Modification, 4*, 57–70

Isaacs, C. D. (1982) 'Treatment of Child Abuse: a Review of the Behavioural Interactions', *Journal of Applied Behaviour Analysis, 15*, 273–94

Isaacs, C. D., Embry, L. H. and Baer, D. M. (1982) 'Training Family Therapists: an Experimental Analysis', *Journal of Applied Behaviour Analysis, 15*, 505–20

Ivancic, M. T., Reid, D. H., Iwata, B. A., Faw, G. D. and Page, T. J. (1981) 'Evaluating a Supervision Programme for Developing and Monitoring Therapeutic Staff-Resident Interactions during Institutional Care Routines', *Journal of Applied Behaviour Analysis, 14*, 95–107

Ivey, A. E., Normington, C. J., Mueller, D. C., Merrill, W. H. and Haase, R. F. (1968) 'Micro-counselling and Attending Behaviour: an Approach to Pre-counsellor Training', *Journal of Counselling Psychology, 15* (Monograph supplement 5)

Iwata, B. A., Bailey, J. S., Brown, K. M., Foshee, T. J. and Alpern, M. (1976) 'A Performance-based Lottery to Improve Residential Care and Training by Institutional Staff', *Journal of Applied Behaviour Analysis, 9*, 417–31

Jeffree, D. and McConkey, R. (1976) *Let me Speak*, Souvenir Press, London

Jeffree, D. M., McConkey, R. and Hewson, S. (1977) *Teaching the Handicapped Child*, Souvenir Press, London

Jencks, C. (1972) *Inequality*, Basic Books, New York

Jenkins, J., Felce, D., Mansell, J. and de Koch, U. (1983) *The Bereweeke Skill Teaching System: Training Workshop Manual*, Health Care Evaluation Research Team, 45–47 Salisbury Road, Southampton SO9 5NH

Johnson, C. A. and Katz, R. C. (1973) 'Using Parents as Change Agents for their Children: a Review' *Journal of Child Psychology and Psychiatry, 14*, 181–200

Johnson, S. M. and Bolstad, O. D. (1973) 'Methodological Issues in Naturalistic Observation', in L. A. Hamerlynck, L. C. Handy and E. J. Marsh (eds) *Behaviour Change*, Research Press, Ill.

Johnson, S. M. and Lobitz, G. (1972) 'Demand Characteristics in Naturalistic Observation', Unpublished manuscript, Eugene, University of Oregon

Joint Board of Clinical Nursing Studies (1978) *Course Evaluation Package* (Occasional Publication No. 2), Joint Board of Clinical Nursing Studies, London

Jones, A. and Robson, R. (1983) 'Within Course Effects of a Training Package for Teachers of the Mentally Handicapped', *Special Education, Forward Trends: Research Supplement, 10*, 17–20

Jones, F. H., Fremouw, W. and Carples, S. (1977) 'Pyramid Training of Elementary School Teachers to Use of Classroom Management "skill package"', *Journal of Applied Behaviour Analysis, 10*, 239–53

Kashima, K. J. (1983) *Improving Maintenance of Parent Teaching: an Intervention Following Participation in a Behavioral Training Program for Parents of Mentally Retarded Children*. Unpublished Master's thesis, University of California, Los Angeles

Katz, R. C., Johnson, C. A. and Gelfard, S. (1972) 'Modifying the Dispensing of Reinforcers: Some Implications for Behaviour Modification with Hospitalized Patients', *Behaviour Therapy, 3*, 579–88

Kazdin, A. E. and Moyer, W. (1976) 'Training Teachers to use Behaviour Modification', in S. Yen and R. W. McIntyre (eds), *Teaching Behavior Modification*, Behaviordelia, Kalamazoo, MI

Keeley, S. M., Shamberg, K. M. and Carbonell, J. (1976) 'Operant Clinical Intervention: Behaviour Management or Beyond? Where are the Data?', *Behaviour Therapy, 7*, 292–305

Kendall, R. E. (1981) 'The present Status of ECT', *British Journal of Psychiatry, 139*, 265–87

Kent, R. N. and O'Leary, K. D. (1977) 'Treatment of Conduct Problem Children: BA and/or Ph.D. Therapists', *Behaviour Therapy, 8*, 653–8

Kiernan, C. and Riddick, B. (1973) *A Draft Programme for Training in Operant Techniques*, Thomas Coram Research Unit, London

Kiernan, C. C. and Wright, E. C. (1973) 'Behaviour Modification with the Severely Mentally Handicapped', *Proceedings of the Royal Society for Medicine, 66*, 1137–46

Kiernan, C., Harlour, S., Sanders, C. and Riddick, B. (1973) *Programme Materials 2*, Thomas Coram Research Unit, London

Kiernan, C. C., Wright, E. C. and Hawks, G. D. (1975) 'The Ward-wide Application of Operant Training Techniques', *Proceedings of the Third Congress of the International Association for the Scientific Study of Mental Deficiency, Vol. 1*, Polish Medical Publishers, Warsaw

Kiernan, C., Jordan, R. and Sanders, C. (1978) *Starting Off: Establishing Play and Communication in the Handicapped Child*, Souvenir Press, London

Kiresuk, T. J. and Sherman, R. E. (1968) 'Goal Attainment Scaling: a General Method for Evaluating Comprehensive Community Mental Health Programmes', *Community Mental Health Journal, 4*, 443–53

Kirton, M. (1976) 'Adaptors and Innovators: a Description and Measure', *Journal of Applied Psychology, 61*, 622–9

Kissel, R. C., Whitman, T. L. and Reid, D. H. (1983) 'An Institutional Staff Training and Self-management Programme for Developing Multiple Self-care Skills in Severely/Profoundly Retarded Individuals', *Journal of Applied Behaviour Analysis, 16*, 395–416

Kistner, J., Hammer, D., Wolfe, D., Rothblum, and Drabman, R. S. (1982) 'Teacher Popularity and Contrast Effects in a Classroom Token Economy', *Journal of Applied Behaviour Analysis, 15*, 85–96

Knight, G., Pickerill, C. and Gale, E. (1985) 'EDY in Health Service Settings', in P. T. Farrell (ed.), *EDY: Its Impact on Staff Training in Mental Handicap*, Manchester University Press, Manchester

Koegel, R. L., Russo, D. C. and Rincover, A. (1977) 'Assessing and Training Teachers in the Generalized Use of Behavior Modification with Autistic Children', *Journal of Applied Behavior Analysis, 10*, 197–205

Koegel, R. L., Glahn, T. J. and Nieminen, G. S. (1978) 'Generalization of Parent-training Results', *Journal of Applied Behaviour Analysis, 11*, 95–109

Kopp, S. (1973) *If you Meet the Buddha on the Road, Kill Him*, Sheldon Press, London

Kraemer, H. C. (1981) 'Coping Strategies in Psychiatric Clinical Research', *Journal of Consulting and Clinical Psychology, 49*, 309–19

Kuna, D. J. (1975) 'Lecturing, Reading, and Modelling in Counsellor Restatement Training', *Journal of Counselling Psychology, 22*, 542–6

Kushlick, A. (1968) 'Social Problems in Mental Subnormality', in: E. Miller (ed.), *Foundations of Child Psychiatry*, Pergamon, London

Lancet Editorial (1981) 'ECT in Britain: a Shameful State of Affairs', *Lancet, 2*, 1207–8

Lang, P. J. and Melamed, B. G. (1969) 'Avoidance Conditioning Therapy for an Infant with Chronic Ruminative Vomiting', *Journal of Abnormal Psychology, 74*, 1–8

Larsen, L. A. and Bricker, W. A. (1968) *A Manual for Parents and Teachers of Severely and Moderately Retarded Children*, IMRID Reports, Vol. 5, No. 22, Nashville, Tennessee

Lawrence, R. M. (1910) *Primitive Psycho-therapy and Quackery*, Constable, London

LeBow, M. D. (1976) 'Applications of Behaviour Modification in Nursing Practice', in M. Hersen, R. M. Eisler and P. M. Miller (eds), *Progress in Behaviour Modification*, Academic Press, London

Levine, F. M. and Tilker, H. A. (1974) 'A Behaviour Modification Approach to Supervision of Psychotherapy', *Psychotherapy: Theory, Research and Practice, 11*, 182–8

Ley, P. (1977) 'Psychological Research on Doctor-Patient Communication', in S. J. Rachman (ed.), *Advances in Medical Psychology*, Pergamon Press, Oxford

Liberman, R. P., Kuehnel, T. G., Kuehnel, J. M., Eckman, T. and Rosenstem, J. (1982) 'The Behavioural Analysis and Modification Project for Community Mental Health: from Inception to Dissemination' in A. M. Jeger and R. S. Slotnik (eds), *Community Mental Health and Behavioural Ecology*, Plenum Press, London

Litow, L. and Pumroy, D. K. (1975) 'A Brief Review of Classroom Group-oriented Contingencies', *Journal of Applied Behaviour Analysis, 8*, 341–7

Lobitz, G. K. and Johnson, S. M. (1975) 'Normal Versus Deviant Children: a Multi-method Comparison', *Journal of Abnormal Child Psychology, 3*, 353–74

Locke, E. A. *et al.* (1981) 'Goal-setting and Task Performance: 1969–1980', *Psychological Bulletin, 90*, 125–52

Locke, H. J. and Wallace, K. M. (1959) 'Short marital-adjustment and prediction tests: their reliability and validity', *Journal of Marriage and Family Living, 21*, 251–5

Loeber, R. (1971) 'Engineering the Behavioural Engineer', *Journal of Applied Behaviour Analysis, 4*, 321–6

Loeber, R. and Weisman, R. A. (1975) 'Contingencies of Therapist and Trainer Performance', *Psychological Bulletin, 82*, 660–88

Lovaas, O. I., Shaeffer, B. and Simmons, J. Q. (1965) 'Building Social Behaviour in Autistic Children by Use of Electric Shock', *Journal of Experimental Research in Personality, 1*, 99–109

Luborsky, L., Chandler, M., Auerbach, A. H., Cohen, J. and Bachrach, H. M. (1971) 'Factors Influencing the Outcome of Psychotherapy: a Review of Quantitative Research', *Psychological Bulletin, 75*, 145–85

Lucero, R. J., Vai, D. J. and Scherser, J. (1968) 'Regulating Operant Conditioning Programmes', *Hospital and Community Psychiatry*, February, 53–4

Lutzker, J. R. (1984) 'Project 12-ways: Treating Child Abuse and Neglect from an

Ecobehavioural Perspective', in R. F. Dangel and R. A. Polster (eds), *Parent Training: Foundations of Research and Practice*, Guildford Press, London

MacKrell, K. (1983) 'Teaching Behaviour Modification and Behaviour Analysis Skills', *Behaviour Analysis, 4*, 2–17

Macmillan, A. and Kelvin, I. (1977) 'Behaviour Modification in Teaching Strategy: some Emergent Problems and Suggested Solutions', *Educational Research, 20*, 10–21

Macmillan, A., Hartley, J. and Stansfeld, R. (1978) 'Behaviour Modification Procedures in a School for the Maladjusted', *Therapeutic Education, 6*, 32–7

McBrien, J. (1978) *Trainee Assessment Form: Guide to Use*. Unpublished document, Hester Adrian Research Centre, University of Manchester

McBrien, J. (1980) *Third Annual Report on the EDY Project to the Department of Education and Science*, Hester Adrian Research Centre, University of Manchester

McBrien, J. (1981) 'Introducing the EDY Project', *Special Education: Forward Trends, 8*, 29–30

McBrien, J. (1982) *Education of the Developmentally Young Mentally Handicapped Child: A Programme of Evaluated Dissemination and Research, Final Report to the Department of Education and Science*, Hester Adrian Research Centre, University of Manchester

McBrien, J. and Edmonds, M. (1985) 'Evaluation of an EDY Training Course in Behavioural Techniques for Staff Working with Severely Mentally Handicapped Children', *Behavioural Psychotherapy*, in press

McBrien, J. and Foxen, T. (1981) *Instructors' Handbook*, Manchester University Press, Manchester

McBrien, J. and Foxen, T. (1985) *The EDY In-service Course for Mental Handicap Practitioners*, in J. Hogg and P. Mittler (eds), *Staff Training in Mental Handicap*, Croom Helm, London

McBrien, J. and Thomas, M. (1981) *Fourth Annual Report on the EDY Project to the Department of Education and Science*, Hester Adrian Research Centre, University of Manchester

McClelland, D. C. (1978) 'Managing Motivation to Expand Human Freedom', *American Psychologist, 33*, 201–10

McConachie, H. (1983) 'Fathers, Mothers, Siblings: how Do they See Themselves?', in P. Mittler and H. McConachie (eds), *Parents, Professionals and Mentally Handicapped People: Approaches to Partnership*, Croom Helm, London

McConkey, R. and Jeffree, D. (1975) 'Partnership with Parents', *Special Education: Forward Trends, 2*, 13–15

McConkey, R. and McEvoy, J. (1983) 'Parental Involvement Courses: Contrasts between Mothers who Enrol and those who Don't', in J. M. Berg (ed.) *Perspectives and Progress in Mental Retardation, Vol. 1, Social, Psychological and Educational Aspects*, University Park Press, Baltimore, MD

McConkey, R. and O'Connor, M. (1982) 'A New Approach to Parent Involvement in Language Intervention Programmes', *Child Care, Health and Development, 8*, 163–76

McMahon, R. J. and Forehand, R. (1984) 'Parent Training for the Non-compliant Child: Treatment Outcome, Generalization and Adjunctive Therapy Procedures', in R. F. Dangel and R. A. Polster (eds), *Parent Training: Foundations of Research and Practice*, Guildford Press, London

McMahon, R. J., Forehand, R. and Griest, D. L. (1981) 'Effects of Knowledge of Social Learning Principles on Enhancing Treatment, Outcome and Generalisation in a Parent Training Programme', *Journal of Consulting and Clinical Psychology, 49*, 526–32

McNamara, E. (1979) 'The Use of Self-reporting in Behaviour Modification in a

Secondary School', *Behavioural Psychotherapy, 7*, 57–66

Madsen, C. H. and Madsen, C. K. (1970) *Teaching/Discipline: Behavioural Principles toward a Positive Approach*, Allyn & Bacon, Boston

Madsen, C. H. and Madsen, C. K. (1973) *Learning and Observational Manual*, Allyn & Bacon, Boston

Madsen, C. H., Becker, W. C. and Thomas, D. R. (1968) 'Rules, Praise, and Ignoring: Elements of Elementary Classroom Control', *Journal of Applied Behaviour Analysis, 1*, 139–50

Margolis, R. B., Sorenson, J. L. and Galano, J. (1977) 'Consumer Satisfaction in Mental Health Delivery Services', *Professional Psychology, 8*, 11–16

Marks, I. M., Hallam, R. S. Connolly, J. and Philpotts, R. (1977) *Nursing in Behavioural Psychotherapy*, Royal College of Nursing, London

Martin, G. L. (1972) *Teaching Operant Conditioning to Psychiatric Nurses, Aids and Attendants*, in F. W. Clark, D. R. Evans and L. A. Hamerlynck (eds), *Implementing Behavioural Programmes for Schools and Clinics*, Research Press, Champaign, Ill.

Martin, J. (1977) 'Implementing the Engineered Classroom', *Academic Therapy, 12*, 197–207

Mathews, A., Teasdale, J., Munby, M., Johnston, D. and Shaw, P. (1977) 'A Home-based Treatment for Agoraphobia', *Behaviour Therapy, 8*, 915–24

Mayhew, G. L. (1979) 'Approaches to Employee Management: Policies and Preferences', *Journal of Organizational Behaviour Management, 2*, 103–11

Medway, F. J. and Forman. S. G. (1980) 'Psychologists' and Teachers' Reactions to Mental Health and Behavioural School Consultation', *Journal of School Psychology, 18*, 338–48

Merrett, F. E. (1981) 'Studies in Behaviour Modification in British Educational Settings', *Educational Psychology, 1*, 13–38

Merrett, F. and Wheldall, K. (1984) 'Training Teachers to Use the Behavioural Approach to Classroom Management: a Review', *Educational Psychology, 4*, 213–31

Milgram, S. (1974) *Obedience to Authority*, Tavistock, London

Miller, A. D. and Wexler, P. (1969) in F. N. Arnhoff, E. A. Rubenstein, J. C. Speisirron (eds), *Manpower for Mental Health*, Aldine, Chicago

Miller, H. C. (1921) *The New Psychology and the Teacher*, Jarrolds, London

Miller, R. and Lewin, L. M. (1980) 'Training and Management of the Psychiatric Aide: a Critical Review', *Journal of Organizational Behaviour Management, 2*, 295–315

Milne, D. L. (1982) 'A Comparison of Two Methods of Teaching Behaviour Modification to Mental Handicap Nurses', *Behavioural Psychotherapy, 10*, 54–64

Milne, D. L. (1983a) 'Some Paradoxes and Findings in the Training of Clinical Psychologists', *Bulletin of the British Psychological Society, 36*, 281–2

Milne, D. L. (1983b) 'Training Occupational Therapy Helpers in Behaviour Therapy', *British Journal of Occupational Therapy*, October, 287–8

Milne, D. L. (1983c) 'The "Hero-innovator" and Nurse Training Interventions: a Systematic Comparison of Two Strategies', Paper presented to the British Association for Behavioural Psychotherapy (BABP), Hull

Milne, D. L. (1984a) 'Ecobehavioural Analysis and Technology,' *Behaviour Analysis, 4*, 2–13

Milne, D. L. (1984b) 'Skill Evaluations of Nurse Training in Behaviour Therapy, *Behavioural Psychotherapy, 12*, 142–50

Milne, D. L. (1984c) 'The Development and Evaluation of a Structured Learning Format Introduction to Behaviour Therapy for Psychiatric Nurses', *British Journal of Clinical Psychology, 23*, 175–85

Milne, D. L. (1984d) 'The Relevance of Nurses' Characteristics in Learning Behaviour Therapy', *Journal of Advanced Nursing, 8*, 175–9

Milne, D. L. (1984e) 'Improving the Social Validity and Implementation of Behaviour Therapy Training for Psychiatric Nurses Using a Patient-centred Learning Format', *British Journal of Clinical Psychology, 23*, 313–14

Milne, D. L. (1984f) 'Learning to Teach Psychology', *Psychology Teaching*, December, 15–20

Milne, D. L. (1985a) 'A Review of the In-service Training of Nurses in Behaviour Therapy', *Behavioural Psychotherapy, 13*, 120–31

Milne, D. L. (1985b) '"The More Things Change the More they Stay the Same": Factors Affecting the Implementation of the Nursing Process', *Journal of Advanced Nursing, 10*, 39–45

Milne, D. L. (1985c) 'An Ecological Validation of Nurse Training in Behaviour Therapy', *Behavioural Psychotherapy, 13*, 14–28

Milne, D. L. (1985d) 'An Observational Evaluation of the Effects of Nurse Training in Behaviour Therapy on the Unstructured Activities of Psychiatric Nurses and Patients', *British Journal of Clinical Psychology 24*, 149–158

Milne, D. L. and Hodd, A. (1985) 'An Observational Study of the Activity and Reactivity of Psychiatric Nurses and Patients', unpublished article available from the author

Milne, D. L. and Mason, H. (1984) 'An Evaluation of Occupational Therapy Helpers as Behaviour Therapists', *Occupational Therapy*, October, 311–14

Milne, D. L., Burdett, C. and Beckett, J. L. (1985a) 'Reducing the Stress and Strain of Psychiatric Nursing by Ward Re-organisation and In-service Training', *Nursing Times* (in press)

Milne, D. L., Burdett, C. and Conway, P. (1985b) 'Review and Replications of a Core Course in Behaviour Therapy for Psychiatric Nurses', *Journal of Advanced Nursing, 10*,137–48

Miron, N. D. (1968) 'Issues and Implications of Operant Conditioning: the Primary Ethical Consideration', *Hospital and Community Psychiatry, 19*, 226–8

Mischel, W. (1968) *Personality and Assessment*, Wiley, New York

Mittler, P. and Mittler, H. (1983) 'Partnership with Parents: an Overview', in P. Mittler and H. McConachie (eds), *Parents, Professionals and Mentally Handicapped People: Approaches to Partnership*, Croom Helm, London

Montegar, C. A., Ried, D. H., Madsen, C. H. and Ewell, M. D. (1977) 'Increasing Institutional Staff to Resident Interactions through In-service Training and Supervisor Approval', *Behaviour Therapy, 8*, 533–40

Moos, R. H. (1974) *Evaluating Treatment Environments*, Wiley, New York

Moos, R. H. (1976) *The Human Context: Environmental Determinants of Behaviour*, Wiley, London

Morris, R. J. (1973) 'Issues in Teaching Behavior Modification to Parents of Retarded Children', paper presented at the 81st Annual Meeting of the American Psychological Association, Montreal, Canada

Morrison, A. and McIntyre, D. (1969) *Teachers and Teaching*, Penguin, Harmondsworth

Morrison, P., Mejia, B. and Miller, D. (1968) 'Staff Conflicts in the Use of Operant Techniques with Autistic Children', *American Journal of Orthopsychiatry, 38*, 647–52

Muir, K. A. and Milan, M. A. (1982) 'Parent Reinforcement for Child Achievement: the Use of a Battery to Maximise Parent Training Effects', *Journal of Applied Behaviour Analysis, 15*, 455–60

Murphy, G. H. and McArdle, M. (1978) 'Behaviour Modification with the Retarded', *Nursing Mirror*, 27 April, 31–4

Murphy, H. A., Hutchinson, J. M. and Barley, J. S. (1983) 'Behavioural School

Psychology Goes Outdoors: the Effect of Organized Games on Playground Aggression', *Journal of Applied Behaviour Analysis, 16*, 29–36

Muslin, H. K., Thurnblond, R. J. and Meschel, G. (1981) 'The Fate of the Clinical Interview: an Observational Study', *American Journal of Psychiatry, 138*, 822–5

Nay, W. R. (1975) 'A Systematic Comparison of Instructional Techniques for Parents', *Behaviour Therapy, 6*, 14–21

Neisworth, J. T. and Moore, F. (1972) 'Operant Treatment of Asthmatic Responding with the Parent as Therapist', *Behaviour Therapy, 3*, 95–9

Nietzel, M. T. and Fisher, S. G. (1981) 'Effectiveness of Professional and Professional Helpers: a Comment on Durlak', *Psychological Bulletin, 89*, 555–65

Novaco, R. W. and Monahan, J. (1980) 'Research in Community Psychology: Analysis of Work Published in the First Six Years of the *American Journal of Community Psychology*', *The American Journal of Community Psychology, 8*, 131–45

O'Dell, S. L. (1974) 'Training Parents in Behaviour Modification: a Review', *Psychological Bulletin, 81*, 418–33

O'Dell, S. L., Flynn, J. and Benlolo, L. (1977) 'A Comparison of Parent Training Techniques in Child Behaviour Modification', *Journal of Behaviour Therapy and Experimental Psychiatry, 8*, 261–8

O'Dell, S. L., Mahoney, N. D., Horton, W. G. and Turner, P. E. (1979a) 'Media-assisted Parent Training: Alternative Models', *Behaviour Therapy, 10*, 103–10

O'Dell, S. L., Tarler-Benlolo, L. and Flynn, J. M. (1979b) 'An Instrument to Measure Knowledge of Behavioural Principles as Applied to Children', *Journal of Behaviour Therapy and Experimental Psychiatry, 10*, 29–34

O'Dell, S. L., Krug, W. W., Patterson, J. N. and Faustman, W. O. (1980) 'An Assessment of Methods for Training Parents in the Use of Time-out', *Journal of Behaviour Therapy and Experimental Psychiatry, 11*, 21–5

O'Dell, S. L., O'Quinn, J. A., Alford, B. A., O'Briant, A. L., Bradlyn, A. S. and Giebanhain, J. E. (1982) 'Predicting the Acquisition of Parenting Skills via Four Training Methods', *Behaviour Therapy, 13*, 194–208

Odum, E. P. (1963) *Ecology*, Holt, Rinehart and Winston, New York

Ohlin, L. F. and Lawrence, W. C. (1959) 'Social Interactions among Clients as a Treatment Problem', *Social Work, 4*, 3–13

O'Leary, K. D. (1972) 'Behaviour Modification in the Classroom; a Rejoinder to Winett and Winkler', *Journal of Applied Behaviour Analysis, 5*, 505–11

O'Leary, K. and O'Leary, S. (eds) (1977) *Classroom Management: the Successful Use of Behaviour Modification*, Pergamon, New York

O'Leary, K. D., O'Leary, S. and Becker, W. C. (1967) 'Modification of a Deviant Sibling Interaction Pattern in the Home', *Behaviour Research and Therapy, 5*, 113–20

O'Leary, S. G. and Dubly, D. R. (1979) 'Applications of Self-control Procedures by Children: a Review', *Journal of Applied Behaviour Analysis, 12*, 449–63

Page, T. J., Iwata, B. A. and Reid, D. A. (1982) 'Pyramidal Training: a Large-scale Application with Institutional Staff', *Journal of Applied Behaviour Analysis, 15*, 335–51

Panyan, M. C. and Patterson, E. T. (1973) 'Teaching Attendants the Applied Aspects of Behaviour Modification: an Empirical Approach', *Proceedings, 81st Annual Convention, American Psychological Association, Montreal*

Panyan, M. C., Boozer, H. and Morris, M. (1970) 'Feedback to Attendants as a Reinforcer for Applying Operant Techniques', *Journal of Applied Behaviour Analysis, 3*, 1–4

Parsonson, B. S., Baer, A. M. and Baer, D. M. (1974) 'The Application of Generalized Correct Social Contingencies: an Evaluation of a Training Programme', *Journal of Applied Behaviour Analysis, 7*, 427–37

Patterson, G. R. (1971) *Families*, Research Press, Champaign, Ill.

Patterson, G. R. (1974) 'Interventions for Boys with Conduct Problems: Multiple Settings, Treatment, and Criteria', *Journal of Consulting and Clinical Psychology, 42*, 471–81

Patterson, G. R. (1980) 'Treatment for Children with Conduct Problems: a Review of Outcome Studies', in S. Feshback and A. Fraczek (eds), *Aggression and Behaviour Change*, Praeger, New York

Patterson, G. R. and Brodsky, G. (1966) 'A Behaviour Modification Programme for a Child with Multiple Problem Behaviours', *Journal of Child Psychology and Psychiatry, 7*, 277–95

Patterson, G. R. and Fagot, B. I. (1967) 'A Re-factorization of Becker's (1960) Scale', *Psychological Record, 17*, 269–378

Patterson, G. R. and Fleischman, M. J. (1979) 'Maintenance of Treatment Effects: Some Considerations Concerning Family Systems and Follow-up Data', *Behaviour Therapy, 10*, 168–85

Patterson, G. R. and Gullion, M. E. (1968) *Living with Children: New Methods for Parents and Teachers*, Research Press, Champaign, Ill.

Patterson, G. R. and Reid, J. B. (1970) 'Reciprocity and Coercion: Two Facets of Social Systems', in C. Neuringer and J. Michael (eds), *Behaviour Modifications in Clinical Psychology*, Appleton-Century-Crofts, New York

Patterson, G. R. and Reid, J. B. (1973) 'Intervention for Families of Aggressive Boys: a Replication Study', *Behaviour Research and Therapy, 11*, 383–94

Patterson, G. R., Littman, R. A. and Hinzey, W. C. (1964) 'Parental Effectiveness as Reinforcers in the Laboratory and its Relations to Child Rearing Practices and Adjustment in the Classroom', *Journal of Personality, 32*, 180–99

Patterson, G. R., McNeal, S., Hawkins, N. and Phelps, R. (1967) 'Reprogramming the Social Environment', *Journal of Child Psychology and Psychiatry, 8*, 181–95

Patterson, G. R., Cobb, J. A. and Ray, R. S. (1970) 'A Social Engineering Technology for Retraining the Families of Aggressive Boys', in H. Adams and L. Unikel (eds), *Georgia Symposium in Experimental Clinical Psychology*, C. C. Thomas, New York

Patterson, G. R., Cobb, J. A. and Ray, R. S. (1972) 'A Social Engineering Technology for Retraining the Families of Aggressive Boys', in H. E. Adams and I. P. Unikel (eds), *Issues and Trends in Behaviour Therapy*, C. C. Thomas, Springfield, Ill.

Patterson, G. R., Reid, J. B., Jones, R. R. and Conger, R. E. (1975) *A Social Learning Approach to Family Intervention: Vol. 1, Families with Aggressive Children*, Castalia Publishing Company, Eugene, Oregon

Patterson, G. R., Chamberlain, P. and Reid, J. B. (1982) 'A Comparative Evaluation of a Parent-training Programme', *Behaviour Therapy, 13*, 638–50

Paul, G. L. (1969) 'Behaviour Modification Research: Design and Tactics', in C. M. Franks (ed.), *Behaviour Therapy: Appraisal and Status*, McGraw-Hill, New York

Paul, G. L. and Lentz, R. J. (1977) *Psychosocial Treatment of Chronic Mental Patients*, Harvard University Press, Cambridge, Mass

Paul, G. L., McInnes, T. L. and Moriotto, M. J. (1973) 'Objective Performance Outcomes Associated with Two Approaches to Training Mental Health Technicians in Milieu and Social-learning Programmes', *Journal of Abnormal Psychology, 82*, 523–32

Peine, H. A. and Howarth, R. (1975) *Children and Parents: Everyday Problems of Behaviour*, Penguin, Harmondsworth

Peine, H. A. and Munro, B. C. (1973) 'Behaviour Management of Parent Training Programmes', *Psychological Record, 23*, 459–66

Perrot, E. (1982) *Effective Teaching: a Practical Guide to Improve Your Teaching*, Longman, London

Peterson, L., Horner, A. L. and Wonderlich, S. A. (1982) 'The Integrity of Independent Variables in Behaviour Analysis', *Journal of Applied Behaviour Analysis, 15*, 477–92

Popper, K. R. (1976) *Unended Quest*, Fontana, London

Porterfield, H. and Blunden, R. (1978) 'Establishing an Activity Period and Individual Skill Training within a Day Setting for Profoundly Mentally Handicapped Adults', *Journal of Practical Approaches to Developmental Handicap, 2*, 10–15

Porterfield, J., Blunden, R. and Blewitt, E. (1980) 'Improving Environments for Profoundly Handicapped Adults', *Behaviour Modification, 4*, 225–41

Porterfield, J., Evans, G. and Blunden, R. (1983) *Working Together for Change: a Service Manager's Guide to Involving Staff and Families in Service Improvement*, Mental Handicap in Wales, Applied Research Unit, Cardiff

Potter, S. (1981) 'Superviseeship', in A. McKendry (ed.), *The Psychology of Acting the Goat*, Capra Press, Oxford

Powdermaker, F. and Grimes, L. (1944) *The Intelligent Parents' Manual*, Penguin, Harmondsworth

Presland, J. (1977) 'Behaviour Modification in Two Schools for Maladjusted Children', *Therapeutic Education, 5*, 26–30

Prieto-Bayard, M. and Baker, B. L. (1985) 'Behavioural Parent Training for Spanish-speaking Families with a Retarded Child', *Journal of Community Psychology*, in press

Quiltich, H. R. (1975) 'A Comparison of Three Staff Management Procedures', *Journal of Applied Behaviour Analysis, 8*, 59–66

Quiltich, H. R., Miller, S. M., McConnell, M. A. and Bryant, S. (1975) 'Teaching Personnel to Implement Behavioural Programmes', *Educational Technology, 15*, 27–31

Raynes, N. V., Pratt, M. W. and Roges, S. (1979) *Organisational Structure and the Care of the Mentally Retarded*, Croom Helm, London

Reid, J. B. (ed.) (1978) *A Social Learning Approach to Family Intervention: II Observations in Home Settings*, Castalia Press, Eugene, Oregon

Reid, D. H. and Whitman, T. L. (1983) 'Behavioural Staff Management in Institutions: a Critical Review of Effectiveness and Acceptability', *Analysis and Intervention in Developmental Disabilities, 3*, 131–49

Reiff, R. (1966) 'Mental Health Manpower and Institutional Change', *American Psychologist, 21*, 540–8

Reisinger, J. J., Frangia, G. W. and Hoffman, E. H. (1976) 'Toddler Management Training: Generalization and Marital Status', *Journal of Behaviour Therapy and Experimental Psychiatry, 7*, 335–40

Repucci, N. D. (1977) 'Implementation Issues for the Behaviour Modifier as Institutional Change Agent', *Behaviour Therapy, 8*, 594–605

Repucci, N. D. and Saunders, J. T. (1974) 'Social Psychology of Behaviour Modification', *American Psychologist*, September, 649–60

Revill, S. and Blunden, R. (1979) 'A Home Training Service for Pre-school Developmentally Handicapped Children', *Behaviour Research and Therapy, 17*, 207–14

Rezin, V. A., Elliott, P. A. and Paschalis, P. (1983) 'Nurse-Patient Interactions in a Token Economy', *Behavioural Psychotherapy, 11*, 225–34

Richards, C. S. (1975) 'The Politics of a Token Economy', *Psychological Reports, 36*, 615–21

Richardson, D. C. and Harlick, L. C. (1975) 'High School Students as Reading Instructors', *Elementary School Journal, 75*, 389–93

Rickard, K. M., Forehand, R., Wells, K. C., Griest, D. L. and McMahon, R. J. (1981) 'A Comparison of Mothers of Clinic Referred Deviant, Clinic Referred

Non-deviant and Non-clinic Children', *Behaviour Research and Therapy, 17*, 201–5

Rioch, M. (1966) 'Changing Concepts of the Training of Therapists', *Journal of Consulting Psychology, 30*, 290–2

Rinn, R. C., Vernon, J. C. and Wise, M. J. (1975) 'Training Parents of Behaviourally Disordered Children in Groups: a Three-year Programme Evaluation', *Behaviour Therapy, 6*, 378–87

Robin, A. L. (1981) 'A Controlled Evaluation of Problem Solving Communications Training with Parent-Adolescent Conflict', *Behaviour Therapy, 12*, 593–609

Robinson, P. W., Newly, T. J. and Ganzell, S. L. (1981) 'A Token System for a Class of Underachieving Hyperactive Children', *Journal of Applied Behaviour Analysis, 14*, 307–15

Robson, C. (1983) 'Evaluation of the Effectiveness of a School-based Intervention', in J. Hogg (ed.), *Advances in Mental Handicap Research, Vol. 3,* Wiley, Chichester

Rogers, C. R. (1951) *Client Centred Therapy*, Constable, London

Rogers, C. R. (1957) 'The Necessary and Sufficient Conditions of Personality Change', *Journal of Consulting Psychology, 21*, 95–103

Rogers-Warren, A. and Warren, S. F. (eds) (1977) *Ecological Perspectives in Behaviour Analysis*, University Park Press, Baltimore

Rose, S. (1974) 'Training Parents in Groups as Behaviour Modifiers of their Mentally Retarded Children', *Journal of Behavior Therapy and Experimental Psychiatry, 5*, 135–40

Russell, P. (1983) 'The Parent's Perspective of Family Needs and How to Meet Them', in P. Mittler and H. McConachie (eds), *Parents, Professionals and Mentally Handicapped People*, Croom Helm, London

Rutter, M., Tizard, J. and Whitmore, K. (1970) *Education, Health and Behaviour*, Longman, London

Salmon, P. (1983) 'Psychologists and the Community: Is Counter-influence Enough?', *Bulletin of the British Psychological Society, 36*, 369–71

Salzinger, K., Feldman, R. and Portnoy, S. (1970) 'Training Parents of Brain-injured Children in the Use of Operant Conditioning Methods', *Behaviour Therapy, 1*, 4–32

Sanders, M. R. (1982) 'The Generalisation of Parent Responding to Community Settings: the Effects of Instructions plus Feedback and Self-management Training', *Behavioural Psychotherapy, 10*, 273–87

Sanders, M. R. and Glynn, T. (1981) 'Training Parents in Behavioural Self-management: an Analysis of Generalisation and Maintenance', *Journal of Applied Behaviour Analysis, 14*, 223–37

Sanders, M. R. and James, J. E. (1983) 'The Modification of Parent Behaviour: a Review of Generalisation and Maintenance', *Behaviour Modification, 7*, 3–27

Sandler, A., Corren, A. and Thurman, S. K. (1983) 'A Training Program for Parents of Handicapped Preschool Children: Effects upon Mother, Father, and Child', *Exceptional Children, 49*, 355–9

Sanson-Fisher, R. and Jenkins, H. J. (1978) 'Interaction Patterns between In-mates and Staff in a Maximum Security Institution for Delinquents', *Behaviour Therapy, 9*, 703–16

Sarasen, S. B. (1967) 'Toward a Psychology of Change and Innovation', *American Psychologist, 22*, 227–33

Schinke, S. P. (1979) 'Staff Training in Group Homes: a Family Approach', in L. A. Hamerlynck (ed.), *Behavioural Systems for the Developmentally Disabled, II*, Bruner Mazel, New York

Schinke, S. P. and Wong, S. E. (1977a) 'Evaluation of Staff Training in Group Homes for Retarded Persons', *American Journal of Mental Deficiency, 82*, 130–6

Schinke, S. P. and Wong, S. E. (1977b) 'Coding Group Home Behaviour with a

Continuous Real-time Recording Device', *Behavioural Engineering, 4*, 5–9

Schnelle, J. F., Traughber, B., Morgan, D. B., Embry, J. E., Binion, A. F. and Coleman, A. (1983) 'Management of Geriatric Incontinence in Nursing Homes', *Journal of Applied Behaviour Analysis, 16*, 235–42

Schortinghuis, N. and Frohman, A. (1974) 'A Comparison of Paraprofessional and Professional Success with Pre-school Children', *Journal of Learning Disabilities, 17*, 245–7

Sebba, J. (1981) 'Intervention for Profoundly Retarded Mentally Handicapped Children through Parent Training in a Preschool Setting and at Home', in P. Mittler (ed.), *Frontiers of Knowledge in Mental Retardation: Vol. 1, Social, Educational and Behavioural Aspects*, University Park Press, Baltimore

Seligman, N. E. P. (1971) *Helplessness*, W. H. Freeman, San Francisco

Shearer, D. E. and Loftin, C. R. (1984) 'The Portage Project: Teaching Parents to Teach their Pre-school Children in the Home', in R. F. Dangel and R. A. Polster (eds), *Parent Training: Foundations of Research and Practice*, Guildford Press, London

Shearer, M. S. and Shearer, D. E. (1972) 'The Portage Project: a Model for Early Childhood Education', *Exceptional Children, 36*, 210–17

Shenk, J. L. (1984) 'Predictors of Joining a Parent Training Program for Spanish Speaking Families with a Mentally Retarded Child', Unpublished Master's Thesis, University of California, Los Angeles

Sheppard, W. C., Shank, S. B. and Wilson, D. (1972) *How to Be a Good Teacher: Training Social Behaviour in Young Children*, Research Press, Champaign, Ill.

Skinner, B. F. (1948) '"Superstition" in the Pigeon', *Journal of Experimental Psychology, 38*, 168–72

Skinner, B. F. (1953) *Science and Human Behaviour*, Free Press, New York

Skinner, B. F. (1954) 'The Science of Learning and the Art of Teaching', *Harvard Educational Review, 29*, 86–97

Skinner, B. F. (1968) *The Technology of Teaching*, Prentice-Hall, New Jersey

Skinner, B. F. (1984) 'The Shame of American Education', *American Psychologist, 39*, 947–54

Sloane, H. N. (1976) *Classroom Management: Remediation and Prevention*, Wiley, New York

Sloane, R. B. *et al.* (1976) 'Patient Characteristics and Outcome in Psychotherapy and Behaviour Therapy', *Journal of Consulting and Clinical Psychology, 44*, 330–9

Solomon, R. W. and Wahler, R. G. (1973) 'Peer Reinforcement Control of Classroom Problem Behaviour', *Journal of Applied Behaviour Analysis, 6*, 49–56

Speidel, G. E. and Tharp, R. G. (1978) 'Teacher-training Workshop Strategy: Instructions, Discrimination Training, Modelling, Guided Practice, and Video Feedback', *Behaviour Therapy, 9*, 735–9

Speltz, M. L., Moore, J. E. and McReynolds, W. T. (1979) 'A Comparison of Standardised and Group Contingencies in a Classroom Setting', *Behaviour Therapy, 10*, 219–26

Spock, B. (1945) *Baby and Child Care*, Book Club Associates, London

Stein, T. J. (1975) 'Some Ethical Considerations of Short-term Workshops in the Principles and Methods of Behaviour Modification', *Journal of Applied Behaviour Analysis, 8*, 113–15

Stern, M. R. and Golden, F. (1977) 'A Partial Evaluation of an Introductory Training Programme in Behavioural Modification for Psychiatric Nurses', *American Journal of Community Psychology, 5*, 23–32

Stevenson, H. C. and Fantuzzo, J. W. (1984) 'Application of the "Generalisation Map" to a Self-control Intervention with School-aged Children', *Journal of Applied Behaviour Analysis, 17*, 207–12

Stoffelmayer, B. E., Lindsey, W. and Taylor, V. (1979) 'Maintenance of Staff

Behaviour', *Behaviour Research and Therapy, 17*, 271–3

Stokes, T. F. and Baer, D. M. (1977) 'An Implicit Technology of Generalisation', *Journal of Applied Behaviour Analysis, 10*, 349–67

Stokes, T. F., Doud, C. L., Rowbury, T. G. and Baer, D. M. (1978) 'Peer Facilitation of Generalisation in a Pre-school Classroom', *Journal of Abnormal Child Psychology, 6*, 203–9

Stolz, S. B. (1981) 'Adoption of Innovations from Applied Behavioural Research: "Does Anybody Care?"', *Journal of Applied Behaviour Analysis, 14*, 491–505

Stones, E. (1966) *An Introduction to Educational Psychology*, Methuen, London

Stones, E. (1979) *Psychopedagogy*, Methuen, New York

Strain, P. S., Steele, P., Ellis, T. and Timm, M. A. (1982) 'Long-term Effects of Oppositional Child Treatment with Mothers as Therapists and Therapist Trainers', *Journal of Applied Behaviour Analysis, 15*, 163–9

Stumphauzer, J. S. and Davis, L. C. (1983) 'Training Mexican–American Mental Health Personnel in Behaviour Therapy', *Journal of Behaviour Therapy and Experimental Psychiatry, 14*, 215–17

Suchman, F. A. (1967) *Evaluative Research*, Russell-Sage, New York

Suckerman, K. R., Hines, P. and Gordon, S. B. (1982) 'A Multi-environment School Mental Health Consultation: Behavioural Skill Training for Teachers and Parents', in A. M. Jeger and R. S. Slotnik, *Community Mental Health and Behavioural Ecology*, Plenum Press, London

Sullivan, A. (1975) '"Don't Move or I'll Modify You"', *Radical Education, 3*, 18–20

Sulzer, B. and Mayer, G. R. (1972) *Behaviour Modification Procedures for School Personnel*, Dryden Press, Hinsdale, Ill.

Sulzer-Azaroff, B., Thaw, J. and Thomas, C. (1975) 'Behavioural Competencies for the Evaluation of Behaviour Modifiers', in W. S. Wood (ed.), *Issues in Evaluating Behaviour Modification*, Research Press, Champaign, Ill.

Tharp, R. G. and Wetzel, R. J. (1969) *Behaviour Modification in the Natural Environment*, Academic Press, New York

Thomas, J. D. (1976) 'Accuracy of Self-assessment of On-task Behaviour by Elementary School Children', *Journal of Applied Behaviour Analysis, 9*, 209–10

Thomas, M. (1985) 'An Introduction to Room Management', in P. T. Farrell (ed.), *EDY: Its Impact of Staff Training in Mental Handicap*, Manchester University Press, Manchester

Thomas, M., Burton, M. and Cullen, C. (1982) 'Take a New Look at your Ward', *Nursing Times*, 23 June, 1068–70

Thompson, T. and Grabowski, J. (1972) *Behaviour Modification of the Mentally Retarded*, Oxford University Press, New York

Tizard, J., Sinclair, I. and Clark, R. V. G. (1975) *Varieties of Residential Experience*, Routledge & Kegan Paul, London

Tornatzky, L. G. and Fergus, E. D. (1982) 'Innovation and Diffusion in Mental Health', in A. M. Jeger and R. S. Slotnik (eds), *Community Mental Health and Behavioural Ecology*, Plenum Press, London

Towell, D. and Dartington, T. (1976) 'Encouraging Innovations in Hospital Care', *Journal of Advanced Nursing, 1*, 391–8

Towell, D. and Harris, C. (eds), (1979) *Innovation in Patient Care*, Croom Helm, London

Trovato, J. and Bucher, B. (1980) 'Peer Tutoring with or without Home-based Reinforcement, for Reading Remediation', *Journal of Applied Behaviour Analysis, 13*, 129–41

Tsoi, M. M. and Yule, W. (1976) 'The Effects of Group Reinforcement in Classroom Behaviour Modification', *Educational Studies, 2*, 129–40

Turnbull, A. P. and Turnbull, H. R. (1982) 'Parent Involvement in the Education of Handicapped Children: a Critique', *Mental Retardation, 20*, 115–20

Ulrich, R. E., Stachnik, T. J. and Marby, J. H. (eds) (1974) *Control of Human Behaviour, Vol. 3: Behaviour Modification in Education*, Scott Foreman, Glenview, Ill.

Valett, R. E. (1970) *Effective Teaching: a Guide to Diagnostic-Prescriptive Task Analysis*, Fearon Publishers, Belmont, CA.

Vadenbos, G. R., Stapp, J. and Kilburg, R. R. (1981) 'Health Service Providers in Psychology', *American Psychologist, 36*, 1395–1418

Wahler, L. O., Cohen, S. E., Breiter, D. E., Daston, P. G., Hirsch, I. S. and Leibowitz, J. M. (1969) 'Teaching Behavioural Principles to Parents of Disturbed Children', in B. G. Guerney (ed.), *Psychotherapeutic Agents: New Roles for Non-professionals, Parents and Teachers*, Holt Rinehart Winston, New York

Wahler, R. G. (1980) 'The Insular Mother: her Problems in Parent-Child Treatment', *Journal of Applied Behaviour Analysis, 13*, 207–20

Wahler, R. G. and Afton, A. D. (1980) 'Attentional Processes in Insular and Non-insular Mothers: Some Differences in their Summary Reports about Child Behaviour Problems', *Child Behaviour Therapy, 2*, 25–41

Wahler, R. G. and Dumas, J. E. (1984) 'Changing the Observational Coding Styles of Insular and Non-insular Mothers', in R. F. Dangel and R. A. Polster (eds), *Parent Training: Foundations of Research and Practice*, Guildford Press, London

Wahler, R. G. and Fox, J. J. (1980) 'Solitary Toy Play and Time-out: a Family Treatment Package for Children with Aggressive and Oppositional Behaviour', *Journal of Applied Behaviour Analysis, 13*, 23–9

Wahler, R. G. and Fox, J. J. (1981) 'Setting Events in Applied Behaviour Analysis: toward a Conceptional and Methodological Expansion', *Journal of Applied Behaviour Analysis, 14*, 327–38

Wahler, R. G. and Graves, M. G. (1983) 'Setting Events in Social Networks: Ally or Enemy in Child Behaviour Therapy?', *Behaviour Therapy, 14*, 19–36

Wahler, R. G., Winkel, G. H., Peterson, R. F. and Morrison, D. C. (1965) 'Mothers as Behaviour Therapists for their Own Children', *Behaviour Research and Therapy, 3*, 113–24

Wahler, R. G., Leske, G. and Rogers, E. S. (1979) 'The Insular Family: a Deviance Support System for Oppositional Children', in L. A. Hamerlynck (ed.), *Behavioural Systems for the Developmentally Disabled: 1 School and Family Environments*, Bruner Mazel, New York

Walker, L. O., Cohen, S. E., Breitner, D. E., Daston, P. G., Hirsch, I. S. and Leibowitz, J. M. (1969) 'Teaching Behavioural Principles to Parents of Disturbed Children', in B. G. Guerney (ed.), *Psychotherapeutic Agents*, Holt, Rinehart and Winston, New York

Walker, H. M. and Buckley, N. K. (1972) 'Programming Generalization and Maintenance of Treatment Effects across Time and across Settings', *Journal of Applied Behaviour Analysis, 5*, 209–24

Wallace, C. J., Davis, J. R., Liberman, R. P. and Baker, V. (1973) 'Modelling and Staff Behaviour', *Journal of Consulting and Clinical Psychology, 41*, 422–5

Ward, J. (1976) 'Behaviour Modification in Education: an Overview and a Model for Programme Implementation', *Bulletin of the British Psychological Society, 29*, 257–68

Ward, M. H. and Baker, B. L. (1968) 'Reinforcement Therapy in the Classroom', *Journal of Applied Behaviour Analysis, 1*, 323–8

Warren, S. F. (1977) 'A Useful Ecobehavioural Perspective for Applied Behavior Analysis', in A. Rogers-Warren and S. F. Warren (eds), *Ecological Perspectives in Behaviour Analysis*, University Park Press, Baltimore, MD

Watson, L. S. (1972) 'The Use of Contingent Reinforcement for Training Staff Members and Parents Working with Autistic and Mentally Retarded Children', in D. A. Primrose (ed.), *Proceedings of the Second Congress of the International*

Association for the Scientific Study of Mental Deficiency, Swetz & Zeittinger, Amsterdam

Watson, L. S. and Bassinger, J. F. (1974) 'Parent Training Technology: a Potential Service Delivery System', *Mental Retardation*, October, 3–10

Watson, L. S. and Uzzell, R. (1980) 'A Programme for Teaching Behaviour Modification Skills to Institutional Staff', *Applied Research in Mental Retardation, 1*, 41–53

Watson, L. S., Gardner, J. M. and Sanders, G. (1971a) 'Shaping and Maintaining Behaviour Modification Skills in Staff Members in an MR Institution: Columbus State Institute Behavior Modification Program', *Mental Retardation, 9*, 39–42

Watson, L. S., Gardner, J. M. and Sanders, C. (1971b) *How to Use Behavior Modification with Mentally Retarded and Autistic Children: Program for Administrators, Teachers, Parents and Nurses*, Behavior Modification Technology, Illinois

Watson, W. H. (1979) 'Resistances to Naturalistic Observation in a Geriatric Setting', *International Journal of Aging and Human Development, 10*, 35–45

Webster-Stratton, C. (1981) 'Modification of Mothers' Behaviours and Attitudes through a Video Tape Modelling Group Discussion Programme', *Behaviour Therapy, 12*, 634–42

Weinrott, M. R., Corson, J. A. and Wilchesky, M. (1979) 'Teacher-mediated Treatment of Social Withdrawal', *Behaviour Therapy, 10*, 281–94

Weitz, S. E. (1981) 'A Code for Assessing Teaching Skills of Parents and Developmentally Disabled Children', *Journal of Autism and Developmental Disorders, 12*, 13–24

Wells, K. C. and Forehand, R. (1981) 'Childhood Behaviour Problems in the Home', in S. M. Turner and H. E. Adams (eds), *Handbook of Behaviour Therapy*, Wiley, New York

Westmacott, E. V. S. and Cameron, R. J. (1981) *Behaviour Can Change*, Globe Education, Basingstoke

Wheldall, K., Merrett, F. E. and Russell, A. (1982) 'The Behavioural Approach to Teaching (B.A.T.) Project', *Behavioural Approaches with Children, 7* (2), 4–10

White, M. A. (1975) 'Natural Rates of Teacher Approval and Disapproval in the Classroom', *Journal of Applied Behaviour Analysis, 8*, 367–72

Whitman, T. L. and Johnston, M. R. (1983) 'Teaching Addition and Subtraction with Regrouping to Educable Mentally Retarded Children: a Group Self-instructional Training Programme', *Behaviour Therapy, 14*, 127–43

Whitman, T. L., Scibak, J. W., Butler, K. M., Richter, R. and Johnson, M. R. (1982) 'Improving Classroom Behaviour in Mentally Retarded Children through Correspondence Training', *Journal of Applied Behaviour Analysis, 15*, 545–64

Wicker, A. W. (1969) 'Attitudes versus Actions: the Relationship of Verbal and Overt Behavioural Responses to Attitude Objects', *Journal of Social Issues, 25*, 41–78

Willems, E. P. (1972) 'The Interface of the Hospital Environment and Patient Behaviour', *Archives of Physical Medicine and Rehabilitation*, March, 115–22

Willems, E. P. (1973) 'Go ye into All the World and Modify Behaviour: an Ecologist's View', *Representative Research in Social Psychology, 4*, 93–105

Willems, E. P. (1974) 'Behavioural Technology and Behavioural Ecology', *Journal of Applied Behaviour Analysis, 7*, 151–65

Willems, E. P. (1979) 'An Ecological Orientation in Psychology', *Merrill-Palmer Quarterly, 11*, 317–43

Williams, C. D. (1959) 'The Elimination of Tantrum Behaviour by Extinction Procedures', *Journal of Abnormal and Social Psychology, 59*, 269–70

Williams, C. and Jackson, M. W. (1975) 'Nurse Training in Behaviour Modification', in C. C. Kiernan and F. P. Woodford (eds) *Behaviour Modification with the*

Severely Retarded, Associated Scientific Publishers, Oxford

Willis, J., Crowder, J. and Morris, B. A. (1972) 'A Behavioural Approach to Remedial Reading Using Students as Behavioural Engineers', in G. Semb (ed.) *Behaviour Analysis and Education*, University of Kansas Press, Lawrence

Wilson, G. T. (1982) 'Psychotherapy Process and Procedure: the Behavioural Mandate', *Behaviour Therapy, 13*, 291–312

Wilson, G. D. and Patterson, J. R. (1968) 'A New Measure of Conservatism', *British Journal of Social and Clinical Psychology, 7*, 264–9

Winnett, R. A. and Winkler, R. C. (1972) 'Current Behaviour Modification in the Classroom: Be Still, Be Quiet, Be Docile', *Journal of Applied Behaviour Analysis, 5*, 499–504

Wodarski, J. S. (1976) 'Procedural Steps in the Implementation of Behaviour Modification Programmes in Open Settings', *Journal of Behaviour Therapy and Experimental Psychiatry, 7*, 133–6

Wolf, M. M. (1978) 'Social Validity: the Case for Subjective Measurement or How Applied Behaviour Analysis is Finding its Heart', *Journal of Applied Behaviour Analysis, 11*, 203–14

Wolf, M. M., Risley, T. R. and Mees, H. (1964) 'Application of Operant Conditioning Procedures to the Behaviour Problems of an Autistic Child', *Behaviour Research Therapy, 1*, 305–12

Wolfe, D. A., St. Lawrence, J., Graves, K., Brehany, K., Bradlyn, D. and Kelly, J. A. (1982) 'Intensive Behavioural Parent Training for a Child Abusive Mother', *Behaviour Therapy, 13*, 438–51

Woods, P. A. and Cullen, C. (1983) 'Determinants of Staff Behaviour in Long-term Care', *Behavioural Psychotherapy, 11*, 4–17

Wright, J., Mathieu, M. and McDonough, C. (1981) 'An Evaluation of Three Approaches to the Teaching of Behavioural Therapy', *Journal of Clinical Psychology, 77*, 326–35

Yates, B. T. (1978) 'Improving the Cost-effectiveness of Obesity Programmes: Three Basic Strategies for Reducing the Cost per Pound', *International Journal of Obesity, 2*, 249–66

Yule, W. (1975) 'Teaching Psychological Principles to Non-psychologists: Training Parents in Child Management', *Journal of the Association of Educational Psychologists, 10*, 5–16

Yule, W. and Carr, J. (1980) *Behaviour Modification for the Mentally Handicapped*, Croom Helm, London

Zaltman, G. and Duncan, R. (1977) *Strategies for Planned Change*, Wiley Interscience, New York

Zangwill, O. (1980) *Behaviour Modification:* A Report of a Joint Working Party to Formulate Ethical Guidelines for the Conduct of Programmes of Behaviour Modification in the NHS, HMSO, London

Zebiob, L. E., Forehand, R. and Resnick, P. A. (1979) 'Parent Child Interactions: Habituation and Resensitization Effects', *Journal of Clinical Child Psychology, 8*, 69–71

Ziarnik, J. P. and Bernstein, G. S. (1982) 'A Critical Examination of the Effect of In-service Training on Staff Performance', *Mental Retardation, 20*, 109–14

Zimbardo, P., Harey, C., Barks, W. and Jaffe, D. (1973) 'Pirandellion Prison: the Mind is a Formidable Jailor', *New York Times Magazine*, April, 38–60

Zimmerman, E. H. and Zimmerman, J. (1962) 'The Alteration of Behaviour in a Special Classroom Situation', *Journal of the Experimental Analysis of Behaviour, 5*, 59–60

INDEX